Applied SOAP: Implementing .NET XML Web Services

Kenn Scribner and Mark C. Stiver

SAMS

20 Indianapolis, Indiana 46290

Applied SOAP: Implementing .NET XML Web Services

Copyright © 2002 by Sams Publishing

All rights reserved. No part of this book shall be reproduced, stored in a retrieval system, or transmitted by any means, electronic, mechanical, photo-copying, recording, or otherwise, without written permission from the publisher. No patent liability is assumed with respect to the use of the information contained herein. Although every precaution has been taken in the preparation of this book, the publisher and author assume no responsibility for errors or omissions. Nor is any liability assumed for damages resulting from the use of the information contained herein.

International Standard Book Number: 0-672-32111-4

Library of Congress Catalog Card Number: 00-110536

Printed in the United States of America

First Printing: October 2001

04	03	02	01		4	3	2	1

Trademarks

All terms mentioned in this book that are known to be trademarks or service marks have been appropriately capitalized. Sams Publishing cannot attest to the accuracy of this information. Use of a term in this book should not be regarded as affecting the validity of any trademark or service mark.

Windows, Windows 2000, Windows XP, .NET, Visual Studio .NET, .NET Framework, Passport, and Hailstorm are registered trademarks of Microsoft Corporation.

Java is a registered trademark of Sun Microsystems, Inc.

Websphere is a registered trademark of IBM, Inc.

Warning and Disclaimer

Every effort has been made to make this book as complete and as accurate as possible, but no warranty or fitness is implied. The information provided is on an "as is" basis. The authors and the publisher shall have neither liability nor responsibility to any person or entity with respect to any loss or damages arising from the information contained in this book or from the use of the programs accompanying it.

ASSOCIATE PUBLISHER
Linda Engelman

ACQUISITIONS EDITOR
Linda Scharp

DEVELOPMENT EDITOR
Laurie McGuire

MANAGING EDITOR
Charlotte Clapp

PROJECT EDITOR
Leah Kirkpatrick

COPY EDITOR
Krista Hansing

INDEXER
Larry Sweazy

PROOFREADER
Wendy Ott

TECHNICAL EDITOR
Scott Seely

TEAM COORDINATOR
Lynne Williams

MEDIA DEVELOPER
Dan Scherf

INTERIOR DESIGNER
Gary Adair

COVER DESIGNER
Gary Adair

PAGE LAYOUT
Gloria Schurick

Overview

Contents

About the Authors

Kenn Scribner is a full-time consultant specializing in distributed applications, COM, Windows programming, and systems architecture. Kenn also instructs for Wintellect (www.wintellect.com), where he wrote both the *XML for Windows Programmers* and *Web Services* courses. He has written or contributed to a number of books, including *Understanding SOAP* (Sams Publishing), *Sams Teach Yourself ATL Programming in 21 Days* (Sams Publishing), *MFC Programming with Visual C++ Unleashed* (Sams Publishing), *Sams Teach Yourself DirectX 7 in 21 Days* (Sams Publishing), and *Professional MFC* (Wrox Press).

Mark C. Stiver is a consulting software engineer with the largest news and business online information service, LexisNexis. Mark has over 12 years of distributed application experience in commercial, industrial, and military software development and is the co-author of *Understanding SOAP* (Sams Publishing). Mark is currently a major contributor to the architecture, design, and development of Web Services for large-scale data warehouse systems.

About the Technical Editor

Scott Seely is a member of the MSDN Architectural Samples team. He is co-author of the "At Your Service" MSDN Voices column with Matt Powell. Besides his work at Microsoft, he has published two books through Prentice Hall: *SOAP: Cross Platform Web Service Development Using XML* and *Windows Shell Programming*. He wrote and maintains a small C++ based SOAP library (http://www.scottseely.com/soap.htm), published under the LGPL.

Dedication

To my mom, who hasn't had a book dedicated in her honor, and to my lovely wife, Judi, and wonderful children Aaron and Katie, who have had three (so far). You make my life rich and complete.

—Kenn Scribner

To my beautiful wife and best friend, Donna, and to my three beautiful children Brendan, Nicholas, and Sydney. My greatest reward as a husband and father is the love that they give so freely.

—Mark C. Stiver

Acknowledgments

I think the best part about writing a book is that you have the opportunity to formally thank everyone who dedicated their time to your effort for little or no reason other than to selflessly help you. It takes an amazing number of people to bring this material to you[em]more than just myself, a computer, and a word processor.

First and foremost, I would like to thank my wonderful wife, Judi, for her patience and support as I wrote on into the night. For far too many evenings I sat and worked on this material, and you can bet we'll catch up on movies and dinners out. To my children I offer my thanks for their support and smiling little faces, even as I tell them I couldn't toss the baseball or kick the soccer ball at that precise moment. We'll be throwing and kicking a lot more now too! I would also like to extend my deepest thanks to Mark and his family, for without their dedication and assistance you would be holding a book half as thick and only one quarter as informative. Thank you, Mark and Donna, for standing with me for "just one more."

I'd like to thank my new friend, Scott Seely, for not only volunteering to help us with this work but also for his friendship and advice. If you happen to find any technical errors in this material, the fault is mine alone and not Scott's (he probably told me to fix it!). This is a far better book because of his assistance with the technical end of .NET XML Web Services.

As I progress through my career, I'm finding myself with more and more to do at any given time. I'd like to thank Dave Pledger and Pat Caruso for their kind offers to give me time to complete this effort. This was no small contribution on their part because of the incredible workload we've sustained to move a new distributed automotive application into the marketplace.

We all should extend a huge "thank you!" to Linda Engelman for spearheading this project once we got started. I fully understand the pressures she is under to bring you the finest .NET information available. Of course, I can't forget to thank Linda Scharp for kicking this project off! We wouldn't be here today without her efforts. But if you want to thank the really hard-working crew, you surely have to thank Laurie McGuire, Charlotte Clapp, Leah Kirkpatrick, Krista Hansing, Larry Sweazy, and Wendy Ott for taking the raw materials I gave them (and they were raw, too) and turning them into the fine production you see here. Thanks to you all. Of course, I know where the real work is done, and that's in the back office, so to all of you there at Pearson that helped this book get out the door, thank you!

I simply must say a hearty "thank you!" to my Wintellect cohorts who were always there to address an issue or two. I gathered many of my thoughts and the organization for this book through the .NET Web Services course they allowed me to author. With any luck I can return the favor by providing knowledge and information, and perhaps even help one of them someday.

And of course there are a number of folks at Microsoft that held their laughter as I asked dozens of questions by e-mail. If I couldn't figure something out, I wrote them. If I couldn't get something to work, I wrote them. But it was nice having them on the team! I'd specifically like to thank Keith Ballinger who not only helped me but also drove the .NET Web Service architecture you'll see in this book. That was a monumental undertaking on his part and one I believe exceptionally well executed. Keith, I will send you that chili I owe you (and I'm hopeful you'll find a cool .NET polo somewhere in a back closet!).

Finally, I buy books, just as you do. But this time I'm on the other side, and for picking up this book and rummaging though its contents I thank you, the reader. I work long and hard hours for my paycheck, and I've met precious few developers who don't. So I know that when you lay down the money to purchase this book, it's hard won money. I truly hope you'll find this material interesting and useful. If you have questions, I'm available at kenn@endurasoft.com. If you like what you read, I thank you. If not, I still thank you and hope you'll drop me a note so I can try to address the issue.

—Kenn Scribner

I want to thank all of the people that made this book possible, starting with my wife, Donna. The sacrifices that she made enabled me to focus on what seemed like an endless labor of coding and writing. I also want to thank my children for patiently waiting for their father to re-emerge from the abyss that we call my den. A huge thank you goes to Kenn Scribner, a great teacher and an even better friend—as always, it's a pleasure working with you. I specifically want to thank the XML Gateway team: Brian Bailar, Brent Ballard, Carol Becher, Nisha Bhatt, Geary Biggs, Caleb Deupree, Doug Heitkamp, Bob Hodgeman, Nick Hughes, Dean Myers, Brian Rambacher, Joe Riess, and Les Tolkkinen. I'd like to give special thanks to Ron Meyer and Chris Cardiff, for leading our team on such a great new adventure. It's unfortunate that I don't have more room on this page to individually thank everyone at LexisNexis who has supported me over the years. I've been extremely fortunate to be surrounded by such a great team of professionals.

I want to thank Microsoft and the .NET development teams for building such a great new platform—the fun is just beginning. I'd also like to thank our technical editor, Scott Seely, for his outstanding contributions to this work. Scott kept us on our toes from day one—there's no question that his diligence has produced a higher quality book.

Thanks to Linda Engelman, Laurie McGuire, Leah Kirkpatrick, Krista Hansing, and the rest of the staff at Sams Publishing. These people worked hard to mold a mere concept into something that can be placed on a shelf.

As always, I want to thank you, the reader. In a myriad of technical books, you've chosen to purchase ours. My hope is that this book will answer a question, provoke a thought, or simply provide some insight. If you have questions or comments, please contact me at mstiver@yahoo.com. Once again, thank you!

—Mark C. Stiver

Author's Note

This book is about the Web Service, and more specifically about the Web Service as implemented by .NET. We tell you how to use .NET to create useful and interesting Web Services. We touch on why Web Services exist and what some alternative architectures might be that incorporate Web Services tomorrow where none exist today. But I wanted to draw your attention to a specific point before you dive into the technical material.

Here is that point. Web Services are about integration. Integration is about collaboration. Collaboration is about strategic partnerships. And strategic partnerships drive the industry as a whole. I'm a techno-wienie, and chances are you are also. But even a techno-wienie such as myself can see that the Web Service may be one of those rare technologies that can change the nature of our business (Bill Gates knows this also, if you happened to see his open letter in the September issue of "MSDN Magazine"). As important as we might believe .NET to be, it's the Web Service that will marry entire industries together as we bring remote corporations into the nth tier of our business layer.

Whether you buy this book, or another, you owe it to yourself to learn what Web Services are all about. Just as the Internet exploded on to the scene in the early 1990s, so will Web Services explode in the early 2000s. I can't say you'll make a few hundred million dollars by creating a startup technology firm, but I can say that those who know and understand Web Services will probably do well in the job market in the not-so-distant future. And maybe some of you will make a few hundred million (just remember your old pals Mark and Kenn). This is a significant technology, and it is yours to use and profit from. We wish you the best of luck as we enter this new world.

Finally, I owe you a technical side note. As I write this, the summer of 2001 draws to a close. At this time, we're all using Beta 2 of the .NET Framework and Visual Studio .NET. The material contained within this book was drawn from experience using the .NET Framework, various magazine articles, the online documentation for .NET, and through many personal interviews and requests for information. We anticipate that very little will change between the second beta and the actual release of .NET to the general public, but there is no guarantee. If you happen to be reading this after the official release of .NET and you find things don't work as we claim, rest assured we're aware of the situation and will correct the book if given an opportunity. Drop me a note (kenn@endurasoft.com) and I will be happy to help you find the correct solution. It is my intention to maintain current code at http://www.endurasoft.com/netws.htm, so drop by my site for some code and updates if you have the chance.

Tell Us What You Think!

As the reader of this book, *you* are our most important critic and commentator. We value your opinion and want to know what we're doing right, what we could do better, what areas you'd like to see us publish in, and any other words of wisdom you're willing to pass our way.

As an associate publisher for Sams, I welcome your comments. You can fax, e-mail, or write me directly to let me know what you did or didn't like about this book—as well as what we can do to make our books stronger.

Please note that I cannot help you with technical problems related to the topic of this book, and that due to the high volume of mail I receive, I might not be able to reply to every message.

When you write, please be sure to include this book's title and author as well as your name and phone or fax number. I will carefully review your comments and share them with the author and editors who worked on the book.

Fax: 317-581-4770

E-mail: `feedback@samspublishing.com`

Mail: Linda Engelman
         Sams
         201 West 103rd Street
         Indianapolis, IN 46290

Introduction

This book is about a new approach to building applications for the Internet--the technology is called Web Services.

Quite a lot of changes have taken place where the Internet is concerned, especially with regard to how information and services can be shared. If you can disregard the typical marketing hype for a short time, you will see that Web Services are really just a new way for applications to share information using existing and proven Internet technologies.

But it doesn't stop with the Internet. Web Services also offer the opportunity for services to be shared between applications on the same machine, within an intranet, or even between devices.

Web Services are all about interoperability, and XML is one of the fundamental enabling technologies behind them. However, XML alone isn't enough--the Simple Object Access Protocol (SOAP) defines a common way for systems to use XML as a communication protocol.

Applying Web Services to SOAP

In our last book, *Understanding SOAP: The Authoritative Solution*, we discussed SOAP from a distributed application and Remote Procedure Call (RPC) perspective, with a strong emphasis on protocol-specific features. Although not everyone will want to learn the ins and outs of SOAP, understanding the implications of the decisions that you make about the protocol will definitely make you a better Web Service developer.

Since the release of *Understanding SOAP*, many new technologies, such as WSDL and UDDI, have emerged to extend the capabilities of SOAP-enabled systems. Several new SOAP implementations have been released as well (the last unofficial count suggested that there are roughly 68 implementations), and the industry is seeing Web Services gain momentum in real-world applications.

Because of many of these changes, we've taken a slightly different tact in this book: We've decided to look at SOAP in a larger context--properly applying SOAP to Web Services. Although SOAP is not the only approach to implementing Web Services, alternatives such as directly using HTTP GET and POST simply aren't as flexible and thus won't be emphasized.

This book devotes more attention to document-oriented messaging than to RPC. Using SOAP as an RPC mechanism is extremely helpful when you're trying to preserve object identity and other features typically supported by current RPC protocols. The fact is, most of the existing implementations are based on the RPC approach, but this is quickly changing. In the business-to-business (B2B) arena, the document-based solution is more direct and much easier to describe in schema languages. We will try to shed some light on the pros and cons of using RPC versus literal XML documents because this will become an interoperability issue as time goes on.

As I've already mentioned, you no longer need to build your own SOAP implementations (I can already hear your cries of disappointment). As you might expect, there are plenty of good implementations for a variety of different programming languages and platforms. The mainstream offerings include Apache's Java SOAP toolkit (originally IBM's SOAP4J), Microsoft's SOAP Toolkit, and several different libraries for Perl, C++, and others.

So why did we choose to write about Microsoft's .NET Framework? Our initial response is because .NET has created an entirely new runtime that's designed specifically for Internet application development. But somewhere deep inside, we know that part of the reason is because .NET is just plain cool. It's especially interesting to those of us who have been doing Windows development on and off for many years. Windows development has had its share of blemishes, not uncommon for a system that has undergone many new face-lifts and architectural changes. .NET represents the playground equivalent of a *do-over*. The developers at Microsoft took a long look at what is working in the industry and improved upon it. The end result is a framework for building applications that simplifies the programming model while still maintaining backward compatibility with existing architectures such as COM.

We've been around long enough to know that there's no panacea in software development. To be a good software developer, it's important to be pragmatic. You need to question why things work the way they do, you need to be critical about the technologies you choose, and you have to be willing to try new things. It's possible that all of these played a part in your decision to pick up and read this book. They definitely contributed to our decision to write this book about Web Services and .NET!

Overall, this book has three main themes. First, it approaches Web Services from an architectural and design standpoint to analyze the issues that must be addressed in this new paradigm, specifically within the .NET Framework. Second, it shows you how to implement Web Services using the .NET Framework and the new Visual Studio .NET tools. Finally, more advanced Web Services and SOAP topics are discussed, including information regarding the W3C's work on the XML Protocol (XMLP).

Today's Enterprise Applications

Software development is a constantly changing art, and programmers have the daunting responsibility of staying up-to-date with the latest trends in technology. The purpose of this book is to teach you how to apply practical solutions to building Web Services using the .NET Framework. The greatest advantage to Web Services is that it applies to so many problem spaces. These problem spaces include complex B2B system integration, networked devices, distributed development, and many others. However, with this promise of interoperability and simplicity comes a great deal of expectations.

Expectations

Many advancements in our field have made software development a much easier task--and, at times, a much harder one. Design methodologies, programming languages, operating systems, network protocols, distributed architectures--all of these and others impact the way we build software. Unfortunately, all of this technology leads to a staggering number of software incompatibilities that become even more apparent when cast upon the Internet backdrop.

The industry has tried to address these incompatibilities in a number of ways. Java addresses the problem from a programming language perspective, allowing applications to be written once and deployed to any number of platforms that support a Java Virtual Machine. Through the use of Java's Remote Method Invocation (RMI) technology, applications can more easily operate in a distributed environment. When considering Java and RMI however, to guarantee interoperability, you are responsible for ensuring that both ends of the connection are running Java. In a controlled environment this could be a viable solution, but the Internet is far from a controlled environment.

Both CORBA and DCOM (DCE/RPC) address the interoperability problem from a networking perspective. Given a common way to encode information into network packets (using Network Data Representation), programming languages become less of an issue. Instead, maintaining compatibility with serialization methods becomes the concern. This usually means that to build compatible components, you are forced to use one particular vendor's implementation. Although the vendors would love this, it would be impossible to get everyone on the Internet to agree to use just one vendor's software.

Web Services offer a layer of abstraction that hides many of the implementation details that so many developers can't seem to disregard. Take programming languages, for example. Programmers tend to gravitate toward one particular language and discount other (possibly competing) languages. Sometimes these observations are based on experience, and sometimes the reasons are purely religious in nature, such as the animal desire to see semicolons and curly braces in code. Regardless of the basis for these feelings, this choice is a fact of life for developers and will not likely ever go away. Certainly, the .NET Framework goes a long way toward marrying diverse programming languages into a common environment--but this is true only on platforms that support .NET. Web Services take this one step further by breaking down the platform barriers to allow heterogeneous systems to interact.

The Internet has introduced technologies that are a sort of common denominator. Interoperability is the driving force behind most of the successful Internet technologies. Without interoperability, a particular technology has little chance of being adopted. Without adoption, even the most interesting technologies become nothing more than graduate research projects. The reason that the Internet has been so successful is the increasingly popular movement toward standardization. It started with the adoption of TCP/IP, the cornerstone of the Internet communication protocols, and has continued with the acceptance of HTTP, XML, and, more recently, SOAP.

In actuality, SOAP isn't considered a standard--at least, not in terms of the W3C. But it is considered *industry accepted*, as can be seen by the enormous development community interest. The fact is, SOAP is currently under the looking glass of the W3C's XML Protocol Activity. In this forum, W3C members get the opportunity to shape the technology into something that addresses the needs of the industry.

Today's Web applications are expected to handle thousands of transactions per minute to solve a wide array of problems. As we build upon an architecture in which applications interact with other applications, the frequency and size of transactions will most definitely grow. This will cause us to think about the Internet in entirely new terms, eventually leading to a metamorphosis in the systems that make up the network. Concerns about reliability, availability, performance, and similar properties will need to be addressed under this new development model.

The Search for Solutions

There's still a lot to learn about distributed computing, and Web Services will force us to extend our knowledge in the Internet space. This time around, however, we'll be forced to think in terms of standards that will allow all kinds of systems to participate.

The most important concept behind Web Services is that software functionality can be shared regardless of the implementation details behind these services. This level of integration is accomplished through loosely coupled services that provide a flexible and responsive architecture for building the next generation of applications.

Who Should Read This Book?

This book is for the intermediate to advanced developer who is new to Web Services. It will show you how to use the .NET Framework and Visual Studio .NET to construct Web Services. It also will help you understand common pitfalls and issues that surround this new architecture. Software engineers, programmers, and Web developers alike will find many of the concepts applicable to their daily development lives when building these systems. As always, our goal is to save you development time by presenting practical information through discussion, examples, and source code.

The examples in this book mostly contain Visual C# code, with an occasional Visual Basic snippet. We chose C# because of its close relationship to Java and C++ programming, which should meet the needs of a fairly wide audience.

The majority of this book is dedicated to the SOAP protocol as it has been implemented within .NET. Although some introductory SOAP information is provided in Chapter 4, ".NET Web

Services and SOAP," we assume that most readers are already familiar with the protocol and are simply looking for new insights when applying SOAP to .NET applications.

Contents of This Book

This book is divided into three sections.

Section 1, "Foundations of Web Services," describes what Web Services are and how the .NET architecture applies to this paradigm.

- Chapter 1, "Web Service Fundamentals," provides a brief explanation of Web Services and tells why they are the future of Web application development.
- Chapter 2, ".NET Architecture and Web Services Components," takes you on a quick tour of the .NET architecture. It also gives you an overview of the Common Language Runtime and specific Web Service components.
- Chapter 3, "Web Services and XML," shows how the .NET architecture integrates XML with the new .NET XML classes.
- Chapter 4, ".NET Web Services and SOAP," explains how SOAP is used to provide a consistent serialization format, fault pattern, and general protocol for Web Services.
- Chapter 5, "Web Service Description and Discovery," details the Web Service Description Language as well as the Universal Description, Discovery, and Integration concepts.

Section 2, "Implementing Web Services," walks you through the ASP.NET and Visual Studio .NET tools.

- Chapter 6, "Web Services in ASP.NET," covers development from the server-side perspective.
- Chapter 7, "Consuming .NET Web Services," shows the latest features provided in Microsoft's newest development environment.

Section 3, "More Advanced Web Services," discusses several issues and provides multiple options to consider when encountering these problems.

- Chapter 8, ".NET Remoting," covers issues such as how SOAP can be used to carry various forms of payloads, encryption, and alternate encoding formats.
- Chapter 9, "Extreme Web Services," closes the book's discussion by establishing a basis for understanding authentication, authorization, entitlements, and digital signatures as they relate to Web Services.
- Chapter 10, ".NET and Web Service Security," overviews the options available when securing your Web Service.

In addition, this book provides reference material in the following appendixes:

- Appendix A—"Example .NET Web Service"

- Appendix B—"Using ATL Server to Create Web Services"

- Appendix C—"XML Protocol and SOAP"

- Appendix D—".NET Web Service Resources"

Version Issues

This book is based on a pre-release version (Beta 2) of Visual Studio .NET and the .NET Framework. It's possible that features of the fully released product could be inconsistent with topics covered in this book. Potential changes to look for include minor organization changes in the .NET libraries, minor parameter changes in classes, and significantly improved documentation.

Regardless of the changes to .NET, the concepts and approaches described in this book will continue to remain valid.

Foundations of Web Services

Web Service Fundamentals

IN THIS CHAPTER

It's pretty hard to pick up a trade magazine these days without seeing a headline about Web Services. With phrases such as "a new paradigm" being proliferated, are we really witnessing the genesis of a new technology?

Unfortunately, the answer isn't black and white—a lot depends on your perspective. Web Services can be used in a wide variety of ways, including these:

- Participating in business-to-business (B2B) transactions
- Exposing software functionality to customers
- Integrating heterogeneous platforms and programming languages
- Providing a simplified platform for product development

What Are Web Services?

Web Services can be described as any functionality that is accessible over the Internet, generally (but not necessarily) using one or more eXtensible Markup Language (XML) messages in the communications protocol. Web Services use the concept of an operation to represent the association of a request message to zero or more response messages. When these operations are combined to satisfy some particular purpose, they form an interface.

The Poor Man's Web Service

The Internet is already flooded with conventional types of Web Services, better known as Web pages. Users are expected to interact with the functionality behind the Web page through typical user-interface widgets such as forms, buttons, and so on.

We already know how to reuse Web functionality by embedding other Web pages into our own pages through frames and links. But this presentation-based approach severely limits the things that you can accomplish. If you embed another Web site within a frame of your own, you generally have no control over the colors, graphics, or other aspects of the presentation. Another problem is that any information entered by a user in the embedded page never gets back to your controlling application. In other words, you're out of the loop!

One way around this is for your application to act as a proxy for the user. Many developers have already written simple applications that navigate to a particular URL, screen-scrape the Web site's HTML for information, and use that information to build new Web content. Consider the following HTML that describes the current weather temperature:

```
<HTML>
   <HEAD>
      <TITLE>Today's Weather</TITLE>
   </HEAD>
   <BODY>
```

```
      <P>City: <B>Los Angeles</B></P>
      <P>State: <B>California</B></P>
      <P>Temperature: <B>83</B></P>
   </BODY>
</HTML>
```

In this case, it would be fairly simple to programmatically locate the temperature value within the markup. However, over an extended period of time using this service, you can be sure that the underlying Web page will change and ultimately break your application. It would be nearly impossible to develop software that could automatically adjust to fluctuations in the type of markup, as shown:

```
<HTML>
<HEAD>
   <TITLE>Today's Weather</TITLE>
</HEAD>
<BODY>
   <TABLE WIDTH="500" CELLPADDING="10" CELLSPACING="15">
      <TR>
         <TD ALIGN="LEFT" VALIGN="MIDDLE" WIDTH="100"><B>City</B></TD>
         <TD ALIGN="LEFT" VALIGN="MIDDLE" WIDTH="200">Los Angeles</TD>
      </TR>
      <TR>
         <TD ALIGN="LEFT" VALIGN="MIDDLE" WIDTH="100"><B>State</B></TD>
         <TD ALIGN="LEFT" VALIGN="MIDDLE" WIDTH="200">California</TD>
      </TR>
      <TR>
         <TD ALIGN="LEFT" VALIGN="MIDDLE" WIDTH="100">
            <B>Temperature</B>
         </TD>
         <TD ALIGN="LEFT" VALIGN="MIDDLE" WIDTH="200">83</TD>
         <TD ALIGN="LEFT" VALIGN="TOP">
            <IMG SRC="sunny.gif" WIDTH="25" HEIGHT="33">
         </TD>
      </TR>
   </TABLE>
</BODY>
</HTML>
```

Now consider integrating multiple systems using this approach. Recall that in the Web Services paradigm, many systems likely could participate in some business process. Because HTML content changes at such a fast pace, you likely will not ever be able to construct a reliable integrated solution.

For example, consider one application that monitors the temperature Web site and another Web site that posts the average speed of traffic on a nearby highway:

```
<HTML>
    <HEAD>
        <TITLE>Interstate Traffic Report</TITLE>
    </HEAD>
    <BODY>
        <CENTER>Average Speed</CENTER>
        <CENTER>67</CENTER>
    </BODY>
</HTML>
```

By relating these two axes of data, the application might be capable of determining whether there is a correlation between sunny days and fast driving. Although it might be an interesting problem to solve, the likelihood of the application working with 24×7 reliability is extremely low. The plain-and-simple fact is that relying on presentation-oriented data leads to a tightly coupled and brittle system.

The question isn't whether the concept of integrating Web content is valid; the problem lies within the information that can be obtained from a source. Without rich content markup, programs don't have much of a chance of locating pertinent information. Of course, this is where XML markup makes an important difference. Given standardized markup that describes information in a particular domain space, an application should always be capable of finding the right data.

Taking the concept of standardized markup into account, Web Services can be better defined as functionality that is accessed over the Web and that provides information in a reliable and predictable manner. In many cases, this predictability will be realized through the use of XML markup for describing information.

Although Web Services are not limited to the following technologies, you will find that a large percentage of Web Service implementations are built upon the Hypertext Transfer Protocol (HTTP), SOAP/XML as a messaging protocol, and Web Services Description Language (WSDL) as a way to describe service interfaces.

The basic idea behind Web Services isn't really new. In many ways, we are just reusing technologies that most of us have used for years. Surprisingly, many developers have already built systems using Web Service techniques, but in a very ad hoc and proprietary way. The main difference is that the industry is now supporting Web Services with standards, tools, and implementations.

First reactions about Web Services usually revolve around performance. Most people recognize that transmitting XML is not the most expeditious way for systems to communicate. So why use XML? We use XML because it provides us with a predictable way to package information that is structured, extensible, and yet still very easy to use—not something that can be said for other packaging protocols. Let's take a closer look.

XML Messages

By nature, interface-based programming enables us to build loosely coupled systems, meaning that the client and Web Service are independent of one another. This has been true in object-oriented programming for many years, within the confines of a particular programming language. Web Services reinforce loosely coupled systems by removing dependence upon a common programming language or even a common platform. This is realized through the use of XML messages, which define the operations inside a Web Service interface.

The importance of this feature is well understood by distributed application developers who have been using systems such as CORBA and DCOM. Historically, building applications on top of binary protocols and their associated runtimes results in a very tight dependency between the client and the server. This forces developers to repeatedly build and distribute new interface components (such as proxies and stubs), which is a very tedious and error-prone process. More importantly, though, XML lets you focus on the interface semantics rather than having to worry so much about synchronizing parameter lists of remote methods.

Syntax Versus Semantics

Recall that *syntax* is the detailed representation of information. It's the way you organize instructions in a programming language or arrange tags in an XML document.

Semantics, on the other hand, refers to the meanings or concepts behind a syntactical representation. Because semantics represents information from a logical standpoint, there might be several ways to syntactically represent that information, all of which should convey the same meaning to the information consumer.

To better contrast syntax and semantics, consider the following sample XML:

```
<ChargeCreditCard>
    <amount>150.00</amount>
    <creditCardNumber>123456789</creditCardNumber>
    <expirationDate>2003-01-31</expirationDate>
</ChargeCreditCard>
```

In this case, the syntax is fairly simple—an XML message consisting of start and end tags, structured with a single root element and its descendants. We could have just as easily used the following text:

```
Please charge $150.00 to credit card number 123456789, which expires January
31, 2003.
```

Semantically, the information represented by both syntaxes allows you to bill someone's credit card, which is really what we're interested in. Obviously, the latter syntax is more pleasing to humans, and the former XML message is much more acceptable for application consumption.

SOAP uses XML to define a syntax, which makes it very easy to represent information in a structured form. However, SOAP also carries some important protocol semantics that allow SOAP processors to serialize/deserialize data, handle faults, and mandate that certain information be present in a message.

As the creator of a Web Service, you have the task of defining your own set of semantics for your Web Service. Some simple semantics might be to get a stock quote or to retrieve the time and temperature. A more advanced semantic might be to schedule a vacation, which includes reserving a hotel room, airfare, and ground transportation. Arriving at a reasonable set of semantics requires you to use standard software engineering practices such as working with domain experts.

The long-term vision of Web Services is for developers to be able to construct applications by integrating one or more units of functionality into a single service (as in the vacation example). The most significant aspect of this model is that you can incorporate distinct units of functionality from a wide variety of sources and successfully complete some larger task or business process. It is like code reuse, without the programming language compatibility problems.

To describe the interaction between Web Services and their clients, it's important to define some terminology that will be used in this context.

Web Service Terminology

The Web Services model uses several terms that help to identify the various roles in a typical Web Service scenario.

A *service provider* is an entity that hosts a Web Service that exposes some functionality. The service provider is responsible for defining the semantics of the service interface as well as constructing the appropriate physical representation as depicted in a Web Service description document.

The service provider can then publish the interface description to a *service registry*. Here, information about the provider and the service are persisted for service discovery. The service registry exposes its own set of interface semantics that allows others to create new entries, update registry information, or query for specific registry parameters. For more detailed information about service registries, refer to Chapter 5, "Web Service Description and Discovery."

At some point after service publication, a *service requestor* (sometimes referred to as the client) can discover the Web Service and its interface description, and bind to this service to fulfill the service requestor's needs.

As you can see from Figure 1.1, three major processes take place. First, the service provider *publishes* service information. Next, the service requestor *finds* the service in the service registry. Finally, the service requestor *binds* to the service to execute some functionality. This *publish, find, and bind* model is consistent with other networking protocols such as DNS.

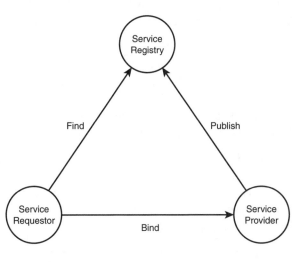

FIGURE 1.1
The Publish, Find, and Bind Model.

Now that you are familiar with the concept of Web Services, let's take a quick tour of how Web Services came about and why.

The Road to Web Services

Most things in software engineering happen for a very good reason—or, at least, we hope so. This is how concepts such as *abstraction* and *encapsulation* have become mainstream. As with any technology, we learn from past mistakes and capitalize upon our successes.

Web Services are no different. They have materialized from a variety of Web technologies that have been proven to work in the widely distributed environment of the Internet. The Internet itself has evolved over the years, spawning many new ideas and concepts that have contributed to the Web Service approach.

Waves of the Internet

Since the beginning of the Internet, many changes have come about in networking technology, security, system scalability, and many other areas of distributed computing. Overall, we believe that the Internet has succumbed to four major waves of development.

The first wave of the Internet started around the 1970s with some very important government research, specifically the Defense Advanced Research Projects Agency (DARPA). This is where Transmission Control Protocol/Internet Protocol (TCP/IP) was born. Its goal was to interconnect computer systems through a complex architecture of networks and subnetworks. Over the years, a variety of physical networks (such as Ethernet) and routing technologies evolved to the point that, in 1990, more than 200,000 computers were interconnected on the Internet.

Although Internet connectivity was one of the most significant achievements in computing, it meant very little without applications to drive it. This is where the second wave of the Internet began (roughly in the 1980s). Tools such as FTP and Telnet gained in popularity by allowing system users to remotely access other computers. Although the tools were crude, compared to today's standards, the underlying protocols that they used where quite elegant.

In the early 1990s, the Internet began to seep into more sophisticated applications and led to the dawn of the Web, which marks the third wave. Browsers—and eventually Java applets—allowed the general consumer to experience interconnected communities of users. Of course, where there are consumers, there are vendors. This spawned more electronic business opportunities, as evidenced by the plethora of electronic storefronts and shopping carts.

All this, of course, has brought about the fourth wave of the Internet, which is the focus of this book—Web Services. Here, the goal is for multiple *diverse* applications to communicate so that they can execute some task. Not only does this improve the user's experience, but it also offers the ability for you to integrate functionality at a much lower cost than developing it all yourself. From the user's standpoint, all of this is orchestrated from a single application. But behind the scenes, one or more additional applications will likely participate. The key is that the applications work while remaining oblivious to vendor-specific technologies being used by the participating services.

Looking back, each wave introduced new Internet standards that facilitated the next wave of development.

Internet Standards

In April 1969, the first Request for Comments (RFC) was published at UCLA (RFC 1), and thus began the process of sharing ideas in computing for a much greater cause. Then, in 1986, the Internet Engineering Task Force (IETF) was officially created. Its charter was (and still is) to evolve the architecture of the Internet using open contributions from the research and development community.

After inventing the Web, Tim Berners-Lee decided to create the World Wide Web Consortium (W3C) in October 1994. The W3C's purpose is to promote interoperability and open forum discussions about the Web and its protocols.

These organizations have led the way to standardization, a process that has resulted in a strong foundation for the Web Service infrastructure.

Several standards are prevalent in current Internet development. Some have existed for years, and others are relatively new, and not necessarily standards. This section summarizes these technologies and shows how they apply to Web Services.

HTTP and SMTP

As stated before, TCP/IP is the foundation of Internet communication protocols. However, TCP/IP without an application is a little like a car without a driver. How an application uses TCP/IP also determines the semantics of that application's protocol.

Application protocols such as HTTP and Simple Mail Transfer Protocol (SMTP) already have predefined semantics and behavior that determine how they should be used. For HTTP, the semantic implies a request/response model designed to serve Web resources such as HTML or JPG files. SMTP, on the other hand, implies a one-way request/acknowledge semantic designed to transmit text-based email messages in a *fire-and-forget* manner.

NOTE

Fire-and-forget is a military warfare term that has been overloaded for networking purposes. We use it to describe the process of sending a message: The sender does not require any acknowledgement that the recipient actually received the message.

In the context of Web Services, these *application protocols* are used to carry additional semantics, such as those specified by SOAP. SOAP, in turn, provides a way for you to define your application semantics that are also carried over these application protocols. This layering of semantics just reemphasizes the flexibility of Web Service protocols.

Because HTTP is the dominant protocol being used for Web Services, let's take a quick look at the two most common aspects of HTTP being exploited, the GET and POST verbs.

The following is a sample HTTP GET request:

```
GET /default.htm HTTP/1.1
Accept: text/*
Host: www.mcp.com
{CR}{LF}
```

In this case, the client is requesting that the www.mcp.com server return the default.htm resource. The client would like to use version 1.1 of the HTTP protocol in this transaction and is willing to accept the resource as some form of text. Notice that the message is terminated by the carriage return/line feed pair following the message.

Many times you need to provide application-specific information to the server that is not represented in the semantics of the HTTP protocol. For instance, you can pass parameters on the URL, as shown:

```
GET /GetStockQuote.asp?symbol=MSFT HTTP/1.1
Accept: text/*
Host: www.mcp.com
{CR}{LF}
```

Given this sample request for obtaining stock quote information, the `symbol` parameter and its value are passed on the query string, and you can expect the server to respond with some form of HTML, such as the following:

```
HTTP/1.1 200 OK
Content-type: text/html

<html><head><title>Microsoft Stock Price</title></head>
<body>
    <b>Microsoft: 80.75</b>
</body>
</html>
```

The server's response contains the HTTP version, a status code and message, and the content type that is associated with the related payload following the carriage return/line feed pair.

However, using the `GET` request is less than optimal when dealing with large and complex parameters. Certain HTTP implementations and older firewalls have been known to truncate URLs based on poorly chosen size limits. URLs also undergo encoding for a large number of characters, which complicates processing procedures.

Instead, we can use the HTTP `POST` verb, which places information within the Body of the request message:

```
POST /GetStockQuote.asp HTTP/1.1
Accept: text/*
Host: www.mcp.com
Content-type: text/xml
Content-length: nnnn


<Symbol>MSFT</Symbol>
```

Similar to the `GET` verb, the `POST` verb also identifies a resource, the version of HTTP, and the content that it expects to receive. However, two additional HTTP fields are provided—`Content-type` and `Content-length`. The two new fields refer to the remainder of the message, which, in this case, happens to carry an XML message.

Here you can see that we are no longer bound by limitations of the URL. There is less character encoding taking place, and we are able to transmit more complicated payloads—this is by far the most helpful aspect of HTTP when used in the Web Service model.

> **NOTE**
>
> Although we generally recommend that you use the POST method, in some situations using GET might make sense. GET is best used for simple semantics that require only minimal message structure and in situations when client applications don't have control over the POST payload.
>
> An example of this is with the Visual Studio .NET test pages that are generated with your Web Services. Because the browser's POST feature does not allow you to place customized information in the message Body, the GET verb comes in very handy.
>
> Also note that your test pages won't support complicated parameter types (same goes for the WSDL for HTTP GET or POST), so you'll be required to manually build a client that can exercise your service in this case.

eXtensible Markup Language (XML)

Although XML has such a wide variety of uses, it makes a great foundation for Web Services for many reasons:

- In a world where global business arrangements are becoming the norm, XML natively supports different character sets through Unicode (UTF-8, UTF-16, and so on).

- XML promotes interoperability in a platform-agnostic way by promoting the convergence of information to a common, vendor-neutral state.

- Probably most importantly, XML is simple.

As we briefly mentioned before, XML is really just syntax for application semantics that you must define. To define semantics and the associated XML syntax for your semantics, you need to establish the appropriate structure and restrictions of your markup—you do this through a schema.

XML Schemas

When you want to describe (and possibly validate) an XML document, you might use a Document Type Definition (DTD), such as this one:

```
<!-- House DTD -->
<!ELEMENT house (address)>
<!ATTLIST house bedrooms CDATA #REQUIRED
                bathrooms CDATA #REQUIRED>
<!ELEMENT address (street, city, state, zip)>
```

```
<!ELEMENT street (#PCDATA)>
<!ELEMENT city (#PCDATA)>
<!ELEMENT state (#PCDATA)>
<!ELEMENT zip (#PCDATA)>
```

As you can see, though, DTDs are limited by their somewhat cryptic syntax and lack of type checking.

In February 2001, the XML Schema specification was promoted to Recommendation status by the W3C. XML schemas not only encapsulate the same feature-function as DTDs, but they also offer complex type checking, all wrapped up in an XML language. This makes XML schemas the preferred method of describing all forms of XML documents, including XML messages. The same example is shown in XML schema format, as follows:

```
<!-- House XML Schema -->
<xsd:schema xmlns:xsd="http://www.w3.org/2001/XMLSchema">
  <xsd:complexType name="AddressType">
    <xsd:sequence>
      <xsd:element name="street" type="xsd:string" />
      <xsd:element name="city" type="xsd:string" />
      <xsd:element name="state" type="xsd:string" />
      <xsd:element name="zip" type="xsd:decimal" />
    </xsd:sequence>
    <xsd:attribute name="bedrooms" type="xsd:positiveInteger" use="required" />
    <xsd:attribute name="bathrooms" type="xsd:positiveInteger" use="required"/>
  </xsd:complexType>

  <xsd:element name="house" type="AddressType" />
</xsd:schema>
```

SOAP

Although SOAP isn't officially an Internet standard, it has been widely adopted by the Internet community, including the Electronic Business XML (ebXML) organization, for its transport and routing layer.

To summarize SOAP in a single word, *packaging* is the most appropriate description. Many developers have created ad-hoc approaches for sending XML messages between their applications. The creators of XML-RPC took the concept to the next level by exposing a publicly available specification for XML messaging. Taking XML-RPC a step further, SOAP basically defines a standard yet extensible way to wrap information in XML so that both ends of the connection (and potentially everything in between) can understand how to open this package. Let's take a quick look at a SOAP request message:

```
<SOAP-ENV:Envelope
   xmlns:SOAP-ENV="http://schemas.xmlsoap.org/soap/envelope/"
```

```
SOAP-ENV:encodingStyle="http://schemas.xmlsoap.org/soap/encoding/">
  <SOAP-ENV:Header>
    <t:transId xmlns:t="http://www.mcp.com/trans">
       87654
    </t:transId>
  </SOAP-ENV:Header>
  <SOAP-ENV:Body>
    <m:GetStockQuote xmlns:m="http://www.mcp.com/stock">
       <Symbol>MSFT</Symbol>
    </m:GetStockQuote>
  </SOAP-ENV:Body>
</SOAP-ENV:Envelope>
```

This simple message shows the general packaging of a SOAP message. The Envelope contains an optional Header and a mandatory Body. The Header is used for out-of-band information that doesn't necessarily apply to the semantics of the message Body. The Body is used to carry the application-specific message content. This is definitely not all that SOAP represents, but it captures the spirit of what SOAP set out to accomplish. We'll leave it to Chapter 4, ".NET Web Services and SOAP," to provide the gory details about the remainder of the SOAP protocol.

WSDL and UDDI

WSDL is the description language that is used to describe how software must interact with a particular Web Service. Clients use WSDL documents to understand the logical structure and the syntax of a Web Service. WSDL also provides message-exchange patterns, service bindings, and references to the location of a service.

Growing in popularity, Universal Description, Discovery, and Integration (UDDI) is one way for the publish, find, and bind process to be accomplished. UDDI servers allow WSDL to be published and propagated across the Internet so that clients can ultimately consume a given service.

Although neither WSDL nor UDDI has been standardized, the industry is giving both the most attention of any similar mechanisms. A great deal more about WSDL and UDDI will be explained in Chapter 5.

Uses for Web Services

At the beginning of this chapter, we briefly mentioned several areas where Web Services can have an impact on the solutions that you build. Let's look at a few of these areas a little closer.

Business-to-Business

One area that clearly deserves attention is in the business-to-business (B2B) paradigm. Most companies today still operate on paper systems. This is due in part to the simplicity and low cost of entry into paper-based systems. For more than two decades, developers have been trying to integrate business processes using a combination of software and communication protocols.

Electronic Data Interchange (EDI) has been the technology of choice for many years. Unfortunately, EDI has been a technology that only large corporations could afford to leverage. Not only was EDI expensive, but it also could require years of effort to become fully integrated into a business process. Although the intentions were good, the complexity of the underlying technologies was not cost-effective for many companies.

When XML took center stage, it became apparent that XML could facilitate the low-cost and simplistic approach that was necessary for the B2B task.

Right around the advent of SOAP, the Organization for the Advancement of Structured Information Standards (OASIS) formed a group to design an XML-based technology that could become the de facto standard for business communication. This effort is known as Electronic Business XML (ebXML) and is sponsored by OASIS and the United Nation's Center for Trade Facilitation and Electronic Business (UN/CEFACT).

Because most of the ebXML group has been working with EDI for years, it had a clear idea of how to build a global electronic marketplace. Initially, the ebXML team set a course to deliver a framework within 18 months of the group's forming. In May 2001, the group did just that.

What was so significant about ebXML was that the ebXML Transport, Routing, and Packaging team began developing an XML-based protocol that did not involve SOAP. Fortunately, before the release in May 2001, the TRP team reevaluated the SOAP specifications and eventually incorporated SOAP and its use with Multipart MIME.

Exposing Functionality to Customers

Although this is a similar topic, don't confuse this type of service with standard B2B operations as addressed by ebXML. Here we're talking about something like a billable service or a deliverable that you expose to a customer through a Web Service.

An example might be the history report of a car—but not just any report, especially not one that is displayed in a Web page. Rather, this information must be provided in XML so that a car dealer can build a used-car evaluation system that automatically approves or rejects trade-ins.

Consumer-related services such as the Hailstorm services being developed by Microsoft provide the capability to store documents, calendar information, and even your favorite Web sites in a common repository.

Integrating Heterogeneous Systems

It's normal for companies to have computing systems dispersed across multiple platforms. This can be the result of system evolution, cost reduction, or varying developer experience. Commonly, it's the result of architectural disagreements between developers that prefer one platform to another.

The typical RPC-like protocols have never proved to be a satisfactory solution to this problem. While it's possible to get disparate systems to communicate, the time involved in doing so usually outweighs the benefits. Why is it so difficult to get disparate systems to communicate? One reason is that vendors choose to deviate from standards to squeeze more performance out of their platforms. Interpretation of standards is another cause of protocol incompatibility, mostly because specifications are complex and have areas of ambiguity that aren't easily resolved without vendor cooperation.

If you can reduce the development time to a manageable amount and remove the vendor-specific protocols, you can capitalize on Web Services in the enterprise in many ways.

We won't try to convince you that Web Service performance is on par with binary protocols—the additional overhead in text processing alone suggests that they're not. But we can tell you that it takes less than a week to get two dissimilar systems communicating using XML and HTTP. And with network and processor speeds rapidly improving, ease of development may be more beneficial than raw speed. Ultimately, you'll have to decide which type of performance means the most to you.

Rapid Development Environment

Web Services can make your project development environment operate faster, for several reasons.

As mentioned before, heterogeneous systems can be hooked together to build a solution. This enables developers to work in their preferred environment, while still allowing them to produce an integrated solution. If at some point you decide to move a service from one platform to another, clients will be unaware of the change, as long as you maintain the same interface. A platform-independent programming environment such as .NET adds to this capability by reducing the amount of code that actually needs to be rewritten.

Web Services also force you to think in terms of interfaces. You don't have to worry about compiling another developer's source code or linking in libraries. Stack traces and memory dumps are partially replaced by traces of XML messages.

This usually has the positive side effect of breaking down services into logical subcomponents. You can then isolate functionality and test it accordingly. Because of this, Web Services can be easier to test. You can fairly easily trace Request messages and save them in text files so that later they can be played back to regression test your interfaces.

Web Services can offer such an improved development environment because of the fundamental Web Service properties. We'll take a look at these next.

Web Service Properties

Many times we become so enamored with new technologies that we don't always realize the benefits and costs of using them. It's important to explore these so that you can make informed decisions about the systems you are building.

Performance

Although there are many types of performance, we are specifically referring to raw communications performance at this point. This type of performance always seems to be one of the first topics that come up in discussions of Web Services. It's a perfectly reasonable concern because we're talking about using a text-based protocol (such as SOAP and XML).

Losses Versus Gains

The fact is, when using XML and HTTP, you definitely sacrifice network performance when compared to binary protocols such as CORBA. Various unofficial tests have shown performance degradation at five times slower (or worse) than a binary protocol. Although most of the performance cost can be attributed to XML parsing, character encoding and socket setup and teardown costs also have an impact. However, as we've already mentioned, network and processor speed improvements will eventually make these concerns nonissues.

But consider what you gain from this loss in performance. First, you gain native Unicode support. By default, XML is designed to accommodate most forms of languages, making it a truly global protocol. This might not be important to you now, but in an Internet economy that has no physical borders, globalization will play an important part in future B2B efforts.

You also gain loose coupling between systems. This is by far one of the most positive aspects about Web Services—and SOAP, in particular. Developers are constantly challenged to work with different operating systems, runtime platforms, programming languages, and so on. Loose coupling enables you to hide the implementation details of a service from the service requestor, giving both parties a great deal of flexibility and choice. This leads to the topic of another type of performance: developer performance. Because Web Services are agnostic to implementation details, programmers have the opportunity to choose the programming environment that makes them the most productive. In a multi–Web Service environment, loose coupling also allows developers to work independently on these services. This helps to improve parallel development efforts.

Finally, you gain an extensible protocol that can grow over time. With so many changes occurring in the Internet, you cannot afford to stagnate. Systems must be capable of adapting faster and faster. Built-in mechanisms for extensibility (as demonstrated in SOAP) are necessary to protect systems from becoming brittle.

Improving the Performance of Web Services

But don't go away feeling that all performance is lost. You can do a few things to improve the overall performance of your application.

One of the most significant ways is to be aware of how you define your interfaces. We tend to think in terms of standard distributed RPC architectures. With these systems, we usually have a distributed runtime that is managing state and maintaining an open connection at all times. RPC architectures do this because setup and teardown of connections takes a significant amount of time. When using protocols such as HTTP for Web Services, you have to plan on connections coming and going to achieve high scalability.

To account for this, you must maximize the amount of information that you transmit on each call. However, this is not always an easy task because you can't afford to change the semantics of an interface just to improve performance. You will need to spend a great deal of design time determining the best way to convey your semantics in the fewest number of messages possible. Just remember, you're better off sending a little too much information than not sending enough and requiring additional round trips.

It's also important to understand the needs of your service's typical service requestor and adjust the interface appropriately. For instance, if you know that a client will typically ask for A and then almost immediately ask for B, maybe your interface should always return B with A, saving that additional round trip. This is a simple but common example in distributed systems development.

You should also be aware that how a service requestor is implemented could make a significant difference in the service requestor's performance. Although you shouldn't care about the service requestor's implementation—and, in most situations, it's out of your control—the fact remains that poor implementations can be directly attributed to lousy performance. A common improvement can be found by using SAX parsers over DOM parsers. There are certainly advantages to each, but, in many cases, SAX will help your applications get faster. Don't be overly discouraged by parsing speed, though; vendors are developing new ways to improve parse times, as you've already seen in newer generations of XML parsers.

User Perceptions

Another client-related area that you might have control over deals with *perceived performance*. This type of performance is directly related to the end user's experience. You can identify these areas for improvement when your XML messages have a direct effect on a user interface. In this case, it might be possible to provide partial user feedback before all transactions in a business process complete. This is similar to the way Web pages are rendered in a browser—as a user, it's helpful to see the first screen of a document while the remainder is downloaded in the background. Be careful when architecting your systems around presentation-oriented behavior—you want to avoid sacrificing semantics for performance whenever possible.

Simplicity

Compared to many of the distributed systems currently in the industry, Web Service dwarfs the others when it comes to simplicity.

Granted, some of the technologies surrounding Web Services have their share of complexities, but XML and HTTP generally are not very difficult to use. Plenty of software is available to use XML and HTTP, not to mention the growing number of SOAP implementations that are freely available (see Appendix D, ".NET Web Service Resources").

Building software to use a Web Service is also very easy. When you understand the semantics of the Web Service, constructing the code to interact with the service is usually straightforward. This is because the programming model for Web Service is fairly simple. It forces you to separate interface from implementation, a concept that is well understood by the object-oriented programming community.

Security

The Internet has brought security to the forefront of everyone's minds. Viruses, hackers, and the like all lead to concerns from both a consumer and a developer standpoint. The question of whether Web Services make you more susceptible to security risks doesn't have a clear answer. On one hand, Web Services don't introduce any new technologies, but they do introduce yet another application of existing technologies that can be attacked.

The Secure Socket Layer (SSL) is one level of security that encrypts SOAP messages at the HTTP transport layer, usually referred to as HTTPS. Without the proper SSL certificate information, an interceptor would have no way of knowing the actual contents of the underlying HTTPS message.

In addition to SSL, a lot of interest has arisen in extending SOAP's security prospects. This has led to a W3C submission called *SOAP Security Extensions: Digital Signature*. In a nutshell, this promotes a standard way to use digital signatures in XML to sign SOAP messages. Although this does not prevent others from peering into your messages or replaying messages to your applications, it does allow you to verify the integrity of the message as well as its origin. To accomplish this, the specification proposes using the SOAP Headers to carry digital signatures that relate to some other portion of the SOAP Envelope.

At this point, the major aspects of security that you should concentrate on are authentication, authorization, and encryption. You can perform authentication in several ways, including using Microsoft's Passport, using client certificates, or implementing your own authentication scheme. In the latter case, SSL remains the definitive mechanism for securing a connection so that you can perform your authentication work.

Reliability and Availability

How many times have you attempted to point your browser to a Web page, only to find nothing but a sleepy status bar followed by that ominous and yet oh-so-familiar HTTP 404 error?

When you consider the amount of network traffic that the Internet carries today and the number of complex systems that must work together to keep the Internet running, it's amazing that this type of error doesn't occur more often. However, for many business processes (such as a financial transaction), even a minor hiccup in the network can cause great damage.

The best way to solve this problem is to use a transport protocol that guarantees delivery. For instance, a message queue that supports ACID transactions can ensure that messages arrive at their destination.

NOTE

Recall that ACID stands for Atomic (interrupted work can be undone), Consistent (resource integrity is preserved), Isolated (it works independent of other transactions), and Durable (the results are permanent).

For many people, this level of reliability is not worth the incompatibilities of message-queuing systems. This is why we're using Web Services in the first place—so that we don't force both ends of a connection to share some proprietary protocol.

Until more sophisticated and standardized systems are put in place, the best recommendation that we can make is to build your systems with the most atomic interfaces possible. This minimizes the sequencing of requests, thus reducing the risk of taking a particular message out of context. And as any distributed application programmer knows, you program defensively for communication problems and deal with exceptions in the most robust way possible, trying to eliminate the possibility of leaving your system in an unstable state. This suggests that, at a bare minimum, you build in mechanisms so that changes can be *backed out*.

Consistency

Although this can be related to reliability and availability, we refer to consistency as the capability of a service requestor to faithfully expect the interface to perform in a manner similar to past requests. In other words, you can't arbitrarily change the semantics or syntax of a published interface without potentially causing problems for clients. And if you are charging for your service, you can be sure that customers will not find change very pleasing.

We mentioned that you shouldn't change the syntax of an interface, and to some extent that's true. However, as discussed earlier, syntax is normally the part of a message that computers can understand. Thus, it's not overly unreasonable to expect SOAP infrastructures to eventually be capable of automatically adjusting for small syntactic changes, assuming that the semantics remain the same.

You've read a lot about Web Services and many of the issues surrounding them. Now it's time to dive into some code and see a Web Service in action.

Creating a Web Service in Visual Studio .NET

In this section, you will see how Visual Studio .NET helps you generate a Web Service, as well as build a consumer application of that service. You will see how WSDL plays a critical part in bringing together the service requestor and the service provider. Finally, you will have an opportunity to use a network-tracing application to analyze request and response SOAP messages.

Creating the Service

In this example, you will create a Persistence application that allows a client to store name/value pairs on the server. Although this implementation of a *property bag* is far from full-featured, you can see how a simple Web Service can bridge the gab between heterogeneous systems wanting to share state information. The following steps walk you through creating a Persistence application:

1. Start a new ASP.NET Web Service project called Ch1WebService—in this case, using C#.

2. Select http://localhost for the location of your service. (This step assumes that you are running a local copy of IIS with the appropriate server extensions.)

3. Look under your system's wwwroot folder (by default located in C:\inetpub\wwwroot), for a folder with the Ch1WebService project name. Within that folder there are several hidden folders and a bin folder that, at this point, should be empty. After you build the project, the bin folder will be populated with the necessary files for your service to execute.

> **NOTE**
>
> Hidden files can be seen by enabling this option under the Tools, Folder Options menu, under the View tab in Windows Explorer.

4. Go back to the Ch1WebService project folder. Among the many files available, there is a Service1.asmx file that is the entry point into your Web Service. You might want to take a look at the contents of this file to see how it is organized.

5. Looking at the Solution Explorer in Visual Studio .NET, note that Service1.asmx is also listed under the Ch1WebService project. To change the name of your service, you must alter the properties of the Service1.asmx file and change it to Persistence.asmx. You will also need to change the contents of this file so that the Class= value reflects the new Persistence service name in this assembly. Finally, you must change the name of the Service1 class in the source code.

6. Press F5 (Debug mode) to see Visual Studio .NET build your project and launch a browser window showing a sample Web page. At the top of the page, you will see a hyperlink to the service description of your service. Notice that there isn't much here because you haven't created any Web-enabled methods yet. You will also see a warning on the page about the default namespace being used; we will assign a real namespace to the service shortly.

7. Close the browser window. Visual Studio .NET should exit Debug mode.

8. Enter the service code. Listing 1.1 shows the final code that will be used for this example.

LISTING 1.1 Form1.cs

```
using System;
using System.Collections;
using System.ComponentModel;
using System.Data;
using System.Diagnostics;
using System.Web;
using System.Web.Services;

namespace Ch1WebService
{
   /// <summary>
   /// Summary description for Persistence.
   /// </summary>
   [WebService(Namespace="http://www.mcp.org/WebServices/Persistence")]
   public class Persistence : System.Web.Services.WebService
   {
      public Persistence()
      {
         //CODEGEN: This call is required by the ASP.NET Web Services Designer
         InitializeComponent();
      }
```

LISTING 1.1 Continued

```
#region Component Designer generated code
/// <summary>
/// Required method for Designer support - do not modify
/// the contents of this method with the code editor.
/// </summary>
private void InitializeComponent()
{
}
#endregion

/// <summary>
/// Clean up any resources being used.
/// </summary>
protected override void Dispose( bool disposing )
{
}

[WebMethod]
public string Get(string myName)
{
   string s;

   try
   {
      // Retrieve the named value from the Application property
      s = Application[myName].ToString();
   }
   catch (Exception e)
   {
      s = e.Message;
   }

   return s;
}

[WebMethod]
public void Put(string myName, string myValue)
{
   try
   {
      // Assign the named value to the Application property
      Application[myName] = myValue;
   }
   catch (Exception)
```

LISTING 1.1 Continued

```
        {
            // do nothing
        }
        return;
    }
  }
}
```

Listing 1.1 takes advantage of the `Application` state-management facilities provided through .NET. This allows you to store name/value pairs across multiple sessions of the service. Of course, this is really only a simulation of persistence and would be better implemented by actually storing the information in a database. With the current code base, the state is simply lost when the IIS service stops executing.

> **NOTE**
>
> As you develop a service, you might find yourself wanting to use the `Session` feature of .NET to maintain state for a specific client.
>
> This is easy enough to do: Just use the `[WebMethod(true)]` attribute on each Web method to enable session state, and use `Session` in place of `Application`.
>
> But be warned—`Session` relies upon HTTP cookies in the transport protocol. When testing with the browser (using HTTP `GET`), your application will perform exactly as you expected because IE will automatically pass cookies back and forth for you. However, client applications like the one you are about to build will not automatically support cookies. Thus, the application will not be capable of maintaining state across Web Service methods because each request will be considered a new session.
>
> Overall, you should avoid using transport-level facilities such as cookies that bleed into application behavior. In other words, cookies don't appear anywhere in the SOAP message, but they can have a significant impact on the behavior of your application. Instead, you should create your own state-management values that are contained within the interface (ideally the SOAP Header) so that, regardless of the transport you choose, clients can always be sure of proper system behavior. Chapter 4 provides more information about modifying the SOAP Header.

Now that you've built a fully functional Web Service, you need to create a client that will access the service through the SOAP protocol.

Creating the Client

You've already seen the standard test Web client that Visual Studio .NET automatically creates for your project. This example shows you how to build a simple Windows application that can interact with your service.

1. Start by creating a new project. This time, though, you want to create a Windows application in C#. Call the project Ch1Client.

2. Place two buttons (named Get and Put) and two text boxes (named myName and myValue) on your form.

3. Next, right-click on References in the Solution Explorer window, and select Add Web Reference from the menu.

4. Click on the Web References on Local Web Server hyperlink, which displays all available services on your machine.

5. Click the Ch1WebService link in the right pane, which displays two additional hyperlinks, View Contract and View Documentation. If you click on the View Contract hyperlink, the WSDL for this service will be displayed. We'll cover this shortly.

6. Click on the Add Reference button to inject the Web Service description into your client project.

7. In addition to the code that is generated by Visual Studio .NET, add the Web Service-specific code fragment as shown in Listing 1.2.

LISTING 1.2 Form1.cs

```csharp
private void Get_Click(object sender, System.EventArgs e)
{
   localhost.Persistence p = new localhost.Persistence();

   System.Windows.Forms.MessageBox.Show(p.Get(this.myName.Text));
}

private void Put_Click(object sender, System.EventArgs e)
{
   localhost.Persistence p = new localhost.Persistence();

   p.Put(this.myName.Text, this.myValue.Text);
   this.myName.Clear();
   this.myValue.Clear();
}
```

Adding the Web reference to your project (see Step 7) enables you to instantiate a `localhost.Persistence` object within the application code. When adding a Web Reference, you are physically including the WSDL file into your application. The compiler also creates a folder in the project (under Web References) called *localhost*, which includes a .CS file that contains a proxy for the service. If the Web Service changes at some point, you can simply right-click on the `localhost` folder and select Update Web Reference option. Be aware that you also might need to update your application code to conform to any new interface changes. However, the compiler will most likely catch these as well.

While we're on the topic of WSDL, take a quick look at the WSDL file shown in Listing 1.3.

LISTING 1.3   Persistence.wsdl

```
<?xml version="1.0" encoding="utf-8"?>
<definitions xmlns:s="http://www.w3.org/2001/XMLSchema"
             xmlns:http="http://schemas.xmlsoap.org/wsdl/http/"
             xmlns:mime="http://schemas.xmlsoap.org/wsdl/mime/"
             xmlns:tm="http://microsoft.com/wsdl/mime/textMatching/"
             xmlns:soap="http://schemas.xmlsoap.org/wsdl/soap/"
             xmlns:soapenc="http://schemas.xmlsoap.org/soap/encoding/"
             xmlns:s0="www.mcp.org/WebServices/Persistence"
             targetNamespace="www.mcp.org/WebServices/Persistence"
             xmlns="http://schemas.xmlsoap.org/wsdl/">
  <types>
    <s:schema attributeFormDefault="qualified" elementFormDefault="qualified"
              targetNamespace="www.mcp.org/WebServices/Persistence">
      <s:element name="Get">
        <s:complexType>
          <s:sequence>
            <s:element minOccurs="1" maxOccurs="1" name="myName"
nillable="true" type="s:string" />
          </s:sequence>
        </s:complexType>
      </s:element>
      <s:element name="GetResponse">
        <s:complexType>
          <s:sequence>
            <s:element minOccurs="1" maxOccurs="1" name="GetResult"
nillable="true" type="s:string" />
          </s:sequence>
        </s:complexType>
      </s:element>
      <s:element name="Put">
        <s:complexType>
          <s:sequence>
```

LISTING 1.3 Continued

```
            <s:element minOccurs="1" maxOccurs="1" name="myName"
nillable="true" type="s:string" />
            <s:element minOccurs="1" maxOccurs="1" name="myValue"
nillable="true" type="s:string" />
          </s:sequence>
        </s:complexType>
      </s:element>
      <s:element name="PutResponse">
        <s:complexType />
      </s:element>
      <s:element name="string" nillable="true" type="s:string" />
    </s:schema>
  </types>
  <message name="GetSoapIn">
    <part name="parameters" element="s0:Get" />
  </message>
  <message name="GetSoapOut">
    <part name="parameters" element="s0:GetResponse" />
  </message>
  <message name="PutSoapIn">
    <part name="parameters" element="s0:Put" />
  </message>
  <message name="PutSoapOut">
    <part name="parameters" element="s0:PutResponse" />
  </message>
  <message name="GetHttpGetIn">
    <part name="myName" type="s:string" />
  </message>
  <message name="GetHttpGetOut">
    <part name="Body" element="s0:string" />
  </message>
  <message name="PutHttpGetIn">
    <part name="myName" type="s:string" />
    <part name="myValue" type="s:string" />
  </message>
  <message name="PutHttpGetOut" />
  <message name="GetHttpPostIn">
    <part name="myName" type="s:string" />
  </message>
  <message name="GetHttpPostOut">
    <part name="Body" element="s0:string" />
  </message>
  <message name="PutHttpPostIn">
    <part name="myName" type="s:string" />
```

LISTING 1.3   Continued

```xml
      <part name="myValue" type="s:string" />
    </message>
    <message name="PutHttpPostOut" />
    <portType name="PersistenceSoap">
      <operation name="Get">
        <input message="s0:GetSoapIn" />
        <output message="s0:GetSoapOut" />
      </operation>
      <operation name="Put">
        <input message="s0:PutSoapIn" />
        <output message="s0:PutSoapOut" />
      </operation>
    </portType>
    <portType name="PersistenceHttpGet">
      <operation name="Get">
        <input message="s0:GetHttpGetIn" />
        <output message="s0:GetHttpGetOut" />
      </operation>
      <operation name="Put">
        <input message="s0:PutHttpGetIn" />
        <output message="s0:PutHttpGetOut" />
      </operation>
    </portType>
    <portType name="PersistenceHttpPost">
      <operation name="Get">
        <input message="s0:GetHttpPostIn" />
        <output message="s0:GetHttpPostOut" />
      </operation>
      <operation name="Put">
        <input message="s0:PutHttpPostIn" />
        <output message="s0:PutHttpPostOut" />
      </operation>
    </portType>
    <binding name="PersistenceSoap" type="s0:PersistenceSoap">
      <soap:binding transport="http://schemas.xmlsoap.org/soap/http"
style="document" />
      <operation name="Get">
        <soap:operation soapAction="www.mcp.org/WebServices/Persistence/Get"
style="document" />
        <input>
          <soap:body use="literal" />
        </input>
        <output>
          <soap:body use="literal" />
```

LISTING 1.3 Continued

```
      </output>
    </operation>
    <operation name="Put">
      <soap:operation soapAction="www.mcp.org/WebServices/Persistence/Put"
style="document" />
      <input>
        <soap:body use="literal" />
      </input>
      <output>
        <soap:body use="literal" />
      </output>
    </operation>
  </binding>
  <binding name="PersistenceHttpGet" type="s0:PersistenceHttpGet">
    <http:binding verb="GET" />
    <operation name="Get">
      <http:operation location="/Get" />
      <input>
        <http:urlEncoded />
      </input>
      <output>
        <mime:mimeXml part="Body" />
      </output>
    </operation>
    <operation name="Put">
      <http:operation location="/Put" />
      <input>
        <http:urlEncoded />
      </input>
      <output />
    </operation>
  </binding>
  <binding name="PersistenceHttpPost" type="s0:PersistenceHttpPost">
    <http:binding verb="POST" />
    <operation name="Get">
      <http:operation location="/Get" />
      <input>
        <mime:content type="application/x-www-form-urlencoded" />
      </input>
      <output>
        <mime:mimeXml part="Body" />
      </output>
    </operation>
    <operation name="Put">
```

LISTING 1.3 Continued

```
    <http:operation location="/Put" />
    <input>
      <mime:content type="application/x-www-form-urlencoded" />
    </input>
    <output />
  </operation>
</binding>
<service name="Persistence">
  <port name="PersistenceSoap" binding="s0:PersistenceSoap">
    <soap:address location="http://localhost/Ch1WebService/Persistence.asmx" />
  </port>
  <port name="PersistenceHttpGet" binding="s0:PersistenceHttpGet">
    <http:address location="http://localhost/Ch1WebService/Persistence.asmx" />
  </port>
  <port name="PersistenceHttpPost" binding="s0:PersistenceHttpPost">
    <http:address location="http://localhost/Ch1WebService/Persistence.asmx" />
  </port>
</service>
</definitions>
```

Starting at the bottom of the file, the service is exposed through three different WSDL ports listed under the <service> element. One port operates on HTTP GET requests; another operates on HTTP POST requests. Most importantly, the third supports the SOAP protocol.

When running the Visual Studio .NET debugger, you've probably already figured out that the test pages generated for your service use the HTTP GET port.

NOTE

Be aware that Visual Studio .NET does not generate test pages for complex interface types. Therefore, you are responsible for manually constructing a test client.

You will also find at the top of the WSDL file an XML schema that describes the logical structure of your Web Service messages. Note that there is only one logical structure for each message, but each port represents a potentially different syntactical representation of each message.

Chapter 5 provides extensive coverage of WSDL, but it's helpful for you to see the types of information that a client application needs to communicate with the service.

At this point, you have learned how the service requestor and service provider are constructed and how they ultimately interoperate. Now let's take a closer look at the actual SOAP transactions that are transmitted over the wire.

Tracing Messages on the Network

When debugging your Web Service in Visual Studio .NET, you might have noticed that the generated test page displays sample messages for SOAP and HTTP GET/POST. At times, you will find it very helpful to see the actual messages that are being sent back and forth between endpoints.

The trace utility (MSSOAPT.EXE), provided with the SOAP Toolkit 2.0 binaries, is a favorite tool. For the trace to work, you need to start a new trace that will listen to a port (usually 8080) and forward requests to port 80, where your local IIS copy should be listening.

You then need to configure your client application to point to the newly created 8080 port. To do this in the sample client that you just created, open the WSDL file that is listed under the Solution Explorer window.

> **NOTE**
>
> Rather than changing the WSDL file, you may prefer to change your code by modifying the p.Url (from Listing 1.2) to point to the new location.

Edit the WSDL file so that the three ports' address value references localhost:8080, as follows:

```
<service name="Persistence">
    <port name="PersistenceSoap" binding="s0:PersistenceSoap">
      <soap:address
➥location="http://localhost:8080/Ch1WebService/Persistence.asmx" />
    </port>
    <port name="PersistenceHttpGet" binding="s0:PersistenceHttpGet">
      <http:address
➥location="http://localhost:8080/Ch1WebService/Persistence.asmx" />
    </port>
    <port name="PersistenceHttpPost" binding="s0:PersistenceHttpPost">
      <http:address
➥location="http://localhost:8080/Ch1WebService/Persistence.asmx" />
    </port>
  </service>
```

> **NOTE**
>
> You don't necessarily have to modify the location of all three bindings. Generally, you're probably interested only in the SOAP binding.

Rebuild and execute your project, and you will see the trace utility capture both the request and the response messages. For example, using the operations that you just built will result in the traces shown in Listings 1.4–1.7.

LISTING 1.4 PUT Request

```
<?xml version="1.0" encoding="utf-8"?>
<soap:Envelope xmlns:soap="http://schemas.xmlsoap.org/soap/envelope/"
               xmlns:xsi="http://www.w3.org/2001/XMLSchema-instance"
               xmlns:xsd="http://www.w3.org/2001/XMLSchema">
  <soap:Body>
    <Put xmlns="www.mcp.org/WebServices/Persistence">
      <myName>phone</myName>
      <myValue>555-1234</myValue>
    </Put>
  </soap:Body>
</soap:Envelope>
```

LISTING 1.5 PUT Response

```
<?xml version="1.0" encoding="utf-8"?>
<soap:Envelope xmlns:soap="http://schemas.xmlsoap.org/soap/envelope/"
               xmlns:xsi="http://www.w3.org/2001/XMLSchema-instance"
               xmlns:xsd="http://www.w3.org/2001/XMLSchema">
  <soap:Body>
    <PutResponse xmlns="www.mcp.org/WebServices/Persistence" />
  </soap:Body>
</soap:Envelope>
```

LISTING 1.6 GET Request

```
<?xml version="1.0" encoding="utf-8"?>
<soap:Envelope xmlns:soap="http://schemas.xmlsoap.org/soap/envelope/"
               xmlns:xsi="http://www.w3.org/2001/XMLSchema-instance"
               xmlns:xsd="http://www.w3.org/2001/XMLSchema">
  <soap:Body>
    <Get xmlns="www.mcp.org/WebServices/Persistence">
```

LISTING 1.6   Continued

```
      <myName>phone</myName>
    </Get>
  </soap:Body>
</soap:Envelope>
```

LISTING 1.7   GET Response

```
<?xml version="1.0" encoding="utf-8"?>
<soap:Envelope xmlns:soap="http://schemas.xmlsoap.org/soap/envelope/"
               xmlns:xsi="http://www.w3.org/2001/XMLSchema-instance"
               xmlns:xsd="http://www.w3.org/2001/XMLSchema">
  <soap:Body>
    <GetResponse xmlns="www.mcp.org/WebServices/Persistence">
      <GetResult>555-1234</GetResult>
    </GetResponse>
  </soap:Body>
</soap:Envelope>
```

This is clearly the only way that you can debug interoperability problems. Sometimes the *unformatted* trace also will be more appropriate because it shows the entire HTTP message, including the Header and the Body.

If you already have some experience with SOAP, you might have noticed that these messages are encoded using the literal form of an XML schema rather than SOAP's special encoding format (see Section 5 of the SOAP specification). This is the default behavior of a Visual Studio .NET–generated Web Service, but it can easily be switched using a Web Service attribute. More about this will be covered in Chapter 6, "Web Services in ASP.NET."

Interface Design Tips

You've already been introduced to interface semantics and the underlying concepts. Hopefully you came away with a clear understanding about the differences between syntax and semantics, and how semantics play such a critical part in building valuable Web Services.

This section presents a few practices that will help you build better Web Service interfaces.

Learning from the Past

It didn't take the software development community very long to figure out that interfaces are one of the best ways to decouple complex systems. This technique has been used for many years, especially in the electronics industry.

For example, consider the RCA jacks on a television. Most people know that there are three separate connectors—one for right channel audio, one for left channel audio, and one for the video signal. Each has a standard color-coding scheme, which makes it very easy to connect components.

You can take away several ideas from this example:

- **Ease of use**—Like the colors on connectors, interfaces should be easily recognizable and understood.

- **Distribution of functionality**—You need to strike a balance between having too many interfaces and having one overly complex and monolithic interface. One wire is easier for a consumer to connect, but if technical challenges of combining signals into a single connector force you to charge $10,000 for your DVD player, nobody wins.

- **Compatibility and overloading**—New components need to maintain compatibility with older interfaces, and new interfaces should be created when old ones no longer meet your needs. This is analogous to the creation of component-video output for DVD players. We needed higher-quality video, but the existing RCA jacks couldn't support the technology. Conversely, just as you wouldn't try to run power to your television through the cable jack, you shouldn't force an interface to accommodate something that it wasn't designed to handle. In the world of electronics, you know when you've done something wrong when smoke billows from your equipment. But with software, the consequences might not be so obvious. You might not realize the problems that you've created until much later, when it is more costly to fix.

Before getting too far into the nuts and bolts of interfaces, we need to come to terms on what an interface really is.

What Is an Interface?

Webster defines an interface as follows:

Interface: (n): A point at which independent systems interact.

However, an interface should be a multitude of things—some are obvious, while others are somewhat intangible.

Naturally, an interface should be interesting to users. This can be done with the content that your interface provides, the speed at which the interface performs, or simply because you offer a reliable service.

The other side of the coin is that a poorly designed interface can interfere with its potential for use. Many good things have fallen to the wayside just because users found it difficult to learn how to make them work.

The bottom line is, proper design of interfaces is a huge responsibility—the interface becomes your *storefront* and establishes how users view your Web Service.

Let's take a moment to slightly modify Webster's definition of an interface. You might suggest that an interface is a *logical* point at which independent systems interact. Why *logical*? It's logical because, as you've already seen, there could be more than one physical representation of an interface. There's no reason why an interface should change just because a developer chooses to use SMTP rather than HTTP.

Another property of your interfaces that you can control is the way that SOAP packages your messages. Deciding whether to use SOAP encoding could have an impact on the capabilities of your interface.

Using SOAP to Encode Information

SOAP defines an encoding style (see Section 5 of the SOAP v1.1 specification) for serializing an information graph as XML. This is an important feature of SOAP that is extremely useful for RPC serialization; it is denoted by using the `encodingStyle="http://schemas.xmlsoap.org/soap/encoding/"` attribute within the Envelope contents. By using SOAP's encoding style, you get some of the following benefits:

- Serialization of objects by value and by reference
- Array serialization, including multidimensional arrays
- Partially transmitted and sparse array serialization

Although you can describe type information using XML schemas, in some cases, you might want to use an XML schema to validate messages entering or leaving your system. Section 5 allows for so many different variations of encoding information, so you will find that it's difficult to generate a schema that covers the exhaustive list of possibilities.

Rather than use the encoding mechanisms as defined by SOAP, you can define message structures that are completely describable in an XML schema.

> **NOTE**
>
> The UDDI framework (as described in Chapter 5) uses the message-based encoding style rather than Section 5 encoding as defined by SOAP.

Interface Versioning

Versioning interfaces requires a syntactical approach to encoding messages. In the case of SOAP, consider the following service example, which retrieves the temperature for a location based on its ZIP code:

```
POST /GetTemperature.asmx HTTP/1.1
Host: www.mcp.com
Accept: text/*
Content-type: text/xml; charset=utf-8
Content-length: nnnn
SOAPAction: "http://www.mcp.com/Temperature/GetTemperature"
{CR}{LF}
<SOAP-ENV:Envelope
    xmlns:SOAP-ENV="http://schemas.xmlsoap.org/soap/envelope/">
    <SOAP-ENV:Body>
        <GetTemperature xmlns="http://www.mcp.com/Temperature">
            <ZipCode>12345</ZipCode>
        </GetTemperature>
    </SOAP-ENV:Body>
</SOAP-ENV:Envelope>
```

In this case, the URI http://www.mcp.com/Temperature is used as the mechanism for identifying an interface from other interfaces. By using XML namespaces, the URI scopes the operation GetTemperature to that interface. In the case of HTTP, the SOAPAction field may also reflect this URI to verify the intent of the message. If SOAPAction is left empty, the HTTP message declares the intent of the request.

Now consider changing the temperature service to accept a city/state pair rather than a ZIP code. You have several options for exposing this new operation.

Creating a New Interface

The first approach that you can take is to create a new URI that represents a completely new interface, as follows:

```
POST /GetTemperature.asmx HTTP/1.1
Host: www.mcp.com
Accept: text/*
Content-type: text/xml; charset=utf-8
Content-length: nnnn
SOAPAction: "http://www.mcp.com/Temperature2/GetTemperature"
{CR}{LF}
<SOAP-ENV:Envelope
    xmlns:SOAP-ENV="http://schemas.xmlsoap.org/soap/envelope/">
    <SOAP-ENV:Body>
        <GetTemperature xmlns="http://www.mcp.com/Temperature2">
            <City>San Jose</City>
            <State>CA</State>
        </GetTemperature>
    </SOAP-ENV:Body>
</SOAP-ENV:Envelope>
```

Here, the URI http://www.mcp.com/Temperature2 has been applied to the XML namespace and SOAPAction field appropriately. This requires you to build a completely new WSDL description and XML schema to describe this new URI.

Adding an Operation to an Existing Interface

The next approach that you can take is to create a new operation name under an existing URI:

```
POST /GetTemperature.asmx HTTP/1.1
Host: www.mcp.com
Accept: text/*
Content-type: text/xml; charset=utf-8
Content-length: nnnn
SOAPAction: "http://www.mcp.com/Temperature/GetTemperatureByCity"
{CR}{LF}
<SOAP-ENV:Envelope
    xmlns:SOAP-ENV="http://schemas.xmlsoap.org/soap/envelope/">
    <SOAP-ENV:Body>
        <GetTemperatureByCity xmlns="http://www.mcp.com/Temperature">
            <City>San Jose</City>
            <State>CA</State>
        </GetTemperatureByCity>
    </SOAP-ENV:Body>
</SOAP-ENV:Envelope>
```

Rather than change the URI http://www.mcp.com/Temperature, you only need to add a new operation for the given WSDL description and XML schema. Because you won't change any of the existing operations in your WSDL file, existing clients will be unaware of the new interface.

Modifying an Existing Operation

Finally, you have the option of modifying an existing operation to facilitate the new functionality.

```
POST /Router.pl HTTP/1.1
Host: www.mcp.com
Accept: text/*
Content-type: text/xml
Content-length: nnnn
SOAPAction: "http://www.mcp.com/Temperature/GetTemperature"
{CR}{LF}
<SOAP-ENV:Envelope
    xmlns:SOAP-ENV="http://schemas.xmlsoap.org/soap/envelope/"
    SOAP-ENV:encodingStyle="http://schemas.xmlsoap.org/soap/encoding/">
    <SOAP-ENV:Body>
        <m:GetTemperature xmlns:m="http://www.mcp.com/Temperature">
            <City>San Jose</City>
            <State>CA</State>
```

```
      </m:GetTemperature>
   </SOAP-ENV:Body>
</SOAP-ENV:Envelope>
```

This can be a more difficult approach than the previous options because your service code must be capable of interpreting the intention of incoming parameters. At times it can be difficult resolving ambiguity in requests.

Using the temperature example, what happens if your service receives a message that has a city, state, and ZIP code. Which parameters take precedence over others? Should you fail the request altogether? What happens when you start mixing mandatory and optional fields? These are all questions that you must answer when you start to change an existing operation.

All these questions lead to the topic of interface complexity.

Interface Complexity

Measuring complexity is a difficult task because it's one of those concepts that is purely based on your perspective. Unfortunately, this means that there's no silver bullet, no recipes that you can apply to guarantee a simple interface.

The following section provides an example to get you thinking about the issues at hand and the options that you have.

Additional Operations Versus Additional Parameters

It is often difficult to determine the best way to expose your system's functionality. Should you create a collection of small, succinct operations? Or possibly create a single, all-inclusive interface that offers a wide variety of parameters? In either case, you can probably fulfill the system requirements. So does it really matter which direction you choose?

Consider the example XML fragment showing a simple request to place an order:

```
<PlaceOrder>
   <partNumber>EVH5150</partNumber>
   <accountNumber>317</accountNumber>
   <quantity>8</quantity>
</PlaceOrder>
```

This is followed by a typical response containing an order number:

```
<PlaceOrderResponse>
   <orderNumber>670221</orderNumber>
</PlaceOrderResponse>
```

When a customer has placed an order, it's reasonable to assume that the customer will want to periodically check the status of the order, as shown in the following request:

```
<CheckStatus>
    <orderNumber>670221</orderNumber>
</CheckStatus>
```

The client can expect a standard status response message:

```
<CheckStatusResponse>
    <status>submitted</status>
</CheckStatusResponse>
```

However, one alternative to having separate operations (and requiring two round trips) is to combine the two operations into a single request:

```
<PlaceOrderAndCheckStatus>
    <partNumber>EVH5150</partNumber>
    <accountNumber>8675309</accountNumber>
    <quantity>7</quantity>
</PlaceOrderAndCheckStatus>
```

The semantics seem simple. The customer is interested in knowing whether the order was automatically shipped at the time it was placed. The response message seems innocent:

```
<PlaceOrderAndCheckStatusResponse>
    <orderNumber>670221</orderNumber>
    <status>submitted</status>
</PlaceOrderAndCheckStatusResponse>
```

Here, we have made a 100% improvement in performance by reducing the process to a single round trip. Therefore, this must be the correct way to design this interface. But wait—what happens when the user needs to check the order status again? Well, you could change the `PlaceOrderAndCheckStatus` operation so that it can accept optional parameters. This allows two types of messages to be valid:

```
<PlaceOrderAndCheckStatus>
    <partNumber>EVH5150</partNumber>
    <accountNumber>8675309</accountNumber>
    <quantity>7</quantity>
</PlaceOrderAndCheckStatus>
```

and

```
<PlaceOrderAndCheckStatus>
    <orderNumber>670221</orderNumber>
</PlaceOrderAndCheckStatus>
```

But because the interface semantics are becoming confusing, what happens if someone tries to place a new order and check the status of an existing order in the same request?

```
<PlaceOrderAndCheckStatus>
    <partNumber>EVH5150</partNumber>
    <accountNumber>8675309</accountNumber>
    <quantity>7</quantity>
    <orderNumber>670221</orderNumber>
</PlaceOrderAndCheckStatus>
```

Should you process the new order and then check status for the second order? Which status do you return? Possibly both? If so, how does the client know which status goes with a particular operation?

```
<PlaceOrderAndCheckStatusResponse>
    <orderNumber>670221</orderNumber>
    <status>submitted</status>
    <status>back order</status>
</PlaceOrderAndCheckStatusResponse>
```

Better yet, instead of allowing this ambiguity to creep into the interface, what if you just deny requests of this nature and inform the client of the poorly formed request? But should you really force clients to discover the interface semantics through trial and error? Generally, if you want a wide audience to use your service, your best bet is to keep the interface simple and spend less time worrying about performance. In cases where performance needs do exist, you should provide good documentation that explains exactly how your interface works and why.

The problem with making the blanket statement that you should be minimizing round trips is that you could end up requiring clients to receive information that they never intended to use. Under normal circumstances, a little bit of extra information is better than the overhead of requiring extra round trips. In some pathological situations in which the payload is extremely large, however, this might not be a fair trade.

Criteria for Managing Complexity

To summarize from the preceding example, here are some general questions that you should ask yourself before you make your final interface decisions:

- How difficult will it be for me to validate an operation's syntax?
- How complex will the server logic need to be for this request to be processed and a intelligible response to be sent?
- Will clients be able to quickly understand the semantics behind this operation?
- How much unrelated information is a client receiving that doesn't pertain to the request?
- How easy will it be for clients to upgrade to newer versions of my interface?
- How many round trips will the client need to make before getting the desired information?

Summary

We've covered a lot of ground in this chapter, touching on many aspects of Web Services to set the stage for the remainder of the book.

By now you should have a better understanding of why semantics are so important to Web Services and what properties contribute to a valuable service. You've also learned about many of the Internet protocols that play a big part in the Web Service paradigm.

You've been introduced to Visual Studio .NET and have seen a working demonstration of its Web Service tools for both clients and servers. It's pretty clear that .NET provides a flexible and robust environment for building and consuming services.

Finally, you explored Web Service interfaces and some of the issues surrounding their development, maintenance, and use.

In the next chapter, you will learn about the Microsoft .NET Framework and how it applies to Web Services. This will provide you with a better understanding of the facilities that .NET provides and will reinforce the topics that were discussed in this chapter.

.NET Architecture and
Web Services Components

IN THIS CHAPTER

Let's start out by stating that .NET is *big*. By *big*, I mean that it consists of a new programming model, languages, memory allocation scheme, classes, types, and much, much, more. Entire books are dedicated to presenting the full list of .NET concepts, so you can see that it would be impossible to describe all of .NET in a single chapter. Instead, this chapter presents aspects of .NET that will help you understand how .NET makes the Web Service development model more approachable than traditional development models.

But before going any further, let's take a look at the motivation behind why the .NET Framework was created.

Motivation for Creating .NET

It seems that every few years, Microsoft introduces a new set of technologies that promise to be the software development equivalent of the Holy Grail. Each step in this journey has revealed some very significant programming models, while at the same time introducing so many new complexities that developers find themselves somewhat perplexed.

The Benefits and Limits of COM

One of the most important technologies that Microsoft introduced was the Component Object Model (COM). From the beginning, COM solved a very specific problem—how to integrate software. COM was designed to allow applications to share code and information through the use of well-defined interfaces. This was made possible through the use of a binary compatibility layer and a fairly standardized type system. COM also abstracted many of the details about DLL usage, shared memory, and threading. Ultimately, COM provided a layer of abstraction that allowed applications to be integrated regardless of the programming language that was used (well, almost).

Eventually applications needed to extend beyond the machine boundary. Client/server, *n*-tier, and peer-to-peer systems are all viable architectures for solving problems. Therefore, Microsoft extended COM so that it could be used across the wire (that is, over a network). Thus, Distributed COM (DCOM) was born. DCOM used DCE/RPC at the core of the protocol, with a few alterations, and extensive distributed services integrated into the runtime environment. The end result allowed clients to access servers through proxy objects that handled the raw communications tasks. In general, this approach allowed the COM developer to automatically distribute functionality across machine boundaries with very little effort.

> **NOTE**
>
> The promise has always been that DCOM makes it a no-brainer for COM developers to build distributed applications. This is partly true because developers don't have to write the network-layer code. However, this lack of exposure to networking can lead to lazy programming that results in a *chatty* interface (requiring excessive round-trips to complete a task).

DCOM worked well in an intranet, where the number of client connections was manageable. By *manageable*, we mean that you can fairly accurately estimate and accommodate the resource requirements needed for your system. Putting firewall issues aside for now, trying to supply enough stateful DCOM connections to Internet clients is next to impossible. Of course, this is why the HTTP request/response protocol has been so successful. The general rule is to set up a connection, service a single atomic request, and tear down the connection, requiring the client, the server, or both to maintain the application's state.

Given the fact that DCOM wouldn't be useful for Internet-sized traffic, Microsoft focused its attention on improving the middle tier. Microsoft began persuading developers to build transactional components that could scale more easily. This led to the introduction of Microsoft Transaction Server (MTS). MTS continued to provide the same functionality as DCOM, but it also provided additional component services such as transaction support. MTS promoted a stateless programming model and attempted to simplify developers' lives by improving middleware facilities such as thread management. Unfortunately, MTS was implemented as a wrapper to COM/DCOM, so it came with its share of inconveniences. In other words, developers had to pay close attention to *how* they used MTS so that applications would work properly under the MTS framework.

With the release of Windows 2000 came COM+—a component runtime that integrated the best of COM and MTS. COM+ solved the deficiencies of MTS by changing the runtime environment so that its management services were an integral part of the runtime. Again, COM+ made a valuable contribution to the runtime environment by providing services for transactions, queuing, security, just-in-time activation, events, and so on.

Other Microsoft Technology Considerations

Despite the capabilities of COM and its descendents, developers are still faced with many troubling issues. Windows has an extremely broad span of development models to choose from. You can build GUI applications using Visual C++ and the Microsoft Foundation Classes (MFC). Visual Basic can generate MTS/COM+ objects for transactional Web applications. The Active Template Library (ATL) can be used to construct Windows NT/2000 services. The list goes on and on.

Most Windows developers like what they do because, for one, they are empowered by the development environment supported by Windows. Microsoft has done a reasonable job of providing technologies that improve software-integration efforts. But this certainly doesn't imply that things are perfect. In actuality, still many issues plague Windows developers:

- **Cross-language compatibility**—Developers must be very explicit about defining interfaces so that they will be compatible with other programming languages. For example, a C++ developer can easily build components that are incapable of being executed from a scripting language such as ASP. The main reason for this incompatibility is that many C++ developers don't choose to implement the IDispatch interface. The root problem, however, is that there are incompatible runtime environments and that there's no common type system imposed upon all objects.

- **Reference counting**—COM uses reference counting to manage the lifetime of objects. From one perspective, reference counting provides a clear and distinct way to control when objects get destroyed. However, this places a huge burden on developers of application code. If you forget to notify the COM runtime (via the `Release()` call) that you are finished with an object, it can result in memory or other forms of resource leaks.

- **COM or Win32**—Developers must ask a more fundamental question when searching for a Windows service—is there a COM object available, or do I need to use the Win32 API? The Win32 API is somewhat antiquated, which has led to an overwhelming number of API calls. In many cases, the same function is copied to a new name (such as `CoInitializeEx`) and performs the same task with some minimal difference. This has made it very difficult for Windows developers to stay current with API changes, and it leads to confusion when choosing an API service.

- **Platform dependence**—The technologies that we've discussed all assume one thing: that you're developing for Windows.

- **Object-oriented programming**—For those of you who are object-oriented programmers, it doesn't matter whether you're using the Win32 API or COM: Neither behaves as a native object in an object-oriented language. If you're a C++ developer, how many times have you wrapped a class around a set of Win32 API functions so that resources (such as *critical sections*) are properly released?

Overall, these technologies have had a great impact on Windows application development, but there's always room for improvement.

A Better Model

Today's competitive industry has stimulated a great improvement in application environments. The successes of Java and Java 2 Enterprise Edition (J2EE) have proven that code can be developed better and in a shorter period of time. This is partly because of the fundamental changes of the runtime (using a virtual machine) and the adoption of a simpler programming language.

But just having a virtual machine doesn't solve all your problems. Other pieces of the puzzle can offer a more robust programming model, one that guarantees interoperability regardless of the programming language that is used. Some of these include the following:

- A common type system
- Memory management and garbage collection
- Cross-language inheritance
- An error/exception-handling model
- A consistent security model
- Platform independence
- A dependable deployment model

This is the .NET Framework, plain and simple. Microsoft's .NET architecture represents years of learning about the difficulties inherent in building applications. Let's take a closer look at the .NET Framework and some of the features that it offers to make Web Service development simple.

The .NET Framework

.NET is like the Switzerland of software—a place where COM objects, Web Services, and components written in many different languages can join together to form a software solution. From the Web Service perspective, the most important aspect to .NET is its adoption of Internet standards such as XML, SOAP, and WSDL. This allows developers to build open architectures that can be extended as these standards evolve.

Let's take a closer look at the components that make up the .NET Framework, starting with the most significant architectural module, the Common Language Runtime.

The Common Language Runtime

The Common Language Runtime (CLR) is the environment in which .NET components exist and execute. The CLR provides memory isolation, type-safety enforcement, just-in-time compiling, memory management, exception handling, COM integration, debugging, security, and much, much more. All these services play a part in creating a safe, secure, and robust environment for your Web Service to execute within. The idea behind the CLR is similar to other virtual machines: It provides a neat and tidy environment for your code to execute within. This keeps your code and the system safe by providing an intermediate layer between them. When this layer exists between the two parties, a wide variety of services can be implemented that make development much easier and more consistent.

The CLR is a virtual machine of sorts, so it requires an instruction set for execution of software. This instruction set is the Microsoft Intermediate Language.

Microsoft Intermediate Language

One of the most significant aspects of the CLR is its complete disregard for programming languages. Stated another way, the CLR views all programming languages compatible with the *Common Language Specification (CLS)* in exactly the same light. It does so by mandating a common denominator language called the *Microsoft Intermediate Language (MSIL)*. MSIL is a platform-independent, object-oriented, high-level language that is compiled into native CPU instructions just before execution. Any programming language that targets the CLR must generate MSIL in accordance with the CLS. This is not to say that a programming language is limited to the CLS functionality definitions. Instead, each programming language may still implement unique language features, with the understanding that these features will not be accessible under the CLR environment.

> **NOTE**
>
> You will see the name Common Intermediate Language (CIL) used in place of MSIL throughout various .NET documentation and articles. CIL is the term used within the Common Language Infrastructure (CLI) specifications that were submitted to the ECMA standards association.

To Web Service developers, this means that it doesn't matter what language you choose to develop with—you can still reap the benefits of the .NET Web Service classes and the supporting framework.

The code fragment shown in Listing 2.1 shows a simple console application written in C#. Although the application doesn't do anything extremely interesting, when comparing it to its associated MSIL code in Listing 2.2, you get a good idea of how the CLR operates.

LISTING 2.1 Hello World in C#

```
using System;

class HelloWorld
{
    public static Int32 Main(string[] args)
```

LISTING 2.1   Continued

```
  {
     Console.WriteLine("Hello, world");
     return 0;
  }
};
```

LISTING 2.2   Hello World in MSIL

```
.class private auto ansi beforefieldinit HelloWorld
       extends [mscorlib]System.Object
{
  .method public hidebysig static int32  Main(string[] args) cil managed
  {
    .entrypoint
    // Code size        16 (0x10)
    .maxstack   1
    .locals ([0] int32 CS$00000003$00000000)
    IL_0000:  ldstr      "Hello, world"
    IL_0005:  call       void [mscorlib]System.Console::WriteLine(string)
    IL_000a:  ldc.i4.0
    IL_000b:  stloc.0
    IL_000c:  br.s       IL_000e

    IL_000e:  ldloc.0
    IL_000f:  ret
  } // end of method HelloWorld::Main

  .method public hidebysig specialname rtspecialname
          instance void  .ctor() cil managed
  {
    // Code size        7 (0x7)
    .maxstack   8
    IL_0000:  ldarg.0
    IL_0001:  call       instance void [mscorlib]System.Object::.ctor()
    IL_0006:  ret
  } // end of method HelloWorld::.ctor

} // end of class HelloWorld
```

The first thing you should recognize are the metadata declarations, denoted by the preceding dot (.) character. These are used to provide extended information to the CLR about the behavior of your code. In contrast, the IL instructions as denoted by the preceding IL_xxxx: Labels are the actual executable instructions of your program.

Starting with the metadata, the .class declaration establishes a privately accessible HelloWorld class. The auto attribute allows the CLR to best determine how fields of the given type should be arranged. By using ansi, you are stating that the CLR should use 8-bit strings to interoperate with unmanaged code. The alternative is to use the unicode attribute to denote that 16-bit strings are to be used, or you can let the CLR choose (based on platform) by using the autochar attribute. The beforefieldinit attribute allows the CLR to use the HelloWorld type without having to initialize the type first. Finally, you see that the HelloWorld type simply extends System.Object, as all CLR objects eventually do.

With the class declaration already in place, we can begin to analyze the Main method. The .method declaration is used to define a method that is publicly accessible (public), that is statically associated with its type rather than on a per-instance basis (static), and that returns a 32-bit signed integer. One additional attribute that you might have noticed is hidebysig. Although the CLR does not use this attribute, tools may use it to determine when to hide methods that have duplicate names (the default behavior) or that have duplicate signatures (hidebysig). The cil attribute is used to denote that the code within the method is written in Common Intermediate Language (CIL). The alternative is to have code written for a native processor or automatically generated by the CLR as with *delegates*. When writing CIL code, the managed attribute is used to explicitly state that the code will be managed by the CLR, where native code will be unmanaged.

In this example, the Main method is where the program begins execution. When compiled, the .entrypoint directive shows the CLR where this single point of execution is located. The .maxstack directive informs the CLR of the largest possible stack size that will be needed for this method. Finally, local variable declarations are created using the .locals directive.

Now that we've covered the metadata in our example, Table 2.1 provides a synopsis of the IL instructions and their usage.

TABLE 2.1 Hello World Instruction Synopsis

Instruction	Definition
ldstr	Allocates a new string object, loads it with a literal string, and pushes it onto the stack.
call	Used for fixed destination address (at link time). In this case, it is used to call WriteLine method under System.Console.
ldc	Loads a constant onto the stack. In this case, we are loading a 4-byte signed integer with the value of 0.

TABLE 2.1 Continued

Instruction	Definition
stloc	Pops a value off the stack and stores it to a local variable. The `stloc.0` instruction loads the first local variable with the `0` just pushed onto the stack.
br.s	Branches to a target using the short (1-byte) form rather than the long (4-byte) form, as denoted by the `br` instruction.
ldloc.0	Loads the first local variable onto the stack.
ret	Returns from the current method to the calling method.

The remaining code in the example is the automatically generated constructor method for the class, which follows a similar pattern.

Of course, this example wasn't very complicated, and it exercised only a small portion of the available instruction set. At a minimum, though, it provides some insight into how the CLR operates. To see the list of instructions in the assembly, we used the ILDASM.EXE application that ships with the .NET Framework. You can locate this program at {.NET Install Path}\Microsoft.NET\FrameworkSDK\Bin.

For more information about the ILDASM.EXE tool or the full IL instruction set, see the references in Appendix D, ".NET Web Service Resources," or your .NET documentation.

Just-in-Time Compiling

The MSIL that we just described is generated by .NET compilers and eventually is converted into native code before execution. For this to take place, the CLR uses a just-in-time compiler (JIT) built specifically for the particular hardware platform. This is considered *just-in-time* because of its lazy compilation model. Rather than compiling the entire application at load time, the JIT compiler builds only a small portion of the application at any given time. Because a particular portion of code may be re-executed (a very common occurrence), the JIT compiler caches compiled code for future reference.

An optional but important verification process may be enforced on the application, depending on security privileges of the software. Although there is some overhead in doing so, this ensures that the application is following the appropriate type safety rules and will not corrupt other portions of the code.

> **NOTE**
>
> When you build and deploy your Web Service code using ASP.NET, the actual exe-
> cutable binary is not created until your service receives its first request. A cached copy
> of your code services subsequent requests. At the point where you need to release a
> new version of your service, you can simply deploy the new code and future requests
> will begin executing the new version. This is a helpful feature that enables you to
> smoothly release new Web Service code at any time.

As was previously mentioned, the CLR can support any number of programming languages
that target it. However, for these languages to interoperate, they require a well-defined and
agreed-upon standard for establishing datatypes. This is defined by the Common Type System.

Common Type System

Through the Common Language Specification, we now have a definition that consistently
describes how type information should be represented in any CLR-compatible programming
language. This greatly reduces interoperability problems that are so prevalent in today's multi-
language systems.

The Common Type System (CTS) is similar to contemporary object-oriented programming
type systems. *Types* in the CTS are defined as having both a data representation and a behavior.
This means that two object instances can be of the same type if they share compatible data representations and behavior. In other words, just because two object instances behave the same
way (that is, implement the same interface) doesn't necessarily mean that they are of the same
type.

.NET uses the concept of *namespaces* to scope (that is, partition) types so that the same type
names can be reused. For instance, the `MyClass` class is scoped to the MyNamespace
namespace:

```
namespace MyNamespace
{
  class MyClass
  {
    public static void Method1()
    {
    ...etc...
    }
  }
}
```

This requires you to use either the `using` notation shown here:

```
using MyNamespace;
...etc...
MyClass.Method1();
```

or fully qualifying type names:

```
MyNamespace.MyClass.Method1();
```

While we're on the topic of types, note that the CTS supports two general forms of types—*value types* and *reference types*.

Value and Reference Types

Value types are user-defined datatypes that mimic the *pass-by-value* behavior of built-in (that is, primitive) datatypes. However, value types may contain methods, fields, and so on. One such example of a value type is the enumeration (see `System.Enum` in the .NET documentation). Value types are considered *sealed*, so you may not derive other types from them. You can apply the `sealed` modifier to your own types so that other classes cannot derive from them.

When you define a value type, the CTS will automatically define an associated *boxed type*. Boxed types are simply references to the value type's content. When you want to use a value type as an object, the runtime can use the boxed type's reference. Put another way, the CTS enables all value types to be treated as objects by automatically creating a reference (that is, boxing) to the type's value. Although different programming languages deal with boxed types in their own way, the basic principle still applies.

For example, consider the code in Listing 2.3.

LISTING 2.3   Value and Reference Types Example

```
using System;

class HelloWorld
{
  public struct SomeValueType
  {
    public int a;
    public int b;
  }

  public class SomeReferenceType
  {
    public int a;
    public int b;
  }
```

LISTING 2.3 Continued

```
public static Int32 Main(string[] args)
{
  SomeValueType svt;
  svt.a = 5;
  svt.b = 10;

  SomeValueType svtRef = svt;
  svtRef.a = 9;

  Console.WriteLine("Value Types: a={0}, b={1}", svt.a, svt.b);
  Console.WriteLine("Value Types: Ref a={0}, b={1}", svtRef.a, svtRef.b);
  Console.WriteLine();

  SomeReferenceType srt = new SomeReferenceType();
  srt.a = 5;
  srt.b = 10;

  SomeReferenceType srtRef = srt;
  srtRef.a = 9;

  Console.WriteLine("Reference Types: a={0}, b={1}", srt.a, srt.b);
  Console.WriteLine("Reference Types: Ref a={0}, b={1}", srtRef.a, srtRef.b);

  return 0;
  }
}
```

When running this example, the following output is generated:

```
Value Types: a=5, b=10
Value Types: Ref a=9, b=10

Reference Types: a=9, b=10
Reference Types: Ref a=9, b=10
```

Here, the SomeValueType struct automatically creates a type in which its instances cannot be modified. At the point the svtRef reference is created, a boxed type reference is used.

In contrast, the same structure implemented as a class (SomeReferenceType), does allow its values to be changed by references.

Let's take a look at how interfaces are applied to the .NET type system.

Interfaces

A common design practice in software development is to separate interface from implementation. CTS interfaces have the same purpose as COM and Java interfaces—to provide a specification or contract for the functionality that a class should provide. The class is ultimately responsible for providing the implementation behind the interface, and it may inherit from more than one interface, when necessary.

Listing 2.4 shows an interface that is implemented by two different classes. In this example, the Arnold and Gump classes are required to implement the Talk() method because they both inherit from the IMovieCharacter interface. The fact that they both implement this interface enables you to declare an IMovieCharacter variable that can reference either of the two class instances. Note that you cannot use the character reference variable before assigning it to either the arnold or the gump instance variables.

LISTING 2.4 Interface Example

```
using System;

namespace MovieCharacterApplication
{
  interface IMovieCharacter
  {
    void Talk();
  }

  class Arnold : IMovieCharacter
  {
    public void Talk()
    {
      Console.WriteLine("I'll be back.");
    }
  }

  class Gump : IMovieCharacter
  {
    public void Talk()
    {
      Console.WriteLine("That's my Jenny.");
    }
  }

  class InterfaceTest
  {
    static void Main(string[] args)
```

LISTING 2.4 Continued

```
    {
      Arnold arnold = new Arnold();
      Gump gump = new Gump();

      IMovieCharacter character;

      character = arnold;
      Console.Write("{0}: ", character.GetType().Name);
      character.Talk();

      character = gump;
      Console.Write("{0}: ", character.GetType().Name);
      character.Talk();
    }
  }
}
```

Methods defined within an interface are, by nature, considered to be publicly accessible; it makes little sense for an interface to have private methods because its sole purpose is to define a contract that other classes will support. For more information about accessibility rules, refer to the "Access Control" section, later in this chapter.

An interface may not contain fields, but it may contain property definitions that contain no implementation, as follows:

```
interface ISomeInterface
{
  void Method1();

  int MyProperty
  {
    get;
    set;
  }
}
```

In this case, an implementing class of ISomeInterface is required to provide both Method1() and get/set implementations for MyProperty.

Classes

Classes define both *methods* and *fields* (also known as member data). The CTS also extends the standard method/field model by adding two new concepts. The first is the notion of a *property*, which is logically just a field that is accessible through get/set methods. The last concept is that of an *event*. An object's events are used to notify other objects that something of importance has taken place—very similar to a callback function.

Running the example code in Listing 2.5 exercises some of these concepts and produces the following output:

```
Calling Constructor
Calling Method1
x=4, y=5, t=12
```

As you would expect, the constructor is called when the new operator is used to instantiate the object, and methods behave as they do in other object-oriented languages.

LISTING 2.5   Fields, Methods, and Properties

```
using System;

namespace ClassApplication
{
  class MyClass
  {
    // fields
    public int x;              // object level
    public static int y = 5;   // class level

    // properties
    private int t;
    public int T
    {
      get
      {
        return t;
      }
      set
      {
        t = value * 2;    // uses the implicit *value* parameter
      }
    }

    // methods
    public MyClass()       // Constructor
    {
      Console.WriteLine("Calling Constructor");
    }

    public void Method1()
```

LISTING 2.5 Continued

```
    {
      Console.WriteLine("Calling Method1");
    }
  }

  class ClassExample
  {
    static void Main(string[] args)
    {
      MyClass mc = new MyClass();
      mc.Method1();

      mc.x = 4;
      mc.T = 6;

      Console.WriteLine("x={0}, y={1}, t={2}", mc.x, MyClass.y, mc.T);
    }
  }
}
```

Properties offer a much safer mechanism for exposing class data than fields do because they enable you to control *how* others interact with your class. This protects your user-defined datatypes by ensuring that true encapsulation is maintained. Certainly, you could have implemented this same behavior using Get and Set methods in your class, but the property feature provides a more standardized approach to solving the problem.

Just as in C++, base classes can define methods as being *virtual*, thus allowing these methods to be overridden by derived classes. In this case, a derived class has the choice to accept the implementation provided by the base class or to provide a new implementation.

We've already discussed CLS interfaces to some extent, which are basically abstract base classes that have no implementation or fields. The true notion of an *abstract class* lies somewhere between an interface and a standard class. An abstract class is a class that contains one or more abstract members (containing no implementation), or a class that is explicitly declared as being abstract. In either case, you may instantiate only a descendant of this class. However, you may create a reference to an existing instantiation. Listing 2.6 demonstrates abstract classes and produces the following output:

```
MyClass::Method1
MyClass::Method2
MyAbstract::Method1
MyClass::Method2
```

LISTING 2.6   Abstract Classes

```
using System;

namespace AbstractClassExample
{
  abstract class MyAbstract
  {
    int x;

    virtual public void Method1()
    {
      Console.WriteLine("MyAbstract::Method1");
    }

    abstract public void Method2();
  }

  class MyClass : MyAbstract
  {
    public void Method1()
    {
      Console.WriteLine("MyClass::Method1");
    }

    override public void Method2()
    {
      Console.WriteLine("MyClass::Method2");
    }
  }

  class Example
  {
    static void Main(string[] args)
    {
      MyClass m = new MyClass();
      // MyAbstract c = new MyAbstract(); // Illegal
      MyAbstract c = m;

      m.Method1();
      m.Method2();

      c.Method1();
      c.Method2();
    }
  }
}
```

The `MyAbstract` class explicitly declares its abstractness and contains a single abstract method. This method provides a default implementation that can be accepted or overridden by a descendant class. Notice in `Main()` that the abstract class cannot be instantiated, but it can be used as a reference to an instance of the derived `MyClass` class. Depending on the reference that you use, `m` or `c`, you get either the derived class behavior or the abstract class behavior, respectively.

Deriving from a class can be a useful technique, especially when you want to inherit some base class functionality. However, note that, unlike C++, multiple-class inheritance is not supported by the CTS. Therefore, programming languages such as C++ that want to target .NET cannot provide this feature through the CLR (that is, as managed code).

Yet another benefit for adopting the CTS is that all class types derive from the base `System.Object` type. This means that all objects are fundamentally the same and, at a minimum, support four basic functions, as shown in Table 2.2.

TABLE 2.2 `System.Object` Methods

Method	Description
`Equals()`	Compares the identity of two objects to see if they are the same instance
`GetHashCode()`	Generates a hash code
`GetType()`	Gets the type of the current instance
`ToString()`	Provides a string representation of the object

One of the greatest benefits to the CLR model is that every datatype in the CLR can be identified or created at runtime using *reflection*. This is how the CLR can properly serialize and remote datatypes, or even just browse type information. Reflection is how .NET is capable of building WSDL files for your services. By inspecting the types that are used in your Web method, the compiler can map .NET types into compatible XML Schema types. This is also how .NET manages to create typed objects on the fly when servicing an incoming service request. More about the System.Reflection namespace will be discussed later in this chapter.

Access Control

As you've already seen in many of the previous examples, types have the capability to set rules that dictate how its members can be accessed. The CTS provides accessibility rules that each language can implement. Table 2.3 shows how C# handles the various levels of member visibility.

TABLE 2.3 Accessibility Rules in C#

Accessibility	Description
Private	Access is limited to the given member's class.
Public	Access is open to any executable code, either internal or external to the type.
Protected	Access is open to derived classes.
Internal	Access is limited to the given assembly.
Protected internal	Access is limited to derived classes within the given assembly.

When overriding virtual methods, you are restricted to using the same accessibility rules as with the virtual method. For example, you cannot change a protected member to a publicly accessible method.

So far, we've taken a very quick tour of the Common Type System and how C# provides CTS facilities to you. You've also seen how assemblies participate in the accessibility rules of sharing datatypes. Assemblies and the managed code that they contain deserve a closer look.

Assemblies and Managed Code

In today's world, when you want to ship Windows applications, you typically build an installation package that incorporates all the DLLs and EXEs that are necessary for the software to run. Unfortunately, there is no guarantee that the version of system files that you built and tested the software with are the ones that will always exist on the executing machine. To resolve this problem, Microsoft introduced the concept of an *assembly*. An assembly contains one or more files that make up the application, but they go much further than this. Assemblies contain a manifest that describes such managed-code metadata as file versions, class dependencies, security information, and so on.

Code that has been targeted for the CLR is considered *managed code*. Because managed code is designed to run under the CLR, it cannot execute on its own. Conversely, unmanaged code (that is, native code) is code that does *not* run within the constraints of the CLR.

An additional feature of managed code is *garbage collection*. This is a process in which the runtime determines that memory needs to be cleaned out; objects are inspected to determine whether they can be removed. In the stateless model of Web Services, XML messages eventually get turned into one or more objects that become input parameters to some Web method. In traditional remoting architectures, clients held an open connection with the server to keep objects alive. DCOM used the notion of reference counting to accomplish this task. With the .NET runtime, this is no longer a concern. Objects can come and go, and the runtime decides when objects should be deleted.

Security

As we've already mentioned, assemblies also provide a variety of security mechanisms. In part, these mechanisms guarantee that your application components cannot be tampered with. Security measures also can be used to properly identify that code being executed is actually your code. Both public key encryption and digital signatures are used to implement these features, and they make the deployment model of .NET much safer and more reliable than current Windows application deployment.

Another important feature in .NET is that of role-based security. If you're at all familiar with Microsoft Transaction Server (MTS) or COM+, you've probably had some exposure to this model. In short, role-based security enables you to configure policies that can be assigned to a particular role. A user may participate in more than one role, thereby having multiple levels of security, depending on what the user is doing.

When you authenticate a Web Service client, you have the capability to assign clients to one or more roles. These roles establish the entitlements that clients have within your system. If you find yourself building a Web Service that requires levels of control to access different methods in your service, you should take a closer look into Window's role-based security model. Refer to Appendix D for more information.

The System Namespace

The System namespace is the mother of all namespaces. Not only does it contain the all-important `Object` type, which all types derive from, but it also contains types that map to the primitive types that are supported by your programming language. For instance, the `System.Int32` type represents a 32-bit signed integer that corresponds with the C# primitive type of `int`.

The System namespace also contains a wide variety of additional namespaces that are used for exception handling, garbage collection, console input/output, and so on.

Let's take a look at several of the namespaces that are more applicable to Web Services.

System.XML

Because Web Services are all about XML, it only makes sense that you should be introduced to the XML classes provided by .NET. Listing 2.7 shows how you can use the DOM interface to load a document and use the XPath feature to locate a particular node in the XML tree.

LISTING 2.7   XML Example

```
using System;
using System.Xml;
```

LISTING 2.7   Continued

```
namespace SystemXMLTest
{
  class MyMain
  {
    static void Main(string[] args)
    {
      XmlDocument doc = new XmlDocument();

      doc.LoadXml("<Employee EmpId='02123'><Name>John Doe</Name><Phone>
                 ➥(919)555-1234</Phone></Employee>");

      XmlNode node = doc.SelectSingleNode("//Name");
      if (node != null)
      {
        Console.WriteLine(node.OuterXml);
      }
    }
  }
}
```

What's even more significant is the System.Xml.Serialization namespace, which contains the XmlSerializer class, as demonstrated in Listing 2.8.

LISTING 2.8   XmlSerializer Example

```
using System;
using System.IO;
using System.Xml;
using System.Xml.Serialization;

namespace SystemXMLSerializerTest
{
  public class SomeClass
  {
    public int a;
    public string s;
  }

  class MyMain
  {
    static void Main(string[] args)
    {
      XmlSerializer ser = new XmlSerializer(typeof(SomeClass));
```

LISTING 2.8   Continued

```
    SomeClass sc = new SomeClass();
    sc.a = 4;
    sc.s = "My class to be serialized";

    ser.Serialize(Console.Out, sc);
  }
 }
}
```

The output generated by this example is as follows:

```
<?xml version="1.0" encoding="IBM437"?>
<SomeClass xmlns:xsi="http://www.w3.org/2001/XMLSchema-instance"
           xmlns:xsd="http://www.w3.org/2001/XMLSchema">
  <a>4</a>
  <s>My class to be serialized</s>
</SomeClass>
```

If you recall how SOAP wants to see information encoded, you might notice that this is not far from that same type of XML serialization.

This is all possible because of the reflection properties of .NET.

System.Reflection

Reflection is the capability to discover or create an object's type information at runtime. This powerful feature is what makes Web Services so much easier to implement in .NET than with a programming language such as C++. Consider the example code in Listing 2.9.

LISTING 2.9   Reflection Example

```
using System;
using System.Reflection;

namespace ReflectionApplication
{
  public class MyReflectableClass
  {
    public int a;
    public string s;

    public void Method1()
    {
      Console.WriteLine("MyReflectableClass::Method1");
    }
  }
```

Listing 2.9 Continued

```
class MyMain
{
    static void Main(string[] args)
    {
        Type t = Type.GetType("ReflectionApplication.MyReflectableClass");

        // Display all fields
        FieldInfo[] fi = t.GetFields();
        for (int i=0; i < fi.Length; i++)
        {
            Console.WriteLine("{0} {1};", fi[i].FieldType.Name, fi[i].Name);
        }

        Console.WriteLine();

        // Display all public methods
        MethodInfo[] mi = t.GetMethods();
        for (int i=0; i < mi.Length; i++)
        {
            Console.WriteLine("{0} {1}();", mi[i].ReturnType.Name, mi[i].Name);
        }
    }
}
```

In this example, `MyReflectableClass` is defined to have two `public` fields and a public method. It's important that these be public members for them to be visible to the reflection engine of the CLR. This program simply loads the type based on its namespace qualified class-name, and it iterates over the fields and methods displaying the following output:

```
Int32 a;
String s;

Int32 GetHashCode();
Boolean Equals();
String ToString();
Void Method1();
Type GetType();
```

Notice that the type information that is associated with the fields and methods is based on the types defined in the System namespace, not the types defined in C#. Also notice that the methods derived from System.Object are also included in the reflection properties of this class.

This runtime binding of types makes it much easier for .NET to map XML messages to their associated C# structures and classes. You will have far less type binding to manually code for your Web Services because .NET does this work for you.

System.Net

The System.Net namespace contains classes for a wide variety of network-related tasks. This includes authentication and authorization, cookie management, and a whole host of other classes. The example in Listing 2.10 shows how the WebClient and WebRequest/WebResponse classes can be used to access the Internet.

LISTING 2.10   System.Net Examples

```
using System;
using System.IO;
using System.Net;
using System.Text;

namespace SystemNetExample
{
  class MyMain
  {
    static void Main(string[] args)
    {
      // WebClient example
      WebClient wc = new WebClient();
      wc.DownloadFile("http://localhost/default.html", "c:\\mycopy.html");

      // WebRequest and WebResponse example
      WebRequest req = HttpWebRequest.Create("http://localhost/default.html");

      // Read up to 500 bytes off of the response stream
      WebResponse resp = req.GetResponse();
      Stream str = resp.GetResponseStream();
      byte[] buffer = new byte[500];
      str.Read(buffer, 0, 500);
      resp.Close();

      // Convert from byte array to char array
      ASCIIEncoding ae = new ASCIIEncoding();
      char[] ca = ae.GetChars(buffer);

      // Display characters
      Console.WriteLine(ca);
    }
  }
}
```

The WebClient class simply makes an HTTP GET request from the specified server to obtain a file and create a local copy. The WebRequest class is used for a similar purpose, but instead of encapsulating the entire download of a file, a WebResponse object must be created. Then the stream associated with this response is read and dumped to the console window.

System.Runtime.Remoting

The System.Runtime.Remoting namespace is used to create distributed applications. Specifically, you can control the configuration, publishing, and use of remote objects.

Web Services

A quick overview of the Web Service features in .NET is in order before you encounter them throughout the rest of this book.

> **NOTE**
>
> For you to use the System.Web.Services classes in your Visual Studio .NET project, you must first add the System.Web.Services.dll reference to your project. Refer to the Solution Explorer window.

Discovery

As the consumer of a Web Service, you might or might not know exactly how to locate a service that you want to use. For instance, if you go out looking for a StockQuote service, it's likely that a standard Web search engine will produce some possible clues. However, you would have to do this manually and feed your program the appropriate information after the service was found.

The idea of *discovery* is more related to programmatic discovery. We would like our applications to be able to locate a service with minimal human intervention.

The System.Web.Services.Discovery namespace contains several classes that ease this process. Chapter 5, "Web Service Description and Discovery," contains more details about the industry-accepted UDDI effort that is solving the discovery problem.

Description

Describing services is just as important as discovering them—maybe even more so. The Web Service Description Language (WSDL), as discussed in Chapter 5, provides a unique structure for organizing Web Service descriptions. The System.Web.Services.Description namespace provides all the necessary classes for interacting with WSDL files.

Protocols

Obviously, SOAP is the predominant protocol for implementing Web Services. However, the System.Web.Services.Protocols namespace contains a variety of classes that enable you to work with a wide range of protocols—from SOAP to MIME to URL-encoded HTTP messages.

Summary

This chapter has concentrated on the .NET Framework, with a particular focus on Web Service–related features and classes.

The .NET Framework is such an improvement over the existing Windows technologies that we're certain that most Windows developers will make the transition to .NET very quickly. Not only does it provide a robust environment for your software to execute within, but it also eases the overall development experience by providing a consistent and well-thought-out design.

Although there are just too many classes to document in a single chapter, we've tried to expose the core System classes that will play a part at some point within your Web Service code.

Chapter 3, "Web Services and XML," extends the discussion of .NET and XML by looking at how these two technologies play such an integral part in the Web Service model.

Web Services and XML

IN THIS CHAPTER

XML is critical to Web Services. It's a fundamental technology; without it, you wouldn't have Web Services—at least, not as they're implemented today.

This is true for two main reasons. First, XML is loosely coupled. That is, XML enables you to loosely bind the client and server, making it easier to change one or both, as well as add versioned information after the initial release. Second, XML is easily interpreted, making it highly interoperable. XML is simply text, so if you can interpret text on your computer system, you can interpret XML. You'll find XML in use in nearly every contemporary computer system available today, and perhaps even in some venerable systems that you used yesteryear. There is a great deal more to it than that, but, in a nutshell, XML is just text in a file or network packet.

> **NOTE**
>
> My observation that XML is merely text is inarguably true. However, XML is becoming increasingly Unicode-aware. Most of the XML documents that you'll see in use today are encoded using either UTF-8 (single-byte Unicode) or UTF-16 (traditional 2-byte Unicode). Therefore, your system needs Unicode capability to truly handle these contemporary XML documents. .NET provides you with this capability, even if you're running on a 16-bit version of Windows, such as Windows 98.

The goal of this chapter is to introduce you to the fundamentals of XML and to dig deeper into XML to show how it plays a role in Web Service implementation. If you're new to XML, Appendix D, ".NET Web Service Resources," points to alternative sources of information that you can examine on your own. If you do know something about XML, you might want to scan this chapter for information that's new to you and skip the parts that you know well. With luck, you'll find something interesting and new, and you'll expand your understanding of XML, with both Web Services and .NET's handling of XML in general.

The true goal of this chapter is to make sure that you understand how XML fits into Web Service processing and to show you how to work with XML using the .NET class hierarchy. You might find that you'll need to modify the XML that your Web Service uses for some reason. If so, you'll use what you've learned from this chapter. We'll start with a discussion of XML as a wire representation, which should explain why XML is so important to Web Services.

XML as a Wire Representation

Whenever you transmit information over a network, that information is ultimately transformed from a binary representation in your computer's memory into another representation that was designed for network use. Perhaps the network representation is a highly efficient binary one, or perhaps its purpose is more general. In any case, you'll probably find that the information's binary format in memory is very different than its network form. The form that it takes for network transmission is called its *wire representation*. This is the form that the data takes when it's transmitted over the network, no matter what the network medium is.

Wire representations, and protocols in general, are often designed to meet specific design criteria, a few of which are listed here:

- Compactness
- Protocol efficiency
- Coupling
- Scalability
- Interoperability

Compactness refers to how terse the network packet becomes while still conveying the same information. Small is usually best. *Protocol efficiency* is related to compactness—you rate efficiency by examining the overhead required to send the payload. The more overhead you require, the less efficient the protocol is.

A protocol's *coupling*, loose or tight, tells you how flexible consumers of the protocol will be if you change things. Loosely coupled protocols are quite flexible and easily adapt to change, while tightly coupled protocols will most likely require significant modifications to both the server and existing clients. Tightly coupled protocols, for example, are those that require (or force) such things as the same in-memory representation or the same processor type to avoid endian issues (byte ordering in multibyte values). Loosely coupled protocols avoid this altogether by abstracting the information to a degree that makes the byte order irrelevant. Converting an integer represented in big or little endian looks the same when represented as a string. The byte order conversion is made by the software handling the protocol, not by the protocol itself.

Scalability addresses the protocol's capability to work with a large number of potential recipients. Some protocols are limited to a handful of consumers, while others handle millions of users easily.

Finally, *interoperability* speaks to the protocol's acceptance on a variety of computing platforms. Will you have to issue network packets to one specific operating system or platform, or is the protocol a bit more general-purpose, enabling you to send information to a wider variety of systems?

Protocols, including XML, generally lie within a continuum of these characteristics. Highly efficient protocols tend to not scale well. Interoperable protocols tend to scale well but are often not as efficient as proprietary protocols. No single protocol does it all, and network

3

WEB SERVICES
AND XML

engineers often make design decisions based upon these and many other criteria. Which protocol you choose depends upon where the protocol falls in the continuum.

XML is both loosely coupled and highly interoperable. In fact, XML is so interoperable that it is nearly ubiquitous. You can send XML to anyone on the planet—not only will that person receive the information, but he'll also be able to interpret and make use of it in nearly every case.

With XML, you pay for loose coupling and interoperability with protocol efficiency and compactness. XML is actually rather inefficient, although you can tailor this by judiciously choosing your element names (fewer characters in element names often yields more efficient XML, even though terseness of the XML was not a design goal of the inventors). Nor is XML particularly compact. XML is text, and, as with any text document, you might be either conservative with your expressiveness or creative yet a bit more verbose. In either case, you are still left with a loosely coupled and interoperable mechanism for encoding information to be transmitted over the wire.

XML and Loose Coupling

If XML isn't terribly efficient, why use it? Because XML is simply text formatted in a specific way. You could make the same argument about HTTP, SMTP, POP3, NNTP, and a host of other such Internet protocols, but they've also proven to be successful. XML works, and it works well—when you transmit information using XML, you're sending text rather than a proprietary protocol that has arbitrary design limitations. DCOM, for example, uses a fairly efficient wire representation but requires the object's server to keep track of the client. To do this, the DCOM client issues "I'm still here" messages to the server every two minutes. After three periods without one of these *ping* messages, the server chops off the object's head and reclaims the resources (memory and such). But imagine making changes to the DCOM wire representation and then trying to field that worldwide… .

Because XML is nothing more than text, with no claims made to object status or association, changes to your XML are rather easily accepted. You still send and receive text; it's just that the element names might have changed or the document layout might have been slightly altered.

XML and Interoperability

The fact that XML is so loosely coupled has undoubtedly been a contributing factor to its wide acceptance throughout the Internet. Nearly every major computing platform available today has some capability to accept and interpret XML. XML is text—and, if your computer can handle text, your computer can handle XML. Palm PCs, cellular telephones, desktop and laptop PCs, and the largest of mainframes all have XML processing capability.

If this is the case, you should expect to be able to send anyone an XML document and know that the recipient can make use of the information. Because this is so, SOAP architects chose XML as the encoding mechanism for the SOAP protocol. XML is a rich and expressive technology that readily lends itself to method parameter serialization. Best of all, everyone understands what has been serialized, regardless of computing platform, and can make use of it.

As you probably already know, it's one thing to create the XML document. It's quite another to interpret the contents using an automated system. You'll require some mechanism to reach into the XML to extract the portions of interest. That mechanism is called XPath. Here we'll move away from "Why is XML good?" toward "How do I use XML?"

Querying XML Elements Using XPath

The previous section "XML as a Wire Representation" provides you with a few reasons why we've seen explosive growth of XML in the past few years, and it told why XML was selected to be a major component of the SOAP protocol. Another factor is the many peripheral XML technologies that make using XML even more attractive. Certainly one of these technologies is *XPath*, which is the language that you use to query an XML document for specific information.

If you work with XML, you're probably somewhat familiar with XPath. If not, here is the basic idea. XPath serves the same purpose as the Structured Query Language (SQL) for database access. With SQL, you establish a search expression and provide that to the database. The database, in turn, searches its tables for the data that you requested and provides you with the results. XPath also establishes search patterns, but instead of accessing a database, you apply the XPath query against an XML document that is contained within an *XML processor*.

XML processors are software components that, when provided an XML document, expose a programmable interface that enables you to work with the XML document in an automated manner. Typically XML processors expose the XML Document Object Model (DOM) or perhaps the Simple API for XML (SAX). The DOM enables you to deal with the XML document as if it were composed of tree nodes. SAX, on the other hand, offers a stream-based approach to accessing the XML information. You take what you need from the stream and discard the rest. (.NET implements another model that you'll examine in the later section ".NET's XML Architecture.")

Because this book is focused on Web Services, we won't go into much detail regarding DOM or SAX, which are general XML topics that merit their own book. If you need a brush-up, or if XML is new to you, I'll explain the basics here. For more information, see the references included in Appendix D.

Essential XML

The engine that drives the Web Service is the Simple Object Access Protocol, or SOAP. SOAP's power is centered on the intrinsic behavior of XML and related XML technologies. To fully appreciate SOAP and its capabilities, it's important to have a good understanding of XML. It is beyond the scope of this book to teach you all you might need to know to use XML effectively. However, it would be unreasonable to assume that you understand all the emerging technologies associated with XML because several of these are still ongoing efforts. Therefore, this section briefly reviews XML to provide the basis for discussion of the newer aspects to XML.

Documents, Elements, and Attributes

An *XML document* is really just a collection of data consisting of both *physical* and *logical* structure. Physically, the document consists of textual information. It contains *entities* that can reference other entities that are located elsewhere in memory, on a hard disk, or, more importantly, on the Web. The *logical structure* of an XML document includes processing instructions, declarations, comments, and elements. XML documents contain ordinary text (as specified by ISO/IEC 10646) that represent markup or *character data*.

The general form of an XML document looks something like this:

```
<?xml version="1.0" ?>
<Car Year="2002">
    <Make>Chevrolet</Make>
    <Model>Corvette<Model>
    <Color>Gunmetal</Color>
</Car>
```

You know that this is an XML document because of the *XML declaration* on the first line that tells you that this document conforms to XML version 1.0. In this example, <Car/> is the *root element* or *document element* of this XML document, <Make/> is just one of the child *elements* contained within <Car/>, and Year is an *attribute* of the <Car/> element.

Any text document is considered a *well-formed* XML document if it conforms to the constraints set forth in the XML specification. For example, one very important constraint is the limitation to one and only one root element in a document. An XML document is considered *valid* if it is well formed, if it has an associated Document Type Definition (DTD) or XML Schema, and if the given instance document complies with this definition. The DTD or XML Schema documents act as a template that the associated XML document must precisely match. If not, there is a problem with the formatting of the instance document, and the entire document is considered not valid.

It is common to find *processing instructions* embedded within the document, but they are not considered part of the document's content. They are used to communicate information to application-level code without changing the meaning of the XML document's content.

The following notation denotes the syntax of *processing instructions*:

```
<?target declaration ?>
```

The processing instruction contains a target followed by one or more instructions, where the target name specifies the application to which the processing instruction is applied. A common target name found in XML documents is the reserved target xml. This enables the XML document to communicate instructions to XML parsers. The most common (but optional) processing instruction used in XML documents is the XML declaration itself.

Recall that an *element* consists of a *start tag*, an *end tag,* and a *value*. But what if you have no value? Do you omit the entire XML element? You could, but it's also useful information to know that an element *could* be there but, in this particular case, you have no value. Rather than using a start and end tag when you have no value to include, you can combine the tags to form an *empty-element tag*:

```
<Car Year="2002">
    <Make>Chevrolet</Make>
    <Model>Corvette<Model>
    <Color>Gunmetal</Color>
    <VehicleID/>
</Car>
```

> **NOTE**
>
> XML is sensitive to case and whitespace when creating element names. Whitespace is never legal in tag names, and tag names that are spelled the same but differ in alphabetical case represent *different* XML elements.

A parent element can theoretically contain an infinite number of child elements, and the same child element can appear multiple times under its parent element as siblings:

```
<Car>
    <Name>Corvette</Name>
    <Name>Speedy<Name>
    <Color>Red</Color>
    <!-- ...etc... -->
</Car>
```

Also, the same element name can appear under different parent elements. In this case, the element <Name appears under the <Car> element as well as the <SoundSystem> element:

```
<Car>
    <Name>Corvette</Name>
    <SoundSystem>
        <Name>Bose</Name>
    </SoundSystem>
</Car>
```

You are not allowed to overlap tags within an XML document. The following document would *not* be considered a well-formed XML document because the <Color> element starts before the <Name> element ends:

```
<Car>
    <Color>3721-<Name>Red</Color>Corvette</Name>
</Car>
```

This example is trying to specify that the color of the car is 3721-Red and the name of the car is RedCorvette. However, this does not meet the XML specification constraints. Instead, it should be rewritten as follows:

```
<Car>
    <Color>3721-Red</Color><Name>RedCorvette</Name>
</Car>
```

Elements can be embedded within values of other elements:

```
<Car>
    <Name>Corvette</Name>
    <Base>MSRP<Price>39,475</Price>with options</Base>
</Car>
```

In this case, the <Price> element was embedded between the first part of the MSRP value and the last part of the with options value. This XML document encoding style is very much discouraged in general practice, however. The most common way to logically view an XML document is as a tree, and having elements embedded within values muddies this model.

Attributes provide more specific information about a particular element. Choosing between using an attribute and using an element can sometimes be a difficult decision. In a lot of cases, either form will work. One approach is to use attributes to denote element classifications based on the problem domain. Or, consider the attribute as a way to insert metadata that tailors the element in some way. Another aspect to using attributes deals with ease of access to data. If you always want to obtain the car's color every time you encounter a Car element, then Color might be a good candidate for an attribute.

> **NOTE**
>
> The SOAP specification uses attributes in a variety of ways. In particular, the id and href attributes are used for unique identifiers and references, respectively. They are part of XLink, which you'll see in the section "Identifying XML Elements Using XLink."

Entity References and CDATA

It is not uncommon for *character data* to contain characters that are used in XML constructs. The following XML does not conform to the XML specification:

```
<Car Year="2002 "The Sleekest Vette Yet"">
    <Name>Corvette</Name>
</Car>
```

The additional quotes in "The Sleekest Vette Yet" corrupt the syntax of the root element. Proper use of *entity references* allows you to instruct parsers to treat data as character data. The preceding example should be changed to this:

```
<Car Year="2000 &quot;The New Millennium&quot;">
    <Name>Corvette</Name>
</Car>
```

Here, the quotes have been replaced by their entity reference and will now be correctly parsed.

The double quote is but one of five characters that must be replaced with their entity references. The other four include the apostrophe (single quote), the ampersand, and the "less than" and "greater than" brackets. This makes sense because the quote characters are used to encapsulate attributes, the ampersand denotes an entity reference, and the brackets form XML element tags. If you use these characters within general text element values, you confuse the XML parser.

CDATA is an alternate form of markup that is better for larger quantities of text to be explicitly described as character data:

```
<Car Year="2002">
    <Model>Corvette</Model>
    <Description><![CDATA["I bet it's fast!"]]></Description>
</Car>
```

Rather than using entity references for each individual character, you can specify that an entire block of text should be treated as character data. This is a nice benefit because you do not need to replace each special character with its entity reference, which can be costly in terms of string manipulations. You simply wrap the text data with the CDATA tag.

There are two limitations to CDATA, however. CDATA sections *cannot* be nested within one another, and you cannot use CDATA within attribute values. CDATA sections cannot be nested because, by XML specification, the end tag of the enclosing CDATA section is considered to be the end tag for the CDATA section. If there were more text after this tag, the XML parser would become confused and would return to you an error when the document was parsed. For attributes, it is not legal XML syntax to specify XML elements within attribute values, and CDATA falls within that ruling. If you happen to have textual data that contains some of the XML special characters, you should use their respective entity reference values instead.

URIs and XML Namespaces

URI, or *uniform resource identifier*, is a generic term used to identify some particular entity or object in the Web world using its string representation. This is the most fundamental addressing scheme of the Web. A perfect use for this uniqueness deals with naming XML elements and attributes so that they don't conflict with one another. This section reviews the characteristics of URIs and namespaces, and describes how they are related when used with your XML documents.

URLs and URNs

Different types of Web resources require different forms of URIs. Specifically, uniform resource locators (URLs) and uniform resource names (URNs) are both forms of a URI (see Figure 3.1). Each has its own syntax designed to fulfill a purpose.

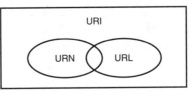

FIGURE 3.1
The relationship between URIs, URNs, and URLs.

URLs are a form of URI used to *locate* a particular resource in the Web world. Basic URL syntax (see RFC 1738) is dependent on the *scheme* to which it applies, but it follows this format:

```
<scheme>:<scheme-specific syntax>
```

One form of a URL is used to specify a Web page located on a Web server, similar to this:

```
http://www.endurasoft.com/educenter.htm
```

In this case, the scheme indicates that the HTTP protocol is to be used to retrieve the HTML text for a particular Web page. By changing just one of the values in this URL, you are specifying a completely different location, resource, or both on the Web.

URNs are another form of URI that provides *persistence* as well as *location-independence*. In a nutshell, a URN uniquely describes some resource that will *always* be available. The following is an example of a URN:

```
urn:foo-bar:foobar.1
```

The exact syntax of URNs is denoted in RFC 2141, but the following is a summary:

urn:*<Namespace Identifier>*:*<Namespace Specific String>*

1. The text "urn:" (uppercase or lowercase) is included.
2. The *Namespace Identifier* consists of letters, numbers, and hyphens (uppercase or lowercase).
3. The *Namespace Specific String* consists of letters, numbers, parentheses, commas, periods, hyphens, and other such characters (uppercase or lowercase).

Efforts are underway to provide Internet protocols for resolving URNs. This would work similar to the way DNS (or other name service) resolves hostnames.

XML Namespaces

In the .NET Framework, namespaces are used routinely to uniquely identify groupings of logically related classes that might have names that coincide with classes within other framework class groupings. XML also uses namespaces, but for a slightly different purpose. Because you are free to create your own XML elements, chances are good that you will happen to select a tag name that someone else has also used. With everyone declaring their own XML element names and attributes, you can expect ambiguous results when trying to combine this data. For example, one system might use the `<Title/>` element when describing a book, while another system might also use `<Title/>` to describe automobile ownership. As long as the XML data from the two systems is never combined within the same XML document, everything is fine. However, if the data ever merges, there is no way to distinguish between the two semantic meanings.

An *XML namespace*, as identified by a URI reference, qualifies element and attribute names within an XML document. This not only avoids name collisions, but it also enables *vocabularies* to be reused. You can think of an XML vocabulary as a published set of element and attribute names common to a particular user domain. SOAP is one such vocabulary, but there are many others.

The following example contains XML that has no associated namespace:

```
<Product>
    <ProductName Type="1">Widget</ProductName>
</Product>
```

To reference a namespace, you must first declare one by creating a *namespace declaration* using this form:

```
xmlns:<Namespace Prefix> = <URI>
```

In the namespace declaration, you specify a *namespace prefix* and the URI of the namespace. The prefix is attached to the local names of elements and attributes so that they are associated with the correct namespace, like so:

```
<pns:Product xmlns:pns="http://www.endurasoft.com/prodns">
    <pns:ProductName pns:Type="1">Widget</pns:ProductName>
</pns:Product>
```

In this case, pns is defined to be the *prefix* and is used to associate Product, ProductName, and Type with the http://www.endurasoft.com/prodns URI. In reality, the URI doesn't necessarily point to anything—its purpose is to provide uniqueness to the namespace.

XML namespaces also provide the concept of a *default namespace* (denoted in XML as xmlns). This enables you to establish a namespace for an element and all its children, thus avoiding the need to use a prefix on each element name.

> **NOTE**
>
> Default namespaces do not apply to attribute names. Instead, attributes must be explicitly prefixed to the desired namespace.

Initially, an XML document has no assigned default namespace, so any elements that are not qualified with a prefix will be locally scoped.

Now consider the following example:

```
<pns:Product xmlns:pns="http://www.endurasoft.com/prodns">
    <pns:ProductName pns:Type="1">Widget</pns:ProductName>
    <ProductLoc xmlns="http://www.endurasoft.com/prodlocns">
        <Building>310</Building>
        <Floor>2</Floor>
        <Room>118</Room>
    </ProductLoc>
    <Cost>495.00</Cost>
</pns:Product>
```

On the first line, the `pns` prefix is created to reference a product URI. This same prefix is used to qualify the `Product` and `ProductName` elements. On the third line, a default namespace is created that references a completely different URI than did the first line. All elements contained within the `ProductLoc` element are scoped to the default namespace and, therefore, require no prefix. However, because `<Cost/>` element is not contained by the `ProductLoc` element and doesn't have a prefix, it is considered locally scoped to the document.

.NET uses namespaces. If you examine the XML used to transfer information between the Web Service and the client, you'd see these namespaces in action. They're simply there to identify a certain XML element as belonging to a logically related group of XML elements that form a vocabulary. But how is the vocabulary itself specified? This is the primary use of the XML Schema.

XML Schemas

As you know, all XML documents must be well formed. For example, tags cannot overlap. They must specify some sort of hierarchy. But often the benefits of producing a well-formed document aren't enough. Saying that the XML elements cannot overlap is not as useful as saying that the XML elements cannot overlap and must follow a specific order or use certain tag names. The XML Schema specification identifies an XML vocabulary that you can use to create other XML vocabularies. In doing so, you tell consumers of your schema how your XML should be constructed to be considered valid by your design.

Understanding XML Schemas

Many times as you develop XML documents, you often need to place constraints on the way data is represented in the document. You might be concerned that a particular set of XML elements follows a specific order, or you might want to identify an XML element as containing text that actually represents a specific datatype, such as a floating point.

To place constraints on data, you must build Document Type Definitions (DTDs) or XML Schemas to provide data about the data, also known as *metadata*. DTDs were an early XML constraint mechanism. And although DTDs are beneficial to many XML applications, they do not have the characteristics necessary for describing constructs such as inheritance or complex datatypes. To overcome these limitations, a working group was formed to produce XML Schemas based on an original draft from Microsoft. The XML Schema specification is divided into two parts. The first part, *XML Schema Part 1: Structures*, proposes a way to structure and constrain document content. The second part, *XML Schema Part 2: Data Types*, provides a way to describe both primitive and complex datatypes within a document.

The XML Schema specification establishes a means by which the XML Schema language describes the structure and content of XML documents. A desirable feature of XML Schemas is the fact that they are represented in XML, so standard XML parsers can be used to *navigate* them.

At this point, you are already familiar with XML and many of the terms used to identify the concepts behind XML. The XML Schema draft defines several new terms that help describe the semantics of using and understanding schemas.

Instances and Schema

An *XML instance document* refers to the document element, including elements, attributes, and content contained within the document, that conforms to an XML Schema. *Instances* in the more general sense may refer to any element (including its attributes and content) that conforms to an XML Schema. An instance that conforms to a schema is considered to be *schema-valid*.

Schemas can be independent XML documents, or they can be embedded inside other XML with references to the schema. Schemas take this form:

```
<xsd:schema xmlns:xsd="http://www.w3.org/TR/xmlschema-1/">
    <!--type definitions, element declarations, etc. -->
</xsd:schema>
```

Definitions and Declarations

A great advantage of schemas is that they enable you to create simple or complex *types* for applying classifications to elements. As in most programming languages, this is called *type definition* and is shown as follows:

```
<xsd:schema xmlns:xsd="http://www.w3.org/TR/xmlschema-1/">
    <xsd:complexType name="Person">
        <xsd:element name="FirstName" type="xsd:string" />
        <xsd:attribute name="Age" type="xsd:integer" />
    </xsd:complexType>
</xsd:schema>
```

The preceding example also shows an *element declaration* (for the element <FirstName/>) and an *attribute declaration* (for the attribute Age) that are local to a particular type named Person.

Beyond participating in the type definition, elements also may be declared as top-level elements of a particular type, as shown in the following example, where BaseballPlayer is a type of Person:

```
<xsd:schema xmlns:xsd="http://www.w3.org/TR/xmlschema-1/">
    <!-- ...Type definition... -->

    <xsd:element name="BaseballPlayer" type="Person" />
</schema>
```

Attributes, however, can be of only simple types, as defined in *XML Schema Part 2: Datatypes*, such as string, boolean, and float.

Target Namespace

Because element and attribute declarations are used to validate instances, it is necessary for them to match the namespace characteristic of a particular instance. This implies that declarations have an association with a *target namespace URI* or *no namespace* at all, depending on whether the instance has a qualified name. For a schema to specify a target namespace, it must use the targetNamespace attribute, as follows:

```
<xsd:schema xmlns:xsd="http://www.w3.org/TR/xmlschema-1/"
  targetNamespace="SomeNamespaceURI">
    <xsd:element name="ElementInNS" type="xsd:string" />
    <xsd:complexType name="TypeInNS">
       <xsd:element name="LocalElementInNS" type="xsd:integer" />
       <xsd:attribute name="LocalAttrInNS" type="xsd:string" />
    </xsd:complexType>
</xsd:schema>
```

As you can see, all global and local elements are associated with SomeNamespaceURI. Lack of the targetNamespace attribute designates that no namespace is associated.

Datatypes and Schema Constraints

Datatypes consist of a *value space*, *lexical space*, and *facets*. The value space is the datatype's permitted set of values, and it can have various properties associated with it. A set of valid literals for a datatype makes up the lexical space of that datatype. Finally, a facet is a single dimension of a concept that enables you to distinguish among different datatypes. Two kinds of *facets* are used to describe datatypes, *fundamental* and *constraining*.

Fundamental facets enable you to describe the order, bounds, cardinality, exactness, and numeric properties of a given datatype's value space.

Constraining facets enable you to describe the constraints on a datatype's value space. Possible constraints include minimum and maximum length, pattern matching, upper and lower bounds, and enumeration of valid values.

The following is the fragment of a *simple type* definition:

```
<xsd:simpleType name="HourType">
   <xsd:restriction base="xsd:integer">
      <xsd:minInclusive value="1" />
      <xsd:maxInclusive value="12" />
   </xsd:restriction>
</datatype>
```

In this case, `HourType` is defined to be of the built-in `integer` datatype and additionally is constrained to values between 1 and 12. This new type can then be used in other type definitions as in the following `Hour` attribute:

```
<xsd:complexType name="Time">
    <xsd:attribute name="Hour" type="HourType" />
    <xsd:attribute name="Minute" type="MinuteType" />
</xsd:complexType>
```

The instance for this type might look something like this:

```
<Time Hour="7" Minute="30" />
```

That was also an example of a *complex type* definition. The complex type definition combines one or more simple types to form something new. Here is another complex type example:

```
<xsd:element name="cars" type="CarsType"/>

<xsd:complexType name="CarsType">
    <xsd:element name="car" type="CarType"
      minoccurs="0" maxoccurs="unbounded"/>
</xsd:complexType>

<xsd:complexType name="CarType">
    <xsd:element name="make" type="xsd:string"/>
    <xsd:element name="model" type="xsd:string"/>
</xsd:complexType>
```

This type can be represented by an instance as follows:

```
<cars xmlns:xsi="http://www.w3.org/TR/xmlschema-1/"
  xsi:noNamespaceSchemaLocation="CarSchema.xsd">
    <car>
        <make>Cheverolet</make>
        <model>Corvette</model>
    </car>
</cars>
```

minOccurs and maxOccurs

Elements and attributes enable you to specify the minimum and maximum number of times that they may appear in the instance. The following example shows how you can force an attribute to appear one and only one time:

```
<xsd:element name="Book">
    <attribute name="Author" type="A" minOccurs="1" maxOccurs="1" />
    <attribute name="Title" type="T" minOccurs="1" maxOccurs="1" />
</xsd:element>
```

The maxOccurs attribute can also be set to unbounded to denote that the element or attribute can appear *many* times. You also can prevent a value from appearing by setting the maxOccurs attribute equal to 0.

Deriving Type Definitions

Similar to the way object-oriented programming languages work, schemas enable you to derive types from other types in a controlled way. When defining a new type, you may choose to *extend* or *restrict* the other type definition.

When extending another type definition, you can introduce additional elements and attributes, as shown in the following example:

```
<xsd:complexType name="Book">
    <xsd:element name="Title" type="xsd:string" />
    <xsd:element name="Author" type="xsd:string" />
</xsd:complexType>

<xsd:complexType name="ElectronicBook">
    <xsd:complexContent>
        <xsd:extension base="Book">
            <xsd:sequence>
                <element name="URL" type="xsd:string" />
            </xsd:sequence>
        </xsd:extension>
    </xsd:complexContent>
</xsd:complexType>
```

Sometimes an instance wants to explicitly indicate its type. To do this, the instance can use the XML Schema instance namespace definition of xsi:type, as follows:

```
<Car xsi:type="SportsCar">
    <Driver>Me</Driver>
</Car>
```

Although this was not an exhaustive coverage of schemas, at least you now should realize the following:

- You can constrain your XML documents and their content using XML Schema.
- The XML Schema specification provides you with a set of built-in datatypes.
- You can use the built-in datatypes or create your own datatypes.
- Schemas may be standalone documents or may be combined within other XML documents.

This information is here because XML Schemas are important to .NET. Let's see why.

3

WEB SERVICES AND XML

.NET Web Services and XML Schemas

If you happen to glance at the SOAP specification, you'll find a section that describes how to encode method parameters, Section 5. This section was necessary when the SOAP specification was introduced because there was no way to otherwise describe the SOAP XML. If you couldn't somehow validate the incoming SOAP packets, you could not extract the method's parameter data and actually invoke the method on your local systems.

Section 5 is becoming far less important today because of the Web Service Description Language (WSDL), as you'll see in detail in Chapter 5, "Web Service Description and Discovery." WSDL serves as an interface description document that you can use to determine what XML information the Web Service will accept. In other words, you can change the XML formatting for your Web Service by changing the way you describe the Web Service in its WSDL file. As it happens, there is a schema embedded within the WSDL file.

This actually makes a lot of sense. If you think about it, handing someone an arbitrary XML document and expecting that person to figure out by inspection just what you're asking him to do is a very complex undertaking, if that person even has enough information to make an informed decision. On the other hand, if you hand that same person a document that outlines the datatypes of your method parameters and the order in which they can be found, you've given that person enough information to decipher the XML instance documents that you intend to transmit.

For this reason, you'll find an XML schema embedded within the WSDL document that describes your Web Service. Essentially, with your WSDL document, you're telling the other side what datatypes you expect and how you want them ordered, as well as how they should appear within the SOAP packet. Web Services are now significantly more flexible.

Now that you know how XML documents are formed and how they are validated, how do you get the values associated with the XML elements back out of the XML document? This is the job of XPath.

We will discuss XPath in some detail, mainly because many people who have worked with XML to some degree still might require a little XPath brush-up. And it's XPath that makes your work easier if you need to reach into a SOAP packet and modify what you find, as you might do with a .NET SoapExtension. Why? Because of interoperability, if nothing else, but you might have other reasons as well, depending upon your individual system requirements. For example, you might want to retrieve a SOAP parameter value and encrypt it.

Let's take a more detailed look at XPath to see what it can offer when you're tweaking XML.

XPath Drilldown

Imagine that you have this XML document you created for yourself to remind you how to access a couple of your favorite Web Services:

```xml
<?xml version="1.0"?>
<Servers>
   <Server name="Gumby">
      <WebService wsdl="?wsdl">
         <Family>Calculators</Family>
         <EndpointURL>http://www.myurl.com/calc</EndpointURL>
      </WebService>
   </Server>
   <Server name="Pokey">
      <WebService wsdl=".wsdl">
         <Family>Time</Family>
         <EndpointURL>http://www.myurl.com/time</EndpointURL>
      </WebService>
   </Server>
</Servers>
```

This totally fictitious XML document describes two imaginary Web Service servers. The first provides some sort of calculator service, based upon the service's family, and the second gives the time. The calculator service sends its WSDL by adding ?WSDL to the endpoint URL, which is how .NET works. The second does the same by concatenating .WSDL, which is how the SOAP Toolkit works. Of course, only two servers are shown in this case. You could have hundreds or more, so the corresponding XML document could grow to be quite large. How will you find the one particular server's information that is of interest to you?

Now let's say that you want to retrieve all the servers that are part of the Time family. You could use this XPath query string:

```
/Servers/Server/WebService[./Family="Time"]
```

The result of this query is a *nodeset*, which is a set of XML elements that match the query. The query itself can be called a *location step*, which can be broken into three parts:

- The *axis*
- The *node test*
- The *predicate*

Let's take a closer look at each.

3

WEB SERVICES
AND XML

The XPath Axis

The axis is optional—in fact, this particular location step has no axis identified. You use the axis to move through the XML document in some other manner than from the top down. This is because the default location step is `child::`, so the XPath query returns, by default, a node-set containing children of the current *context node*. The context node is the current XML element that you happen to be examining, which, in this case, is the root or document element. Other possible axes include `ancestor::`, `parent::`, `following::`, and a myriad of other possible values, all shown in Table 3.1.

TABLE 3.1 XPath Axis Values

Axis	Purpose
ancestor	Ancestors of the context node, including the root node if the context node is not already the root node
ancestor-or-self	Same as ancestor, but includes the context node
attribute	Attributes of the context node (context node should be an element)
child	All (immediate) children of the context node
descendant	All children of the context node, regardless of depth
descendant-or-self	Same as the descendant, but includes the context node
following	All nodes following the context node, in document order
following-or-sibling	Only sibling nodes following the context node, in document order
namespace	Namespace of the context node (the context node should be an element)
parent	Immediate parent of the context node, if any (that is, not the root node)
preceding	Similar to the following, except returns preceding nodes in document order
preceding-sibling	Same as preceding, but for sibling nodes only
self	The context node itself

You probably noticed the term *document order* mixed into Table 3.1. Document order refers not to the ordering and hierarchy of XML elements, but instead to the literal order in which the element is found in the document, whether it is a parent, sibling, or whatever. Essentially, when you access nodes in document order, you're flattening any hierarchy that might be present.

The XPath Node Test

The node test is effectively a road map that shows the element names in progression, from the start of the document to the particular element in question. It's literally a path from the document element (the root XML element) to the data that you're testing for inclusion into the result nodeset. XPath, as usually implemented, is often more efficient if you specify the complete element path. However, you could have written the example location step as this:

```
//WebService[./Family="Time"]
```

The initial double slash, `//`, tells the XPath processor to start at the document element, search recursively for the `<WebService/>` element, and, after finding it, execute the predicate.

The XPath Predicate

The predicate, sometimes referred to as the *filter*, is a Boolean test that you apply to make a final decision about the particular XML element that XPath is examining. If the predicate returns a `true` result, the XML element is added to the result nodeset. If not, the element is discarded from the nodeset. Essentially, you're fine-tuning an XML element filter. For example, given the two servers shown in the example XML document, the initial nodeset returned from the axis yields both servers, as does the result of the node test. That is, both `<Server/>` elements have children `<WebService/>` elements. It's the predicate that distinguishes them, in this case, because only the second server, Pokey, exposes a Time family Web Service.

The node test, being a pathway into the XML document, is sensitive to both the alphabetical case and the namespace of the particular XML element shown in the path. That is, imagine that you mistyped the example location step in this manner:

```
/servers/server/webservice[./family="Time"]
```

The resulting nodeset would be empty, whereas before it contained the element for the Pokey server. Notice in the second XPath query that all the text is lowercase, which is why it would fail.

To help with XPath query generation, we wrote the application that you see in Figure 3.2. The *XPathExerciser* is a utility that enables you to load an XML document, display its contents so that you can see what your queries should produce, type in an XPath location step, and display the resulting nodeset using a tree control.

You'll examine the source code for the XPathExerciser when we discuss .NET's XML handling capabilities, starting with the upcoming section ".NET and XPath." This is a tool that you truly will use because you can never be too expert at recording XPath expressions.

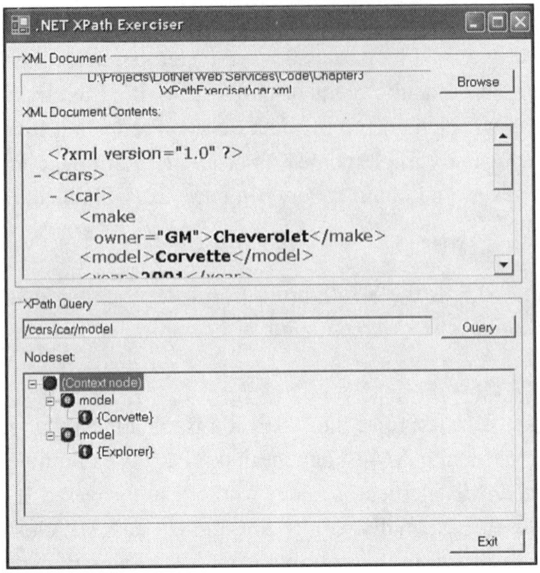

FIGURE 3.2

The XPathExerciser user interface.

XPath Operators

XPath is a language all its own. Like any programming language, XPath has a set of operators. The operators represent intrinsic capabilities that XPath can perform upon request—you see these listed in Table 3.2.

TABLE 3.2   XPath Intrinsic Operators

Operator	Purpose
/	Child operator, which selects child nodes or specifies the root node
/ /	Recursive descent, which looks for a specified element at any depth
.	Current context node (akin to C++ this or VB me)
..	Shorthand notation for parent of current context node (akin to moving up a file directory)
*	Wildcard, which selects all elements regardless of their element name
:	Namespace operator (same use as in XML proper)
@	Attribute operator, which prefixes an attribute name
@	Attribute wildcard (when used alone), which is semantically equivalent to *
+	Addition indicator

TABLE 3.2 Continued

Operator	Purpose
-	Subtraction indicator
*	Multiplication indicator
div	Floating-point division indicator
mod	Modulo (remainder from a truncating division operation)
( )	Precedence operator
[ ]	Operator that applies a filter (akin to a Boolean test)
[ ]	Set subscript operator (akin to an array index specification)

Not too much in Table 3.2 should be too surprising. The square brackets, [and], indicate either an array or a filter pattern depending upon how you use them. The single period, ., indicates the current context node, much like the same operator does in a Windows file path. The same is true for the dual period, ... The @ indicates an attribute. Otherwise, you have operators that you would expect to see, such as the wildcard operator, *, and mathematical operations.

Returning to the previous example, you could locate all the SOAP Toolkit Web Services stored in the XML document using this XPath location step:

```
/Servers/Server/WebService[./@wsdl=".wsdl"]
```

You could accomplish the same task with these two location steps:

```
//WebService[./@wsdl=".wsdl"]
```

```
/Servers/*/*[./@wsdl=".wsdl"]
```

If some of the servers had no wsdl attribute but others did, you could test merely for the presence of the attribute, like so:

```
/Servers/Server/WebService[./@wsdl]
```

In this case, the nodeset would contain both servers shown in the example XML document, but this is only because both servers have a wsdl attribute. If one server had no wsdl attribute, the predicate would fail for that particular node, and that XML element would be removed from the result nodeset.

XPath Intrinsic Functions

In addition to operators, XPath has an entire suite of intrinsic functions that it exposes to help with your queries. There are a lot of these, so the more commonly used functions are distilled in Table 3.3.

3

WEB SERVICES
AND XML

TABLE 3.3 Commonly Used XPath Intrinsic Functions

Operator	Purpose
ceiling()	Is the smallest integer not less than the argument
count(nodeset)	Gives the number of nodes in the nodeset argument
contains(string,string)	Returns true if the first argument contains the second
false()	Always returns a Boolean false
floor()	Is the largest integer not greater than the argument
last()	Gives the context size (number of nodes in context node set)
local-name()	Returns the local name of the first node (document order)
name()	Returns the QName of the first node (document order)
node()	Returns true for any type of node
not()	Indicates a logical negation
number(object)	Converts object to a number
position()	Gives the index number of the node within the parent
starts-with(string,string)	Returns true if the first argument starts with the second
string(object)	Turns object into a string
sum(nodeset)	Converts nodeset to numerical values and adds them
true()	Always returns a Boolean true

For a complete list of XPath intrinsic functions, you should refer to a good XPath reference. You'll probably find that these functions will handle most of your XPath needs, however.

Using the Web Service server example, you could identify the first server, or an arbitrary server, using this location step:

```
/Servers/Server[position()="1"]
```

Similarly, you find the last server like so:

```
/Servers/Server[last()]
```

If you want all the servers but the last one, you query the document in this way:

```
/Servers/Server[not(position()=last())]
```

Many people want to locate XML information within a document based upon string values or string searches. Say, for example, that you want all the servers that have names starting with the letter *G*:

```
/Servers/Server[starts-with(string(./@name),"G")]
```

Of course, this will return the Gumby server's XML information.

As you can see, you can produce a wide variety of queries, especially if you combine an axis with a node test and a filter. This becomes important later if you need to crack open a SOAP packet to examine and modify the contents by hand.

SOAP uses another XML technology called XPointer. Let's now turn to that technology and see what it offers the Web Service.

Identifying XML Elements Using XLink

As you gain experience with XML, you'll find that hierarchical relationships between data elements lend themselves to XML serialization rather naturally. XML is quite happy with a parent/child or sibling/sibling relationship between data elements. But what do you do if the data isn't hierarchical by nature?

A classic example of this is the linked list. The nodes in a linked list, by definition, have no hierarchical relationship. You could argue in favor of a sibling/sibling relationship, but recall that XML doesn't specify ordering of elements. To XML, this document arrangement

```
<element1/>
<element2/>
```

is semantically the same as this arrangement:

```
<element2/>
<element1 />
```

XML doesn't distinguish between the two unless you consider their document order—and this ordering is considered tenuous, at best. Because we're talking about a linked list, which has a definite ordering in memory, we need to be a bit more concrete. In this case, XPLink is employed.

XLink uses two attributes, href and id, to identify the semantic links between elements. Actually, XLink is a great deal more than what is discussed here. We'll discuss XLink only with respect to its use in the SOAP protocol, as you'll see in Chapter 4, ".NET Web Services and SOAP." You could use XLink to link elements in completely different XML documents, for example, but you needn't go that far for Web Service purposes.

Let's look at XLink by example. Imagine that you have the linked list that you see in Figure 3.3.

You'll actually revisit the linked list in the next chapter when we tie XLink to SOAP, as well as in Chapter 6, "Web Services in ASP.NET," where you'll send a linked list to a Web Service for processing. Here, though, it's important to note that you have four nodes, with the usual components—a head node, a tail node, and intermediate nodes. The tail node has its "next" link set to null, or nothing, to indicate that there is no more data.

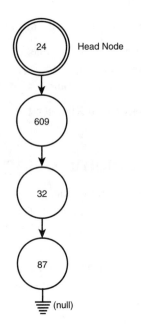

FIGURE 3.3

Conceptual image of a linked list.

In code, this linked list is made up of nodes:

```
class Node
{
    int iValue;
    Node pNext;
}
```

In XML, we create XML elements representing the list nodes and link them so that the current node "points" to the next node using the href attribute:

```
<node head="true">
    <iValue>24</iValue>
    <pNext href="#node2" />
</node>
<node root="true" id="node2">
    <iValue>609</iValue>
    <pNext href="#node3" />
</node>
<node root="true" id="node3">
    <iValue>32</iValue>
    <pNext href="#node4" />
</node>
```

```
<node id="node4">
   <iValue>87</iValue>
   <pNext xsi:null="true" />
</node>
```

Each corresponding "next" node has an id attribute that is identical to the href of the previous node. Note that the href attribute precedes the actual id value with a pound sign, #. This indicates that the link is contained within this document instead of some external reference.

A head attribute also was created for this example. This identifies the node as the starting point—without it, you wouldn't necessarily know which node was the starting point. It's true that you could look at all the <pNext/> elements and figure it out, but adding the attribute makes for faster processing. SOAP has a similar concept that you'll read about in the next chapter.

To tie off the list, we added the xsi:null attribute. This comes directly from XML schema, where you can identify a value as null or nothing using this construct. Of course, you must tie off the list—that is required as part of the basic linked list abstract datatype. To do otherwise would invite your code to randomly walk through memory until you hurt yourself. The same requirement applies to the XML list serialization—hence, the attribute.

As the XML list representation indicates, XLink is a necessary technology for serializing Web Services. After all, if you think about it, the methods that you send into the remote Web Service method are roughly equivalent to a linked list. They're not linked in the traditional sense, but they do have some association, if only because they belong to the same remote method. SOAP looks at your method parameters and, in some cases, will serialize them using XLink.

XML Transformations

The final XML-based technology mentioned here handles how you transform XML from one vocabulary into another. That is, you can change one XML document format into another very easily using the *eXtensible Stylesheet Language with Transforms* (XSLT). Actually, we've already looked at a major component of XSLT—XPath. What we'll do here, briefly, is combine XPath with the XML style sheet vocabulary to change XML from one form into another.

Why would we want to do this in a Web Service book? After all, .NET does all the soapy stuff, right? Well, that's true, in a way. But you might have noticed that three versions of SOAP are available (1.0, 1.1, and 1.2). The SOAP specification states that you should return a version mismatch error if you receive a SOAP packet indicating that the packet is formed using a version of SOAP that you don't handle. But you might want to work with Web Services or clients that expect another version. If you accept a SOAP packet that .NET cannot handle (an old SOAP version, for example), you can easily intercept the packet using a .NET SoapExtension and then can transform it into something .NET can handle. We're simply showing you how to take SOAP in one form and convert it to another, in case you ever need to do so.

> **NOTE**
>
> This is by far *not* the most common use of XSL and XSLT. In the vast majority of the cases we've seen, people are using XSLT to turn XML documents into an HTML representation for display purposes. You'll probably never have to actually transform XML from one version of SOAP to another, especially given Microsoft's aggressive acceptance of the SOAP standard. But this transformation, no matter how unlikely, is still a valid use of the XSLT technology. This use simply relates XML and XSLT to SOAP and Web Services. However, you might find that if you use Web Services often and long enough, you'll want to access a Web Service that will require you to modify your SOAP packets for one reason or another, and XSLT is an excellent alternative for doing so.

> **NOTE**
>
> As I write this, the latest SOAP working draft specification has just been released. Therefore, my prediction that you might use XSL to transform SOAP 1.1 packets into SOAP 1.2 packets isn't necessarily so far-fetched. Luckily, the differences in the protocol versions aren't significant enough, for the most part, to truly merit XSL transformation. However, two clichés come to mind—"You never know" and "Never say never".... .

Before diving in, another caveat should be mentioned: XPath and XSL/XSLT are huge topics that merit books of their own, and many are available. What we intend to present here is just enough to get you working with the technology. For an in-depth view, definitely pick up a good reference.

XSLT Drilldown

XSLT combines XPath expressions with *templates*. A template combines a nodeset returned from a specific XPath location step and produces output based upon the contents of the template. More often than not, the template uses the results obtained from the nodeset as input.

Let's say that you were given this XML document:

```
<?xml version="1.0"?>
<Parts>
    <Part vehicle="Corvette" manufacturer="GM">
        <Number>3972178</Number>
        <Desc>Special Hi-Perf Camshaft</Desc>
```

```
        <MinYear>1970</MinYear>
        <MaxYear>1972</MaxYear>
        <Comment>LT-1, Solid Lifters</Comment>
    </Part>
    (More part elements...)
</Parts>
```

This document is clearly parts-centric. What if you want an XML document that is vehicle-centric? Would you need to create that from scratch? Well, assuming that all (or some) of the data that you require is already contained in the parts XML document, you wouldn't—you could use XSLT to transform it from the parts-centric view to the vehicle-centric view rather easily.

Let's do just that. The vehicle XML document needs to look like this:

```
<?xml version="1.0"?>
<Vehicles>
    <Vehicle>
        <Make/>
        <Model/>
        <Parts>
            <Part>
                <Number/>
                <Description/>
                <ModelYears/>
            </Part>
        <Parts>
        <Additional parts elements here)
    </Vehicle>
</Vehicles>
```

The XSL style sheet to accomplish this is shown in Listing 3.1.

LISTING 3.1 Example XSL Style Sheet

```
<?xml version="1.0"?>
<xsl:stylesheet xmlns:xsl="http://www.w3.org/1999/XSL/Transform"
    version="1.0">
<xsl:output method="xml"/>

<xsl:template match="/">
    <Vehicles>
        <xsl:apply-templates select="Parts"/>
    </Vehicles>
</xsl:template>
```

LISTING 3.1   Continued

```
<xsl:template match="Parts">
   <Vehicle>
      <Make><xsl:value-of select="Part/@manufacturer"/></Make>
      <Model><xsl:value-of select="Part/@vehicle"/></Model>
      <Parts>
         <xsl:for-each select="Part">
            <Part>
               <Number>
                  <xsl:value-of select="Number"/>
               </Number>
               <Description>
                  <xsl:value-of select="Desc"/>
                  <xsl:text>: </xsl:text>
                  <xsl:value-of select="Comment"/>
               </Description>
               <ModelYears>
                  <xsl:value-of select="MinYear"/>
                  <xsl:text> to </xsl:text>
                  <xsl:value-of select="MaxYear"/>
               </ModelYears>
            </Part>
         </xsl:for-each>
      </Parts>
   </Vehicle>
</xsl:template>

</xsl:stylesheet>
```

If you run the XML file and style sheet through Internet Explorer, you might not get the output that you expect. Internet Explorer will execute the transformation, but it will not display the result as XML. If you're interested in viewing the actual transformed output, it's best to run the XML document and style sheet through a program designed to execute the style sheet and save the resulting output to a file for later recall. You'll get an application that does just this when you get to .NET in the upcoming section ".NET and XSL."

XSL is an XML vocabulary, which is to say that your XSL style sheets will be XML documents in their own right. Many elements are associated with XSL; Table 3.4 gives you the more commonly used XSL instructions.

TABLE 3.4 Commonly Used XSL Vocabulary Elements

Operator	Purpose
`<apply-templates/>`	Tells the XSL processor to apply all appropriate templates to the nodeset
`<call-template/>`	Invokes a template by name
`<choose/>`	Uses multiple conditional testing (use with when and otherwise)
`<for-each/>`	Applies a template repeatedly to all nodes in the nodeset
`<if/>`	Is a conditional construct (has no `else` clause—use `<choose/>` instead)
`<number/>`	Inserts a formatted integer into the output document
`<otherwise/>`	Is a default conditional expression used in conjunction with `<choose/>`
`<output/>`	Specifies serialization of the result tree
`<sort/>`	Sorts output nodes (used to rearrange output document)
`<stylesheet/>`	Is the XSL style sheet document (root) element
`<template/>`	Is the template tag (identifies and encapsulates template)
`<text/>`	Inserts literal text into the output document
`<value-of/>`	Copies the node of the input document to the output document
`<when/>`	Is an optional conditional expression used in conjunction with `<choose/>`
`<when/>`	Is an optional conditional expression used in conjunction with `<choose/>`

Here you see the XSL document element, `<xsl:stylesheet/>`, as well as the XSL workhorse, `<xsl:template/>`. The style sheet element encapsulates the style sheet itself, while the template element identifies what could be referred to as XSL subroutines. In fact, they're not subroutines, but you could view them that way and not be terribly incorrect. Although we didn't show the XSL elements related to variables, XSL does have the capability of passing variables and parameters between templates. Because they're so powerful, let's look at XSL templates in a bit more detail.

3

WEB SERVICES AND XML

XSL Templates

Listing 3.1 provided two templates, one for the document element and one for the <Parts/> element. We could have created more templates, one for each <Part/> node and children, but instead we elected to dig more deeply into the original XML document using <xsl:for-each/>. This simply made the template a bit easier to read.

The template itself is the cookie cutter that XSL will use to create the newly formatted document. For each template that you include within your style sheet, you'll receive formatted output. The key is to set up the templates so that they operate on the nodeset returned from the match attribute. If you know that many XML nodes will match the template, but you want to constrain the use of some of those nodes, you can also apply the mode attribute to the template:

```
<xsl:template match="/">
   ...
   <xsl:apply-templates select="Parts" mode="Engine" />
   <xsl:apply-templates select="Parts" mode="Body" />
   ...
</xsl:template>

<xsl:template match="Parts" mode="Engine">
   (Something to do with engine parts...)
</xsl:template>

<xsl:template match="Parts" mode="Body">
   (Something to do with body parts...)
</xsl:template>
```

Essentially, mode enables you to process original document nodes many times, with each processing iteration producing a different result.

Notice that we also used the XSL instruction <xsl:apply-templates/>. This tells XSL to go through its template collection and, for any of the input XML nodes that match the templates, produce the output. The key is to create XPath expressions that draw from the XML document the precise nodeset that you want to work with.

The template is the key to transforming the original XML document. After you establish the XPath expression that will pull the set of nodes of interest, you insert the new XML document structure within the template. For each XML node XSL finds that matches the template, it spits out a copy of the resulting template into the new XML document.

At this point, you've reviewed enough XML to move into .NET. Although it's entirely possible to write .NET-based Web Services all day long and never need to access their XML nature, it's also very likely that you'll find a minor change to some part of your SOAP packet to be useful.

In that case, you'll find yourself using some or all of the technologies described here. If you're comfortable with what has been discussed so far, let's now talk about XML within .NET.

.NET's XML Architecture

.NET's core XML architecture (at least, as of Beta 2) is as you see it in Figure 3.4. This is slightly different than it was for Beta 1, in which the XPathNavigator in Figure 3.4 was called XmlNavigator. The basic layout is somewhat the same, however.

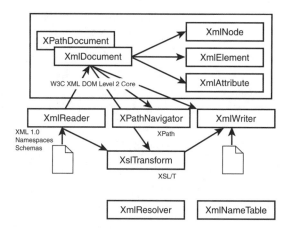

FIGURE 3.4
.NET's core XML architecture.

The main XML class that you'll use here is XPathNavigator. With this class, you can move through the XML document, using movement commands such as MoveToNext() and MoveToFirstChild(). Or, as the name suggests, you can provide the XPathNavigator an XPath query, and it will return to you an iterator that represents the nodeset returned from the query. Although it isn't discussed here, you have XML DOM Level 2 support using XmlDocument. We won't use XmlDocument here because we'll be primarily interested in XPath queries, and XPathDocument is optimized for quick searches. It might be helpful to know that XmlDocument exists if you're used to working with the XML DOM. However, we will be interested in using other .NET XML classes, starting with the .NET class that enables you to read XML data from a stream.

Reading XML Data

If you have an XML file on disk, XPathNavigator will accept the file's filename and path, and will happily load the file for processing. .NET, however, is stream-based, so it might not be surprising to find that .NET has an XML class designed for reading XML streams. This class is `XmlReader`, and if you have a stream that you know represents XML data, you can wrap that stream with a reader and it will manage movement through the stream in an XML-friendly fashion.

To see `XmlReader` in action, let's simulate the file read that `XPathNavigator` performs when loading XML data. Imagine that you have an XML file called Activities.xml. To load this file into .NET, and to demonstrate `XmlReader`, you would use this code:

```
FileStream fstmActivities =
                new FileStream("Activities.xml",FileMode.Open);
XmlTextReader xrdActivities = new XmlTextReader(fstmActivities);
```

Note that `XmlReader` is an abstract class; you don't use it directly. Instead, you use a class derived from `XmlReader`, such as `XmlTextReader`. And although you could load the file directly into `XmlTextReader`, the stream-based constructor was used in this brief example simply because that's how you'll accept the SOAP information from .NET when processing a `SoapExtension`.

`XmlReader` gives you a fast, forward-only XML data stream. `XmlTextReader` is ideal for quickly determining whether your XML document is well-formed and allowing you to progress through the document. You'll see an example of `XmlTextReader` in action in the next section, "Writing XML Data."

Writing XML Data

If there is a .NET `XmlReader`, then there probably should be an equivalent writer. In fact, there is—not surprisingly, its class name is `XmlWriter`. And, like `XmlReader`, `XmlWriter` is an abstract class that must be implemented in a derived class. For `XmlWriter`, the only class provided by .NET for this is `XmlTextWriter`.

`XmlTextWriter` also accepts a stream in its constructor, and it is to this stream that `XmlTextWriter` will write the XML that is created or otherwise slated for output. Listing 3.2 shows both `XmlTextReader` and `XmlTextWriter` in action.

LISTING 3.2   Reading and Writing XML Data Using .NET Framework Classes

```
using System;
using System.IO;
using System.Text;
using System.Xml;

namespace RdrWtr
{
```

LISTING 3.2   Continued

```csharp
/// <summary>
/// Summary description for Class1.
/// </summary>
class Class1
{
    static void Main(string[] args)
    {
        try
        {
            // Create a file stream
            FileStream fstmXmlOut = new FileStream("MyXML.xml",
                                                FileMode.Create);

            // Create an encoding
            UTF8Encoding objEncoding = new UTF8Encoding();

            // Create an XML text writer
            XmlTextWriter objXmlWriter =
                        new XmlTextWriter(fstmXmlOut,objEncoding);

            // Create some XML
            objXmlWriter.WriteStartDocument();
            objXmlWriter.WriteStartElement("m",
                                        "Employees",
                                        "http://www.myurl.com");
            objXmlWriter.WriteAttributeString("xmlns",
                                            "m",
                                            null,
                                            "http://www.myurl.com");

            // Write an employee element
            objXmlWriter.WriteStartElement("m",
                                        "Employee",
                                        "http://www.myurl.com");
            objXmlWriter.WriteStartAttribute("m",
                                            "id",
                                            "http://www.myurl.com");
            objXmlWriter.WriteString("175-A15");
            objXmlWriter.WriteEndAttribute();
            objXmlWriter.WriteStartElement("m",
                                        "Name",
                                        "http://www.myurl.com");
            objXmlWriter.WriteString("Kenn Scribner");
            objXmlWriter.WriteEndElement(); // Name
```

LISTING 3.2   Continued

```
objXmlWriter.WriteStartElement("m",
                               "Title",
                               "http://www.myurl.com");
objXmlWriter.WriteString("Code Gecko");
objXmlWriter.WriteEndElement(); // Title
objXmlWriter.WriteEndElement(); // Employee

// Write another employee element
objXmlWriter.WriteStartElement("m",
                               "Employee",
                               "http://www.myurl.com");
objXmlWriter.WriteStartAttribute("m",
                                 "id",
                                 "http://www.myurl.com");
objXmlWriter.WriteString("129-B68");
objXmlWriter.WriteEndAttribute();
objXmlWriter.WriteStartElement("m",
                               "Name",
                               "http://www.myurl.com");
objXmlWriter.WriteString("Mark Stiver");
objXmlWriter.WriteEndElement(); // Name
objXmlWriter.WriteStartElement("m",
                               "Title",
                               "http://www.myurl.com");
objXmlWriter.WriteString("Code Godzilla");
objXmlWriter.WriteEndElement(); // Title
objXmlWriter.WriteEndElement(); // Employee

// Finish off the document
objXmlWriter.WriteEndElement(); // Employees

// Flush it to the file
objXmlWriter.Flush();
objXmlWriter.Close();
fstmXmlOut.Close();

// Create a file stream
FileStream fstmXmlIn = new FileStream("MyXML.xml",
                                      FileMode.Open);

// Create an XML text writer
XmlTextReader objXmlReader = new XmlTextReader(fstmXmlIn);

while (objXmlReader.Read())
```

LISTING 3.2 Continued

```csharp
        {
           switch (objXmlReader.NodeType)
           {
              case XmlNodeType.XmlDeclaration:
                 Console.WriteLine("<?xml version=\"1.0\"?>");
                 break;

              case XmlNodeType.Element:
                 Pad(objXmlReader.Depth);
                 Console.Write("<{0}", objXmlReader.Name);
                 if ( objXmlReader.HasAttributes )
                 {
                    bool bAttr =
                            objXmlReader.MoveToFirstAttribute();
                    while ( bAttr )
                    {
                       Console.Write(" {0}=\"{1}\"",
                                  objXmlReader.Name,
                                  objXmlReader.Value);
                       bAttr = objXmlReader.MoveToNextAttribute();
                    } // while
                 } // if
                 Console.WriteLine(">");
                 break;

              case XmlNodeType.Text:
                 Pad(objXmlReader.Depth);
                 Console.WriteLine(objXmlReader.Value);
                 break;

              case XmlNodeType.EndElement:
                 Pad(objXmlReader.Depth);
                 Console.WriteLine("</{0}>", objXmlReader.Name);
                 break;

              default:
                 break;
           } // switch
        } // while

        // Close the file
        objXmlReader.Close();
        fstmXmlIn.Close();
     } // try
```

LISTING 3.2   Continued

```
      catch (Exception ex)
      {
         Console.WriteLine("Exception: {0}\n",ex.Message);
      } // catch
   }

   static void Pad(int iDepth)
   {
      for ( int i = 0; i < iDepth; i++ )
      {
         Console.Write("    ");
      } // for
   }
  }
}
```

As you see in Listing 3.2, we provide XmlTextReader and XmlTextWriter with streams instead of asking them to open the files directly. This is again because you'll be given streams of XML when dealing with SOAP from within .NET in Chapter 6.

Creating XML elements with XmlTextWriter is a simple matter of deciding what type of element to create and then writing the element information to the stream using the XmlTextWriter method that is most appropriate. We used the combination of WriteStartElement(), WriteString(), and WriteEndElement(), but you could have also used WriteElementString() or created entirely different sorts of elements, like those dedicated to a DTD or comment.

After we created the XML file, we read it back into memory and displayed it on the console screen using XmlTextReader. In this case, to format the output in more familiar terms, we determine what type of element XmlTextReader is currently indicating and spit out formatted text accordingly. We treated the start of an element differently than we treated the content or ending element tag, for example.

It's nice having XmlTextReader and XmlTextWriter, but they work at a rather low level when it comes to dealing with XML. Next you'll see how to move up the abstraction hierarchy and work with XML at a slightly higher level.

Navigating XML with .NET

When people who know .NET think of navigating an XML document, they probably think of XPathDocument and XPathNavigator before XmlReader and XmlWriter. This is because these two XPath classes provide you with the capability to deal with the XML document in a couple different ways. First, you can access the XML information using a *pull model*. That is, you obtain XML information when you request it. Second, you have the option of providing an XPath location step to extract a nodeset, which you access using XPathNodeIterator. In most cases, you'll probably use a combination of the two.

Pulling XML Element Information with .NET

If you are familiar with XML and XML technologies, you've undoubtedly heard of SAX, the Simple API for XML. We even mentioned it earlier in the chapter. SAX is a stream-based approach to reading XML information. You create callback functions that the SAX parser will invoke when it senses information that you're interested in accepting. That is, if you create a callback function for the start of an element tag, SAX will invoke your callback function whenever it reads a starting tag. This is a *push model* because SAX is shoving XML your way as it encounters the information within the document.

.NET, however, works the other way. .NET provides you with a water fountain instead of a fire hose, and you can sip from the fountain when you want. As you sip (read XML element information), more information is readied for your next request. You pull in more information as you're ready.

The .NET XPath classes expose a window into which you examine the XML. Whenever you're working with these classes, it's important to remember that you are working with only a single XML element at any one time. To work with another XML element, you must move the "window." If you're new to .NET and .NET's XML handling capabilities, this is probably the hardest concept to comprehend. This is most likely because of the nature of the classes—by appearance, you perform an element-based action upon the entire XML document, which at first seems odd.

For example, say that you have an instance of XPathNavigator, which contains an XML document. At first, it seems odd to execute code written like this:

```
' objXPN is an instance of XPathNavigator that contains
' an XML document
Dim strElementValue As String = objXPN.Value
```

This seems odd because it isn't apparent that when you ask for the "value" of the XPathNavigator, you're really asking for the value associated with the XML element that the XPathNavigator object is currently referencing (the XML element in the "window"). If you "pull" more data, by executing XPathNavigator's MoveToNext() method, for example, the XML element sitting in the window will change and you'll retrieve the value for that element rather than the initial element.

When you're comfortable with the pull model, however, it makes a lot of sense. With SAX, whenever one of your callback methods is invoked, you must deal with that piece of data then and there. If you want that information cached in any way, you implement the caching. With

XPathNavigator, though, the data waits for you. When you're ready for more data, just pull in more data. We'll demonstrate this more graphically in the next section, ".NET and XPath," where you'll learn about retrieving a nodeset using XPath only to recursively examine the nodeset as the results are displayed in a .NET Windows Forms tree view.

.NET and XPath

You've already done the hard work if you've created and debugged the XPath query that you intend to apply to an XML document contained within XPathDocument. To execute the query, you create an instance of the associated XPathNavigator and execute its Select() method. Select() accepts as input the XPath location step as a string and returns in response an instance of XPathIterator. You then use XPathIterator to rummage through the nodeset.

The code that you'll need to perform the XPath query is simply this:

```
Dim objNodeItr As XPathNodeIterator = _
                    objXPathNav.Select({XPath query text})
```

Of course, a bit more is involved to set up the objects, but making the Select() call is about all you really need. Given the iterator, you can access all the nodes in the nodeset, extracting data from each as necessary.

To demonstrate this, we created a utility, called XPathExerciser, to write and test XPath queries. A portion of the Windows Forms application is shown in Listing 3.3.

LISTING 3.3 XPath Queries Using XPathNavigator

```
Private Sub cmdQuery_Click(ByVal sender As System.Object, _
                    ByVal e As System.EventArgs) _
                    Handles cmdQuery.Click
    ' Execute the query
    Try
        ' Check for text
        If txtQuery.Text.Length >= 1 Then
            ' Perform the query
            Dim objNodeItr As XPathNodeIterator = _
                        m_objXPathNav.Select(txtQuery.Text)
            If Not objNodeItr Is Nothing Then
                ' Iterate through the nodeset and display in the
                ' tree control
                FillNodesetTree(objNodeItr)
            Else
                ' No nodes to add...
                tvwNodeSet.Nodes.Add("No nodes returned fromXPath query...")
            End If
        End If
```

LISTING 3.3 Continued

```
    Catch ex As Exception
        ' Show error
        MsgBox(ex.Message, _
                MsgBoxStyle.Critical, _
                "XPath Exerciser Error")
        tvwNodeSet.Nodes.Clear()
        tvwNodeSet.Nodes.Add(New TreeNode("***Error executing XPath query...",
                                    6,
                                    6))
    End Try
End Sub


Private Sub FillNodesetTree(ByVal objNodeItr As XPathNodeIterator)
    ' Clear the tree
    tvwNodeSet.Nodes.Clear()

    ' Cut off screen update
    tvwNodeSet.BeginUpdate()

    ' Create the root node
    Dim node As TreeNode = New TreeNode("(Context node)", 6, 6)
    tvwNodeSet.Nodes.Add(node)

    ' Advance through the nodeset
    While objNodeItr.MoveNext
        AddTreeNode(objNodeItr.Current, node)
    End While

    ' Update screen
    tvwNodeSet.EndUpdate()
End Sub


Private Sub AddTreeNode(ByRef objCurrXMLNode As XPathNavigator, _
                    ByRef nodParent As TreeNode)
    Try
        ' Create the new node
        Dim node As TreeNode
        Select Case objCurrXMLNode.NodeType
            Case XPathNodeType.Text
                nodParent.Nodes.Add(New TreeNode(objCurrXMLNode.Name & _
                            "{" & objCurrXMLNode.Value & "}", 2, 2))
                Exit Sub

            Case XPathNodeType.Comment
```

LISTING 3.3 Continued

```
        nodParent.Nodes.Add(New TreeNode(objCurrXMLNode.Name & _
                        "{" & objCurrXMLNode.Value & "}", 4, 4))
        Exit Sub

    Case XPathNodeType.Attribute
        nodParent.Nodes.Add(New TreeNode(objCurrXMLNode.Name & _
                        "{" & objCurrXMLNode.Value & "}", 3, 3))
        Exit Sub

    Case XPathNodeType.Root
        node = New TreeNode("{root}", 1, 1)

    Case Else
        node = New TreeNode(objCurrXMLNode.Name, 0, 0)

End Select

' Add ourselves to the tree
nodParent.Nodes.Add(node)

' Look for attributes
Dim objNodeClone As XPathNavigator
If objCurrXMLNode.HasAttributes Then
    objNodeClone = objCurrXMLNode.Clone
    objNodeClone.MoveToFirstAttribute()
    AddTreeNode(objNodeClone, node)
    While objNodeClone.MoveToNextAttribute
        AddTreeNode(objNodeClone, node)
    End While
End If

' Find children
objNodeClone = objCurrXMLNode.Clone
If objNodeClone.HasChildren Then
    objNodeClone.MoveToFirstChild()
    AddTreeNode(objNodeClone, node)
    While objNodeClone.MoveToNext()
        AddTreeNode(objNodeClone, node)
    End While
End If
Catch ex As Exception
    ' Show error
    MsgBox(ex.Message, _
        MsgBoxStyle.Critical, _
        "XPath Exerciser Error")
```

LISTING 3.3 Continued

```
    tvwNodeSet.Nodes.Clear()

    tvwNodeSet.Nodes.Add(New TreeNode("***Error executing XPath query...",
                            6,
                            6))


    End Try
End Sub
```

XPathExerciser enables you to select an XML file against which you want to apply XPath queries. XPathExerciser then displays the file in the Web Browser ActiveX control after you've browsed for your particular XML file. Then, with the file in hand, you type in your XPath query and click the Query button. If things go well, the tree control displays the resulting nodeset. If this operation sounds familiar, it should. As you might remember, the XPathExerciser user interface was presented in Figure 3.2.

What is important to see from Listing 3.3 is the combination of XPath and pull methods, such as MoveToFirstChild() and MoveToNext(). Note also that, given an instance of XPathNavigator, you can recursively read the XML element information and build a tree view.

> **NOTE**
>
> This book was written with the second beta version of Visual Studio .NET and the .NET Framework. As of this second beta, an issue exists with ActiveX and COM inter-operability: If the source files were created on the *Windows XP* operating system (originally called *Whistler*) and later were transferred to an older version of Windows, the source files will be modified by Visual Studio .NET and the reference to the ActiveX control will be dropped. When Visual Studio .NET drops the ActiveX control, it also drops any sibling controls (controls at the same user interface scope, such as when grouped on a form or group box). Therefore, we have included two versions of XPathExerciser, one for XP and one for other versions of Windows. The executable itself executes without error in either case, and you can mix and match executables at will. Just the source and project files present problems.

.NET and XLink

You might be wondering if special support for XLink is built into the .NET Framework. There is, but it requires a bit of additional overhead.

`XPathNavigator` has a method, `MoveToId()`, that is designed to work with `id` attributes. The additional overhead mentioned is that the `id` attribute must be explicitly defined in the XML DTD or schema that is associated with your XML document. If you have no DTD or schema, `MoveToId()` won't work for you. However, you still may use XPath to search for all elements with an `id` attribute, or even an `id` attribute containing a specific identifying value.

.NET and XSL

The final general-purpose XML technology we mentioned is XSL, and .NET supports XSL through its `XSLTransform` class. If you load an XML document into an instance of `XPathDocument` and then load an XSL style sheet into `XSLTransform`, you can run the style sheet in this manner:

```
objXSL.Transform(objXMLDoc,null,objWriter);
```

Here, `objXSL` is the `XSLTransform` instance, `objXMLDoc` is the `XPathDocument`, and `objWriter` is the `XmlTextWriter` that you'll use to persist the changes.

To provide a useful demonstration of transformations within the .NET Framework, we created the XSLExerciser application, whose user interface you see in Figure 3.5. If you browse for an XML file and an associated style sheet, you can click the XForm button to execute the transform. If you've elected to save the results, the new XML document will be recorded within the file that you specified. You can also view the output either as text or as XML contained within the Web Browser control.

FIGURE 3.5

The XSLExerciser user interface.

Listing 3.5 shows you how to handle the transform action itself. The code that you see is executed when you click the XForm button. You don't need to load any files until you actually want to perform the transformation, so if you need to adjust the style sheet, as often happens, you can do so easily and retransform the document.

LISTING 3.4   XPath Queries Using XPathNavigator

```
private void cmdXForm_Click(object sender, System.EventArgs e)
{
   try
   {
      // Open the original XML document
      m_objXMLDoc = new XPathDocument(m_strXMLPath);

      // Open the stylesheet
      XslTransform objXSL = new XslTransform();
      objXSL.Load(m_strXSLPath);

      // Create a stream to contain the results
      m_stmOutput = new MemoryStream();

      // Create and overlay an XML writer
      ASCIIEncoding objEncoding = new ASCIIEncoding();
      XmlTextWriter objWriter = new XmlTextWriter(m_stmOutput,
                                                  objEncoding);

      // Do the transform
      objXSL.Transform(m_xpdXMLDoc,null,objWriter);

      // Save output as a string
      byte[] bytes = m_stmOutput.ToArray();
      m_strXMLOutput = objEncoding.GetString(bytes);

      // Check to see if we need to save the file...
      if ( optSave.Checked && m_strOutPath.Length > 0 )
      {
         FileStream fstmXMLOut = new FileStream(m_strOutPath,
                                                FileMode.Create);
         m_stmOutput.Position = 0;
         TextReader objTRFrom = new StreamReader(m_stmOutput);
         TextWriter pbjTWTo = new StreamWriter(fstmXMLOut);
         twTo.WriteLine(trFrom.ReadToEnd());
         twTo.Flush();
         fstmXMLOut.Close();
      } // if

      // Close the stream
      m_stmOutput.Close();
```

LISTING 3.4 Continued

```
    // Enable the UI
    cmdView.Enabled = true;

    // Show results
    lblResults.ForeColor = SystemColors.ControlText;
    lblResults.Text = "Transformation successful, now click View";
} // try
catch (Exception ex)
{
    // Show results
    lblResults.ForeColor = Color.Red;
    lblResults.Text = "Transformation Unsuccessful";

    MessageBox.Show(ex.Message,
                    "XSLExerciser Error",
                    MessageBoxButtons.OK,
                    MessageBoxIcon.Error);
} // catch
}
```

A lot of this code you saw previously. One thing that we do differently is to create a memory-based stream, into which we shove the transformed XML:

```
// Create a stream to contain the results
m_stmOutput = new MemoryStream();
```

We do this because we then have the transformed XML in one location, ready to display or store into a file.

No single book has everything that you'll need to work with a technology as diverse as XML. However, a few books are well worth examining to gain a bit more detail regarding this fascinating and pliant tool. Unfortunately, as of this printing, no .NET-specific XML books are available, but hopefully this chapter has given you the basics that you'll need to move forward into the .NET world.

Summary

This chapter began with a discussion of XML and how it suits Web Services well as a wire protocol. For example, XML is loosely coupled and lends itself to a high degree of interoperability.

We then moved into some of the XML technologies that are necessary to help you work with Web Services and, more specifically, the SOAP protocol, if you have to dip into the SOAP packets to adjust their contents. For example, we looked at how XPath helps you dig out information from within the XML document. You establish a location step and hand that to the XPath processor, which returns to you a nodeset if any of the XML elements match your query. We looked at how the XPath axes and intrinsic functions add power to your searching capability.

We then moved to XLink, which enables you to link XML elements that don't have natural hierarchical relationships. Two attributes, href and id, enable you to link the XLink elements. The href attribute "points" to the element with a matching id attribute.

The final general XML technology considered was XSL, which you can use to transform XML from one form to another. This might be necessary to transform SOAP from one version to another; the latest SOAP specification (1.2) was released just as this book was written. The main programmable feature that XSL presents is the template, in which an XPath query extracts a nodeset that is then transformed according to the contents of the template.

We finally turned to .NET and .NET's handling of XML. You learned about all the .NET XML classes necessary to deal with the XML technologies discussed in the first half of the chapter. XmlReader and XmlWriter, for example, read and write XML to and from streams. XPathDocument and the related XPathNavigator enable you to traverse the XML content using either XPath queries or pull-model methods such as MoveToFirstAttribute().

This chapter also provided several useful .NET applications that not only help you learn how the .NET XML classes are used but also serve as useful utilities by themselves. Hopefully you might find XPathExerciser and XSLExerciser are useful beyond the covers of this book.

Now it's time to move beyond simple XML and see how it's used in conjunction with the SOAP protocol. Chapter 4 discusses the SOAP protocol and tells how information is converted from memory into XML to be transmitted over the network.

3

WEB SERVICES
AND XML

.NET Web Services and SOAP

IN THIS CHAPTER

As you learned in Chapter 1, "Web Service Fundamentals," SOAP is a critical technological component in the .NET Web Service scheme. SOAP in general defines a mechanism for encoding information into an XML wrapper. For Web Services, SOAP gets a bit more specific when it facilitates the mappings between method signatures and the XML document.

The basic idea behind the use of the SOAP protocol, as it was originally envisioned, is to interpret a remote method's parameter values at runtime and stuff those values into an XML document. The XML data is then transported to the remote server using the HTTP protocol (other transport protocols are also used, albeit currently outside .NET). If you use SOAP in this manner, you are using the SOAP protocol as an implementation of a more general concept, the invocation of some remote method (implemented as a Web Service). The Remote Procedure Call (RPC) protocol has the same objective: to carry local computer information to a remote computer, even information that might not make sense to a remote system without some conversion (for example, addresses of data to their textual equivalents). This allows the remote computer to execute the remote method on your behalf and return a result.

In this chapter, you'll explore SOAP in some detail to see how it acts as a messaging protocol. To SOAP, the concept of an RPC protocol has a specific meaning. .NET, however, actually uses the SOAP protocol in a dual fashion. It uses SOAP to carry the information back and forth as SOAP messages or as true SOAP RPC calls, depending on how you configure your Web method.

After learning why SOAP is quickly becoming so successful in the industry, you'll dive into the protocol itself to see specifically how SOAP carries remote method information to and from a Web Service. You'll also learn how .NET employs the protocol.

Why Is SOAP Needed?

This innocent-looking question is actually a very good one to ask. RPC protocols grew from research in the mid-1980s that had roots all the way back to Tim Berners-Lee and his description of TCP/IP—and even the invention of Ethernet itself, circa 1970 by Bob Metcalfe, later of 3Com fame. The concept of distributed computing dates back farther than that. The creators of the ENIAC envisioned that one day large numbers of computers would be linked to solve very complex problems.

In the case of RPC and SOAP, the distributed computing issue is simply one of consuming resources on a remote computer as if the remote computer and the calling (local) machine were the same machine. The goal is to seamlessly tie the distributed systems together so that when you call a given method, you don't know (and presumably don't care) whether the call is actually handled by a remote system. In real-world situations, you very often do care, if only because the call latency is greatly increased. It simply takes longer for the method to complete its task. For the purposes of discussing SOAP as a protocol, however, let's ignore those issues and imagine that SOAP, as an RPC protocol actually does seamlessly integrate distributed systems. In critical cases when this model breaks down, you'll find the issue noted in the text.

Why Do You Need to Understand SOAP?

This is also a very good question. After all, given the power of .NET, should you be concerned about underlying protocols .NET uses? As an analogy, when you bring up your email client, do you care how your email is sent or how attachments to your email messages are encoded?

You could make an excellent argument that you don't need to understand SOAP to program Web Services today. .NET handles the details for you. You write the code that .NET requires to handle the Web Service, or the invocation of the Web Service, if you're writing client-side code. Then .NET takes care of the serialization aspects as well as the transmission of the information back and forth. As you'll see in Chapter 5, "Web Service Description and Discovery," you don't require the more complex aspects of the SOAP protocol because you tell the world what your packets look like using the Web Service Description Language (WSDL).

Those complex SOAP encoding practices were required when client and server had to agree on a protocol using static code. WSDL allows for dynamic packet layout and description—at least, from an early binding perspective—rendering the deeper encoding structures less necessary and even obsolete. This is so because the RPC style of encoding is going out of fashion in favor of the wider range of encoding possibilities that WSDL document/literal encoding offers. You are free to encode information as you see fit rather than blindly follow the SOAP specification itself—at least as far as Section 5 is concerned.

> **NOTE**
>
> In this case, the term *early binding* refers to tying the client code to the Web Service when the code is compiled. With .NET, the WSDL is read to create proxy source code that is compiled into the client. Dynamic proxy generation, to be used for truly late bound Web Services at runtime, is certainly a possibility but is not currently supported by .NET. It is an alternative offered by the SOAP Toolkit, however, if you require this capability.

But if you really examine what you intend to do, the "why do I care" façade breaks down. Returning to our analogy, an email consumer doesn't need to understand the details associated with the Internet email protocols—or email attachment encoding, for that matter. But developers need to understand these protocols to write code that uses them directly. Blindly trusting infrastructure might get you 80% of the features you require. After all, the infrastructure was designed to satisfy the needs of the general populace. That other 20% or so requires the true ingenuity that comes from understanding the lower levels of the technology.

This chapter won't make you an expert on SOAP, but it will give you the understanding that you'll require to write professional grade Web Services and clients. So back to the initial question—why SOAP? Let's explain it in this way... .

The SOAP Advantage

Probably the best-known RPC protocol is DCE-RPC, which is the Distributed Computing Environment's implementation. Many Unix environments use DCE-RPC, as does Microsoft Windows (which modified it slightly to handle object references across machines to support DCOM). DCE-RPC requires the use of a port mapper, which you'll find listening (monitoring network traffic) on TCP/UDP Port 135. Whenever you want to access a remote computer using DCE-RPC, you access the remote system's port mapper and request a socket address. The actual distributed communication then takes place over the assigned port.

The issue here is actually one of security, when your business-critical servers are safely tucked behind a firewall. For DCE-RPC to work, not only do you have to open Port 135 to the world for port-mapping purposes, but you also need to have a range of other socket addresses available for the general public to use for RPC communications. This very often leads to an opening through which some 13-year-old will ruin your crucial data as well as your day. So it isn't surprising to find nearly every business IT guru locks Port 135 and almost every other port. The one universal exception is Port 80, or Port 443 for secure sockets.

Port 80 is the network socket port used by HTTP, at least as it is nominally configured (Port 8080 is often used to manage the Web server, and HTTP is also spoken there). As you probably already know, the Hypertext Transfer Protocol (HTTP), is the lower-level network protocol used to shuttle Hypertext Markup Language (HTML) documents around the Internet. HTTP is the transport protocol for Web pages, and because you can bet that practically every corporate vice president likes to surf the Net, you'll probably find Port 80 open through any firewall you'll likely encounter.

This is SOAP's secret weapon and one of the sources of its power. It's almost unheard of to find someone blocking Port 80 with a corporate firewall, so SOAP (as bound to HTTP) should pass through corporate firewalls untouched.

The other source of SOAP's power is the fact the information transported by the HTTP protocol is actually XML (which is why Chapter 3, "Web Services and XML," dealt so heavily with XML within the .NET Framework). To be more specific, the content type of the HTTP packet is text/xml. The remainder of this chapter is dedicated to uncovering the XML format that SOAP uses to serialize method parameter information, starting with the SOAP XML object model.

The SOAP XML Object Model

SOAP itself doesn't deal with objects. Frankly, the *object* in "simple *object* access protocol" lends itself merely to the formation of a catchy name. Actually, SOAP as destined for RPC purposes was designed to translate a method's parameters from its native binary form and carry those parameters as XML information to the remote server. There, a corresponding SOAP processor would pull the XML information and return it to its binary state for processing. Information that would associate the method with some object (C++, Java, SmallTalk, or whatever) would be metadata to SOAP and would have to be encoded separately from the method itself.

In a sense, SOAP *does* have an *object model*, however. SOAP is XML, as defined by an XSD schema, so it really consists of XML elements. But these elements can be thought of in terms of objects, with each object having a distinct purpose. In that light, the SOAP object model consists of three main objects:

- The SOAP Envelope
- The SOAP Header
- The SOAP Body

The SOAP Envelope forms the root document element of the SOAP XML packet. As such, one of its primary jobs is to convey the XML namespace information used when the packet was serialized. Of course, because the Envelope is the XML root document element, the other two SOAP objects (also XML) must be serialized within the Envelope. Thus, its other main task is to encapsulate the SOAP information for any given SOAP RPC invocation.

The SOAP Header is an optional piece of the object model that carries information necessary to process the request that isn't found in the method's signature. Here you'll commonly find public key encryption information, transactional sequence identifiers, information needed by the various actors processing the message, and other metadata that the remote SOAP processor will require to manage the remote request.

The SOAP Body is where the action takes place. Here you find the method and its parameters stored as XML. The remote SOAP processor rips through the SOAP Body and converts the XML parameter information back to a native format for processing. The bulk of this chapter targets the SOAP Body and the formatting of various method parameters and constructs.

Given this brief introduction, let's look at the objects themselves in more detail, starting with the SOAP Envelope.

The SOAP Envelope

The SOAP Envelope, as serialized by .NET, is shown in Listing 4.1.

4

.NET WEB
SERVICES AND
SOAP

LISTING 4.1 The .NET SOAP Envelope Encoding

```
<?xml version="1.0"?>
<soap:Envelope xmlns:soap="http://schemas.xmlsoap.org/soap/envelope/"
 xmlns:soapenc="http://schemas.xmlsoap.org/soap/encoding/"
 xmlns:tns="http://tempuri.org/"
 xmlns:types="http://tempuri.org/encodedTypes"
 xmlns:xsi="http://www.w3.org/2001/XMLSchema-instance"
 xmlns:xsd="http://www.w3.org/2001/XMLSchema">
    <soap:Header/>
    <soap:Body/>
</soap:Envelope>
```

Serialization refers to the process of turning actual method parameter information at the time that the Web Service is invoked into a SOAP XML packet. In this case, you see only the namespaces associated with the XML. You'll see example parameters serialized throughout the remainder of this chapter. Here, though, the stage is set for deserialization. You see that the XML is framed according to the SOAP specification (the soap namespace) and encoded (data is serialized) using constructs outlined in the SOAP encoding schema (soapenc). The W3 Committee's XML Schema datatypes are also specified using the xsd and xsi namespaces (integers, floating-point values, strings, and so on). You'll find XML elements throughout the XML document identified using these namespaces as well as other Web Service–specific namespace values.

The SOAP Envelope literally serves as a wrapper for the really important information. You might imagine the Envelope acting as a postal envelope that encloses a letter or other correspondence. But that analogy actually breaks down a bit because an envelope that you use to send something to Aunt Millie also requires an address and postage. The SOAP Envelope certainly doesn't require a stamp; more importantly, the SOAP Envelope doesn't specify an address.

Perhaps a better analogy is to think of the SOAP Envelope as if it were a three-ring binder that you stuff with papers and notes. Inside the binder you'll insert cardboard tab sheets to separate various groups of notes and information. The tab sheets in the SOAP binder's case are the Header and the Body, as well as any custom elements you might create.

SOAP `encodingStyle` Attribute

Returning to SOAP itself, one thing that you'll find missing from the .NET packet in Listing 4.1 is the soap:encodingStyle attribute. If this attribute were serialized within the Envelope tag, the contents of the XML document would be serialized according to the value associated with the attribute. In most cases, this would be according to the SOAP schema found at http://schemas.xmlsoap.org/soap/envelope/ (this URL would be the value of the attribute):

```
soap:encodingStyle=" http://schemas.xmlsoap.org/soap/envelope/"
```

Some other value would indicate another serialization encoding, such as a different XML vocabulary for some or all of the XML packet, encryption of portions of the packet, or possibly some other serialization rule change.

NOTE

The first beta of .NET did not allow you to choose the encoding style. However, versions of .NET from Beta 2 onward allow you to select the encoding style that you prefer. If you want to follow the SOAP specification to the letter, you can choose to apply the `System.Web.Services.Protocols.SoapRpcService` attribute to your remote method. The resulting SOAP packets will then fully comply with the SOAP specification.

Because the attribute is missing from the serialization, you really don't know much at all about the encoding style of the contents, at least as indicated by the SOAP XML that you see in Listing 4.1. It's the WSDL that actually tells you all you need to know, so the omission of the attribute at the .NET SOAP packet level is really by design rather than by error.

However, if you later modify the SOAP XML stream that .NET provides to you (a technique that you'll see in Chapter 6, "Web Services in ASP.NET"), you might need to add this attribute to convey the relevant encoding information to the recipient of the packet.

The SOAP Envelope, as you've learned, provides a wrapper for the SOAP information necessary to convey the Web Service information. Inside the Envelope, you'll find the Header and Body of the method call. Let's turn to those objects now, starting with the SOAP Header.

The SOAP Header

Because the SOAP Header is an optional object, you might or might not find header information serialized in a given SOAP packet. But if there is header information, all of that information must be serialized within the SOAP Header object, which must be the first (XML) child of the Envelope element. That's where you'll find it, but what is it used for?

Well, in a nutshell, the SOAP Header is used to transmit auxiliary information relevant to the Web Service processing that isn't part of the method signature. For example, imagine that you have a Web Service that specifies the toppings and crust style of the pizza that you intend to order (in C#):

```
OrderInfo OrderPizza(int[] toppings, int[] crust, PaymentInfo pi);
```

For this example, assume that the OrderInfo structure contains delivery information such as order confirmation, delivery timeline, and so on. The integer arrays contain integers that enumerate the various toppings and crusts available to you. The payment information structure contains payment data, such as a credit card number.

The Web Service, in this case, accepts your pizza order (presumably, you called another Web Service before this to establish your identity and delivery information). But it isn't a stretch to believe that there should be some sort of encryption associated with this invocation. That is, as the customer, you probably want to see at least the payment information, if not the entire packet, encrypted.

The fact that the payment information is encrypted could be verified using the encodingStyle attribute, but an alternate (and probably better) design might be to include public key information necessary to decrypt the payment data as SOAP Header information. This is the strategy used by the *SOAP Digital Signatures* specification, found at http://www.w3.org/TR/ SOAP-dsig/ (we won't go into SOAP digital signature processing here—it's important to see only that the cypher information is transmitted within the SOAP Header at this point). What the pizza chef is interested in knowing is that you placed an order. What the pizza-ordering software is concerned with is the integrity of the payment information, which is *orthogonal* to the method signature. That is, decryption keys are (obviously) important to the processing of the pizza order, but the cypher information isn't actually necessary to make the pizza from a toppings and crust perspective.

The arrangement and contents of the header are specific to the Web Service. If the information is well-formed XML and otherwise adheres to the SOAP specification, you can put anything in there that you want using any XML vocabulary that you want. Anyone who wants to insert Header information may do so, but you'll all use the single SOAP Header XML element. As a result, each child element within the Header *must* be qualified using a namespace. After all, you have to be able to pull the header information back out again; to do that reliably, you'll need the associated namespace. One example of a very complex SOAP Header can be found in the SOAP Digital Signature specification. Luckily, most header entries are not this complex. Other simpler examples might include these:

- Transaction IDs
- Packet sequence values
- Causality IDs (deadlock prevention)
- Authentication information
- Session identification information
- Message routing information
- Other Web Service method metadata

This isn't an exhaustive list, to be sure, but it hopefully gives you an idea of the types of things that SOAP headers typically convey.

According to the SOAP specification, one rule to follow, though, is to keep the header information self-contained. That is, the XML in the header should not somehow refer to the SOAP Body. This allows SOAP processing software to analyze and deal with header information without necessarily processing the body. In practice, this rule is sometimes broken to allow for more generic services. For example, a notable exception to this rule is provided by the SOAP Digital Signature specification. But there is a clear need to indicate body contents if you're encrypting a portion of the body using public key information found in the header. For all intents and purposes, the header elements should be self-contained, at least within the header element.

SOAP Header Attributes

As with the SOAP Envelope, the SOAP Header has attributes that you apply to indicate that certain behavior is desired or required. For example, it doesn't make sense for a Web Service to process encrypted SOAP Body information if it cannot decipher the encryption algorithm or digital key. You might see two predefined SOAP Header element attributes and another attribute applied to Header elements from time to time.

The Header `mustUnderstand` Attribute

The SOAP Header attribute that you see used most often is `soap:mustUnderstand`, and its intent and use is probably relatively obvious. If you apply this attribute to a given SOAP Header element, the recipient is bound, according to the SOAP specification, to return a fault packet if it does not actually understand the Header information:

```
soap:mustUnderstand="true"
```

Note that the SOAP 1.1 specification tells you to use values of `0` and `1`, but the W3 Schema specification has subsequently been updated, so Boolean values for `true` and `false` are now also potentially serialized as the strings `"true"` and `"false"`. Either value should be respected by the receiver, although there is no universal guarantee that this will be the case.

You don't need to provide the attribute if the header information is optional. That is, if you intend to use a `mustUnderstand` value of `false`, you alternatively could have not included the attribute at all. The default condition for SOAP Header elements is that `mustUnderstand` is `false`.

The Header `actor` Attribute

As it happens, SOAP is actually quite expressive with respect to the varieties of XML serializations that you can use to express similar things. Because of this, SOAP is good for many more tasks than just RPC. In fact, when it's used for RPC purposes, SOAP constrains the packet serialization rather tightly. When it's used for general-purpose data transmission, such as for messaging, SOAP is much more flexible.

One of the things that messaging systems are interested in achieving is transmission of a message from stop to stop, with each stop adding or removing pieces of the message as it travels from source to destination. These stops have a more formal name: *actor*. You will also find actors that are not the ultimate recipient of the SOAP message referred to as *intermediaries*, but they are not referenced as such in the SOAP specification itself.

The contents of the message, contained within the SOAP Body, are typically directed to a particular actor. Intermediate processing can and does take place usually through modifications to the SOAP Header. As the SOAP packet moves from actor to actor, each actor reviews the SOAP Header and twiddles the bits as necessary. What the actors do with the Header information and how many actors are involved is entirely up to the designers of the particular Web Service.

One thing that the actors must do, however, is adjust the `actor` attribute as the SOAP packet moves from stop to stop. The `actor` attribute's value is actually the URI of the next stop in the message path. There is a special URI for "next":

`http://schemas.xmlsoap.org/soap/actor/next`

At a minimum, each actor is required to strip its own URI from the `actor` attribute and replace the attribute value with the URL of the next actor, or with the special "next" destination URI, if that is more appropriate. What "next" specifically means is that this header is intended for the recipient of the message. Any additional Header child elements, messages may be reviewed based on URI. Any Header child elements intended for the recipient must be removed by the recipient from the Header before processing continues. The Header child elements represent a contract between the entity that last held the message and the current recipient.

The concept of an actor isn't typically associated with RPC-style communications. With RPC, you're usually more interested in sending information to a specific endpoint. Messages, on the other hand, often bounce around the Internet until they wind their way to their ultimate destination—at least, the potential for this style of communication is possible. This is actually the purpose of the SOAP Routing Protocol (see `http://www.gotdotnet.com/team/xml_wsspecs/ soap-rp/default.html`) and is beyond the scope of this chapter.

The SOAP `root` Attribute

If you've read the SOAP specification regarding the SOAP `root` attribute and wondered what it means by "object serialization graph," you're not alone! This attribute can actually be applied to elements in either the SOAP Header or the Body, and very often what it means depends upon where you find it.

If you serialized a linked list within the SOAP Body as a method parameter, that linked list would have a head node. As you serialize the list, you march through the nodes of the list, converting their in-memory representation to XML. One mechanism that you can use to indicate which list node was actually the first is to apply the SOAP `root` attribute to that XML element:

```
soapenc:root="true"
```

Again, the SOAP specification refers to using values of `0` and `1`, but the W3 XML Schema specification has been updated since the publication of the SOAP specification, so `true` and `false` are also appropriate. The SOAP processing software on the receiving end can then scan the XML for this attribute and begin deserialization proceedings with that element.

Applying the `root` attribute to the head node of a linked list is relatively intuitive. But the `root` attribute has another purpose. The SOAP Header element can possibly have one or more child XML elements. If you serialize many (related) Header child elements, from an XML perspective, they all appear at the same level within the document—children of the Header element. Yet it is conceivable that not all the Header elements have equal importance. So there is a potential conflict, depending upon how you serialize Header elements: You would normally assume that XML elements at the same level would be of equal importance, yet, from a SOAP Header perspective, this might not be the case. If this is so—and this depends entirely on what you intend to serialize—you have the option of inserting the SOAP `root` attribute to one or more of the Header element's child elements to promote its importance. The attribute simply provides a mechanism to make one or more elements stand out from the rest.

The SOAP Header is somewhat free-form. You can shove nearly anything in the Header itself and rest assured that you've followed the SOAP specification. The SOAP Body, however, can be a bit more constrained if you're not using WSDL document/literal encoding. It's also where the actual packet payload is recorded, so it's a critical SOAP object. Let's see how the SOAP Body is constructed.

The SOAP Body

If you're using a network protocol at all, you're probably using it to send data from one network address to another. Some overhead is associated with any network protocol, and SOAP is no exception. In general, though, the protocol should efficiently convey the data from one network location to the other. This is the primary responsibility of the SOAP Body object, the workhorse of the SOAP protocol.

If you're using SOAP in the general case, such as for messaging purposes, the SOAP specification loosely defines the arrangement of items in the Body. On the other hand, if you are using SOAP for RPC purposes, the SOAP specification cranks down the serialized XML and describes it in very precise terms.

When the SOAP specification was introduced, tightly constrained RPC serialization made perfect sense. If you and someone else wanted to share remote methods, you had to agree in no uncertain terms on how the method's parameters would be arranged within the XML document. Otherwise, how would you know what you were getting? (Remember, the intention was to *automate* the process.)

Today, the hefty SOAP RPC serialization rules have less impact because the WSDL explicitly tells the recipient how the XML is formatted. As a result, you can make simplifications to the parameter serialization, at least if you're dealing with a WSDL-enabled site. If you're not, you (and .NET) will need to revert to the SOAP RPC encoding rules. This section is important to you if you're at all interested in interoperability, at least in the near term (until WSDL 1.1 is adopted by the other sites that you intend to deal with). So let's dive in—we'll start with some terms that the SOAP specification provides to describe certain XML constructs and parameter use models.

SOAP Body Serialization Terminology

When you serialize method parameter information that is stored in the local computer's memory into another format for transmission, you often have to adopt a new vocabulary to describe the serialization process or the results. SOAP is no different. The SOAP specification describes several terms that are often used to describe serialized SOAP packets.

Many terms overlap. For example, a simple value will generally be embedded and, therefore, will be single-reference and locally scoped. In plain English, that means that the simple value, which would be something like an integer, will be recorded deep within the XML element hierarchy and will only ever be accessed by processes working with its parent or siblings. We're really referring to where in the XML document you'll find the integer value and who can access it. Embedded values are typically sent to the remote system by value, whereas independent elements are often how data is sent by reference, such as data accessed in memory by a pointer or output parameters.

Table 4.1 addresses most of the important SOAP terms. Probably the most important set of terms to understand is the difference between simple and compound values. A simple value is a method parameter value passed by value to the remote method; it is usually an integer, a floating point, or a string value. Compound values, on the other hand, refer to how structures and arrays are serialized in the SOAP XML stream. SOAP differentiates between the structure and the array by identifying how you access the elements within the compound value. Structure members are accessed by name, while array elements are accessed by position. When you see how SOAP encodes method parameter data, you'll understand why these concepts were described in this manner.

TABLE 4.1   SOAP Terminology

Term	Definition
Value	A string, a name of measurement (number, date, enumeration, and so on), or a composite of several simple types. All values are of specific datatypes.
Simple value	A value without named parts (specific strings, enumerations, and so on).
Compound value	An aggregation of relations to other values (struct or array).
Accessor	A particular related value contained within a compound value (distinguished by either name [struct] or ordinal value [array]).
Array	A compound value in which ordinal position distinguishes member values.
Struct	A compound value in which accessor name distinguishes member values.
Simple type	A class of simple values, such as strings, integers, enumerations, and so on.
Compound type	A class of compound values, such as a struct definition that could be filled with different accessor values.
Locally scoped	An accessor that has a distinct name within that (compound) type but that is not distinct with respect to other types (such as struct members).
Universally scoped	An accessor whose name is based upon a URI, in whole or in part, directly or indirectly, so that the name alone is sufficient to identify the accessor, regardless of the type (that is, qualified by a namespace URI, such as Header entries).
Single reference	An accessor that can be only directly accessed (that is, a value passed by a value). It is typically embedded.
Multireference	An accessor that can be indirectly accessed, whether accessed in this manner actually or potentially (that is, a value passed by a reference). It is typically independent.
Embedded	An element that appears within an independent element (such as XML elements that are grandchildren or that are further descended from the SOAP Header or Body).
Independent	An element that appears at the top level of a serialization (such as immediate children of the SOAP Header or Body).

The SOAP specification itself is relatively easy to read and understand, as long as you know what the verbiage is referring to. Before applying these terms to the serialization of some remote methods, let's look at a couple Body element attributes that you'll find useful.

SOAP Body Attributes

The SOAP Body attributes, like those of the SOAP Header, are usually applied to subordinate XML elements rather than the Body element itself. Some of the attributes are designed specifically for certain serialization conditions, such as for encoding arrays. But two attributes in particular are used quite often when serializing strings or general compound values. These attributes are actually related—they're used to link XML elements that aren't necessarily hierarchically related.

The SOAP `id` and `href` Attributes

The id and href attributes really come from XLink (http://www.w3.org/TR/xlink/, Section 5.4), which is actually used to link external elements to a given XML document. In SOAP's case, their use is narrowed to link XML elements. An example will best illustrate this.

Let's return to the linked list. Imagine that you have a linked list in your computer's memory that you want to ship to some remote computer for processing. For brevity, assume that it has only two nodes and takes this form (shown in C#):

```
public class Node
{
    public int iData;
    public Node pNext;
}
```

Using this class, suppose that you created one node and assigned its iData member to the value 27. Then you created a second node and set its iData member to 54. To link the nodes, you assigned the first node's pNext member so that it referenced the second node, and the second node's pNext pointer was set to null:

```
Node pHead = new Node();
pHead.iData = 27;
Node pTail = new Node();
pTail.iData = 54;
pHead.pNext = pTail;
pTail.pNext = null;
```

When this data structure is serialized in a SOAP packet, the SOAP Body would take this form (if serialized according to Section 5 of the SOAP specification, assuming that the remote method is called ConsumeList(Node pNode)):

```
<soap:Body>
   <m:ConsumeList xmlns:m="http://tempuri.org">
      <pNode href="#node1"/>
   <m:ConsumeList>
   <m:Node xmlns:m="www://tempuri.org" soapenc:root="true" id="node1">
      <iData>27</iData>
      <pNext href="#node2"/>
   </m:Node>
   <m:Node xmlns:m="www://tempuri.org" id="node2">
      <iData>54</iData>
      <pNext xsi:null="true"/>
   </m:Node>
</soap:Body>
```

The id and href attributes are italicized for emphasis. Although this is an example of a compound value serialization, something we've not covered yet, it does show how values that are not hierarchically related are associated with each other (few would claim that a linked list was an example of a hierarchical data structure!). The input method parameter pNode "points" to the value for pHead, and pHead's pNext value "points" to pTail, as you'd expect. The # used within the href's attribute value indicates that the linkage is internal to the current document rather than being linked to some external source.

The serialization of this linked list example could actually take many different forms, depending upon the WSDL associated with the particular Web Service. For example, this particular linked list could have been serialized as an array of integers, if you knew this beforehand and could therefore later extract the list. If you're serializing according to SOAP Section 5 rules (used for RPC), then you'll see the SOAP packet serialized very much as you've seen here. Armed with what you've seen so far, let's see how SOAP actually serializes your Web Service data.

SOAP Remote Method Serialization

Although you could arrange things within the SOAP Body nearly any way you want, the SOAP specification gives a precise format for serializing RPC information destined for the remote system. The basic SOAP Request packet format has the method information serialized as the first child of the SOAP Body element, like so:

```
<soap:Body>
   <m:ReverseString xmlns:m="http://tempuri.org">
      (Embedded single reference parameters here)
   </m:ReverseString>
   (Independent multi-reference accessors here)
</soap:Body>
```

The method element is an independent element because it is the immediate child of the SOAP Body opening tag. In fact, for RPC purposes, the method element should also be the first child element to simplify deserialization. Other independent elements may follow (as you've seen with the linked list example previously).

Note that the method element has a namespace. What the method namespace URI text consists of is often immaterial to SOAP. SOAP may care only that it is unique throughout the SOAP packet. (*You* might care, however, for interoperability purposes, or the URI might be used to arbitrate overloaded methods, in which case SOAP *does* care.) Because a namespace is applied to this element, it is globally scoped (another one of those SOAP terms).

When the remote server receives this SOAP packet, it extracts the method name, checks to see if it can handle that method, and examines the SOAP XML to see if the required parameters have been provided. Assuming that things are correct, the server then executes the method (reversing a string, in this case) and returns the results of the method. The SOAP Response packet looks a lot like the Request packet:

```
<soap:Body>
    <m:ReverseStringResponse xmlns:m="http://tempuri.org">
        <return>(Method return value here)</return>
        (Embedded single reference parameters here)
    </m:ReverseStringResponse>
    (Independent multi-reference accessors here)
</soap:Body>
```

As you see, you can still have returned values (embedded or independent multireference), but the method's return value is encoded as the first (embedded) child of the method response element. The XML tag name, in this case, doesn't matter—only the position within the XML document matters. Traditionally, though, this element is named return or response, but this is by convention rather than by specification.

Directed Data Flow

You've probably guessed that data has an associated directional component. It can go from your local computer to the remote computer only; if this is the case, the data is referred to as [in] data. You could be expecting data from the server, which is annotated by the [out] moniker. Data also can go both ways, which is [in, out] data. The notation "in," "out," and "in, out" comes from the Interface Definition Language attributes that tell the COM serialization code more precisely how to encode the data for transmission. (Of course, in .NET, you don't have COM, but the concepts and markings remain.)

For example, if you're expecting [out] data, the serialization code doesn't need to put anything into the Request packet. You're not sending data to the server; you're expecting the server to return information to you. Thus, the [out] data would be serialized within the Response packet alone.

The C# language has these same concepts, by the way. In C#, you occasionally might employ the ref and out method parameter attributes to optimize the way the Common Language Runtime (CLR) deals with memory and data. C#'s out attribute equates to [out] data, while the ref attribute indicates [in, out] data. If you omit either attribute from the method signature, the data is passed by value to the method as [in] data.

This directed nature has a direct bearing on the serialization of the method parameters. [in] data is by value and, therefore, encoded as embedded elements of the Request method element. [in, out] data is, by nature, multireference and, therefore, is encoded as independent elements within the SOAP Body. [out] data is also independent and multireference, although this reasoning might not at first be apparent. The [out] data is independent and multireference because when you call the remote method, you provide the .NET serialization code with a reference to the variable that it will populate with the [out] data. As soon as you see the word *reference*, you should think "independent multireference SOAP serialization."

> **NOTE**
>
> This is one place where .NET diverges from the SOAP specification a bit. .NET serializes referenced information as embedded by default. .NET uses SOAP more as a messaging protocol than as a true SOAP RPC protocol, and the fact that the referenced parameters are embedded is noted in the WSDL generated for your Web Service. In other words, what you're seeing in this chapter is how the SOAP specification tells you to serialize RPC information, but this isn't the only way you can do it. It's important to know this because sometimes you might need to interoperate with third-party Web Services that don't emit WSDL 1.1 or that otherwise expect you to provide SOAP RPC-encoded parameter information. At least you'll know what the XML might have to look like to be fully interoperable.

> **NOTE**
>
> .NET serializes information according to Sections 5 and 7 of the SOAP specification, if you need it to do so (again, for interoperability purposes). The .NET SoapRpcMethodAttribute class enables you to force SOAP Specification Sections 5 and 7 encoding rules for specific Web methods. It actually forces the WSDL encoding style to RPC (versus Literal), which triggers the alternative .NET serialization code.
>
> If you want the entire Web Service class to follow Section 5 and Section 7 encoding rules, you should apply the SoapRpcService attribute to the class as a whole.

4

.NET WEB
SERVICES AND
SOAP

You now know how SOAP would have you serialize the method itself. The method element encapsulates the parameter information that you're sending to the Web Service or receiving back as output data. We'll turn now to how SOAP serializes simple parameter values.

SOAP Serialization of Simple Datatypes

Because SOAP is based on XML, SOAP inherently "understands" the simple datatypes noted by the *W3 Schema Specification, Part 2* (`http://www.w3.org/TR/xmlschema-2/`). If you're writing SOAP serialization software, you'll be very interested in these datatypes and their XML representations. In this case, though, .NET handles the details for you, so the entire suite of datatypes isn't shown here. They include all the datatypes that you would expect, such as strings, various kinds of integers and floating-point values, some XML-specific information (such as the `QName`, or namespace-qualified name), and dates and times.

SOAP rolls the W3 datatypes into a collection that it refers to as the *simple datatypes*. The other members of this collection include enumerations and byte arrays.

Serializing W3 Datatypes

As a rule, single-reference W3 datatypes are serialized as plain XML elements. The tag names match the parameter name given by the method signature. For example, consider this method:

```
int Add(int A, int B);
```

If the values for A and B were 17 and 12, respectively, the corresponding SOAP packet would look very much like this:

```
<soap:Body>
    <m:Add xmlns:m="http://tempuri.org">
        <A>17</A>
        <B>12</B>
    </m:Add>
</soap:Body>
```

A and B are embedded elements (children of the method signature) serialized in the order specified in the method signature, from left to right (A before B, in the XML document order).

In this example, the parameters are integer values, but they could just have easily been time durations, dates, times, URIs, floats, or something else. These all generally serialize in this way, at least if they are [in] parameters, as shown in this example.

The one exception is the string, which can be serialized as either an embedded an or independent element. For example, consider this method:

```
string ReverseString(string X);
```

Blindly encoding this, as indicated by the SOAP specification, would yield something very much like this Body serialization:

```
<soap:Body>
    <m:ReverseString xmlns:m="http://tempuri.org">
        <X href="#str0"/>
    </m:ReverseString>
    <m:string xmlns:m="http://tempuri.org" id="str0">
        Hello, World!
    </m:string>
</soap:Body>
```

In many cases, though, the string is used as an [in] parameter, so you have the option of optimizing the serialization a bit to embed the string value:

```
<soap:Body>
    <m:ReverseString xmlns:m="http://tempuri.org">
        <X>Hello, World!</X>
    </m:ReverseString>
</soap:Body>
```

The optimization here is that you don't have to hunt for the str0 identifier to discover what text the string contained. This saves you an additional XPath query .NET takes advantage of this optimization, for example.

If the simple value is [in, out], then it should be serialized as an independent, multireference accessor. The serialization format is as you see it in the first string example. To provide a second example, imagine that you have this method:

```
bool CheckPressure(ref int iPressure);
...
int iPres = 330;
bool bOver = CheckPressure(ref iPres);
```

This method triggers some (imaginary) code to check pressure in some vessel. If the pressure exceeds the pressure provided in the iPressure parameter, the method returns a true value. In either case, imagine that the method returns the actual pressure within the vessel in the iPressure parameter. The addition of the ref attribute tells you that the method can consume the incoming pressure value and modify the contents of the parameter variable upon return. Data goes in, and potentially different data comes back out.

The resulting SOAP packet for this method would look something like this:

```
<soap:Body>
    <m:CheckPressure xmlns:m="http://tempuri.org">
        <iPressure href="#p0"/>
    </m:CheckPressure >
```

```
<m:iPres xmlns:m="http://tempuri.org" id="p0">
   330
</m:iPres>
</soap:Body>
```

A possible Response packet would then appear like this:

```
<soap:Body>
   <m:CheckPressureResponse xmlns:m="http://tempuri.org">
      <return>false</return>
      <iPressure href="#p0"/>
   </m:CheckPressure >
   <m:iPres xmlns:m="http://tempuri.org" id="p0">
      297
   </m:iPres>
</soap:Body>
```

For this example, then, iPres would contain the value 297 (even though it started with the value 330), and the bOver variable would contain the value false.

All the W3 datatypes are serialized in this manner, but you're still left with enumerations and byte arrays. Let's turn first to enumeration serialization.

Serializing Enumerations

SOAP's answer to enumeration serialization is actually relatively intuitive. As you might know, enumerations are represented in memory at runtime as integer values. Only in your source code do you actually use the textual representation. For example, consider this enumeration:

```
enum Colors { Red = 0, Green, Blue };
```

In memory, anywhere you used the Red enumeration value, the computer would use the value 0. Green is 1, and Blue is 2.

SOAP simply reverts back to using the textual value. Consider a method signature like this:

```
void FavoriteColor( Colors eColor );
```

The resulting SOAP Request packet would look a lot like this:

```
<soap:Body>
   <m:FavoriteColor xmlns:m="http://tempuri.org">
      <eColor>Blue</eColor>
   </m:FavoriteColor>
</soap:Body>
```

Of course, this packet shows you an embedded, single-reference value. The method parameter could also have been tagged as a ref parameter, in which case the independent, multireference serialization rules apply.

Serializing Byte Arrays

So what do we mean by a byte array? Well, suppose that you had a 1K text buffer into which a user typed some information. You could serialize that as a string, but you could also serialize it as a buffer. If you chose to maintain its buffer nature, you would serialize the contents of the buffer as an array of bytes. Another example would be an image or perhaps a public key used for encryption and decryption purposes. These would also be serialized as an array of bytes.

Because we're talking about a binary large object (BLOB), the SOAP rules for array serialization can be set aside in favor of a simpler mechanism. In this case, you simply convert the bytes to Base64 and then record the converted data within the parameter's XML element.

This brings up another issue, however. Some characters are "special," according to XML. They include <, >, ', ", and &. If you blindly shove bytes that happen to represent these characters into your XML document, the XML parser will croak and return a parse error. It would be a shame to sustain a round trip to the remote server only to find that you shipped it malformed XML!

You have a couple options. For one, you can check each type in the array for special character status; if a given character is special, you can substitute its *entity reference*. Table 4.2 shows you the special characters and their respective entity reference values.

TABLE 4.2 XML Special Characters and Their Entity Reference Values

Special Character	Entity Reference
<	&lt;
>	&gt;
'	&apos;
"	&quot;
&	&amp;

This works, but you'll do a lot of looping through your buffers to search for the special characters. Moreover, when you find one, you will have to insert 4 to 6 bytes for each byte of special character. This means that you'll need to split your buffer and play memory games. This can be done, but it's expensive and time-consuming.

An alternative is to use the XML CDATA section:

```
<![CDATA[(byte array here)]]>
```

The CDATA section is used in XML to protect blocks of free-form text that should not be parsed. So, you can insert special characters here to your heart's content. The only overhead that you'll have is to insert the byte array text into the CDATA section and strip it out again. You also can't embed CDATA sections because the first grouping of the characters]]> terminates the entire section. This also means that you can't allow random text encoded within a CDATA section to contain these characters. At least, this character sequence isn't very common, so, in most cases, you will have no problem.

However, the SOAP specification recommends using Base64 encoding. The advantage to this is the resulting textual stream is suitable for transmission over the Internet and is guaranteed to pass through firewalls and servers unmolested. Some firewall and server software packages modify incoming text, for various reasons. Modifications to your byte array could be catastrophic, however, so you will likely see SOAP packets with large amounts of buffer data using this encoding scheme.

Base64 is a *Multipurpose Internet Mail Extension* (MIME) encoding. It's typically used to encode email attachments because SMTP servers are particularly touchy about certain textual values and characters. Base64 encoding replaces each byte with a "safe" textual representation. Although the specific algorithm isn't terribly important here, the fact that you have this option is important. You'll essentially run your buffer through a Base64 encoder, only to receive back more text. But the text that you get back won't trigger substitutional or executional code in firewalls and SMTP servers (SMTP is administered through a command line, so it understands commands and carriage returns, and executes the commands on demand). Your buffer will grow by approximately 33%, but it is safe from firewall and server molestation. If you are interested in the Base64 algorithm, you'll find it listed in RFC 2045, "Multipurpose Internet Mail Extensions (MIME), Part One: Format of Internet Message Bodies," or in *Understanding SOAP*, by Scribner and Stiver.

If you applied the Base64 algorithm to the text "Hello World," you would get this value:

```
SGVsbG8gV29ybGQ=
```

To take the example further, assume that you have this C# code:

```
void SendBytes(byte[] bytes);
...
byte[] bytes = {0x48, 0x65, 0x6c, 0x6c, 0x6f, 0x20,
                0x57, 0x6f, 0x72, 0x6c, 0x64}; // "Hello World"
SendBytes(bytes);
```

The resulting SOAP packet would look like this:

```
<soap:Body>
   <m:SendBytes xmlns:m="http://tempuri.org">
      <bytes href="#p0"/>
   <m:SendBytes>
   <m:bytes xsi:type="xsd:base64inary" id="p0">
```

```
      SGVsbG8gV29ybGQ=
   </m:bytes>
</soap:Body>
```

Of course, as with strings, you have the option of optimizing this to embed the byte array:

```
<soap:Body>
   <m:SendBytes xmlns:m="http://tempuri.org">
      <bytes xsi:type="xsd:base64inary">
         SGVsbG8gV29ybGQ=
      </bytes>
   <m:SendBytes>
</soap:Body>
```

And with the serialization of the byte array, you've seen how SOAP encodes simple datatypes! It really has been pretty easy to see how SOAP handles these datatypes. But not everything is so simple when it comes to compound datatypes, as you'll see in the next section.

SOAP Serialization of Compound Data Types

When you consider how difficult it must be to write a system that can serialize any array or structure you can invent, you can see why a discussion of the compound datatype encodings can get so detailed. After all, there is an infinite set of arrays and structures out there, yet .NET must accept anything that you code for SOAP serialization.

So how do the .NET system programmers do it? How do you write code that accepts whatever array or structure you pass in?

Well, it helps if you're clever. But you also can rely upon the SOAP standard. If you take a close look at how arrays and structures are created in memory, you'll find patterns that you can exploit and shortcuts that you can take based on the way .NET (or any system) stores data in memory. So although it's not a simple task, it's also not an overly complex one when you see how things work.

To review a moment, remember that, to SOAP, structs are compound types whose constituent elements are accessed by name. Arrays, on the other hand, are accessed by position (array element ordinal). The result of this is that when you serialize arrays, you use generic XML tag names. With structs, though, you have to carry over the names provided by the structure's designer. The honest truth is that structures are easier to serialize, so let's start there.

SOAP struct Serialization

Before we get to the details, let's take a look at an example. Imagine that you have this structure:

```
public struct PartInfo
{
   public string strPartID;
```

```
    public int iQtyOnHand;
    public string strPartLocation;
}
```

Here, you have some sort of part that you happen to be tracking. Notice that you are providing structure data by value, but you have the option of multireferenced strings, depending on how you want those serialized (optimized or not). The integer value will always be serialized as an embedded parameter because it is passed within the structure itself by value.

Next let's put the struct to work by implementing this code:

```
// Function prototype...
bool RecordPartInfo(PartInfo pi);

...

PartInfo piMyPart = new PartInfo();
piMyPart.strPartID = "002-AS-3220-1";
piMyPart.iQtyOnHand = 17;
piMyPart.strPartLocation = "Bin 3741";
RecordPartInfo(piMyPart);
```

Assuming that the RecordPartInfo() method resides on another computer as a Web Service (which is actually accessed via a local proxy), the resulting SOAP Request Body might appear very much like this:

```
<soap:Body>
    <m:RecordPartInfo xmlns:m="http://tempuri.org">
       <pi>
          <strPartID>002-AS-3220-1</strPartID>
          <iQtyOnHand>17</iQtyOnHand>
          <strPartLocation>Bin 3741</strPartLocation>
       </pi>
    <m:RecordPartInfo>
</soap:Body>
```

The structure data is embedded within the method element because it was passed into the method by value. We'll change the method signature a bit to allow for passing by reference:

```
// Function prototype...
bool RecordPartInfo(ref PartInfo pi);

...

RecordPartInfo(ref piMyPart);
```

As a result, we should obtain a slightly different SOAP Request Body:

```
<soap:Body>
    <m:RecordPartInfo xmlns:m="http://tempuri.org">
       <pi href="#s0"/>
    <m:RecordPartInfo>
```

```
    <m:PartInfo xmlns:m="http://tempuri.org" id="s0">
        <strPartID>002-AS-3220-1</strPartID>
        <iQtyOnHand>17</iQtyOnHand>
        <strPartLocation>Bin 3741</strPartLocation>
    </m:PartInfo>
</soap:Body>
```

Note that the string serialization is optimized. The packet could have appeared like this:

```
<soap:Body>
    <m:RecordPartInfo xmlns:m="http://tempuri.org">
        <pi href="#s0"/>
    <m:RecordPartInfo>
    <m:PartInfo xmlns:m="http://tempuri.org" id="s0">
        <strPartID href="#s1" />
        <iQtyOnHand>17</iQtyOnHand>
        <strPartLocation href="#s2" />
    </m:PartInfo>
    <string id="s1">002-AS-3220-1</string>
    <string id="s2:>Bin 3741</string>
</soap:Body>
```

In this case, we've simply made the strings independent elements instead of embedded elements. Moving the string data from embedded elements to independent elements signifies that the string values are more global in scope. You might do this, say, when reusing the same string value in a couple of places in the method signature (that is, the strings are multireference). It's important to realize that there are many ways to serialize method signature information, and you might or might not have to tweak the XML coming from (or into) .NET to allow for interoperability. You'll see how to accomplish this in Chapter 6.

With this example under your belt, let's take a slightly closer look at how SOAP tells you to serialize structure information.

Embedded Versus Independent

The decision to serialize the struct information as embedded within the method element or as independent data depends entirely upon how the structure is passed into the method. Information passed by value is generally serialized as embedded data, while information passed by reference is serialized as independent elements. The format of the resulting SOAP packet is different, and sometimes you will need to tweak your packet layout to satisfy a third-party Web Service that assumes that the structure information is serialized in a certain form.

Named Parts

Note also that the XML tag names have meaning when serializing structure data. That's because you can "reach into" the structure and pull out a specific piece of information:

```
int x = piMyPart.iQtyOnHand;
```

The "quantity on hand" value is accessed by its name, iQtyOnHand. This is a different access model than the access model for arrays. With arrays, the data is extracted by ordinal position (the element's offset into the array). You might believe that this makes array encoding easy, but array encoding is actually the most complex part of the SOAP specification.

SOAP Array Serialization

When serializing arrays, it's important to remember that arrays come in different shapes and sizes. For example, there is the single-dimension array, the multiple-dimension array, and the partial, jagged, and sparse array. Other forms of arrays exist, but these are the types that the SOAP specification is concerned with. Let's start with some general concepts.

Array Serialization General Concepts

With arrays, you'll need to know whether there is an associated variable name (provided through the schema) because the encoding differs if you have the name. For example, consider this array:

```
int[3] i = {0,2,4};
```

If you have the variable name i, the array would be encoded as such:

```
<m:i soapenc:arrayType="xsd:int[3]"
  xmlns:m="http://tempuri.org>
    <int>0</int>
    <int>2</int>
    <int>4</int>
</m:i>
```

Without the variable name (and schema), however, you'll need to use the SOAP Array element:

```
<soapenc:Array soapenc:arrayType="xsd:int[3]">
    <int>0</int>
    <int>2</int>
    <int>4</int>
</soapenc:Array>
```

In either case, it's important to know that all arrays in SOAP are derived from soapenc:Array and that, if you have an associated schema with your method, the arrays that you specify there must be derived from the SOAP Array element:

```
<element name="i" type="soapenc:Array"/>
```

You probably also noticed that SOAP conveys the size and dimension of the array through its use of the soapenc:arrayType attribute:

```
<soapenc:Array soapenc:arrayType="xsd:int[3]">
```

You'll see this concept repeated in the next few sections.

Single-Dimension Array

The previous section, "Array Serialization General Concepts," actually provided you with your first SOAP array serialization example:

```
int[3] i = {0,2,4};
```

This serialized to the following:

```
<m:i soapenc:arrayType="xsd:int[3]"
  xmlns:m="http://tempuri.org>
    <int>0</int>
    <int>2</int>
    <int>4</int>
</m:i>
```

The SOAP `arrayType` attribute tells you there are three elements to this array, and all three have been serialized (0, 2, and 4). Notice that the element names are simply the datatype associated with the values—this is in keeping with the notion that array values are accessed by position rather than by name. You couldn't access them by name in this case even if you wanted to because they're (clearly) all named the same.

A good question to ask at this point would be something like, "What if I don't have all three values assigned when I serialize the array?" This leads to the concept of a partial array, which is covered next.

Partially Transmitted Array

Partially transmitted arrays are simply arrays that do not have all their element values assigned, or at least are not entirely transmitted within the same SOAP packet. To conserve resources, SOAP provides you with a mechanism to indicate this partially completed nature.

For example, take a look at this code:

```
int[3] j;
j[1] = 27;
j[2] = 54;
```

In this case, `j[0]` has not been assigned a value, so it remains, whatever the default value for the language happens to be. With C#, that's a special form of `null` that the compiler recognizes to be the unassigned value.

The SOAP serialization for this array would be something like this:

```
<m:j soapenc:arrayType="xsd:int[3]"
  soapenc:offset="[1]"
  xmlns:m="http://tempuri.org>
    <int>27</int>
    <int>54</int>
</m:j>
```

As you see, we have added the `soapenc:offset` attribute to tell which array element contains the first assigned array elemental value. Other values proceed from this position. We simply serialized the next value after the first, and this would continue for the remaining array elements. But what if there is a break in the action?

Sparse Arrays

This "break in the action" is often the case with a type of array known as the sparse array. Any array could have uninitialized elements, but this is especially common with arrays with large upper bounds, or when a given number dominates the matrix (such as with the diagonal in image transformation matrices). For example, consider this example:

```
int[1000] k;
k[301] = 43;
k[572] = 76;
k[893] = 109;
```

In this case, the array k is declared to be 1000 elements large, but we have used only 3 of those elements. It would be very wasteful to send all 1000 elements to a remote server with values for only 3 elements.

SOAP handles this by using the `soap:position` attribute:

```
<m:k soapenc:arrayType="xsd:int[1000]"
  xmlns:m="http://tempuri.org>
    <int soap:position="[301]">43</int>
    <int soap:position="[572]">76</int>
    <int soap:position="[893]">109</int>
</m:k>
```

You know that it is a sparse array because the `arrayType` attribute tells you that there are 1000 elements but only 3 have been serialized (and you have their values and element position information as well).

The serialization of both partially transmitted arrays and sparse arrays also holds true for multidimensional arrays. That is, you can easily have multidimensional arrays that are partially transmitted, sparse, or both. Now let's see how multidimensional arrays are encoded in SOAP.

Multidimensional Arrays

Only a couple differences exist between single-dimension and multiple-dimension arrays when it comes to SOAP serialization. First, the array bounds change. Second, you serialize information in row-major format. Let's look at this example:

```
int[,] z = {{5,67},{7,21},{92,4}};
```

The z array is a two-by-three array (two columns, three rows), and its SOAP serialization would look something like this:

```
<m:z soapenc:arrayType="xsd:int[2,3]"
  xmlns:m="http://tempuri.org>
   <int>5</int>
   <int>67</int>
   <int>7</int>
   <int>21</int>
   <int>92</int>
   <int>4</int>
</m:z>
```

Essentially, you store all the columns from the first row before moving to the second row, and so on. You know how large the array is based on the bounds provided with the `arrayType` attribute. If you have no values for certain elements, you'll need to be informed of this by the use of either the `offset` or the `position` attributes, or both. Otherwise, you have to assume that all the data is present. If you later find out that there isn't enough information, you can return an error or you can assume default values (SOAP encodes default values very efficiently—it omits them entirely!).

You should be aware of one other case of array serialization: the jagged array.

Jagged Arrays

A jagged array is an array of arrays, and it gets the name "jagged" from the fact that each constituent array is probably not the same size as the others. This is unlike a multidimensional array, which has constant bounds.

Let's again turn to an example:

```
int[][] q = {new int[2], new int[4], new int[3]};
q[0][0] = 4;
q[0][1] = 7;
q[1][0] = 15;
q[1][1] = 72;
q[1][2] = 6;
q[1][3] = 167;
q[2][0] = 1;
q[2][1] = 90;
q[2][2] = 659;
```

It's nasty-looking, that's true, but take a look at how SOAP might serialize the q array:

```
<m:q soapenc:arrayType="xsd:int[][3]"
  xmlns:m="http://tempuri.org>
   <int href="#a0"/>
   <int href="#a1"/>
   <int href="#a2"/>
</m:q>
```

4

.NET WEB
SERVICES AND
SOAP

```
<soapenc:Array soapenc:arrayType="xsd:int[2]" id="a0">
    <int>4</int>
    <int>7</int>
</soapEnc:Array>
<soapenc:Array soapenc:arrayType="xsd:int[4]" id="a1">
    <int>15</int>
    <int>72</int>
    <int>6</int>
    <int>167</int>
</soapenc:Array>
<soapenc:Array soapenc:arrayType="xsd:int[3]" id="a2">
    <int>1</int>
    <int>90</int>
    <int>659</int>
</soapenc:Array>
```

Actually, you might also see the q array serialized using embedded elements, depending on what system performed the serialization. In that case, another valid SOAP serialization would be as follows:

```
<m:q soapenc:arrayType="xsd:int[][3]"
  xmlns:m="http://tempuri.org>
    <soapenc:Array soapenc:arrayType="xsd:int[2]">
        <int>4</int>
        <int>7</int>
    </soapEnc:Array>
    <soapenc:Array soapenc:arrayType="xsd:int[4]">
        <int>15</int>
        <int>72</int>
        <int>6</int>
        <int>167</int>
    </soapenc:Array>
    <soapenc:Array soapenc:arrayType="xsd:int[3]">
        <int>1</int>
        <int>90</int>
        <int>659</int>
    </soapenc:Array>
</m:q>
```

Of course, it gets a lot more complicated than this, but you're generally dealing with variations on a theme. For example, you could have a jagged array of structs, or you could have a partially transmitted multidimensional array of strings. It just depends. SOAP is flexible enough to serialize these things, but aren't you glad that .NET does it for you?

You've seen just enough SOAP to understand what will be sent to the Web Service and returned to you for local processing. .NET handles the details for you—at least, in most cases.

> **NOTE**
>
> Most of the time you can—and should—let .NET handle the SOAP serialization for
> you. .NET works well. But in some cases you might be dealing with Web Services that
> aren't supported by .NET (Apache, WebSphere, and so on). You might find small
> interoperability issues with using these or other Web Services. Microsoft is working
> hard to eliminate inconsistencies with other major vendors, but it's a large Internet
> out there. The possibility still exists that your SOAP serialization code (within .NET)
> and the remote end's won't sync up. If this is the case, you'll need to tweak SOAP
> yourself using .NET's SoapExtension or work through one of the many SOAP-related
> .NET attribute classes, which you'll see in Chapter 6.

At this point, you've seen how SOAP would format binary data for transmission. If things
work as they should, you'll see XML with data inside going back and forth, client to server.
But in the real world, things break. How do you tell the client that you had an error? This is
the task of the SOAP Fault.

SOAP Faults

SOAP returns an error to the client in a very specific manner—it specifies a fault packet. The
SOAP Fault is really an element of the SOAP Body, and it takes the following form:

```
<soap:Envelope>
   <soap:Body>
      <soap:Fault>
         (Fault information)
      </soap:Fault>
   </soap:Body>
</soap:Envelope>
```

The SOAP Fault information consists of four elements, two of which are optional:

- `<soap:faultcode/>`
- `<soap:faultstring/>`
- `<soap:faultactor/>` (optional)
- `<soap:detail/>` (optional)

The `faultcode` element contains an enumerated value that indicates the type of fault:
`MustUnderstand`, `VersionMismatch`, `Client`, and `Server`. `MustUnderstand` must be returned
if the client issues a SOAP Header with the `mustUnderstand` attribute and the server truly
doesn't understand what to do with the Header. `VersionMismatch` must be returned if the
SOAP namespace URI is not understood by the SOAP processor, such as when a SOAP 1.1

processor receives a SOAP 1.2 packet. `Client` and `Server` are used to return errors related to client formatting or parameter issues (`Client`), or server-side failures (`Server`). SOAP's intention for this element is to allow the client or server to use this information in an automated manner to deal with the fault.

SOAP fault codes are extensible. `MustUnderstand`, `VersionMismatch`, `Client`, and `Server` are all generic errors that are commonly tailored with more specific information. The value placed in the `<soap:faultcode/>` element indicates the more generic error code on the left, with each more detailed code being separated by a dot:

`Server.DivideByZero`

The `faultcode` is contrasted by the `faultstring` element, whose use is to provide a meaningful, human-readable error message. The string itself can contain nearly anything (XML special characters excluded if left unreferenced).

The `faultcode` and `faultstring` elements are required to exist within the SOAP Fault packet. The `faultactor`, however, is optional because not all SOAP packets use actors. As you might recall, a SOAP actor is a recipient of a SOAP message. The actors open the message and examine the Header(s). If the message has reached the final actor (the destination), the recipient acts upon the message itself. If there is an error along the way, the actor that exposed the error places its URI within the `faultactor` element.

The final SOAP Fault element, `detail`, is actually a free-form element into which anything can be placed to further identify the error, as long as it's well-formed XML. If the Web Service had a problem processing the SOAP Body, it is required to use this element. Otherwise, this element is optional. The contents are identified by namespace so that you'll know what to expect:

```
<soap:Body>
   <soap:Fault>
      <faultcode>Server.DivideByZero</faultcode>
      <faultstring>Divide by Zero Error</faultstring>
      <detail>
         <m:Error xmlns:m="http://tempuri.org">
            <message>Divide by Zero Error, assembly myassembly.dll,
                  ➥ method TryMe()</message>
            <errorcode>RPC_S_FP_DIV_ZERO (1769)</errorcode>
         </m:Error>
      </detail>
   </soap:Fault>
</soap:Body>
```

With the SOAP Fault, you've completed your whirlwind tour of the SOAP protocol. Before jumping into .NET Web Service code from a high-level perspective, which you'll do in

Chapter 6, let's look at some low-level .NET SOAP serialization classes and see what services they provide.

.NET SOAP Classes

.NET provides a complex yet elegant system that you can use to implement Web Services. From a programming model perspective, a Web Service in .NET is little more than a method in a class. You simply slap on a couple attributes, and, *voilà*—you have a Web Service. And that's a good thing. We want that. But it's also nice to look under the hood to see what's running this machine.

The .NET `SoapFormatter` Class

`SoapFormatter` is one workhorse .NET SOAP class. Its purpose in life is to format a generic .NET object using a SOAP format, given a stream. The class itself has several methods, but the two most interesting are `Serialize()` and `Deserialize()`. `Serialize()` takes as input both a stream into which the SOAP output will be formatted and an object to format. `Deserialize()` takes the stream from which an object will be created.

To demonstrate SOAP formatting in .NET, Listing 4.2 provides you with a short C# console application that formats the jagged array example into a SOAP format, saves it to disk, and deserializes the array.

LISTING 4.2   `SoapFormatter` Demonstration

```
using System;
using System.IO;
using System.Runtime.Serialization.Formatters.Soap;

namespace SoapSerializer
{
    /// <summary>
    /// Summary description for SoapSerializerTester.
    /// </summary>
    class SoapSerializerTester
    {
        bool Serialize(string strPath, Object objStuff)
        {
            bool bReturn = true;
            try
            {
                // Create a file stream
                FileStream fstmOutput = new FileStream(strPath,
                                                FileMode.Create);
```

LISTING 4.2 Continued

```
        // Create the formatter we'll associate
        // with this stream
        SoapFormatter sfmtFormatter = new SoapFormatter();

        // Serialize and save the object
        sfmtFormatter.Serialize(fstmOutput,objStuff);

        // Close the file stream
        fstmOutput.Close();
    } //try
    catch(Exception e)
    {
        Console.WriteLine("{0}",e.Message);
        bReturn = false;
    } // catch

    return bReturn;
}

Object Deserialize(string strPath)
{
    Object objReturn = null;
    try
    {
        // Create a file stream
        FileStream fstmInput = new FileStream(strPath,
                                            FileMode.Open);

        // Create the formatter we'll associate
        // with this stream
        SoapFormatter sfmtFormatter = new SoapFormatter();

        // Deserialize and return the object
        objReturn = sfmtFormatter.Deserialize(fstmInput);

        // Close the file stream
        fstmInput.Close();
    } //try
    catch(Exception e)
    {
        Console.WriteLine("{0}",e.Message);
        objReturn = null;
    } // catch
```

LISTING 4.2   Continued

```
        return objReturn;
    }

    static void Main(string[] args)
    {
        try
        {
            // Create an instance...
            SoapSerializerTester sst1 =
                        new SoapSerializerTester();

            // Create a jagged array to serialize/
            // deserialize
            int[][] q = {new int[2], new int[4], new int[3]};
            q[0][0] = 4;
            q[0][1] = 7;
            q[1][0] = 15;
            q[1][1] = 72;
            q[1][2] = 6;
            q[1][3] = 167;
            q[2][0] = 1;
            q[2][1] = 90;
            q[2][2] = 659;

            // Serialize the jagged array
            if ( !sst1.Serialize("c:\\out.txt",(Object)q) )
            {
                Console.WriteLine("Failed to serialize object...");
                return;
            } // if

            int[][] r = (int[][])sst1.Deserialize("c:\\out.txt");
            if ( (Object)r == null )
            {
                Console.WriteLine("Failed to deserialize object...");
                return;
            } // if

            // Write results...
            Console.WriteLine("Result was {0}",r.ToString());
            Console.WriteLine(" [0][0] = {0}",r[0][0]);
            Console.WriteLine(" [0][1] = {0}",r[0][1]);
            Console.WriteLine(" [1][0] = {0}",r[1][0]);
            Console.WriteLine(" [1][1] = {0}",r[1][1]);
```

LISTING 4.2   Continued

```
            Console.WriteLine(" [1][2] = {0}",r[1][2]);
            Console.WriteLine(" [1][3] = {0}",r[1][3]);
            Console.WriteLine(" [2][0] = {0}",r[2][0]);
            Console.WriteLine(" [2][1] = {0}",r[2][1]);
            Console.WriteLine(" [2][2] = {0}",r[2][2]);
            Console.ReadLine();
        } // try
        catch (Exception e)
        {
            Console.WriteLine("{0}",e.Message);
        } // catch
    }
  }
}
```

If you run this code and open `out.txt`, you'll find the SOAP output shown in Listing 4.3.

LISTING 4.3   `SoapFormatter` Output SOAP XML

```
<SOAP-ENV:Envelope
  xmlns:xsi="http://www.w3.org/2001/XMLSchema-instance"
  xmlns:xsd="http://www.w3.org/2001/XMLSchema"
  xmlns:SOAP-ENC="http://schemas.xmlsoap.org/soap/encoding/"
  xmlns:SOAP-ENV="http://schemas.xmlsoap.org/soap/envelope/"
  SOAP-ENV:encodingStyle="http://schemas.xmlsoap.org/soap/encoding/"
  xmlns:a1="http://schemas.microsoft.com/clr/ns/System">
  <SOAP-ENV:Body>
    <SOAP-ENC:Array SOAP-ENC:arrayType="a1:Int32[][3]">
        <item href="#ref-2"/>
        <item href="#ref-3"/>
        <item href="#ref-4"/>
    </SOAP-ENC:Array>
    <SOAP-ENC:Array id="ref-2" SOAP-ENC:arrayType="xsd:int[2]">
        <item>4</item>
        <item>7</item>
    </SOAP-ENC:Array>
    <SOAP-ENC:Array id="ref-3" SOAP-ENC:arrayType="xsd:int[4]">
        <item>15</item>
        <item>72</item>
        <item>6</item>
        <item>167</item>
    </SOAP-ENC:Array>
    <SOAP-ENC:Array id="ref-4" SOAP-ENC:arrayType="xsd:int[3]">
        <item>1</item>
```

LISTING 4.3   Continued

```
            <item>90</item>
            <item>659</item>
        </SOAP-ENC:Array>
    </SOAP-ENV:Body>
</SOAP-ENV:Envelope>
```

The output is quite faithful to the SOAP specification! Note that the array is of type `Int32` rather than `int`, but this is a result of .NET serializing .NET datatypes. If the remote Web Service cannot handle `Int32` datatypes (or cannot map them to 32-bit integers), you might have to adjust the SOAP packet as it leaves your local machine.

.NET SOAP Framing Classes

We won't discuss all the .NET SOAP packet framing classes in great detail here. We'll save the details for Chapter 6, where you'll see a lot of code that uses those classes as you create Web Services and twiddle with the SOAP formatting without having to drop into raw XML to make changes.

> **NOTE**
>
> These classes are called *framing classes* because they support the frame, or the layout, of the SOAP packet. This is a contrast to the actual serialization classes that manage the serialization and formatting of data that is to be placed into the SOAP packet (`SoapFormatter` being one such class).

Nonetheless, Table 4.3 identifies several of the major classes and their uses within the .NET Web Service framework.

TABLE 4.3   .NET SOAP Packet Framing Classes

Class	Purpose
WebMethodAttribute	Identifies a given class method as one that is specifically anointed with Web Service status and that establishes some basic SOAP and WSDL information.
WebServiceAttribute	Identifies a given class as one that supports Web Services and that establishes some basic SOAP and WSDL information.
SoapAttribute	Provides default functionality of the SOAP-based attributes (there are several).

TABLE 4.3 Continued

Class	Purpose
SoapBinding	Allows you to tailor several aspects of the SOAP and WSDL XML, such as the SOAP and SOAP Encoding namespaces, the HTTP transport, and the WSDL binding.
SoapBodyBinding	Allows you to tailor other aspects of the SOAP and WSDL XML, such as the WSDL parts and document style (literal or rpc).
SoapExtension	Provides a point of extensibility within the .NET Web Service framework that allows you to access (and modify) the raw SOAP XML.
SoapFault	Encapsulates (and returns to the client) a SOAP fault packet.
SoapHeader	Encapsulates a given SOAP Header entry.
SoapHeaderBinding	Allows you to tailor other aspects of the SOAP and WSDL XML, such as the WSDL parts and the SOAP mustUnderstand status (true or false).
SoapMessage	Encapsulates the SOAP packet (used from within SOAP extensions).
SoapMethodAttribute	Used to tweak the SOAP XML (request and response namespaces and so on). This attribute creates literal SOAP (non–Sections 5/7 formatted). This class is related to SoapRpcMethodAttribute, which gives you the same functionality but uses the rpc WSDL document style (forces use of Sections 5/7 for SOAP serialization).

Other important SOAP classes exist, but these are the common ones that you'll most likely use when creating your .NET Web Services. You'll see these classes again in Chapter 6, where you'll use them when actually creating SOAP packets for transmission to the remote system.

Summary

This chapter's goal was to introduce you to the SOAP protocol. It began with a discussion regarding why the SOAP protocol is so important to the Web Service and the Internet as a whole. It also addressed some of the advantages that SOAP has over other proprietary protocols.

The chapter then described the SOAP XML object model and the SOAP Envelope, Header, and Body, and it described how these objects support RPC. It also mentioned that the SOAP Envelope encapsulates the (optional) Header and Body, that the Header conveys metadata that is orthogonal to the method or header fault information, and that the Body contains the serialized method information itself or body fault information.

Much of the chapter dealt with the serialization of data—how you transform binary information in the computer's memory into an XML format. We looked at serializing both simple and compound datatypes. Simple types include such things as integers, floating-point values, strings, enumerations, and dates and times. Compound values include structs and arrays.

Finally, the chapter discussed several of the .NET SOAP support classes and even provided a demonstration application program that managed to serialize a jagged array into a SOAP XML packet and then store it on disk for later recall.

The next chapter takes you through the next step. At this point, you've seen how the Web Service encodes the data for transmission, but how do you know where to send the information? What's out there that you can use? And when you discover what's available, how does that particular Web Service want the SOAP XML formatted? These and other burning questions are addressed by turning this page... .

Web Service Description and Discovery

IN THIS CHAPTER

Two significant technologies have emerged in the Web Service arena, each with a specific purpose but benefiting one another.

First and foremost is the Web Service Description Language (WSDL), an XML language that is used to describe the logical message structure, syntax, and network properties of a Web Service. Just as distributed objects or remote methods are described with IDL, you need a mechanism for describing services in such a way that clients can easily (and programmatically) determine the service's message format, available network endpoints, and supported transport protocols. This is exactly what WSDL is used for, and it does so in a layered and extensible way that allows it to adjust to changes in the Internet landscape.

The second critical technology is Universal Description, Discovery, and Integration (UDDI), a specification for using a variety of well-defined SOAP messages to publish and locate services. Simply creating the description of a service is usually not enough; publishing this description to others becomes as important to consumers of Web Services as domain name servers (DNS) are to Internet applications.

Let's take a closer look at these two important technologies.

Web Service Description Language

Since SOAP's conception, the designers planned for it to support a type system—the one they chose was XML Schema. The SOAP specification enables you to describe type information in one of two ways.

NOTE

Section 5 of the SOAP specification defines one possible way to encode SOAP messages, specifically with regard to arrays, references, structs, and so on. This plays a part in self-describing messages—information such as jagged arrays must be described within the message because you don't know the size of its contents until serialization time. A similar parallel can be drawn with polymorphic types.

The first way relies on the use of the `xsi:type` attribute within your SOAP messages. In this way, each message can be self-describing so that the receiving end understands how to interpret the message parameters and their associated types.

NOTE

Recall that the `xsi` prefix used in `xsi:type` is simply a reference to the XML Schema instance URI. You use this to annotate elements in a SOAP message with type information.

The second option enables the sender and receiver to rely on some form of schema to be referenced from an external but unspecified source (at least, as far as the SOAP specification is concerned). In this case, the sender and the receiver are interacting based on a well-defined contract of types.

Unfortunately, an XML schema alone doesn't tell you all the information that you need about a Web Service. As far as SOAP serialization is concerned, an XML schema datatype is sufficient. But other aspects to Web Services need to be addressed—thus, WSDL was created.

The Abstract and the Concrete

WSDL is an XML language that uses several layers of abstraction to describe a Web Service in a very modular way. More specifically, WSDL has a vocabulary that enables you to create independent datatype definitions, abstract message definitions, and service definitions. After they're defined, the abstractions can be bound to concrete message formats, transport protocols, and endpoints to complete the overall package.

Listing 5.1 shows a sample WSDL document used to describe a temperature service.

LISTING 5.1 Sample WSDL Document

```xml
<?xml version="1.0"?>
<definitions name="Temperature"
      targetNamespace="http://www.mcp.com/temperature.wsdl"
      xmlns:tns="http://www.mcp.com/temperature.wsdl"
      xmlns:xsd1="http://www.mcp.com/temperature.xsd"
      xmlns:soap="http://schemas.xmlsoap.org/wsdl/soap/"
      xmlns="http://schemas.xmlsoap.org/wsdl/">
  <types>
    <schema targetNamespace="http://www.mcp.com/temperature.xsd"
          xmlns="http://www.w3.org/2001/XMLSchema">
      <element name="TemperatureRequest">
        <complexType>
          <all>
            <element name="zipCode" type="int"/>
          </all>
        </complexType>
      </element>
      <element name="TemperatureResponse">
        <complexType>
          <all>
            <element name="temperature" type="int"/>
          </all>
        </complexType>
      </element>
```

LISTING 5.1   Continued

```
        </schema>
    </types>

    <message name="GetTemperatureInput">
        <part name="body" element="xsd1:TemperatureRequest"/>
    </message>
    <message name="GetTemperatureOutput">
        <part name="body" element="xsd1:TemperatureResponse"/>
    </message>

    <portType name="TemperaturePortType">
        <operation name="GetTemperature">
            <input message="tns:GetTemperatureInput"/>
            <output message="tns:GetTemperatureOutput"/>
        </operation>
    </portType>

    <binding name="TempSoapBinding" type="tns:TemperaturePortType">
        <soap:binding style="document"
                      transport="http://schemas.xmlsoap.org/soap/http"/>
        <operation name="GetTemperature">
            <soap:operation soapAction="http://www.mcp.com/GetTemperature"/>
            <input>
                <soap:body use="literal"
                      namespace="http://www.mcp.com/temperature.xsd"
                      encodingStyle="http://schemas.xmlsoap.org/soap/encoding/"/>
            </input>
            <output>
                <soap:body use="literal"
                      namespace="http://www.mcp.com/temperature.xsd"
                      encodingStyle="http://schemas.xmlsoap.org/soap/encoding/"/>
            </output>
        </operation>
    </binding>

    <service name="TemperatureService">
        <documentation>Get your current temperature</documentation>
        <port name="TemperaturePort" binding="tns:TempSoapBinding">
            <soap:address location="http://www.mcp.com/temperature.temp.asmx"/>
        </port>
    </service>
</definitions>
```

The basic idea behind this service is to allow a client to provide a ZIP code and receive the current air temperature for that region.

Although the service is simple, the representative WSDL description is somewhat verbose. At first, this verbosity of markup might be somewhat intimidating, but a closer look reveals that WSDL was designed for extensibility and modularity, with less emphasis on human consumption. But don't get the impression that WSDL is strictly for programmatic use. In fact, when you understand the major structures and how they tie together, you will be able to quickly assimilate just about any service description.

Definitions

WSDL uses the `<definition>` root element as a container for all the abstract and concrete definitions used to describe a service. The following snippet shows the root `<definitions>` element and XML namespace declarations used in Listing 5.1.

```
<?xml version="1.0"?>
<definitions name="Temperature"
        targetNamespace="http://www.mcp.com/temperature.wsdl"
        xmlns:tns="http://www.mcp.com/temperature.wsdl"
        xmlns:xsd1="http://www.mcp.com/temperature.xsd"
        xmlns:soap="http://schemas.xmlsoap.org/wsdl/soap/"
        xmlns="http://schemas.xmlsoap.org/wsdl/">
```

Notice that WSDL enables you to optionally specify a definition name as well as a `targetNamespace`. In this case, the target namespace is `http://www.mcp.com/temperature.wsdl`, which is also associated with the namespace prefix `tns` (sometimes referred to as *this namespace*) to qualify properties of this service definition. The WSDL namespace, `http://schemas.xmlsoap.org/wsdl/`, is set as the default namespace and thus applies to all unqualified elements.

> **NOTE**
>
> The `targetNamespace` attribute carries the same semantic meaning as defined in the XML Schema specification. Refer to Appendix D, ".NET Web Service Resources," for more information about XML Schema.

Other namespaces that are used include the SOAP extensions for WSDL (`http://schemas.xmlsoap.org/wsdl/soap/`) and, finally, the namespace referencing the XML schema containing the temperature service type definitions (`http://www.mcp.com/temperature.xsd`).

> **NOTE**
>
> Recall that the namespace prefixes that are used are used only to associate an element or attribute with a URI. For instance, some examples use the tns prefix to reference a WSDL document, while other examples use the s0 prefix as generated by Visual Studio .NET. The prefix name isn't important, but its associated URI is.

Types

The <types> element is used to contain schemas or external references to schemas that describe the datatype definitions used within the WSDL document. WSDL uses XML Schema (XSD) as its standard form of type definition; however, one of the extensibility features of WSDL allows for other schema languages to be utilized. At this time, though, it is strongly recommended that you use the XML Schema language for the following reasons:

- XML Schema provides a rich language for defining types using polymorphism, regular expressions, facets, and so on.

- XML Schema has strong industry support, including a growing set of publicly available tools for reading and creating XML schemas.

- XML Schema is the preferred type mechanism for SOAP.

WSDL enables you to optionally specify up to one <types> section within a Web Service description. Within this section, you can describe as many schemas as you want. You also can exclude the schemas altogether and simply reference external schemas as described later in this section.

As previously noted, WSDL uses abstractions to provide you with greater flexibility and reuse when defining services. The types that you define in WSDL are abstract descriptions of messages that can be serialized on the network. Sometimes these types map directly to the actual message format (how it is serialized on the wire), and other times they just represent the *idea* behind the message, not necessarily matching any form of serialization.

Because of this, when simply looking at the schema of a message, you cannot be sure how it will be represented on the wire. This determination can be made only at the point that the message is physically serialized to the network, based on binding information provided elsewhere in the service description.

As an example, consider the types from Listing 5.1:

```
<types>
    <schema targetNamespace="http://www.mcp.com/temperature.xsd"
        xmlns="http://www.w3.org/2001/XMLSchema">
```

```
        <element name="TemperatureRequest">
          <complexType>
            <all>
              <element name="zipCode" type="int"/>
            </all>
          </complexType>
        </element>
        <element name="TemperatureResponse">
          <complexType>
            <all>
              <element name="temperature" type="int"/>
            </all>
          </complexType>
        </element>
      </schema>
</types>
```

In this case, the request message `TemperatureRequest` could be serialized as an
HTTP `GET` request using an encoded URL such as `http://www.mcp.com/`
`TemperatureRequest?zipCode=12345`. Or, the request could be serialized as a SOAP
request using the literal XSD layout:

```
<SOAP-ENV:Envelope
      xmlns:SOAP-ENV="http://schemas.xmlsoap.org/soap/envelope/">
   <SOAP-ENV:Body>
      <TemperatureRequest xmlns="http://www.mcp.com/temperature.xsd">
         <zipCode>12345</zipCode>
      </TemperatureRequest>
   </SOAP-ENV:Body>
</SOAP-ENV:Envelope>
```

Or, even further, the request could be serialized as a SOAP request using the SOAP encoding
constructs (in this case, using the `xsi:type` identification):

```
<SOAP-ENV:Envelope
      xmlns:SOAP-ENV="http://schemas.xmlsoap.org/soap/envelope/"
      xmlns:xsd="http://www.w3.org/2001/XMLSchema"
      xmlns:xsi="http://www.w3.org/2001/XMLSchema-instance">
   <SOAP-ENV:Body
         SOAP-ENV:encodingStyle="http://schemas.xmlsoap.org/soap/encoding/">
      <m:TemperatureRequest xmlns:m="http://www.mcp.com/temperature.xsd">
         <zipCode xsi:type="xsd:int">12345</zipCode>
      </m:TemperatureRequest>
   </SOAP-ENV:Body>
</SOAP-ENV:Envelope>
```

In each example, the same logical information is communicated, but we've used completely
different syntactical or concrete representations.

5

WEB SERVICE DESCRIPTION AND DISCOVERY

As you will see later in this section, proper organization of the service definitions will enable you to define your abstract types once and then use them for defining one or more concrete messages across multiple WSDL files.

After you have defined the appropriate types for your messages, the next step is to lay out your message structure.

Messages

Messages are abstract collections of typed information cast upon one or more logical units, used to communicate information between systems. In other words, a message can be broken into smaller *parts*, with each part representing an instance of a particular type.

Consider the following Web method that uses the RPC form of a SOAP message:

```
[WebMethod()]
[System.Web.Services.Protocols.SoapRpcMethod()]
public float Divide(int numerator, int denominator)
{
  return ((float)numerator)/denominator;
}
```

The associated WSDL `DivideSoapIn` message shows the two separate numerator and denominator parts:

```
<message name="DivideSoapIn">
  <part name="numerator" type="xsd:int" />
  <part name="denominator" type="xsd:int" />
</message>
```

In the case of RPC-like serialization, a message consists of one or more message parts and uses the `type` attribute to reference a particular type:

```
<message name="DivideRequest">
  <part name="numerator" type="xsd:int"/>
  <part name="denominator" type="xsd:int"/>
</message>
```

The second approach to defining messages and their parts is to construct the entire message as one large part, as found when using SOAP for message-based purposes:

```
[WebMethod()]
public float Divide(int numerator, int denominator)
{
  return ((float)numerator)/denominator;
}
```

This results in the following WSDL:

```
<message name="DivideSoapIn">
    <part name="parameters" element="tns:Divide" />
</message>
```

Here, `tns:Divide` is a type that has been defined as follows:

```
<xsd:element name="Divide">
  <xsd:complexType>
    <xsd:sequence>
      <xsd:element minOccurs="1" maxOccurs="1" name="numerator"
                   type="xsd:int" />
      <xsd:element minOccurs="1" maxOccurs="1" name="denominator"
                   type="xsd:int" />
    </xsd:sequence>
  </xsd:complexType>
</xsd:element>
```

In this case, the `Divide` element is defined in the schema and is referenced through the use of an `element` attribute on the message `<part>`.

Types that you reference can exist in three main locations:

- Service definition's `<types>` section
- XML Schema datatypes schema (for example, `xsd:int`)
- Other XML Schema files

For simple Web Services that use RPC, the most commonly used types (simple types) will be referenced from XSD. However, as Web Services become increasingly more complex, message-based SOAP will be more appropriate, thus suggesting that complex schemas will be created. The choice of whether schemas will be directly incorporated inside a WSDL document or imported depends on the likelihood that someone will want to reuse a particular type.

Visual Studio .NET generates multiple definitions of messages for your service, one for each protocol—SOAP, HTTP GET, and HTTP POST. In some cases, these messages contain the exact same information (with the exception of the `name` attribute). This will happen when the logical parts of each message are of simple types and the SOAP message is treated as an RPC method.

At this point, you have messages with one or more parts that reference type information. The next step is to associate these messages with logical operations for your Web Service.

Operations

By definition, a Web Service exposes one or more operations that a service requestor might want to execute. WSDL uses the `<operation>` element to define abstract actions or verbs that a client can request from the service provider.

Notice that the WSDL-defined `<operation>` element should not be confused with the `<binding>`'s `<operation>` element or SOAP's extension of WSDL that also uses an `<operation>` element. These will be covered later in this section.

Operations can be used in a Web Service in four fundamental ways (or patterns):

- Request/response
- Solicit/response
- One-way
- Notification

The first two patterns are basically the same, differing only by who instigates the call. In the request/response pattern, a client requests that some action be taken from a particular service provider. Obviously, this is the typical way that Web Services will be used in the foreseeable future, mostly because current infrastructures are better designed for this kind of interaction.

The solicit/response model is initiated by the service provider, which expects a response from a client. You might see this pattern used in the same way that callback functions are used in standard programming practices, especially in an intranet or server farm model. This approach is less likely to be used for Internet clients, at least with HTTP, because most clients have no means of receiving requests from outside their firewall. It's possible that this type of implementation might become popular if interest in the SMTP transport protocol grows.

In both the request/response and solicit/response cases, the caller expects a response message or a fault message. Recall that, when using SOAP, you may only have a response or a fault message, but not both.

The last two patterns parallel the first two, in that they differ only by the endpoint that instigates the originating call. In the case of a one-way message, the client sends a message to the service provider in a fire-and-forget manner, expecting no response. An example of this might be motion sensors in a security system. Upon activation, each sensor sends a message to a central monitoring station that triggers an alarm.

In this scenario, the sensor doesn't care if its message ever arrived at the monitoring station because there's probably nothing more that it can do about the intrusion. On the other hand, the monitoring station might question why it hasn't received a message from the sensor for some period of time. This lack of interaction might cause the alarm to be sounded for fear of system tampering.

In the notification pattern, the service provider sends a fire-and-forget message to a client, expecting no response. This type of messaging is used by services that want to notify clients of events. An example might be a control unit in a car dashboard. The temperature gauge, speedometer, and tachometer could all be driven by independent messages sent by the control unit. This is analogous to the *publish and subscribe* model, in which the control unit publishes all the events that it makes available. Then each gauge subscribes to those events that it wants to display.

It's also possible that a service might want to offer more than one operation pattern, based on the type of operation that the service is exposing. For instance, a stock quote service might offer a registration operation that allows clients to subscribe to particular ticker symbols. This type of operation would probably use the request/response pattern.

Then, at periodic intervals throughout the day, the service could send the client updated stock information. This could be patterned after the notification operation because it probably isn't imperative that the service know whether the client actually received the information.

Listings 5.2–5.5 show sample operations that represent the four patterns.

LISTING 5.2   Request/Response Operation

```
<operation name="SubscribeStock">
  <input message="tns:SubscribeStockSoapIn" />
  <output message="tns:SubscribeStockSoapOut" />
  <fault name="faultone" message="tns:SubscribeStockSoapOneFault" />
  <fault name="faulttwo" message="tns:SubscribeStockSoapTwoFault" />
</operation>
```

LISTING 5.3   Solicit/Response Operation

```
<operation name="Callback">
  <output message="tns:CallbackSoapOut" />
  <input message="tns:CallbackSoapIn" />
  <fault name="faultone" message="tns:CallbackOneSoapFault" />
</operation>
```

LISTING 5.4   One-Way Operation

```
<operation name="TriggerAlarm">
  <input message="tns:TriggerAlarmSoapIn" />
</operation>
```

LISTING 5.5   Notification Operation

```
<operation name="AdjustSpeedometer">
  <output message="tns:AdjustSpeedometerSoapOut" />
</operation>
```

As you've seen, operations are used to organize input and output messages to orchestrate the communication between systems. An additional level of organization takes place, in which operations are collected to form a *port type*.

> **NOTE**
>
> The optional name attribute that is associated with each input and output message is used to uniquely identify messages within a particular port type. Default names are automatically assumed for input and output messages that do not explicitly provide a name.
>
> Fault message names must be unique only within the scope of the given operation.

Port Types

Port types are nothing more than a named set of operations. The port type is used to bind the collection of logical operations to an actual transport protocol (such as SOAP).

For example, a calculator service might have the following port type definition (where the s0 namespace prefix references the target namespace) as shown in Listing 5.6.

LISTING 5.6 Port Type Definition

```
<portType name="CalculatorSoap">
  <operation name="Add">
    <input message="s0:AddSoapIn" />
    <output message="s0:AddSoapOut" />
  </operation>
  <operation name="Subtract">
    <input message="s0:SubtractSoapIn" />
    <output message="s0:SubtractSoapOut" />
  </operation>
  <operation name="Multiply">
    <input message="s0:MultiplySoapIn" />
    <output message="s0:MultiplySoapOut" />
  </operation>
  <operation name="Divide">
    <input message="s0:DivideSoapIn" />
    <output message="s0:DivideSoapOut" />
  </operation>
</portType>
```

> **NOTE**
>
> The mandatory `name` attribute that is associated with each `portType` provides unique `portType` identification within the WSDL document.

If you look at the WSDL that Visual Studio .NET generates for your service, you will notice that a `portType` is created to accommodate each of three protocols—SOAP, HTTP `GET`, and HTTP `POST`. This is because different messages are created for each protocol as well. These messages are indirectly associated with the port type through their respective operations.

For the aforementioned groups of operations to be associated with a particular protocol, a *binding* must be used. The next section discusses these.

Bindings

Bindings enable you to associate port types to the actual transport protocols that are used to carry your messages. In the case of the calculator service, you will see in Listing 5.7 that the binding applies a `type="s0:CalculatorSoap"` to qualify it with the previously defined port type.

LISTING 5.7   Binding Definition

```
<binding name="CalculatorSoap" type="s0:CalculatorSoap">
  <soap:binding transport="http://schemas.xmlsoap.org/soap/http"
                style="document" />
  <operation name="Add">
    <soap:operation soapAction="http://tempuri.org/Add" style="document" />
    <input>
      <soap:body use="literal" />
    </input>
    <output>
      <soap:body use="literal" />
    </output>
  </operation>

  <!-- etc... -->

  <operation name="Divide">
    <soap:operation soapAction="http://tempuri.org/Divide" style="document" />
    <input>
      <soap:body use="literal" />
    </input>
    <output>
      <soap:body use="literal" />
```

LISTING 5.7   Continued

```
    </output>
  </operation>
</binding>
```

> **NOTE**
>
> Both name and type are mandatory fields for the binding. The name uniquely identi-
> fies the binding within the WSDL document.

WSDL defines several *extensibility elements* that allow additional information to be injected
into a service description.

In the case of SOAP, the `<binding>` element is required for you to specify the type of transport
being used and the style of SOAP serialization that will be applied:

```
<soap:binding transport="http://schemas.xmlsoap.org/soap/http"
              style="document" />
```

The `style` attribute denotes either the RPC-based or the document-based forms. When using
the `rpc` style with SOAP encoding, you should expect to see the message `<parts>` using the
`type` attribute. There is also an assumed return value for any RPC-based usage, per the SOAP
specification.

In the document-based form, where `style` is set to `document`, standard schema messages are
expected and no semantics concerning return values are implied.

In either case, the `style` attribute acts as the default behavior for operations that are contained
within the binding. However, each operation has the option of overriding this value.

As you might expect, protocols other than SOAP can extend the binding information as well.
For example, the HTTP `GET` protocol would specify this:

```
<http:binding verb="GET" />
```

As already mentioned, a binding contains `<operation>` elements that enable you to provide
more specific details about a particular operation. For instance, some SOAP implementations
(other than .NET) might require very specific use of the `SOAPAction` HTTP header field to
properly process a request. The `<soap:operation>` element enables you to denote a `soapAction`
as well as the specific `style` of messaging that it needs. Recall that you can specify either `rpc`
or `document` styles.

Another extensibility element used for SOAP is that of the `<soap:body>` element. We've already covered how messages can consist of one or more message parts. The `<soap:body>` element lets you specify how those message parts should appear in the `<Body>` of the serialized SOAP request or response.

An optional `parts` attribute on `<soap:body>` exists that is used to denote where certain portions of the message are located within the serialized message. Unless you are using a transport protocol (such as multipart/related MIME) that breaks a message body into multiple parts, you may omit this attribute, which implies that all parts exist in a single message.

The `use` attribute denotes whether the message body will use `literal` or `encoded` encoding. With `literal` encoding, the datatype that the message part references will be serialized according to its exact representation in the type definition (that is, the schema). This means that the schema could be used to validate an instance of each individual message part. When using the `encoded` form, the additional `encodingStyle` attribute is used to denote the specific way that the message is serialized. For instance, SOAP messages that follow the SOAP specification's Section 5 encoding style would reference the `http://schemas.xmlsoap.org/soap/encoding/` URI. Again, the encoded form will need to be used only when applying the `System.Web.Services.Protocols.SoapRpcMethod()` Web method attribute to your .NET code.

Although bindings bring together the abstract messages with the concrete protocols used to serialize those messages, a few minor details still haven't been nailed down. This is where `<port>`s and `<service>`s close the loop in the WSDL definition.

Ports

Ports are very simple; they define the address location where a binding can be found. Consider the following example:

```
<port name="CalculatorSoap" binding="s0:CalculatorSoap">
  <soap:address location="http://www.mcp.com/Calculator/Calculator.asmx" />
</port>
```

As you can see, the port links the binding just described to an address that is defined by an extensibility element—in this case, `<soap:address>`. Here, a mandatory location URI must be provided to denote the physical endpoint that clients must use to connect to the service.

NOTE

The location that you specify in the address contains an explicit transport protocol reference (such as `http:`) that should be compatible with the transport protocol URI that you specified in your binding. In other words, if you are using an HTTP transport protocol, your location had better be HTTP or HTTPS.

Services

Finally, we are at the last portion of the WSDL document, the `<service>` element. Because each Web Service may support multiple bindings (one for SOAP, one for HTTP GET, and so on), you should expect a single service to contain a collection of ports as shown in Listing 5.8.

LISTING 5.8 Service Definition

```
<service name="Calculator">
  <port name="CalculatorSoap" binding="s0:CalculatorSoap">
    <soap:address location="http://www.mcp.com/Calculator/Calculator.asmx" />
  </port>
  <port name="CalculatorHttpGet" binding="s0:CalculatorHttpGet">
    <http:address location="http://www.mcp.com/Calculator/Calculator.asmx" />
  </port>
  <port name="CalculatorHttpPost" binding="s0:CalculatorHttpPost">
    <http:address location="http://www.mcp.com/Calculator/Calculator.asmx" />
  </port>
</service>
```

This has the semantic equivalent of stating that the calculator service is accessible through SOAP, HTTP GET, and HTTP POST. And it's up to the client to decide which port to use. Therefore, as the developer of a Web Service, you should make sure that your service provides the same functionality and semantics, regardless of the port that is used.

In the case of .NET, a single entry point (Calculator.asmx) can respond to all three types of message formats (SOAP, HTTP GET, and HTTP POST). However, there is no requirement that these all be the same—in some cases, they will not be the same.

Imports

We mentioned earlier that WSDL enables you to create modular WSDL documents by separating the abstract messages from the other portions of the document.

You may specify zero or more `<import>` elements in your WSDL document, to incorporate external definitions. Two attributes are required for you to do this. The first is the `namespace` attribute, which enables you to establish a namespace for your incoming definitions. The second is the `location` attribute, which specifies the exact location of the WSDL to be imported.

Proper use of this construct enables you to create WSDL documents that contain only type information. You then can import those datatypes into one or more separate WSDL files, to reuse the type definitions. The import feature is not limited to datatypes, so other definitions can be modularized:

- Datatypes

- Messages
- portTypes
- Bindings
- Services
- Extended language definitions

Parsing WSDL

By this point, you might be overwhelmed with the number of details that are associated with WSDL documents. Yet, without some of this complexity, it would be difficult for WSDL to accommodate every possible way that someone might create a Web Service.

If you need to programmatically operate on WSDL documents, some tools will make things a little easier on you. The Microsoft .NET Framework Class Library contains all the necessary types for you to create and format a WSDL document. The System.Web.Service.Description namespace is the first piece in the WSDL puzzle.

Consider the following C# code fragment:

```
ServiceDescription desc = ServiceDescription.Read("c:\\Calculator.wsdl");
MessagePart part = desc.Messages[0].Parts[0];

MessageBox.Show(part.Name.ToString());
MessageBox.Show(part.Element.Name.ToString());
```

This simple example reads the Calculator.wsdl file using the static Read method on the ServiceDescription type. After the service description is loaded and the ServiceDescription object model is populated, you can begin to iterate over the individual pieces of the document.

In the case of this example, the first message part is located and its associated name and element type are displayed.

The Client's Point of View

We've focused a lot on how you create WSDL documents, but we haven't discussed how service requestors use the WSDL to learn about your service.

In most cases, clients want to view your WSDL document starting with the <service> element and working backward through the definitions.

A client starts by evaluating the services that are being described by this WSDL document. Assuming that the desired service exists (by inspecting the <service> element's name), the client can proceed to analyze the potential ports that it might choose to use.

However, the `<port>` element alone doesn't provide enough information for a client to programmatically determine which port to use. This is because clients might be looking for specific transport protocol support, the serialization method, or other related parameters.

Therefore, the client must inspect each binding that has been associated with a port, to find a transport that the client is willing to work with. At this point, the client might need to further qualify the service by navigating deeper into the object model, possibly to determine what serialization model the service uses.

For clients using Visual Studio .NET, the typical process of parsing and working with WSDL is fairly simple. As you saw in Chapter 1, "Web Service Fundamentals," by adding a *Web reference* to your project, .NET takes a snapshot of the WSDL document, by default, and provides you with a copy that is used to interact with the given service.

This brings up an interesting topic—how do you find a Web Service in the first place? Certainly, if you're developing a service or working with someone who's developing a service, the answer is simple. But if you are in the market for a service and don't quite know where to find one, then UDDI is the solution.

Universal Description, Discovery, and Integration

Before a consumer can begin using a Web Service, he must be able to locate that service. This problem has been solved many times under similar paradigms. For example, consider DNS, which is programmatically queried to resolve domain names to IP addresses. Another example, but one that requires manual intervention, is that of a Web search engine. With Web search engines, the obvious goal is to find Web sites that contain content or metadata that matches your search terms. UDDI has this same basic intent and purpose, but it is used for discovering Web Services.

What Is UDDI?

Like most of the technologies described in this book, UDDI is just a specification. But the ideas behind UDDI will have a significant impact on the way you distribute information about Web Services.

Originally, UDDI was promoted as a public repository for Web Service information. Although this is still the case, there are many good reasons why you might want to offer a private UDDI registry for your internal organization use. Not only does this promote service reuse, but it also can act as a single point where service documentation is guaranteed to exist.

UDDI uses the notion of an *operator site* to act as a repository for Web Service information. Operator sites are just implementations of the UDDI specification, potentially hosted on a diverse array of systems. A collection of operator sites offers a Web-based registry for locating just about any published Web Service. More specifically, the registries contain information about a company and its publicly exposed interfaces.

Although these sites generally are designed to be interrogated with the UDDI SOAP interfaces, companies such as IBM and Microsoft have also provided Web pages that provide a user interface to their respective UDDI registries. This just makes it easier for users to manually inspect the registry without requiring a separate client application.

Currently, UDDI is one of the few large-scale Web Service applications in existence today, which means that you can learn a great deal from the UDDI approach and its various implementations.

How UDDI Works

UDDI promotes the *publish*, *find*, and *bind* usage pattern shown in Figure 5.1. In this model, service providers are responsible for publishing information about their Web Service to the registry. Service requestors, on the other hand, can query the registry to find a service that is applicable to their needs. Finally, after a service has been located in the registry, the service requestor can bind to the service and begin using it.

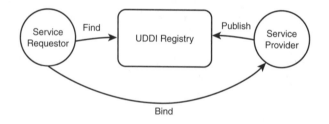

FIGURE 5.1
UDDI's Publish, Find, and Bind model.

One of the most interesting properties of UDDI is that it is one of the first publicly available specifications to utilize SOAP. The UDDI 1.0 specification was released in September 2000, and, more recently, the UDDI 2.0 specification was released in June 2001. Although UDDI does not incorporate all aspects of the SOAP v1.1 specification (such as the serialization model), it uses the same basic Envelope/Body messaging model.

In particular, UDDI has the following properties:

- The SOAP Envelope/Body model is followed, but SOAP Headers are not supported. Any requests that contain SOAP Headers may be processed, with the Headers simply being ignored. However, if a Header entry contains the mustUnderstand attribute, the request will be rejected because the server cannot uphold the mustUnderstand stipulation as defined in SOAP v1.1.

- SOAPAction must contain an empty string surrounded by double quotes.
- SOAP actors are not supported, so any request that contains SOAP Headers with the actor attribute will be rejected.
- The standard SOAP encoding mechanism (Section 5 of the SOAP v1.1 specification) is not supported. UDDI requests must use structure as depicted in the UDDI specification. Any requests that contain an encodingStyle attribute will be rejected.
- Default namespaces may be used to qualify elements contained within the Body of a message.

NOTE

Section 5 of the SOAP specification allows certain elements (such as those contained in a compound type such as a struct) to be represented as unqualified elements. These elements must have no associated namespace, which makes using default namespaces slightly more complicated.

There were many reasons behind why UDDI took this approach, mostly related to performance. Because UDDI was one of the first major Web Services, its designers wanted to ensure that implementations of UDDI could withstand high usage.

For UDDI to ensure that correct and secure information is stored in and retrieved from its repository, a security model was put in place.

UDDI and Security

UDDI supports both inquiry and publisher interfaces, so operator sites are required to implement an authentication scheme to protect published information. Users must sign up with the operator site to establish appropriate credentials before using the secured interfaces. This requires users to follow manual procedures (outside the UDDI API) to acquire an account.

General querying of the UDDI registry can be performed across a standard HTTP connection. However, if you intend to publish information, you currently are required to use SSL.

In addition, authentication tokens are used to maintain authenticated access to the registry. Because each operator site generates its own tokens, you should avoid trying to use these tokens across different implementations. In other words, if you authenticate against operator site A, don't try to get operator site B to accept site A's token.

One of the most fundamental concepts behind UDDI and its implementation is that of the tModel.

tModels

A tModel identifies the specifications and versions of the specifications that your Web Service conforms to. Among its several purposes, this primarily aids service requestors in locating compatible interfaces that can be integrated into their applications.

To uniquely identify tModels, a tModelKey that is represented by a universally unique identifier (UUID) is used. UDDI also employs the use of a businessKey, serviceKey, and bindingKey to identify business, service, and binding data respectively.

You can relate this approach to finding a COM object in the Windows registry. Given a UUID (or GUID if you prefer), you can find a particular implementation.

You can locate information in a repository in several ways, and three query patterns have been provided.

Query Patterns

The UDDI API provides three patterns for finding information in the repository. The first is the *browse* pattern (denoted by the operations beginning with `find_`), which allows you to search the registry for specific information such as tModelKeys, as seen in `find_binding`.

The second pattern is called *drilldown* and can be recognized by the `get_` prefix. Assuming that you found some pertinent information with the browse pattern, you can then drill down to find additional details.

Finally, the *invocation* pattern allows a client to use the binding information stored in the UDDI repository, to contact the Web Service. Once located, the binding information is cached and reused until the service changes locations. At this point, the UDDI registry can again be consulted, and new binding information can be used to contact the service again.

Let's take a closer look at these patterns.

Browsing

UDDI defines a query pattern for browsing registry data based on simple query principles. These queries include the following:

- `find_binding`
- `find_business`
- `find_service`
- `find_tModel`

Consider the XML Schema fragments for the `find_binding` message, as shown in Listing 5.9.

LISTING 5.9 find_binding XML Schema

```
<xsd:element name="find_binding" type="uddi:FindBinding" />
<xsd:complexType name="FindBinding">
  <xsd:sequence>
    <xsd:element minOccurs="0" maxOccurs="1" name="findQualifiers"
                 type="uddi:FindQualifiers" />
    <xsd:element minOccurs="1" maxOccurs="1" name="tModelBag"
                 type="uddi:TModelBag" />
  </xsd:sequence>
  <xsd:attribute name="generic" type="xsd:string" use="required" />
  <xsd:attribute name="maxRows" type="xsd:int" use="optional" />
  <xsd:attribute name="serviceKey" type="xsd:string" use="required" />
</xsd:complexType>

<xsd:complexType name="FindQualifiers">
  <xsd:sequence>
    <xsd:element minOccurs="0" maxOccurs="unbounded" name="findQualifier"
                 type="xsd:string" />
  </xsd:sequence>
</xsd:complexType>

<xsd:complexType name="TModelBag">
  <xsd:sequence>
    <xsd:element minOccurs="1" maxOccurs="unbounded" name="tModelKey"
                 type="xsd:string" />
  </xsd:sequence>
</xsd:complexType>
```

Given this as the base message structure, you should notice that the findQualifiers are completely optional. If they are not provided in the message, the following default qualifiers will be used:

- Left-most name-match behavior
- Case-insensitive matching
- Sorting by ascending names (primary sort order)
- Sorting by descending dates (secondary sort order)

A tModelBag (or any other xxxBag, for that matter) is simply a collection or list. In this case, it's a list of tModelKeys.

You should also notice that both generic and serviceKey are mandatory fields, so your search will automatically be limited by the given service key.

The `find_service` message schema, as shown in Listing 5.10, shows how the categoryBag and tModelBag structures are used to provide multiple (logically ANDed) terms.

LISTING 5.10 `find_service` XML Schema

```
<xsd:element name="find_service" type="uddi:FindService" />
<xsd:complexType name="FindService">
  <xsd:sequence>
    <xsd:element minOccurs="0" maxOccurs="1" name="findQualifiers"
                 type="uddi:FindQualifiers" />
    <xsd:element minOccurs="0" maxOccurs="1" name="name" type="xsd:string" />
    <xsd:element minOccurs="0" maxOccurs="1" name="categoryBag"
                 type="uddi:CategoryBag"/>
    <xsd:element minOccurs="0" maxOccurs="1" name="tModelBag"
                 type="uddi:TModelBag" />
  </xsd:sequence>
  <xsd:attribute name="generic" type="xsd:string" use="required" />
  <xsd:attribute name="maxRows" type="xsd:int" use="optional" />
  <xsd:attribute name="businessKey" type="xsd:string" use="required" />
</xsd:complexType>

<xsd:complexType name="CategoryBag">
  <xsd:sequence>
    <xsd:element minOccurs="0" maxOccurs="unbounded" name="keyedReference"
                 type="uddi:KeyedReference" />
  </xsd:sequence>
</xsd:complexType>
```

Listings 5.11 and 5.12 show sample calls for the `find_binding` and `find_service` queries, respectively.

> **NOTE**
>
> The following UUIDs have been generated for example only and do not represent actual keys in the UDDI registry.

LISTING 5.11 Sample `find_binding` Query

```
<SOAP-ENV:Envelope
     xmlns:SOAP-ENV="http://schemas.xmlsoap.org/soap/envelope/">
  <SOAP-ENV:Body>
    <find_binding serviceKey="D9F9C0E1-C286-11d4-AC39-000000000000"
          generic="1.0" maxRows="3"
```

LISTING 5.11 Continued

```
            xmlns="urn:uddi-org:api">
        <findQualifiers>
          <findQualifier>caseSensitiveMatch</findQualifier>
          <findQualifier>sortByNameAsc</findQualifier>
        </findQualifiers>
        <tModelBag>
          <tModel>uddi:7711A981-C287-11d4-AC39-000000000000</tModel>
        </tModelBag>
      </find_binding>
    </SOAP-ENV:Body>
</SOAP-ENV:Envelope>
```

LISTING 5.12 Sample `find_service` Query

```
<SOAP-ENV:Envelope
      xmlns:SOAP-ENV="http://schemas.xmlsoap.org/soap/envelope/">
    <SOAP-ENV:Body>
      <find_service businessKey="D9F9C0E1-C286-11d4-AC39-000000000000"
            generic="1.0" xmlns="urn:uddi-org:api">
        <findQualifiers>
          <findQualifier>sortByNameDesc</findQualifier>
        </findQualifiers>
        <name>temperature</name>
      </find_service>
    </SOAP-ENV:Body>
</SOAP-ENV:Envelope>
```

By using a few simplesearch terms, you can locate enough service information to proceed to the drill-down step.

Drilling Down

After you have discovered your intended key, most likely by using one of the browse calls, you can get more detailed information about the key by using one of the following drill-down methods:

- `get_bindingDetail`
- `get_businessDetail`
- `get_businessDetailExt`
- `get_serviceDetail`
- `get_tModelDetail`

Although their names are really self-describing, let's take a closer look at a few of these methods.

Consider the `get_serviceDetail` example, as shown in Listing 5.13.

LISTING 5.13 Sample `get_serviceDetail` Query

```
<SOAP-ENV:Envelope
    xmlns:SOAP-ENV="http://schemas.xmlsoap.org/soap/envelope/">
  <SOAP-ENV:Body>
    <get_serviceDetail generic="1.0" xmlns="urn:uddi-org:api">
      <serviceKey>D9F9C0E1-C286-11d4-AC39-000000000000</serviceKey>
      <serviceKey>A9F9C0E1-C286-11d4-AC39-000000000000</serviceKey>
    </get_serviceDetail>
  </SOAP-ENV:Body>
</SOAP-ENV:Envelope>
```

Here, you will receive the `serviceDetail` information as described by the schema in Listing 5.14.

LISTING 5.14 `serviceDetail` Structure

```
<xsd:element name="serviceDetail" type="uddi:ServiceDetail" />
<xsd:complexType name="ServiceDetail">
  <xsd:sequence>
    <xsd:element minOccurs="0" maxOccurs="unbounded" name="businessService"
                 type="uddi:BusinessService"/>
  </xsd:sequence>
  <xsd:attribute name="generic" type="xsd:string" use="required" />
  <xsd:attribute name="operator" type="xsd:string" use="required" />
  <xsd:attribute name="truncated" type="uddi:Truncated" use="optional" />
</xsd:complexType>

<xsd:simpleType name="Truncated">
  <xsd:restriction base="xsd:string">
    <xsd:enumeration value="true" />
    <xsd:enumeration value="false" />
  </xsd:restriction>
</xsd:simpleType>
```

Each drill-down operation returns an `xxxDetail` structure that contains the specific information for that particular aspect of the service. The one other detail information that you should see involves the invocation pattern.

Invoking

Upon calling the get_binding operation and receiving the bindingDetail structure, you can dissect the one or more associated bindingTemplates contained within, as described by the schema in Listing 5.15.

LISTING 5.15   bindingDetail Structure

```
<xsd:element name="bindingDetail" type="uddi:BindingDetail" />
<xsd:complexType name="BindingDetail">
  <xsd:sequence>
    <xsd:element minOccurs="0" maxOccurs="unbounded" name="bindingTemplate"
                 type="uddi:BindingTemplate" />
  </xsd:sequence>
  <xsd:attribute name="generic" type="xsd:string" use="required" />
  <xsd:attribute name="operator" type="xsd:string" use="required" />
  <xsd:attribute name="truncated" type="uddi:Truncated" use="optional" />
</xsd:complexType>

<xsd:complexType name="BindingTemplate">
  <xsd:sequence>
    <xsd:element minOccurs="0" maxOccurs="unbounded" name="description"
                 type="uddi:Description" />
    <xsd:choice minOccurs="1" maxOccurs="1">
      <xsd:element name="accessPoint" type="uddi:AccessPoint" />
      <xsd:element name="hostingRedirector" type="uddi:HostingRedirector" />
    </xsd:choice>
    <xsd:element minOccurs="1" maxOccurs="1" name="tModelInstanceDetails"
                 type="uddi:TModelInstanceDetails" />
  </xsd:sequence>
  <xsd:attribute name="serviceKey" type="xsd:string" use="optional" />
  <xsd:attribute name="bindingKey" type="xsd:string" use="required" />
</xsd:complexType>

<xsd:complexType name="AccessPoint" mixed="true">
  <xsd:attribute name="URLType" type="uddi:URLType" use="required" />
</xsd:complexType>

<xsd:simpleType name="URLType">
  <xsd:restriction base="xsd:string">
    <xsd:enumeration value="mailto" />
    <xsd:enumeration value="http" />
    <xsd:enumeration value="https" />
    <xsd:enumeration value="ftp" />
    <xsd:enumeration value="fax" />
    <xsd:enumeration value="phone" />
```

LISTING 5.15   Continued

```
    <xsd:enumeration value="other" />
  </xsd:restriction>
</xsd:simpleType>

<xsd:complexType name="HostingRedirector">
  <xsd:attribute name="bindingKey" type="xsd:string" use="required" />
</xsd:complexType>
```

The `accessPoint` is used as an address to the Web Service, such as a URL or an email address. If no `accessPoint` is provided, a `hostingRedirector` can be provided to point you to another `bindingTemplate` that should contain an address.

Now that you understand how to query and locate a Web Service, consider how a service may be published to the UDDI registry.

Publishing

Rather than cover each operation in gory detail, you've gathered enough of a basic understanding of the UDDI architecture and design. This list simply provides the publishing API calls and some associated descriptions:

- **get_authToken**—Obtains an authentication token. This token must be used with other publishing calls.
- **discard_authToken**—Invalidates a previously existing authentication token.
- **get_registeredInfo**—Obtains information about a given individual.
- **save_binding**—Creates or modifies a `bindingTemplate`.
- **delete_binding**—Deletes a `bindingTemplate` from a `bindingTemplates` collection.
- **save_business**—Creates or modifies a `businessEntity`.
- **delete_business**—Deletes business information (for example, `businessEntity`) from the UDDI registry.
- **save_service**—Creates or modifies `businessService` information.
- **delete_service**—Deletes a `businessService` from a `businessServices` collection.
- **save_tModel**—Creates or modifies a tModel.
- **delete_tModel**—Deletes a tModel or, at a minimum, flags it for future deletion, depending on whether the tModel is being referenced multiple times.

Be aware that all publishing calls require the use of SSL to ensure that a secure update can be made to the registry.

Private Operations

For groups thatplan to build a UDDI repository, some API calls are used for administrative operations such as registry replication. This topic is beyond the scope of this discussion, so see the UDDI documentation referenced in Appendix D for more details.

Summary

WSDL is the current mechanism for describing services, and it is well supported by the .NET suite of tools. WSDL provides a modular design that enables you to organize definitions according to your reuse needs. By associating abstract datatypes and messages with concrete transport protocols and address locations, you have the ultimate flexibility in defining how your services should be structured and exposed.

UDDI, on the other hand, enables you to locate Web Services and their respective WSDL documents. Through a simple publish, find, and bind usage pattern, both service requestors and providers have a simple mechanism for sharing service metadata.

Please refer to Appendix D for further reading about WSDL and UDDI.

Chapter 6, "Web Services in ASP.NET," explores the construction of Web Services with ASP.NET.

Implementing Web Services

PART

II

Web Services in ASP.NET

IN THIS CHAPTER

This chapter addresses the Web Service, as implemented by ASP.NET. Here you start to use the technologies and concepts presented thus far in this book.

Previous chapters laid down the theoretical or applied background information that you need to understand why you'll add a specific attribute to your Web method or to know what must be happening behind the scenes when you create a proxy for your client application.

The chapter starts with a discussion of .NET's architecture to show you how Web Services are supported by .NET—and, more specifically, by ASP.NET. From there, you'll create Web Services and change their SOAP serialization formats using other .NET classes. We'll then talk about debugging and deployment, concluding with an examination of most of the .NET Web Service classes. We'll begin our journey with .NET's architecture.

Web Service Processing in .NET

Before talking about ASP.NET, this is a good time to show .NET's architecture as a whole. Web Services and ASP.NET fill a part of the picture, but they require assistance from nearly all parts of the .NET architecture. Figure 6.1 gives you what Microsoft calls the "Big Picture."

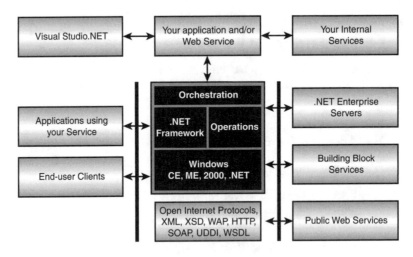

FIGURE 6.1
"Big Picture" .NET architecture.

Your Web Service sits atop the .NET Framework, unless you're using BizTalk, in which case you'll work with .NET through the BizTalk orchestration layer. .NET itself works with the Windows operating system, including COM+ and Microsoft's Internet Information Server (IIS), to provide a rich host environment for Web Services. Ultimately, .NET Web Services are built upon Internet standards such as HTTP and XML.

ASP.NET fits into the .NET Framework block of the big picture. Let's drill down another level and see how ASP.NET fits into that block.

ASP.NET Web Service Architecture

Figure 6.2 shows you the ASP.NET architecture, at least as viewed by Web Services.

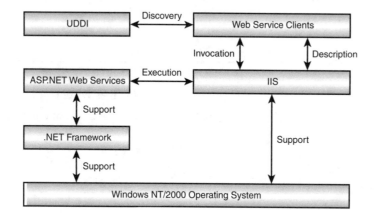

FIGURE 6.2
ASP.NET's Web Service architecture.

ASP.NET actually sits between IIS and the .NET Framework to process Web Service requests through its *HTTP pipeline*. Although the HTTP pipeline is not specifically shown in Figure 6.2, this is what ASP.NET uses to intercept Port 80 network traffic and assign the various packets to handlers. You have many handlers active at any given time; one type is dedicated to Web Services (created through WebServiceHandlerFactory).

Web Service requestors send their SOAP Request packets to your Web Service's URL. At that time, IIS intercepts the HTTP request and shuttles it to ASP.NET's ISAPI extension. From there, it's examined to see if it is a Web Service packet. The service requestor accesses the Web Service at least twice—once to request the service's WSDL file, and many times thereafter to invoke the service.

As it happens, Web Services aren't the only consumers of SOAP packets. .NET also provides for *remoting*, which is loosely analogous to DCOM.

.NET Remoting Versus .NET Web Services

Within .NET, you can issue SOAP Request and Response packets in two ways. Web Services provide for the traditional SOAP view of the loosely coupled remote method. You discover what services are available through UDDI and DISCO (Discovery of Web Services), learn how a given service operates using WSDL, and communicate with the service using SOAP.

.NET remoting, on the other hand, optionally uses the SOAP protocol as a communication tool, but its goal is to more tightly bind .NET objects to their remote counterparts. As such, it is more tightly coupled than the pure Web Service. A solid bond exists between the local and the remote objects, and both maintain state. Table 6.1 lays out the essential differences between remoting and Web Services.

TABLE 6.1   .NET Remoting Compared to .NET Web Services

Remoting	Web Services
Primarily for .NET to .NET	Primarily for .NET to other systems
High .NET fidelity	May be used .NET to .NET, but remoting may be preferred
Binary-style communication (using SOAP or a true binary protocol)	Rich SOAP/XML processing
Essentially .NET DCOM	Loosely coupled Internet standard protocol
Can use HTTP, TCP, or SMTP	Tied to HTTP (initial release)
Remote object activation (supports events)	Remote method execution
Endpoints configured using XML-based configuration file	Discovered using UDDI

Table 6.1 suggests that .NET remoting is useful for object activation, such as waking a remote assembly for processing, while Web Services support a more bare-bones approach by allowing a remote method to be invoked.

.NET remoting and .NET Web Services are not the same, and they're used for different purposes. Although this is but the slightest overview of .NET remoting, you have at least heard the term and have seen some of the essential differences between the two. You'll see more of .NET Remoting in Chapter 8, ".NET Remoting."

Let's now turn our attention to the Web Service, starting with the basics. We'll take a look at what Visual Studio .NET creates for you and how those files play a role to bring your Web Service to life.

Web Services and Visual Studio .NET

This book really isn't about using Visual Studio as a tool. It's about developing code designed to work within the .NET Framework. You created your first .NET Web Service in Chapter 1, "Web Service Fundamentals." Even so, it's probably worth discussing more detailed aspects of the project that Visual Studio .NET created for you.

> **NOTE**
>
> Before we get too far, developers often wonder if they can create .NET Web Services outside Visual Studio .NET. Although creating a Web Service project isn't rocket science, it also isn't as easy as creating a console application. You can't just whip out a quick Notepad source file and compile it using the command-line compiler. You have several source files to deal with, including some that are strange if you're used to pre–.NET versions of Visual Studio. You'll also need to work with IIS to expose your Web Service to the world. If a couple button clicks can do all that for you, why avoid the productivity gain?

So let's look at what Visual Studio .NET provides you when you create the initial file set. We'll look at what files are created, why they're created, and what you should do to make the basic Web Service source code more useful.

The Visual Studio Web Service Project

Visual Studio .NET makes creating Web Services so simple that it's easy to dive right into writing the implementation code. But it's usually worth the time to stop and examine precisely what Visual Studio has provided whenever you create projects using a new version of the product. Using wizard-generated code without understanding the code is a recipe for disaster— often you'll change a seemingly innocuous setting or line of code, and the entire project will fail to compile or execute. To complicate matters further, Visual Studio .NET creates additional files for the Web Service that you need to understand to properly control the Web Service's operation and flow.

When you create a new Web Service using Visual Studio .NET, your Web Service project files, for the most part, are placed in C:\inetpub\wwwroot\<project name>. The Visual Studio .NET solution files that describe your Web Service project are created and saved in C:\My Documents\Visual Studio Projects\<project name>. The file that you'll be most interested in will be named Service1.asmx.cs or Service1.asmx.vb. All the default filenames and their uses are shown in Table 6.2. Note that the filenames shown here reflect a C#–based project, but the same files are valid for a Visual Basic .NET project, with the substitution of the .vb file extension in lieu of the .cs extension. *<pname>* represents the project name.

TABLE 6.2   Visual Studio .NET Web Service Project Files

Filename	*Purpose*
AssemblyInfo.cs	Source file for general assembly information, such as a description, copyright statement, build number, and so on. This file takes the place of the Version resource in Visual Studio 6.
Global.asax	Source file for Web Service–wide event notifications provided by HttpApplication. This file is actually established as a redirector, establishing the Global.asax.cs file as the "code-behind" file.
Global.asax.cs	Source file for global HttpApplication event interception, such as when the application starts up and shuts down, when new sessions begin and end, and when requests are serviced.
Service1.asmx	Source file for the Web Service itself. This file is actually established as a redirector, establishing the Service1.asmx.cs file as the "code-behind" file.
Service1.asmx.cs	Source file for the Web Service itself. This file is where you place the code that handles the Web Service invocations.
Web.config	This is the same file that you'll find used with ASP.NET to control the HTTP handlers associated with the Web Service, tracing, session-state settings, custom error messages, and so on.
<pname>.csproj	This is the main Visual Studio .NET project file, containing build settings and configuration information.
<pname>.csproj.webinfo	This file tells remote instances of Visual Studio .NET where to find the actual project file. You'll use this when opening remote Web Service project files for editing and compilation.
<pname>.vsdisco	DISCO files in general are a type of file that Microsoft uses to identify local system Web Services. The .vsdisco file is an enhanced version of the DISCO file.
<pname>.sln	Visual Studio .NET's solution file, which acts as a collection container for subordinate but related project files.
<pname>.suo	The solution option file (binary format and not editable by hand).

Feel free to add files as necessary—the files shown in Table 6.2 are what Visual Studio .NET provides to you when you create the project. If you had created the project by hand, you would need to create many of these files yourself. For example, you'll need to create the .cs, .config, .vsdisco, and .asmx files (the other files are used only by Visual Studio .NET).

Visual Studio .NET not only created the project files for you, but it also created the IIS virtual directory and anointed your project with IIS Application status. This means that your Web Service is "live"—at least, after you compile the source files for the first time. Creating a Web Service project by hand also forces you to deal with IIS and its administrative applications. Isn't using Visual Studio .NET quite a bit easier?

With a couple mouse clicks and a few typed characters, you now have a Web Service project to your credit. Let's open the primary source file Service1.asmx.cs or Service1.asmx.vb, and massage it a bit.

Moving Away from "Hello World"

After Visual Studio .NET creates the Web Service project files for you, it displays a form that you can use to build a user interface. The first thing that you should do is close this window! Web Services don't have user interfaces. Instead, click the upper-left button in the Solution Explorer window to view the source code, as shown in Figure 6.3.

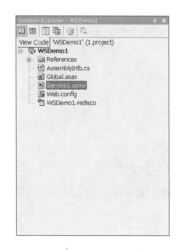

FIGURE 6.3
Visual Studio .NET's Solution Explorer window.

This button opens Service1.asmx.?? as a C# or Visual Basic .NET source file for editing. Its initial state for C# is shown in Listing 6.1. For those interested in the Visual Basic .NET file, you'll find that shown in Listing 6.2.

LISTING 6.1   Initial C# Web Service Source Code

```csharp
using System;
using System.Collections;
using System.ComponentModel;
using System.Data;
using System.Diagnostics;
using System.Web;
using System.Web.Services;

namespace Ch6WebService
{
    /// <summary>
    /// Summary description for Service1.
    /// </summary>
    public class Service1 : System.Web.Services.WebService
    {
        public Service1()
        {
            //CODEGEN: This call is required by the ASP.NET Web Services Designer
            InitializeComponent();
        }

        #region Component Designer generated code
        /// <summary>
        /// Required method for Designer support - do not modify
        /// the contents of this method with the code editor.
        /// </summary>
        private void InitializeComponent()
        {
        }
        #endregion

        /// <summary>
        /// Clean up any resources being used.
        /// </summary>
        protected override void Dispose( bool disposing )
        {
        }

        // WEB SERVICE EXAMPLE
        // The HelloWorld() example service returns the string Hello World
        // To build, uncomment the following lines then save and build the project
        // To test this web service, press F5
        //      [WebMethod]
```

LISTING 6.1 Continued

```
//      public string HelloWorld()
//      {
//          return "Hello World";
//      }
    }
}
```

LISTING 6.2 Initial VB.NET Web Service Source Code

```
Imports System.Web.Services

Public Class Service1
    Inherits System.Web.Services.WebService

#Region " Web Services Designer Generated Code "

    Public Sub New()
        MyBase.New()

        'This call is required by the Web Services Designer.
        InitializeComponent()

        'Add your own initialization code after the InitializeComponent() call

    End Sub


    'Required by the Web Services Designer
    Private components As System.ComponentModel.Container

    'NOTE: The following procedure is required by the Web Services Designer
    'It can be modified using the Web Services Designer.
    'Do not modify it using the code editor.
    <System.Diagnostics.DebuggerStepThrough()> Private Sub InitializeComponent()
        components = New System.ComponentModel.Container()
    End Sub

    Protected Overloads Overrides Sub Dispose(ByVal disposing As Boolean)
        'CODEGEN: This procedure is required by the Web Services Designer
        'Do not modify it using the code editor.
    End Sub

#End Region
```

Listing 6.2 Continued

```
' WEB SERVICE EXAMPLE
' The HelloWorld() example service returns the string Hello World.
' To build, uncomment the following lines then save and build the project.
' To test this web service, ensure that the .asmx file is the start page
' and press F5.
'
'<WebMethod()> Public Function HelloWorld() As String
'    HelloWorld = "Hello World"
' End Function
```

```
End Class
```

You'll want to do at least three things with these files at this point:

- Add a descriptive clause to your WSDL file
- Change the target namespace associated with your Web Service
- Remove the reference to "Hello World" and insert your own Web methods

To add a descriptive clause to your WSDL file, which will be automatically generated by .NET upon request, you add the `WebService` attribute to your `System.Web.Services.WebService` class. Consumers of your Web Service will see this description when they download your service's WSDL file. To do this, modify the `WebService` attribute by adding a `Description` initializer:

```
[WebService(Description="This is a description of my first C# Web Service!")]
public class MyWebService : System.Web.Services.WebService
{
    (Web Service code here)
}
```

or

```
<WebService(Description:="This is a description of my first Visual
➥ Basic.NET Web Service!")> _
Public Class MyWebService Inherits System.Web.Services.WebService
    (Web Service code here)
End Class
```

The resulting WSDL file will have a `<documentation/>` element added to the `<service/>` element that you saw in Chapter 5, "Web Service Description and Discovery":

```
<documentation>This is a description of my first Visual Basic.NET
➥ Web Service!</documentation>
```

The target namespace is also configured through the `WebService` attribute:

```
[WebService(Description="This is a description of my first C# Web Service!",
    Namespace="http://www.myurl.com/ ")]
```

or

```
<WebService(Description:="This is a description of my first Visual
➥ Basic.NET Web Service!", _
    Namespace:="http://www.myurl.com/ ")>
```

This modifies the target namespace as defined in the WSDL <definitions/> element, as well as within the <types/> element:

```
targetNamespace="http://www.myurl.com/mywebservice"
```

To create Web methods, you add public methods to your Web Service class, and to those methods you apply the WebMethod attribute. There is *nothing special* about the HelloWorld() method! Visual Studio .NET generated HelloWorld() simply to provide you with an example method that you can easily tailor to your specific needs.

However, much is special about the WebMethod attribute. Let's take a closer look.

The WebMethod Attribute

When you begin creating Web Services that are more detailed and functional than simple HelloWorld() knock-offs, you soon realize that you will most often add the functionality through .NET's Web Service and SOAP attributes. The second attribute that we'll examine in this chapter, WebMethod, is designed to tailor the operation of the method itself.

WebMethod allows you to enable session-state management and caching, initiate a COM+ transaction, alter the WSDL associated with this method, and provide a descriptive comment regarding the method. Table 6.3 gives you a few of the most-used settings of this attribute.

TABLE 6.3 WebMethod Commonly Used Settings

Setting	Purpose
BufferResponse	Determines whether the response is buffered. In general, you'll buffer responses unless you're returning very large amounts of data (if left unbuffered, the data is streamed to the service requestor as it is generated).
CacheDuration	Establishes the length of time that the response should be held in cache. Caching is fine, but note that your requests and responses will be cached for the duration that you specify, so it's best to not cache large data sets.
Description	Provides a textual description for the method that is written to the WSDL for service requestor use.

TABLE 6.3   Continued

Setting	Purpose
EnableSession	Provides for session-based state management. Note that this requires HTTP cookies, which the service requestor might not support. This also slightly degrades performance.
MessageName	Allows you to directly alias the method's name in the WSDL file. Normally the name associated with the method signature is used, but if you create polymorphic methods, you can rename the method as seen by the service requestor.
TransactionOption	Allows you to specify the level of COM+ transactional support desired for this method. The usual COM+ transactional levels apply, from none to requiring a new transaction for each invocation.

BufferResponse, CacheDuration, and EnableSession are used to work directly with ASP.NET. TransactionOption ties your method into the COM+ transactional runtime environment. The other two, Description and MessageName, are used to tailor the WSDL that the service requestor sees when accessing your Web Service.

For example, imagine that you added this method to your Web Service:

```
<WebMethod()> _
Public Function Foo() As String
   Foo = "This is Foo():
End Function
```

The resulting WSDL <operation/> element, contained within the <portType/> element that you saw in Chapter 5, would look like this, by default:

```
<operation name="Foo">
   </input message="s0:FooSoapIn" />
   </output message="s0:FooSoapOut" />
</operation>
```

However, you could modify the WebMethod attribute like this:

```
<WebMethod(Description:="My Foo() Method",_
   MessageName:="FooManChoo")> _
Public Function Foo() As String
   Foo = "This is Foo()"
End Function
```

Then the resulting WSDL appears like this:

```
<operation name="Foo">
    <documentation>My Foo() Method</documentation>
    </input name="FooManChoo"
      message="s0:FooManChooSoapIn" />
    </output name="FooManChoo"
      message="s0:FooManChooSoapOut" />
</operation>
```

Ultimately, you'll use .NET Web Service attributes, for the most part, to tweak and adjust your WSDL. This results in direct changes to the SOAP wire representation that .NET will produce when your method serializes the parameters. WebMethod isn't the only attribute that you'll find necessary to create real-world Web Services, as you'll see.

Controlling the SOAP Serialization Format

You have other tools that you can use to modify the SOAP wire representation. .NET provides you these so that you can customize the SOAP for any number of reasons, the most important of which is for interoperability. The Web Service world is finding that standards are generally solidifying, but some things are still in flux. Sometimes you might need to tailor SOAP to fit a certain mold, such as when you want to create a Web Service that meets preexisting WSDL. Other times, you might want to create SOAP that specific existing clients expect, perhaps to minimize .NET migration side effects.

A couple of primary mechanisms exist for modifying the SOAP stream. For example, you might add the SoapMethodAttribute or the related SoapRpcMethodAttribute to explicitly modify the SOAP stream. Or, you might employ data-shaping techniques to implicitly change the wire representation. Let's look at each in some detail.

SOAP Method Attributes

As you recall from Chapter 5, WSDL is capable of describing documents that fall into two major types of SOAP message formats, literal and rpc. literal allows you to describe free-form SOAP, as you might do when sending messages between the service provider and requestor. rpc, on the other hand, is more restrictive and formats the SOAP packet according to Sections 5 and 7 of the SOAP specification.

This is also the difference between SoapMethodAttribute and SoapRpcMethodAttribute. The former assigns the literal SOAP use style, while the latter assigns the rpc style. Table 6.4 shows the aspects of the SOAP stream that you can modify using SoapMethodAttribute.

TABLE 6.4 `SoapMethodAttribute` Commonly Used Settings

Setting	Purpose
Embedded	Determines whether the datatype of the parameters is to be explicitly encoded in the <types/> WSDL element.
ResponseXmlElementName	Allows you to explicitly set the SOAP Response element's local name.
ResponseXmlNamespace	Allows you to explicitly set the SOAP Response element's namespace.
ReturnXmlElementName	Allows you to set the XML element name for the method's return value (will default to __return).
SoapAction	Allows you to directly establish the SoapAction HTTP Header.

`SoapRpcMethodAttribute` has a different set of settings, as you can see in Table 6.5.

TABLE 6.5 `SoapRpcMethodAttribute` Commonly Used Settings

Filename	Purpose
Action	Allows you to directly establish the `SoapAction` HTTP Header.
Binding	Allows you to explicitly set the SOAP WSDL binding, which is similar to specifying which interface the method belongs to. Note that you must specify more than just the default binding by using `WebServiceBindingAttribute`.
OneWay	Causes the Web Service server to issue an HTTP 202 message to the service requestor, indicating that the Web server is processing. This allows the service requestor to continue processing without any acknowledgement that the Web server is actively processing the request.
RequestElementName	Allows you to set the XML element name for the method's SOAP Request element.
RequestNamespace	Allows you to explicitly set the SOAP Request element's namespace.
ResponseElementName	Allows you to set the XML element name for the method's SOAP Response element.
ResponseNamespace	Allows you to explicitly set the SOAP Response element's namespace.

Although the settings that you can administer through either attribute differ by name, they have the same purpose, for the most part. You can adjust the SoapAction HTTP Header and specify the XML used to name the Request and Response elements. Both of these can be critical to interoperability or to tailor your WSDL to meet a specific interface specification.

> **NOTE**
>
> Remember that SoapRpcServiceAttribute can be applied to the entire class, alleviating the need for you to set these parameters for each Web method that the class exports.

> **NOTE**
>
> SoapMethodAttribute and SoapRpcMethodAttribute have a similar purpose, but they do not reside in the same Common Language Runtime namespace. SoapMethodAttribute is found in System.Runtime.Remoting.Metadata, while SoapRpcMethodAttribute is found in System.Web.Services.Protocols.

> **NOTE**
>
> An attribute similar to SoapMethodAttribute is SoapDocumentMethodAttribute, which is found in System.Web.Services.Protocols. It also has the same methods and properties as SoapRpcMethodAttribute, as shown in Table 6.5. The difference is that SoapMethodAttribute is remoting-based and SoapDocumentMethodAttribute is Web Service–based. Either will work to provide a document-based SOAP packet versus an RPC-based one.

For an example, consider this Web method:

```
[WebMethod]
[SoapRpcMethodAttribute(Action="http://www.myurl.com/#barnone",
   RequestNamespace="http://www.myurl.com/")]
public string Bar()
{
    return "This is Bar()";
}
```

When you browse the WSDL for this method, you'll find that the `<soap:operation/>` and `<input/>` elements under the WSDL `<operation/>` element look like this:

```
<soap:operation soapAction="http://www.myurl.com/#barnone"
  style="rpc" />
<input>
  <soap:body use="encoded"
    namespace="http://www.myurl.com/"
    encodingStyle="http://schemas.xmlsoap.org/soap/encoding" />
</input>
```

The resulting SOAP Request would then be created so that the `Bar()` method's independent element would have the appropriate namespace applied:

```
<soap:Body>
  <m:Bar xmlns:m="http://www.myurl.com/" />
</soap:Body>
```

The other settings for both `SoapMethodAttribute` and `SoapRpcMethodAttribute` operate in a similar manner. Simply apply the attribute and desired setting, and .NET will create both the WSDL and the SOAP packets according to your design.

Let's relate this back to the SOAP specification. Ultimately, you'll need to decide how you want the SOAP packets formatted. If you are sure that other systems accessing your Web Service are capable of reading the WSDL that .NET generates for you, you are probably finished and can disregard the details that follow. However, that might not always be the case, and you might sometimes be very concerned about how your Web Service packets are serialized. Why? The primary reason is interoperability, but you also might be given a WSDL snippet (as an interface document) and asked to reproduce the WSDL and the underlying SOAP packets using .NET and .NET Framework classes.

The SOAP specification has two main sections that deal with parameter encoding and RPC use. Section 5 deals with the serialization of method parameters—this is where you learn to serialize an array, for example. Section 7 talks about RPC SOAP, where the SOAP XML is specifically tied to HTTP and the request and response packets are very tightly constrained. Table 6.6 associates the WSDL settings with the corresponding SOAP packet styles. This is also where you see the power of WSDL: You can have document-centric (free-form) SOAP packets floating around the Internet, but as long as you described them using WSDL, a client should be capable of consuming your customized SOAP packet and making sense of the method parameters you serialized.

TABLE 6.6 SOAP Body Serialization Style Settings

Parameter Encoding	Section 7	Document
Per Section 5 of the SOAP specification	`SoapRPCMethod` or `SoapRPCService`	Use `SoapDocumentMethod` or `SoapDocumentService` using `Use=Encoded`
Free-form	Not available	Use `SoapDocumentMethod` or `SoapDocumentService` using `Use=Literal`

Table 6.6 essentially is telling you is that if you want both Section 5 and Section 7 encoding behavior from .NET, you need to apply either `SoapRpcMethod` or `SoapRpcService` to your Web Service. You can follow Section 7 only by using these two methods, but you can follow Section 5 to a greater or lesser degree using all the attributes. For example, you can nail down the SOAP XML using the `Encoded` SOAP Body style (this refers to the generated WSDL), or you can go totally free-form and let the WSDL describe the document by using the `Literal` attribute setting.

`Literal` and `Encoded` are WSDL SOAP Body-style settings that significantly affect the look and feel of your resulting SOAP packets. .NET—or, at least, the code generated by Visual Studio .NET, favors a totally free-form SOAP packet that relies upon the embedded XSD schema in the WSDL file to describe the XML that is to be shipped between the client and the server and back again. The bottom line is that another Web Service that can read and interpret your WSDL information will probably benefit the most from a `Literal`-encoded document. However, if you're dealing with Web Services that work with an older WSDL or that don't work with WSDL at all, you have to fall back on the SOAP specification and Section 5 encoding using `Encoded`. We'll revisit this in the next chapter, "Consuming .NET Web Services," when we map the WSDL to the proxy.

One aspect of SOAP packet formatting is completely up to your object-oriented design rather than just .NET. You choose what parameters are provided to your Web Service and also how those parameters will be formatted. This is called *data shaping*, and it is the topic of the next section.

Data Shaping

Let's create a more complex Web Service to use as a data-shaping example. Let's say that you want to ship into a Web Service a linked list. You could do nearly anything with the list, but, for demonstration purposes, let's reverse the nodes. We'll make the head node the tail, and the tail will turn into the head node. Listing 6.3 gives you the C# code for this.

LISTING 6.3 Reversing a Linked List Service in C#

```csharp
public class Node
{
    public int iVal;
    public Node pNext;
}

[WebMethod]
[SoapRpcMethodAttribute()]
public Node ReverseAList(Node pList)
{
    Node pHead = pList;
    try
    {
        // Reverse the list and return
        Node pNext = null;
        Node pCurr = pHead.pNext;
        pHead.pNext = null;
        while ( pCurr.pNext != null )
        {
            // Rewire this node
            pNext = pCurr.pNext;
            pCurr.pNext = pHead;
            pHead = pCurr;

            // Grab the next node
            pCurr = pNext;
        } // while

        // Wire up the new head node
        pCurr.pNext = pHead;
        pHead = pCurr;
    } // try
    catch (Exception)
    {
        // Simply return null...
        pHead = null;
    }

    return pHead;
}
```

Notice that we've used `SoapRpcMethodAttribute` to signify that this method should follow the encoding specification for SOAP RPC. This means that the SOAP XML will be encoded so that the individual nodes are serialized as independent elements:

```
<soap:Body>
    <tns:ReverseAList>
        <pList href="#id1" />
    </tns:ReverseAList>
    <types:Node id="id1" xsi:type="types:Node">
        <iVal xsi:type="xsd:int">int</iVal>
        <pNext href="#id2" />
    </types:Node>
    <types:Node id="id2" xsi:type="types:Node">
        <iVal xsi:type="xsd:int">int</iVal>
        <pNext href="#id3" />
    </types:Node>
    <types:Node id="id3" xsi:type="types:Node">
        <iVal xsi:type="xsd:int">int</iVal>
        <pNext href="#id4" />
    </types:Node>
    <types:Node id="id4" xsi:type="types:Node">
        <iVal xsi:type="xsd:int">int</iVal>
        <pNext xsi:null="1" />
    </types:Node>
</soap:Body>
```

However, the SOAP packet will change radically if we use the `SoapMethodAttribute` instead. This creates a more document-centric SOAP XML packet:

```
<soap:Body>
    <ReverseAList xmlns="http://tempuri.org">
        <pList>
            <iVal>int</iVal>
            <pNext>
                <iVal>int</iVal>
                <pNext>
                    <iVal>int</iVal>
                    <pNext xsi:nil="true" />
                </pNext>
            </pNext>
        </pList>
    </ReverseAList>
</soap:Body>
```

In the previous case, we're shaping the data using a C# class, `Node`, in conjunction with the .NET SOAP attributes. But the data might take a form of its own, depending upon how you declare things. For example, consider this structure:

```
public struct Address
{
    public string Street1;
    public string Street2;
    public string City;
    public string State;
    public string Zip;
}
```

This is a relatively straightforward structure. Using `SoapMethodAttribute`, it would serialize like this, assuming that you sent this structure by reference to a method called `FillAddress()`:

```
<soap:Body>
    <FillAddress xmlns="http://tempuri.org">
        <pAddr>
            <Street1>string</Street1>
            <Street2>string</Street2>
            <City>string</City>
            <State>string</State>
            <Zip>string</Zip>
        </pAddr>
    </FillAddress>
</soap:Body>
```

Now make a subtle change. Remove the street strings and replace them with their own structure, like this:

```
public struct Street
{
    public string Street1;
    public string Street2;
}

public struct Address
{
    public Street Street;
    public string City;
    public string State;
    public string Zip;
}
```

Now the same method would serialize the SOAP XML like this:

```
<soap:Body>
    <FillAddress xmlns="http://tempuri.org">
        <strName>string</strName>
        <pAddr>
            <Street>
```

```
            <Street1>string</Street1>
            <Street2>string</Street2>
        </Street>
        <City>string</City>
        <State>string</State>
        <Zip>string</Zip>
    </pAddr>
  </FillAddress>
</soap:Body>
```

By changing the data structures used, you get different SOAP XML serializations. You can also adjust things by using `ref` to pass structures and classes by reference, as well as to serialize using the different .NET SOAP attributes, as in the linked list example.

Further Web Service SOAP Packet Customizations

You can make a few other customizations to the SOAP XML, if you need to do so. Although you might not often need to resort to these techniques, at least .NET provides you with alternatives.

Wrapped Versus Bare Parameters

If you elect to follow the SOAP specification and use Section 5 encoding, simply select the appropriate attribute from Table 6.6 and force the SOAP Body style to be `Encoded`. However, if you're creating SOAP packets that are more free-form ("document" style), you can easily constrain the methods so that they can be independent (bare) or serialized as embedded elements within the method's SOAP struct (wrapped). You do this by applying one of the `ParameterStyle` enumerated values from `SoapDocumentMethodAttribute` to your Web-enabled method.

> **NOTE**
>
> Remember, you're deciding what your SOAP packets should look like because you're *not* following Section 5 of the SOAP specification. You can let things default, or you can tailor them to suit your needs—it's up to you.

For example, imagine that you want to generate a SOAP packet that looked like this (don't laugh—you might actually *need* this someday):

```
<?xml version="1.0" encoding="utf-8"?>
<soap:Envelope xmlns:soap="http://schemas.xmlsoap.org/soap/envelope/"
 xmlns:xsi="http://www.w3.org/2001/XMLSchema-instance"
 xmlns:xsd="http://www.w3.org/2001/XMLSchema">
```

```
<soap:Body>
    <strInput xmlns="http://www.myurl.com/bareparms2">Testing...</strInput>
    <pt xmlns="http://www.myurl.com/bareparms2">
        <x>5</x>
        <y>10</y>
    </pt>
</soap:Body>
</soap:Envelope>
```

If you look closely, this is a very different-looking packet. The difference might seem minor, but it has a profound effect upon the receiver. Do you see a method element in this SOAP XML? No, normally, you would expect something like this:

```
<?xml version="1.0" encoding="utf-8"?>
<soap:Envelope
 xmlns:soap="http://schemas.xmlsoap.org/soap/envelope/"
 xmlns:xsi="http://www.w3.org/2001/XMLSchema-instance"
 xmlns:xsd="http://www.w3.org/2001/XMLSchema">
    <soap:Body>
        <WrapParms2 xmlns="http://www.myurl.com/wrapparms2">
            <strInput>Testing...</strInput>
            <pt>
                <x>5</x>
                <y>10</y>
            </pt>
        </WrapParms2>
    </soap:Body>
</soap:Envelope>
```

In this case, the italicized lines indicate the method's SOAP struct, which "wraps" the method parameters. The question is really one of normalcy—what is normal for the SOAP that you want to ship back and forth? What do you want the SOAP packets to *look* like?

To better demonstrate this, take a look at Listing 6.4. Five methods have been created, the first four of which are most interesting to this discussion. Listing 6.4 shows you a C# Web Service that tailors its SOAP packets as described. Included is the SoapDumper SoapExtension that we'll discuss later in the section "Adding a SOAP Extension," so that you can see the SOAP as it is generated. However, all that code has been removed for brevity purposes. If you're a Visual Basic .NET fan, don't worry. The equivalent Web Service has been included with the source code for this chapter (VBParamEncoder).

LISTING 6.4   C# Parameter-Encoding Web Service

```
using System;
using System.Collections;
```

LISTING 6.4 Continued

```
using System.ComponentModel;
using System.Data;
using System.Diagnostics;
using System.Web;
using System.Web.Services;
using System.Web.Services.Protocols;
using System.IO;
using System.Xml.Serialization;

namespace CSParmEncoder
{

    (SoapExtension code removed for brevity...)

    public class Service1 : System.Web.Services.WebService
    {

        (Code removed for brevity...)

        public struct Point
        {
            public int x;
            public int y;
        }

        [SoapDocumentMethodAttribute("http://www.myurl.com/wrapparms",
            Use=System.Web.Services.Description.SoapBindingUse.Literal,
            ParameterStyle=System.Web.Services.Protocols.SoapParameterStyle.
            ➥Wrapped)]
        [WebMethod]
        [SoapDumper()]
        public string WrapParms(string strInput, Point pt)
        {
            string strReturn = string.Format("The input string was '{0}',
                ➥ and the point values were {1} and {2}",strInput,pt.x,pt.y);
            return strReturn;
        }

        [SoapDocumentMethodAttribute("http://www.myurl.com/wrapparms2",
            RequestNamespace="http://www.myurl.com/wrapparms2",
            ResponseNamespace="http://www.myurl.com/wrapparms2",
            Use=System.Web.Services.Description.SoapBindingUse.Literal,
```

LISTING 6.4   Continued

```
        ParameterStyle=System.Web.Services.Protocols.SoapParameterStyle.
          ➥Wrapped)]
[WebMethod]
[SoapDumper()]
public string WrapParms2(
    [System.Xml.Serialization.XmlElementAttribute(
        ➥Namespace="http://www.myurl.com/wrapparms2",
        ➥IsNullable=false)]string strInput,
    [System.Xml.Serialization.XmlElementAttribute(
        ➥Namespace="http://www.myurl.com/wrapparms2",
        ➥IsNullable=false)]Point pt)
{
    string strReturn = string.Format("The input string was '{0}',
          ➥ and the point values were {1} and {2}",strInput,pt.x,pt.y);
    return strReturn;
}


[SoapDocumentMethodAttribute("http://www.myurl.com/bareparms",
    Use=System.Web.Services.Description.SoapBindingUse.Literal,
    ParameterStyle=System.Web.Services.Protocols.SoapParameterStyle.
      ➥Bare)]
[WebMethod]
[SoapDumper()]
public string BareParms(string strInput, Point pt)
{
    string strReturn = string.Format("The input string was '{0}',
          ➥ and the point values were {1} and {2}",strInput,pt.x,pt.y);
    return strReturn;
}


[SoapDocumentMethodAttribute("http://www.myurl.com/bareparms2",
    RequestNamespace="http://www.myurl.com/bareparms2",
    ResponseNamespace="http://www.myurl.com/bareparms2",
    Use=System.Web.Services.Description.SoapBindingUse.Literal,
    ParameterStyle=System.Web.Services.Protocols.SoapParameterStyle.
      ➥Bare)]
[WebMethod]
[SoapDumper()]
public string BareParms2(
    [System.Xml.Serialization.XmlElementAttribute(
        ➥Namespace="http://www.myurl.com/bareparms2",
        ➥IsNullable=false)]string strInput,
```

LISTING 6.4 Continued

```
    [System.Xml.Serialization.XmlElementAttribute(
      ➥Namespace="http://www.myurl.com/bareparms2",
      ➥IsNullable=false)]Point pt)
  {
    string strReturn = string.Format("The input string was '{0}',
          ➥ and the point values were {1} and {2}",strInput,pt.x,pt.y);
    return strReturn;
  }


  [SoapDocumentMethodAttribute("http://www.myurl.com/renameparms",
      Use=System.Web.Services.Description.SoapBindingUse.Literal,
      ParameterStyle=System.Web.Services.Protocols.SoapParameterStyle.
        ➥Wrapped)]
  [WebMethod]
  [SoapDumper()]
  [return: XmlElement("MyUniqueReturnValueElementName",IsNullable=false)]
  public string RenameParms(
    [XmlElement("InputString")] string strInput, // normally "strInput"
    [XmlElement("InputPoint")] Point pt) // normally "pt"
  {
    string strReturn = string.Format("The input string was '{0}',
          ➥ and the point values were {1} and {2}",strInput,pt.x,pt.y);
    return strReturn;
  }
 }
}
```

The four methods of interest here are WrapParms(), WrapParms2(), BareParms(), and
BareParms2(). We'll turn to RenameParms() in the next section, "Renaming the SOAP XML
Elements." The "wrapped" methods use the Wrapped parameter style setting, so the parameters
are serialized within the method struct. The "bare" methods likewise use the Bare method
parameter style setting. The difference between the original and the revised methods (the methods with names ending with the letter 2) is one of namespace application. You might not want
the default namespace http://tempuri.org; if not, the revised methods show you how to
change this for both the method and any parameters.

Let's see what the code in Listing 6.4 does. We'll show the SOAP output for each method in
turn. First, here's the WrapParms() SOAP request packet:

```
<?xml version="1.0" encoding="utf-8"?>
<soap:Envelope
 xmlns:soap="http://schemas.xmlsoap.org/soap/envelope/"
 xmlns:xsi="http://www.w3.org/2001/XMLSchema-instance"
```

```
xmlns:xsd="http://www.w3.org/2001/XMLSchema">
   <soap:Body>
      <WrapParms xmlns="http://tempuri.org/">
         <strInput>Testing...</strInput>
         <pt>
            <x>5</x>
            <y>10</y>
         </pt>
      </WrapParms>
   </soap:Body>
</soap:Envelope>
```

And here's the `WrapParms()` SOAP response packet:

```
<?xml version="1.0" encoding="utf-8"?>
<soap:Envelope
 xmlns:soap="http://schemas.xmlsoap.org/soap/envelope/"
 xmlns:xsi="http://www.w3.org/2001/XMLSchema-instance"
 xmlns:xsd="http://www.w3.org/2001/XMLSchema">
   <soap:Body>
      <WrapParmsResponse xmlns="http://tempuri.org/">
         <WrapParmsResult>The input string was 'Testing...',
           ➥and the point values were 5 and 10</WrapParmsResult>
      </WrapParmsResponse>
   </soap:Body>
</soap:Envelope>
```

First, note the namespace that is applied to the method struct as well as the return struct—it's the default namespace. If you execute `WrapParms2()`, you get this request SOAP packet from .NET:

```
<?xml version="1.0" encoding="utf-8"?>
<soap:Envelope
 xmlns:soap="http://schemas.xmlsoap.org/soap/envelope/"
 xmlns:xsi="http://www.w3.org/2001/XMLSchema-instance"
 xmlns:xsd="http://www.w3.org/2001/XMLSchema">
   <soap:Body>
      <WrapParms2 xmlns="http://www.myurl.com/wrapparms2">
         <strInput>Testing...</strInput>
         <pt>
            <x>5</x>
            <y>10</y>
         </pt>
      </WrapParms2>
   </soap:Body>
</soap:Envelope>
```

And you get this SOAP response packet:

```xml
<?xml version="1.0" encoding="utf-8"?>
<soap:Envelope
 xmlns:soap="http://schemas.xmlsoap.org/soap/envelope/"
 xmlns:xsi="http://www.w3.org/2001/XMLSchema-instance"
 xmlns:xsd="http://www.w3.org/2001/XMLSchema">
    <soap:Body>
        <WrapParms2Response xmlns="http://www.myurl.com/wrapparms2">
            <WrapParms2Result>The input string was 'Testing...',
              ➥ and the point values were 5 and 10</WrapParms2Result>
        </WrapParms2Response>
    </soap:Body>
</soap:Envelope>
```

The only notable difference between the SOAP output of the two "wrapped" methods is the XML namespace, but that can make a big difference to the recipient of the SOAP packet.

Now let's turn to the "bare" methods. The first, BareParms(), simply serializes the parameters as independent elements within the SOAP Body. The effect of that, however, is to remove the method struct element, as you'll see. Here is the BareParms() SOAP request packet:

```xml
<?xml version="1.0" encoding="utf-8"?>
<soap:Envelope
 xmlns:soap="http://schemas.xmlsoap.org/soap/envelope/"
 xmlns:xsi="http://www.w3.org/2001/XMLSchema-instance"
 xmlns:xsd="http://www.w3.org/2001/XMLSchema">
    <soap:Body>
        <strInput xmlns="http://tempuri.org/">Testing...</strInput>
        <pt xmlns="http://tempuri.org/">
            <x>5</x>
            <y>10</y>
        </pt>
    </soap:Body>
</soap:Envelope>
```

And here's the associated SOAP response packet:

```xml
<?xml version="1.0" encoding="utf-8"?>
<soap:Envelope
 xmlns:soap="http://schemas.xmlsoap.org/soap/envelope/"
 xmlns:xsi="http://www.w3.org/2001/XMLSchema-instance"
 xmlns:xsd="http://www.w3.org/2001/XMLSchema">
    <soap:Body>
        <BareParmsResult xmlns="http://tempuri.org/">The input string was
          ➥ 'Testing...', and the point values were 5 and 10</BareParmsResult>
    </soap:Body>
</soap:Envelope>
```

Again, you see the default namespace URI (isn't "tempuri" some sort of Japanese food? [Yes, I'm joking.]). Again, because XML systems are sensitive to namespaces, you are free to change the namespace associated with the SOAP XML elements that you serialize. So, if you then execute `BareParms2( )`,you see this SOAP request packet come from .NET:

```
<?xml version="1.0" encoding="utf-8"?>
<soap:Envelope
 xmlns:soap="http://schemas.xmlsoap.org/soap/envelope/"
 xmlns:xsi="http://www.w3.org/2001/XMLSchema-instance"
 xmlns:xsd="http://www.w3.org/2001/XMLSchema">
    <soap:Body>
        <strInput xmlns="http://www.myurl.com/bareparms2">Testing...</strInput>
        <pt xmlns="http://www.myurl.com/bareparms2">
            <x>5</x>
            <y>10</y>
        </pt>
    </soap:Body>
</soap:Envelope>
```

Finally, here is its associated SOAP response packet:

```
<?xml version="1.0" encoding="utf-8"?>
<soap:Envelope
 xmlns:soap="http://schemas.xmlsoap.org/soap/envelope/"
 xmlns:xsi="http://www.w3.org/2001/XMLSchema-instance"
 xmlns:xsd="http://www.w3.org/2001/XMLSchema">
    <soap:Body>
        <BareParms2Result xmlns="http://www.myurl.com/bareparms2">The input
        ➥string was 'Testing...', and the point values were 5 and 10
        ➥</BareParms2Result>
    </soap:Body>
</soap:Envelope>
```

Although it is entirely conceivable that you'll never need to monkey with the SOAP to this degree, it's nice to know that you can do this through .NET, and you won't require a `SoapExtension` to adjust the XML by hand.

You should know about one more data-shaping technique, just in case you find yourself in need of such a trick. .NET normally serializes the parameter's methods according to their names in the method signature, and rightly so. But it turns out that you can rename the SOAP elements—let's see how that is done.

Renaming the SOAP XML Elements

Listing 6.4 provided five methods, but we've described only four so far. The fifth modifies the SOAP XML elements themselves, in case you need to conform to an existing Web Service.

The method signature looks like this (from Listing 6.4):

```
public string RenameParms(
    [XmlElement("InputString")] string strInput, // normally "strInput"
    [XmlElement("InputPoint")] Point pt) // normally "pt"
{
    string strReturn = string.Format("The input string was '{0}',
        ➥ and the point values were {1} and {2}",strInput,pt.x,pt.y);
    return strReturn;
}
```

Of course, the italicized lines show you how the XML element names are changed at runtime when the SOAP serialization commences (SOAP request packet shown):

```
<?xml version="1.0" encoding="utf-8"?>
<soap:Envelope
 xmlns:soap="http://schemas.xmlsoap.org/soap/envelope/"
 xmlns:xsi="http://www.w3.org/2001/XMLSchema-instance"
 xmlns:xsd="http://www.w3.org/2001/XMLSchema">
    <soap:Body>
        <RenameParms xmlns="http://tempuri.org/">
            <InputString>Testing...</InputString>
            <InputPoint>
                <x>5</x>
                <y>10</y>
            </InputPoint>
        </RenameParms>
    </soap:Body>
</soap:Envelope>
```

The corresponding SOAP response packet looks like this:

```
<?xml version="1.0" encoding="utf-8"?>
<soap:Envelope
 xmlns:soap="http://schemas.xmlsoap.org/soap/envelope/"
 xmlns:xsi="http://www.w3.org/2001/XMLSchema-instance"
 xmlns:xsd="http://www.w3.org/2001/XMLSchema">
    <soap:Body>
        <RenameParmsResponse xmlns="http://tempuri.org/">
            <MyUniqueReturnValueElementName>The input string was
            ➥ 'Testing...', and the point values were 5 and 10
            ➥</MyUniqueReturnValueElementName>
        </RenameParmsResponse>
    </soap:Body>
</soap:Envelope>
```

As I mentioned, you might never need this power and flexibility, but if you ever do, you'll be very glad that .NET baked in this capability.

There is also another mechanism to change the SOAP XML packet rather radically, and that is to add a SOAP Header. .NET makes this easy by providing several attributes designed for this specific task.

Adding SOAP Headers

Very few real-world Web Services will likely operate without the assistance of SOAP Headers. SOAP Headers provide you with an outlet for storing security and encryption information, authentication data, and transactional and sequential processing instructions. Anything that is orthogonal to the method itself is a candidate for a Header. It isn't too surprising, therefore, to find that .NET provides an easy mechanism to assist you with SOAP Header processing. True to .NET form, this support comes primarily in the form of attributes, although a .NET class is designed specifically to support Header data.

There is a singular surprising aspect to using the .NET SOAP Header classes, however. .NET attributes do not need to be static. .NET attributes do not need to be hard-coded values—they can be quite dynamic and can change at runtime, depending on the current situation. This is also the nature of the .NET SOAP Header attributes. How do they work?

Header Processing

The primary .NET SOAP Header attribute is `SoapHeaderAttribute`, and it is related to the `SoapHeader` class. These two work in concert to provide you with the dynamic SOAP Header operation that you'll need when making your Web Service more realistic.

> **NOTE**
>
> The service provider specifies the use of the Header, even though the service requestor completes the Header information and establishes the required understanding of the Header data. If this seems backward, consider that it really stems from the fact that if the service requestor arbitrarily assigned SOAP Headers to the Web Service, the likelihood that the Web Service will actually understand the Header would be practically nonexistent. The Web Service "knows" what it needs, and it tells the service requestor what Headers must be established via the service's WSDL file.

The first step is to create a class that will handle the Header data:

```
Public Class Header1
    Inherits System.Web.Services.Protocols.SoapHeader

    Dim strHeader As String
```

```
    Public Property Header() As String
        Get
            Header = strHeader
        End Get
        Set(ByVal Value As String)
            strHeader = Value
        End Set
    End Property
End Class
```

Remember to add the System.Web.Services.Protocols namespace to your source file, or it will not compile properly. Next, declare a public class member that is derived from the Header class that you just created:

```
<WebService()> _
Public Class Service1
    Inherits System.Web.Services.WebService

    Public m_foo As Header1

    ...
End Class
```

Finally, tell .NET that your Web method will use the Header. Note that if you did not set the Required Header setting to false, you will need to set the Header's DidUnderstand attribute to true within your method:

```
<WebMethod(), _
  SoapHeader("m_foo")> _
  Public Function Foo() As String
      m_foo.DidUnderstand = True
      Foo = m_foo.Header
  End Function
```

or

```
<WebMethod(), _
  SoapHeader("m_foo", Required:=false)> _
  Public Function Foo() As String
      Foo = m_foo.Header
  End Function
```

Note that the SoapHeaderAttribute's Required setting corresponds to the SOAP Header's mustUnderstand attribute.

The equivalent C# code is shown in Listing 6.5.

LISTING 6.5 SOAP Header Processing in C#

```csharp
[WebService()]
public class Service1 : System.Web.Services.WebService
{
    public Header1 m_foo;

    ...

    [WebMethod]
    [SoapHeader("m_foo")]
    public string Bar()
    {
        m_foo.DidUnderstand = true;
        return m_foo.Header;
    }
}
```

You probably have noticed that we've used a string as the datatype for the Header itself. This is required and is done by design.

> **NOTE**
>
> The Header's datatype must always be a string, or it must be converted to a string before serialization. The .NET SOAP Header class will serialize string values to the SOAP XML stream only at runtime. In fact, your source code will not even compile if the datatype is something other than a string.

If you merely add the SOAP Header as shown, you'll get a Header that is issued from the service requestor to the service provider through the SOAP Request packet. But what if you want a Header that runs both ways or that goes from the provider to the requestor alone? That's the topic of the next section.

Specifying SOAP Header Direction

Actually, providing direction to SOAP Headers in .NET is quite simple, and it involves the same SoapHeaderAttribute that you've already seen. When you specify the use of the Header with the Web method, just add the Direction setting:

```csharp
[WebMethod]
    [SoapHeader("m_foo", Direction=SoapHeaderDirection.InOut)]
    public string Bar()
```

```
{
    m_foo.DidUnderstand = true;

    string strTemp = m_foo.Header;
    m_foo.Header = "Return to Sender";
    return strTemp;
}
```

The italicized portion of the Web method specifies the direction of the Header, which is managed by the SoapHeaderDirection enumeration: In, Out, and InOut.

Additional SOAP Headers

You can add as many Headers as you require by following the steps that you saw to add the first Header. All the Headers, when they are deserialized by .NET, are added to the SoapHeadersCollection, which you can access at runtime. If a third-party service requestor inadvertently sends more Headers than you expect and none is required, you can examine this collection to determine what Headers were issued and what you might need to do with the additional information, if anything.

If all the .NET SOAP attributes and classes that you've seen so far don't provide the interoperable SOAP packets that you require, or if you're interested in doing something more exotic, the next section is probably just what you need. The .NET SoapExtension is the ultimate in flexibility and control when it comes to serializing your SOAP packets.

Adding a SOAP Extension

In essence, a SoapExtension class allows you to dig into the SOAP XML that .NET has produced or just received so that you can alter the contents or otherwise perform necessary processing. For example, with a SoapExtension, you might use XPath to extract a SOAP XML element, encrypt it, and return it to the XML stream before it leaves your computer. Or, when you receive a SOAP packet, you might scan the contents to see if additional resources will be required to process the request and, if so, marshal those resources in advance.

To create a SoapExtension, you derive a new class from SoapExtension and override the necessary virtual methods. To hook the extension into your Web methods, you also create a custom attribute based on SoapExtensionAttribute, as you'll see in the next section.

Extension Stream Processing

First, you'll need to create the class that manages the extension. Table 6.7 provides you with the virtual SoapExtension methods that you'll need to override, while Table 6.8 similarly shows the virtual methods for SoapExtensionAttribute.

TABLE 6.7   SoapExtension Virtual Methods

Setting	Purpose
ChainStream	Provides you access to the memory buffer that .NET is using to hold the SOAP Request or Response.
GetInitializer	Allows you to provide a .NET type through the SoapExtension attribute at runtime, allowing for polymorphic operation.
Initialize	Uses the .NET type issued through the SoapExtension attribute (cached by GetInitializer()).
ProcessMessage	This is where the action takes place. You access the SOAP XML streams and perform whatever tasks are appropriate.

TABLE 6.8   SoapExtensionAttribute Virtual Methods

Setting	Purpose
ExtensionType	Returns the type of the SOAP extension
Priority	Establishes the priority of the SOAP extension

In Chapter 10, ".NET and Web Service Security," we'll deal with encryption and SoapExtensions. For now, we'll simply flush the contents of the XML stream to a disk file for analysis. You'll find the code for this in Listing 6.6.

LISTING 6.6   SoapExtension Processing in C#

```csharp
[AttributeUsage(AttributeTargets.Method)]
public class SoapDumperAttribute : SoapExtensionAttribute
{
    private string m_strFilename = "C:\\SoapLog.txt";
    private int m_iPriority = 0;

    public override Type ExtensionType
    {
        get
        {
            return typeof(SoapDumper);
        }
    }

    public override int Priority
    {
        get
```

LISTING 6.6 Continued

```
    {
        return m_iPriority;
    }
    set
    {
        m_iPriority = value;
    }
}

public string LogFile
{
    get
    {
        return m_strFilename;
    }
    set
    {
        m_strFilename = value;
    }
}
}

public class SoapDumper : SoapExtension
{
    // Streams we'll use. The "old" stream is what .NET is using, and the
    // "new" stream is what we want to present to .NET
    private Stream m_stmOld;
    private Stream m_stmNew;

    // The file where we'll save the log information
    private string m_strLogFile;

    // Provide the implementation for GetInitializer(). Note it takes
    // two overrides to do so. The initializer is where we'll ship in
    // a log file name other than the default.
    public override object GetInitializer(Type serviceType)
    {
        return GetType();
    }

    public override object GetInitializer(LogicalMethodInfo
            methodInfo, SoapExtensionAttribute attribute)
    {
        return ((SoapDumperAttribute)attribute).LogFile;
    }
```

Listing 6.6   Continued

```
// Provide the implementation for Initialize()
public override void Initialize(object initializer)
{
   m_strLogFile = (string) initializer;
}

// Provide the implementation for ProcessMessage(). This is
// where we determine what state we're currently processing
// under and take action based upon that state.
public override void ProcessMessage(SoapMessage message)
{
   switch (message.Stage)
   {
      // Called before the SOAP packet is created
      case SoapMessageStage.BeforeSerialize:
         break;

      // Called after the SOAP packet is created
      case SoapMessageStage.AfterSerialize:
         LogOutput(message);
         break;

      // Called before the incoming SOAP packet is interpreted
      case SoapMessageStage.BeforeDeserialize:
         LogInput(message);
         break;

      // Called after the incoming SOAP packet is interpreted
      case SoapMessageStage.AfterDeserialize:
         break;

      default:
         throw new Exception("invalid stage");
   }
}

// Provide the implementation for ChainStream()
public override Stream ChainStream( Stream stream )
{
   m_stmOld = stream;
   m_stmNew = new MemoryStream();
   return m_stmNew;
}
```

LISTING 6.6   Continued

```
    public void LogOutput( SoapMessage message )
    {
        m_stmNew.Position = 0;
        FileStream fstmLog = new FileStream(m_strLogFile,
                        FileMode.Append, FileAccess.Write);
        StreamWriter stmLog = new StreamWriter(fstmLog);
        stmLog.WriteLine("--------------------------------- SOAP
                Response at " + DateTime.Now);
        stmLog.Flush();
        Copy(m_stmNew,fstmLog);
        fstmLog.Close();
        m_stmNew.Position = 0;
        Copy(m_stmNew,m_stmOld);
    }

    public void LogInput( SoapMessage message )
    {
        Copy(m_stmOld,m_stmNew);
        FileStream fstmLog = new FileStream(m_strLogFile,
                        FileMode.Append, FileAccess.Write);
        StreamWriter stmLog = new StreamWriter(fstmLog);
        stmLog.WriteLine("=================================== SOAP
                        Request at " + DateTime.Now);
        stmLog.Flush();
        m_stmNew.Position = 0;
        Copy(m_stmNew,fstmLog);
        fstmLog.Close();
        m_stmNew.Position = 0;
    }

    void Copy(Stream stmFrom, Stream stmTo)
    {
        TextReader trFrom = new StreamReader(stmFrom);
        TextWriter twTo = new StreamWriter(stmTo);
        twTo.WriteLine(trFrom.ReadToEnd());
        twTo.Flush();
    }
}

[WebService()]
public class Service1 : System.Web.Services.WebService
{
    ...
    [SoapDumper(LogFile=@"C:\\out.txt")]
```

LISTING 6.6   Continued

```
   public string Bar()
   {
      return "This is Bar()";
   }
}
```

The `SoapExtensionAttribute` is there to allow you to establish a given Web method as extended by using its class name:

```
[SoapDumper(<optional filename and priority>)]
public string Bar()
{
    ...
}
```

The meat of the extension is handled by `SoapExtension::ProcessMessage()`:

```
public override void ProcessMessage(SoapMessage message)
{
   switch (message.Stage)
   {
      case SoapMessageStage.BeforeSerialize:
         // Do something useful...
         break;

      case SoapMessageStage.AfterSerialize:
         // Do something useful...
         break;

      case SoapMessageStage.BeforeDeserialize:
         // Do something useful...
         break;

      case SoapMessageStage.AfterDeserialize:
         // Do something useful...
         break;

      default:
         throw new Exception("invalid stage");
   }
}
```

Using `ProcessMessage()` is a lot like flying a model airplane or driving a remote control car, if you've ever tried either. When the airplane is flying away or the car is driving away from you, your controls behave as you'd expect. Right is right, and left is left. However, if the airplane is flying or the car is driving toward you, left and right on your control yoke or steering wheel are reversed. It's the same with ProcessMessage(). If you're using the extension on the server, the Request is deserialized and the Response is serialized. This seems reasonable; if you are the Web Service, you extract the incoming SOAP parameters through deserialization and return the Response through a serialized SOAP packet.

As it happens, though, you can use the SoapExtension on the service requestor side, as you'll see in Chapter 7, "Consuming .NET Web Services." When you do, you'll find that the roles of serialization and deserialization are reversed. You serialize the Request and deserialize the Response. In the case of SoapDumper, from Listing 6.6, this means that you'll need to reverse the roles of LogInput() and LogOutput().

It's also true that with SoapDumper, we merely streamed the XML to a file for later review. This is handy at times, but the real purpose of the SoapExtension is to allow you to access the SOAP packet while the SOAP is being processed by .NET.

Modifying the XML

As you saw in Chapter 3, "Web Services and XML," with .NET, you work with XML via a stream. This dovetails nicely with the SoapExtension because ChainStream() provides you exactly this—access to the XML stream when executing ProcessMessage(). With SoapDumper, it's possible to divert the incoming SOAP XML stream to a new memory-based stream. While working within ProcessMessage(), it would be possible to then access the stream as XML by using it as input to the constructors for XmlTextReader or XmlNodeReader. For example, this code gives you access to the XML, using the memory stream created in Listing 6.6:

```
XmlTextReader xtr = new XmlTextReader(m_stmNew);
```

Given the XML stream reader, you can process the SOAP XML using the techniques that you saw in Chapter 3. You'll see a more detailed example of this in Chapter 9, when we pull a single SOAP parameter and encrypt it.

Errors and the SOAP Fault

Errors and abnormal processing termination are a fact of life. With luck, your users didn't uncover a latent bug. But at any time you might lose a connection to your database server or encounter some other runtime-based situation that manages to murder your Web Service.

These situations are managed in Web Services through the SOAP Fault packet, which you saw in Chapter 4, ".NET Web Services and SOAP." Within .NET, you can take two main paths to issue a SOAP Fault packet: You allow .NET to create one for you, or you take matters into your own hands and issue one yourself. Let's see how you accomplish both.

Default .NET SOAP Fault Processing

If you want to maintain the standard SOAP Fault behavior that .NET provides, simply don't handle exceptions. It's the exception that is key to .NET SOAP Fault processing. Whenever .NET handles an exception when processing Web Services, it records the execution stack at the time, digs out the exception code and associated error message, and translates those into a SOAP Fault packet. If you do catch exceptions, be sure to `throw` them again if you want the default .NET fault behavior.

Customized SOAP Faults Using `SoapException`

On the other hand, not all errors will be system-level errors. Some errors—and, in fact, probably *most* errors—will be application-level errors. When this is the case, and if you need to issue a SOAP Fault Response to the client, you can do so easily by throwing a new `SoapException`.

For example, imagine that your Web Service kept track of the number of times that it was invoked per requestor. If a specific number of requests was exceeded without new payment arrangements, you want to return an application-level fault that informs the requestor that you'll not process more requests until it provides adequate payment.

In Visual Basic .NET, you would execute the following code:

```
Throw New SoapException("Number of invocations exceeded," &
➥"additional payment is required", _
New XmlQualifiedName("Client.InvocationsExceeded"))
```

The same exception in C# would be this:

```
throw new SoapException("Number of invocations exceeded," +
➥" additional payment is required",
        new XmlQualifiedName("Client.InvocationsExceeded"));
```

Note that you'll need to add both the System.Web.Services.Protocols and System.Xml namespaces. If you haven't added a reference to the System.Xml assembly, you'll need to do that as well.

Web Service State Management

Because .NET Web Services are based upon `System.Web.Services.WebService`, they share the capability to access the ASP.NET `Session` and `Application` objects. We won't say that there is never a reason to use a `Session` object with a Web Service, but if you feel that your design calls for `Session` access, you should review your design. What you're saying is this— your Web Service maintains state across method invocations. How would you necessarily know which possible client to associate this state with? Yes, there are ASP.NET tools to help you do this, but from a design and best-practices standpoint, it's better to create stateless Web Services.

But notice that we mentioned the `Session` object, not the `Application` object. Application-wide state isn't necessarily bad, although you might want to lock down global variable access if you're not using the provided `Application` object. To make things a bit simpler, we recommend keeping application-wide state in the `Application` object.

The `Application` object is like a name-value dictionary that ASP.NET provides you, to make it easier to store temporary state. For example, this (C#) code stores a hit counter in the `Application` object:

```
Application["Hits"] = iHits + 1;
```

To retrieve the hit counter value, you reverse the equation and cast the result:

```
iHits = Application["Hits"];
```

In this case, the name is `Hits` and the associated value is an integer representing the actual count. This works well, but only as long as the Web Service's associated assembly is loaded into memory. As soon as the assembly is removed from memory, all knowledge of the hit counter, as an example, is lost. Therefore, you'll need to store your application state in a durable resource, such as a database.

If you've done some Web design work before, that probably isn't too surprising. But an obvious question is, when do you load and save the application state? How are you notified that the application is activating or deactivating so that you can take the appropriate action?

The answer is the Web Service's global.asax file, or perhaps the *code-behind* file global.asax.cs or global.asax.vb. In this file, you'll find several useful event methods, but the two most interesting to this discussion are the events that fire when the application initializes and unloads:

```
protected void Application_Start(Object sender, EventArgs e)
{

}
```

and

```
protected void Application_End(Object sender, EventArgs e)
{

}
```

In these event methods, you can do nearly anything. Listing 6.7 shows you a technique for storing the application state in a database.

LISTING 6.7   Web Service State Management

```csharp
using System;
using System.Collections;
using System.ComponentModel;
using System.Web;
using System.Web.SessionState;
using System.Data;
using System.Data.OleDb;

namespace AppState
{
    /// <summary>
    /// Summary description for Global.
    /// </summary>
    public class Global : System.Web.HttpApplication
    {
        protected void Application_Start(Object sender, EventArgs e)
        {
            // Create a new (empty) dataset
            DataSet ds = new DataSet();

            // Pull the connection string
            string strConn = System.Configuration.ConfigurationSettings.
                        ➥AppSettings["ConnectionString"];

            // Create the search string
            string strSQL = string.Format("SELECT * FROM AppState");

            // Create the connection, command,
            // and adapter objects
            OleDbConnection objConn = new OleDbConnection(strConn);
            OleDbCommand objCmd = new OleDbCommand(strSQL,objConn);
            OleDbDataAdapter objAdapter = new OleDbDataAdapter(objCmd);

            // Connect to the database and execute SQL query
            objConn.Open();

            // Fill DataSet with the results, if any
            objAdapter.Fill(ds,"AppState");

            // Check for data...we'll look at the id column...
            Application["Hits"] = ds.Tables[0].Rows[0][1].ToString();
        }
```

LISTING 6.7 Continued

```
protected void Session_Start(Object sender, EventArgs e)
{

}

protected void Application_BeginRequest(Object sender, EventArgs e)
{

}

protected void Application_EndRequest(Object sender, EventArgs e)
{

}

protected void Session_End(Object sender, EventArgs e)
{

}

protected void Application_End(Object sender, EventArgs e)
{
    // Create a new (empty) dataset
    DataSet ds = new DataSet();

    // Check for data...we'll look at the id column...
    ds.Tables[0].Rows[0][0] = 1;
    ds.Tables[0].Rows[0][1] = (int)Application["Hits"];

    // Pull the connection string
    string strConn = System.Configuration.ConfigurationSettings.
                    ➥AppSettings["ConnectionString"];

    // Create the search string
    string strSQL = string.Format("SELECT * FROM AppState");

    // Create the connection, command,
    // and adapter objects
    OleDbConnection objConn = new OleDbConnection(strConn);
    OleDbCommand objCmd = new OleDbCommand(strSQL,objConn);
    OleDbDataAdapter objAdapter = new OleDbDataAdapter(objCmd);

    // Connect to the database and execute SQL query
    objConn.Open();
```

LISTING 6.7 Continued

```
        // Update the database
        OleDbCommandBuilder objCmdBlder =
                    new OleDbCommandBuilder(objAdapter);
        objAdapter.Update(ds,"AppState");
    }
  }
}
```

The code you see in Listing 6.7 writes the total number of Web Service "hits" to the database when the application terminates. This enables you to read that value back in when the application reinitializes. This is useful for counters and such things, but there are potentially many reasons to store application state information between instances of the Web Service.

Debugging and Deployment

Creating a Web Service is interesting by itself, but the goal is to expose the Web Service to the Internet. This naturally brings up the topics of debugging and deployment. How do you debug a .NET Web Service? How would you deploy one? If you've been working with .NET for some time, you've probably noticed that .NET tries hard to make your life easier, at least with respect to developing software. Web Service debugging and deployment are no different, as you'll see.

Debugging

.NET Web Service debugging is a two-step process. After you have worked out the kinks in your code so that it compiles successfully, you still have no guarantee that the Web Service will execute properly. It's here that you tackle the first debugging step—examine the .asmx file in the Browser.

Visual Studio Web Service Browser Output

The first thing that will break your Web Service is simply this: If you can't generate the WSDL for your service, you can't take that service online. You often might find that you can get Web Service code to compile without generating WSDL because of runtime concerns, or perhaps you neglected to mark your method as a public WebMethod. Errors of this kind usually pop up when you try to create a proxy to test the Web Service. It's therefore a good idea to examine the Web Service response to the HTTP GET command, as you saw in Chapter 1.

To do that, move the mouse's cursor to your Web Service's .asmx filename in the Solution Explorer window, and click the right mouse button. When you do, Visual Studio .NET presents you with a context menu, one option of which is View in Browser. If you select this option,

Visual Studio .NET issues the HTTP GET command to your Web Service; if things work as they should, you'll see the HTML associated with the Web Service appear in a browser window (as you see in Figure 6.4).

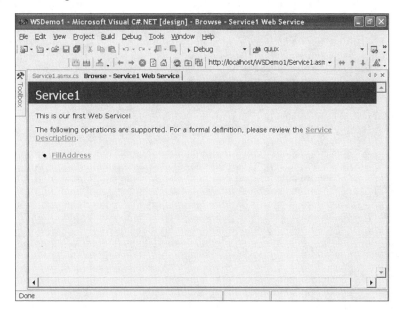

FIGURE 6.4
Correctly implemented Web Service browser output.

If things don't go as planned, you'll see an error message displayed. This error message is quite informative and useful, as you can see from Figure 6.5. In this case, we changed the Address structure example from the "Data Shaping" section to include a secondary structure and tried to serialize it using SoapRpcMethodAttribute. The .NET architecture does not support serialization of secondary structures when using RPC-style SOAP, hence the error. (You can serialize nested *classes*, however!)

Quite often the error message that you see in the browser output is enough to trigger your actions to correct the deficiency. If not, at least you have a clue that you can use to seek an answer.

Remote Debugging

After you have a Web Service that compiles and generates WSDL, you're ready to create service requestors to further test the Web Service. If you've compiled your Web Service assemblies using the Visual Studio .NET Debug configuration, you'll have everything you'll need to remotely debug your Web Service (assuming that you've also compiled the service requestor using the Debug configuration).

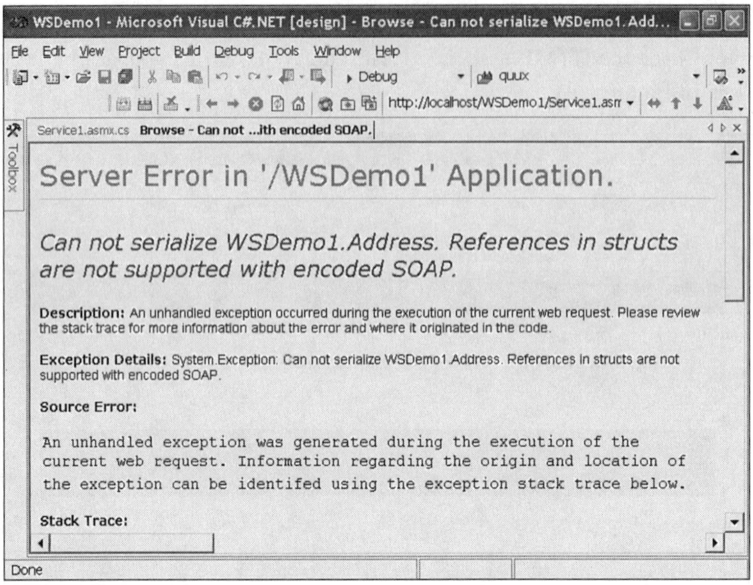

FIGURE 6.5
Erroneous Web Service browser output.

When you're executing your service requestor code, place a breakpoint at the location in your client code where you invoke the Web Service. From there, simply single-step into the remote method using Visual Studio .NET's debugger toolbar or by pressing the F11 key. That's all there is to it!

Remember that you'll need to compile a release version of your Web Service for deployment, or you run the risk of others debugging your Web Service for you. You'll also want to edit your Web.config file to deactivate dynamic debugging by changing the debug attribute of the `<compilation/>` XML element to `false`.

.NET Web Service Deployment

Speaking of deployment, now that you have your Web Service compiled and tested, how *do* you get it into production? You might take one of several approaches, depending upon your needs:

- Copy the assemblies and support files to the remote server by hand
- Create the Web Service project on the remote computer, and compile it in place
- Create a Web Setup Project for the Web Service

We'll look at each in turn to examine strengths and weaknesses.

Deploy Web Service Files by Hand

.NET was designed and built for many reasons, but certainly one of the reasons .NET is so strong is that its deployment model for general-purpose assemblies is so simple. If you are installing a traditional desktop application that is composed of .NET Windows Forms assemblies, your job is as easy as copying the files to the client machine. No fancy registration is required unless you want the assemblies to be available for other applications; in that case, you register those with the Global Assembly Cache. The traditional COM object registration is not part of the .NET installation model, and DLL woes are gone as well.

Thus, it probably isn't surprising to find that you can simply copy your Web Service assemblies to the server using simple file-transfer techniques. Traditionally, if you can use that word with .NET today, Web Service files go under `c:\inetpub\wwwroot\<project name>`, but that's a convention, not a rule. What's really important is that, when you copy the files, you establish the Web Service under IIS and provide IIS with the Web Service's virtual directory. It's also important to remember that .NET expects all required assemblies to reside in a \bin subdirectory, found within the main application's directory. Some of your Web Service files, therefore, will go in the main Web Service directory, and some will go into the application's \bin subdirectory. Table 6.9 outlines the files that you'll require and where they should be copied.

TABLE 6.9   Deployed Web Service Files and Locations

Filename	Location
Global.asax	Application directory
Web.config	Application directory
<application>.vsdisco	Application directory
<application>.asmx	Application directory
Assemblies	Application \bin subdirectory

After you've established the virtual directory and copied these files to the server, your Web Service will be active and ready to service requests.

> **NOTE**
>
> You'll also need the .NET Framework installed on the server for .NET–based Web Services to run.

If the process just described sounds somewhat complicated, especially if you're new to Web programming, don't despair. The other deployment alternatives are more effective and easier to use.

Create the Web Service Project on the Remote Computer

This is a feature of Visual Studio .NET that I find exciting: You can create and manage projects on remote computers. Although long-distance compilation is probably about as satisfying as any long-distance relationship, the mere fact that you can do this is amazing. This also means that you've automatically deployed your Web Service even as you've created the project.

Creating a remotely held Web Service project with Visual Studio .NET is actually a relatively simple proposition. In most cases, all you'll need to do is create the project normally, substituting the name of the remote computer in for `localhost`. You should keep a couple things in mind, however.

First, you must have access to the remote computer and be authorized to create files remotely. Although this is more of an administrative matter than anything else, it can easily keep you from accomplishing the task if the proper credentials aren't in place.

Also, if you don't share the IIS default directory (c:\inetpub\wwwroot), you'll need to use the FrontPage Extensions to gain access. This generally doesn't pose a significant difficulty, and the FrontPage Extensions are installed for you when you install the .NET Framework. They'll be there if you need them. If you need to use the Extensions, you'll be denied access to the server and will be shown an error dialog box. This dialog box allows you to select the Extensions as a secondary mode of access. Select the Extensions as the primary access mode, and close the dialog box to continue.

After the project is created on the remote system, you deal with it as if it were a local project. Make your source file edits, change some properties or rename some files, and compile. When everything compiles correctly and generates WSDL, your Web Service is ready to go.

Create a Visual Studio .NET Web Setup Project

This is the preferred method for Web Service deployment because it ships not only your Web Service assemblies but also the system assemblies, with their correct versions. For this option, you'll create an additional Visual Studio .NET project that is designed specifically to copy your Web Service to the remote server and configure it for use. You create this project in the same way as other projects, by selecting the File menu's New Project option.

After selecting the New Project option, you choose the Setup and Deployment Projects folder. From the choices available to you, which might vary from one version of Visual Studio .NET to another, choose the Web Setup Project. You now give the project a name and close the New Project dialog box by clicking the OK button. You can see this in Figure 6.6.

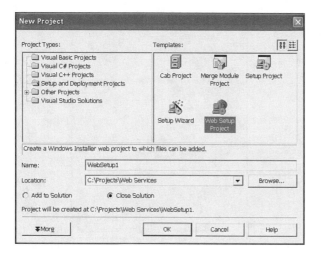

FIGURE 6.6
Visual Studio .NET's New Project Creation dialog box.

Visual Studio .NET will grind a moment and open the new project for you. At this point, you can add the Web Service projects associated with the Web Services that you want to deploy. To do this, select Add (Existing) Project from the File menu, and locate the project or projects that you want to insert and deploy.

Now you've added the projects related to the Web Services, but you still must explicitly configure the Setup project to include the Web Services themselves in the setup file. You do this by clicking the right mouse button when the cursor is sitting atop the Setup project's name in the Solution Explorer window. From the resulting context menu, select the Add menu item. Your response to the resulting dialog box should be Add Project Output Group, which you see in Figure 6.7.

You'll generally want to add Primary Output (assemblies and dependent DLLs) and Content Files (Global.asax, Web.config, and so on), but you also might want to add Debug Symbols if you plan to debug the service after deployment. After selecting the files in the output list control, click OK to close the Add Project Output Group dialog box and build the project normally.

The Setup project's output will be a Windows Installer file (.msi), which you can copy to any server and execute to install the files locally there. This .msi file is no different than any other .msi file that you might find or create, and it's just as easy to use.

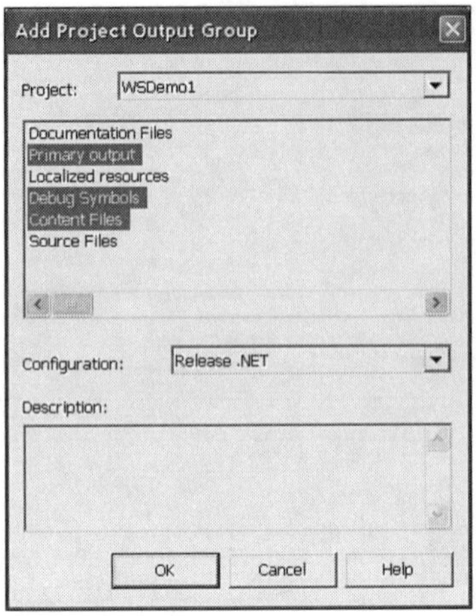

FIGURE 6.7
Visual Studio .NET's Add Project Output Group dialog box.

Web Services and Best Practices

This final section is brief but important. We're not sure that the industry has necessarily decided upon a complete set of "best practices" for Web Services, but here are some things to consider.

First, the old adage that "to people with hammers, everything is a nail" also holds true for Web Services. I often see people designing Web Services into their distributed applications simply because they can. Web Services are powerful, it is true, but they are a tool that you, as a designer, use as you would any other. Use them where they make sense. If you have distributed resources that you need to access, if you need a loosely coupled system, or if you have any other compelling reason, use a Web Service. If you can achieve the same functionality in a local setting, you'll probably be happier in the long run because of the increased performance of the local object or system.

That brings up a second point. Always remember that a Web Service involves a network. You'll sustain not just a single round trip for a Web Service invocation, but quite possibly several, depending upon what you are doing and how much data you're passing back and forth. So, you need to consider latency, loss of signal, quality of service, and all the other aspects of network-based computing.

To minimize round trips, try to design Web Service methods that encapsulate as much as is possible into the single method call. In other words, reduce dependencies between Web Service invocations by passing as much of the data as possible in one invocation (ideally, *all* of the required data is sent).

Finally, even though you can modify the XML stream, it's generally best to let .NET handle your SOAP formatting. You've seen some powerful tools in this chapter that enable you to really customize your SOAP packets. But if you have no true need to do so, perhaps because the Web Service or client can read and interpret WSDL, then avoid making packet customizations simply because you can. Keep your source code—and your SOAP—as simple as possible.

Summary

The generic files that Visual Studio .NET creates for you when you build a new Web Service project aren't generally too useful for real-world Web Services, although they do provide a great starting point. You'll want to initiate modifications to lead the Web Service source away from the basic "Hello World" model. For example, this chapter showed how to add your own target namespace and description, as well as remove the HelloWorld() method and add your own methods.

The chapter looked in some detail at the WebMethod attribute and some of the functions that it provides. Probably the three biggest are MessageName, Description, and TransactionOption. The first two modify your WSDL output, while the third enlists COM+ transactional support for your Web Service.

Looking at WebMethod raised another issue—how to modify the look and feel of the SOAP wire representation from within your .NET source code. You can arm yourself with SoapMethodAttribute or SoapRpcMethodAttribute, for example, or you can take a slightly different approach and use data-shaping techniques.

.NET provides a class designed specifically to support Headers, SoapHeader, and a related attribute, SoapHeaderAttribute. You write the Header functionality into a class derived from SoapHeader and then apply the Header to a specific Web method using the Header attribute.

The powerful SoapExtension allows you to access and alter the SOAP XML stream that .NET will ultimately pass to your Web Service. You create a custom attribute for your extension and apply that attribute to each Web method targeted for extension processing.

The SoapException class is a mechanism for issuing SOAP Faults and application-level faults. Any unhandled Web Service exception causes .NET to return a SOAP Fault to the client.

Deploying your Web Service is your end goal, but first you must debug it. Debugging encompasses two main phases—checking for WSDL output and performing remote debugging. Deployment is accomplished by copying necessary files by hand to the remote server and handling the associated IIS administration, by creating the Web Service project directly on the target machine, or by creating a Web Setup project and creating a Windows Installer file that you deploy.

Ultimately, this chapter has focused on the Web Service itself. But communication takes two parties, a sender and a receiver. The next chapter digs into the service requestor more deeply and exposes tips and tricks that you can use when creating Web Service clients on your own.

Consuming .NET Web Services

IN THIS CHAPTER

So far, you've looked at the more glamorous aspects of Web Services. You've looked at the SOAP protocol, .NET's handling of the Web Service through ASP.NET, and WSDL and UDDI. But, as important as those are, without a consumer—a client—the Web Service is useless. You've seen only half of the story!

This chapter deals with the client side of the equation. Here you'll create applications that consume Web Services, as well as more interesting Web Services than you've seen so far.

When I create client applications, I use Visual Studio. Many people we know who have been working with .NET for a couple years tend to write code in an editor and use the .NET command-line compilers. (Yes, .NET has been around a couple years as a well-kept secret.) It's one thing to create small console-based test applications. It's an entirely different problem to create full-fledged Windows Forms apps. With those, you'll want to establish the precise location of controls, which is more difficult without the visual tools. We've come a long way in the 10 short years that Windows has existed! We have nice tools, and we like them.

What do Windows Forms applications have to do with Web Services? Nothing, by themselves. The point is, though, that you'll soon be writing applications that you intend to sell, and those applications will most likely increasingly use Web Services. This chapter really tries to show you how applications are created within the .NET Framework, as well as how you attach Web Services to those applications.

Visual Studio .NET Web Service Support

Visual Studio .NET is fully Web Service–aware. Because of this, Visual Studio .NET has many features and functions that make life with Web Services easier. You saw some of these in the previous chapter, "Web Services in ASP.NET," where Visual Studio .NET not only created your Web Service projects but also connected to them through the Internet Information Service Web server as Web applications. You also saw how easy it was to deploy Web Services, and I mentioned that you can even create projects on remote systems. This is one powerful tool.

But there's more.

One nice feature is that Web Services are easily integrated into your client applications by associating the Web Service with a *Web reference*. Like traditional references, which bring additional .NET assemblies or legacy COM objects into your application's execution context, the Web reference brings the Web Service into your application by generating proxies (which you see as source code in your project) necessary to connect to and communicate with the remote system.

When you drop the Projects menu in Visual Studio .NET, available only when the project is loaded, you'll see the Web References menu item. In fact, you saw this in Chapter 5, "Web Service Description and Discovery," where you looked at finding Web Services through UDDI.

With the Web reference, you have the capability of discovering Web Services at design time. You might discover them at runtime someday using .NET, although this capability isn't currently built into .NET.

What Visual Studio .NET does for you is create source code that acts as a *proxy*. In other words, to your application the Web Service is a local capability, and you actually compile the proxy into your code. The proxy, however, is merely a shunt for the remote service. The proxy accepts the input parameters, converts them to XML/SOAP, sends them to the Web Service, and waits for the results. Figure 7.1 shows this in action.

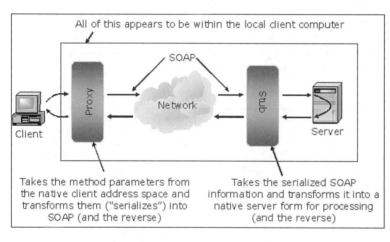

FIGURE 7.1

Web Services communication components.

NOTE

You don't have to use Visual Studio .NET to create your proxy source code. You can use the wsdl.exe utility that comes with the .NET Framework. We're not going to discuss this tool more deeply because Visual Studio .NET does the proxy generation for you. However, if you need the command-line option, wsdl.exe is available. Using the command-line argument /? will provide help for other required and optional command-line arguments.

NOTE

If you used the initial .NET beta, you might already be familiar with wsdl.exe. It was updated and renamed from webserviceutil.exe in the original beta.

Another nice thing that Visual Studio .NET does for you is provide the Server Explorer. The Server Explorer enables you to access other remote servers and ascertain their status, SQL capability, and availability of Web Services. This is nice when developing Web Services because you can work from one place, yet access the remote systems through something other than Web Service means. This feature is useful probably only for servers under your control (security reasons). Still, you can easily check status and access those remote systems for which you do have authorization.

Finally, one of the most amazing things that Visual Studio .NET enables you to do is remotely debug Web Services. If you create a Web Service on one computer, add a Web reference to it from another, and later decide to debug the Web Service, you'd be stuck without some remote debugging capability. However, from the client system, you can single-step into the Web Service and watch it execute just as if the code were compiled and executed locally. This is a feature that you'll use repeatedly as you develop Web Services.

> **NOTE**
>
> Remote debugging is something that you do want to disable when you bring your Web Service online. To disable remote debugging, simply change the debug setting in the web.config file. It defaults to `true`, but setting it to `false` will completely disable remote debugging for this Web Service.

This completes your quick-and-painless introduction to Visual Studio .NET from a Web Service developer's standpoint. Let's jump into the client end of Web Services to how to add Web references in more detail and examine the resulting proxy code.

Consuming Web Services

At the time this book was written, the second beta of Visual Studio .NET had just been released. Publicly available Web Services based upon .NET Beta 2 were not commonplace. Most available Web Services, if they were .NET–based, produced Service Description Language (SDL) instead of Web Service Description Language (WSDL). The non–.NET Web Services that were available, usually created with IBM and Apache tools, were all WSDL 1.0–compliant, whereas .NET Beta 2 expected WSDL 1.1–compliant services. It was difficult to find a true Web Service to present to you!

But this industrious author found one—a simple calculator Web Service based upon Visual Basic .NET. You can't do much: add, subtract, multiply, and divide—and, at that, only with long (32-bit) values instead of double (floating-point) values. The URL for this Web Service should be `http://dotnet.securedomains.com/eyesoft/ws/b2/calc/SimplCalc.asmx`.

To obtain the WSDL for this, you would concatenate ?WSDL to the end of the Web Service URL.

Let's examine the service's WSDL file briefly, to correlate what you see in the WSDL file with what is generated for you in the proxy file. An abbreviated copy of the WSDL is shown in Listing 7.1. From this, you can see that there are four methods, all dealing with long values.

LISTING 7.1   SimpleCalc's Web Service WSDL

```
<?xml version="1.0" encoding="utf-8"?>
<definitions xmlns:s="http://www.w3.org/2001/XMLSchema"
xmlns:http="http://schemas.xmlsoap.org/wsdl/http/"
xmlns:mime="http://schemas.xmlsoap.org/wsdl/mime/"
xmlns:tm="http://microsoft.com/wsdl/mime/textMatching/"
xmlns:soap="http://schemas.xmlsoap.org/wsdl/soap/"
xmlns:soapenc="http://schemas.xmlsoap.org/soap/encoding/"
xmlns:s0=http://tempuri.org/" targetNamespace="http://tempuri.org/"
xmlns="http://schemas.xmlsoap.org/wsdl/">
  <types>
    <s:schema attributeFormDefault="qualified"
              elementFormDefault="qualified"
              targetNamespace="http://tempuri.org/">
      <s:element name="Add">
        <s:complexType>
          <s:sequence>
            <s:element minOccurs="1" maxOccurs="1"
                name="a" type="s:long" />
            <s:element minOccurs="1" maxOccurs="1"
                name="b" type="s:long" />
          </s:sequence>
        </s:complexType>
      </s:element>
      <s:element name="AddResponse">
        <s:complexType>
          <s:sequence>
            <s:element minOccurs="1" maxOccurs="1"
                name="AddResult" type="s:long" />
          </s:sequence>
        </s:complexType>
      </s:element>
      ...
      <s:element name="long" type="s:long" />
    </s:schema>
  </types>
  <message name="AddSoapIn">
    <part name="parameters" element="s0:Add" />
```

7

**CONSUMING .NET
WEB SERVICES**

LISTING 7.1   Continued

```
  </message>
  <message name="AddSoapOut">
    <part name="parameters" element="s0:AddResponse" />
  </message>
  <message name="SubtractSoapIn">
    <part name="parameters" element="s0:Subtract" />
  </message>
  <message name="SubtractSoapOut">
    <part name="parameters" element="s0:SubtractResponse" />
  </message>
  <message name="MultiplySoapIn">
    <part name="parameters" element="s0:Multiply" />
  </message>
  <message name="MultiplySoapOut">
    <part name="parameters" element="s0:MultiplyResponse" />
  </message>
  <message name="DivideSoapIn">
    <part name="parameters" element="s0:Divide" />
  </message>
  <message name="DivideSoapOut">
    <part name="parameters" element="s0:DivideResponse" />
  </message>
  ...
  <portType name="SimpleCalcSoap">
    <operation name="Add">
      <documentation>Add two numbers</documentation>
      <input message="s0:AddSoapIn" />
      <output message="s0:AddSoapOut" />
    </operation>
    <operation name="Subtract">
      <documentation>Subtract two numbers</documentation>
      <input message="s0:SubtractSoapIn" />
      <output message="s0:SubtractSoapOut" />
    </operation>
    <operation name="Multiply">
      <documentation>Multiply two numbers</documentation>
      <input message="s0:MultiplySoapIn" />
      <output message="s0:MultiplySoapOut" />
    </operation>
    <operation name="Divide">
      <documentation>Divide two numbers</documentation>
      <input message="s0:DivideSoapIn" />
      <output message="s0:DivideSoapOut" />
    </operation>
```

LISTING 7.1 Continued

```
  </portType>
  ...
  <binding name="SimpleCalcSoap" type="s0:SimpleCalcSoap">
    <soap:binding transport="http://schemas.xmlsoap.org/soap/http"
      style="document" />
    <operation name="Add">
      <soap:operation soapAction="http://tempuri.org/Add"
      style="document" />
      <input>
        <soap:body use="literal" />
      </input>
      <output>
        <soap:body use="literal" />
      </output>
    </operation>
  ...
  </binding>
  ...
  <service name="SimpleCalc">
    <port name="SimpleCalcSoap" binding="s0:SimpleCalcSoap">
      <soap:address location="http://dotnet.securedomains.com/eyesoft/
                              ➥ws/b2/calc/SimpleCalc.asmx" />
    </port>
    ...
  </service>
</definitions>
```

We edited the WSDL to shorten it up a bit. For example, we I removed all the references to
HTTP bindings, both for HTTP GET and POST, and we removed the schema references for the
Subtract(), Multiply(), and Divide() methods because they were similar to the Add()
method. Enough is shown in Listing 7.1 to see what will happen when you reference this Web
Service.

Let's look at the Add() method now. The WSDL <types/> element tells you this:

```
<s:element name="Add">
  <s:complexType>
    <s:sequence>
      <s:element minOccurs="1" maxOccurs="1"
        name="a" type="s:long" />
      <s:element minOccurs="1" maxOccurs="1"
        name="b" type="s:long" />
    </s:sequence>
  </s:complexType>
</s:element>
```

The interesting portion of this WSDL snippet are italicized. Here you see that `Add()` expects a couple of parameters, one called a and one called b, both of which are long values. This element, `Add`, is rolled up into a message called *AddSoapIn*:

```
<message name="AddSoapIn">
  <part name="parameters" element="s0:Add" />
</message>
```

This specifies the input to the `Add()` method. There is a similar definition for the output, which is combined with the input to `Add()` in the WSDL `<portType/>` element:

```
<operation name="Add">
  <documentation>Add two numbers</documentation>
  <input message="s0:AddSoapIn" />
  <output message="s0:AddSoapOut" />
</operation>
```

The operation is then identified in a SOAP binding:

```
<binding name="SimpleCalcSoap" type="s0:SimpleCalcSoap">
  <soap:binding transport="http://schemas.xmlsoap.org/soap/http"
    style="document" />
  <operation name="Add">
    <soap:operation soapAction="http://tempuri.org/Add"
    style="document" />
    <input>
      <soap:body use="literal" />
    </input>
    <output>
      <soap:body use="literal" />
    </output>
  </operation>
...
</binding>
```

You now know the `Add()` method is bound to the SOAP protocol and that it has two input parameters, a and b, both of which are long values.

Finally, you assign the binding to a service called SimpleCalc, where you find its endpoint:

```
<service name="SimpleCalc">
  <port name="SimpleCalcSoap" binding="s0:SimpleCalcSoap">
    <soap:address location="http://dotnet.securedomains.com/eyesoft/
                              ➥ws/b2/calc/SimpleCalc.asmx" />
  </port>
...
</service>
```

The Web Service's WSDL is highlighted here to correlate what you see in the WSDL to what appears in the proxy code Visual Studio .NET will generate for you when you add the Web reference to your application. Let's talk briefly about the application before adding the Web reference so that you see how the Web Service will be used.

We created an application that optionally consumes the SimpleCalc Web Service. Not surprisingly, the application is named Calculator, and its user interface is shown in Figure 7.2.

FIGURE 7.2

The Calculator user interface.

As you see from Figure 7.2, you have the option of making calculations using local resources or the Web Service. This is the code that you'll execute when you add two numbers:

```
// Add
if ( m_bLocal )
{
   // Local addition
   m_lAccumulator = lX + lY;
} // if
else
{
   // Remote addition
   m_lAccumulator = m_pxyCalc.Add(lX,lY);
};
```

The local addition should be straightforward—you simply add the two numbers and display the results. The remote case, however, uses the Web Service through its proxy. Let's see how to create the proxy source code and add that to the project.

Creating the Web Reference

The Web Service proxy is added to your project by selecting the Web Service as a Web reference. You're probably already accustomed to pulling other .NET assembly references and legacy COM objects into your application. This was necessary to work with XML in

Chapter 3, "Web Services and XML," for example. There, you needed to add a reference to the System.Xml assembly.

You'll add a Web reference in nearly the same manner as you add a traditional reference. In Visual Studio .NET, select the Web References item from the Projects menu to display the dialog box that you see in Figure 7.3.

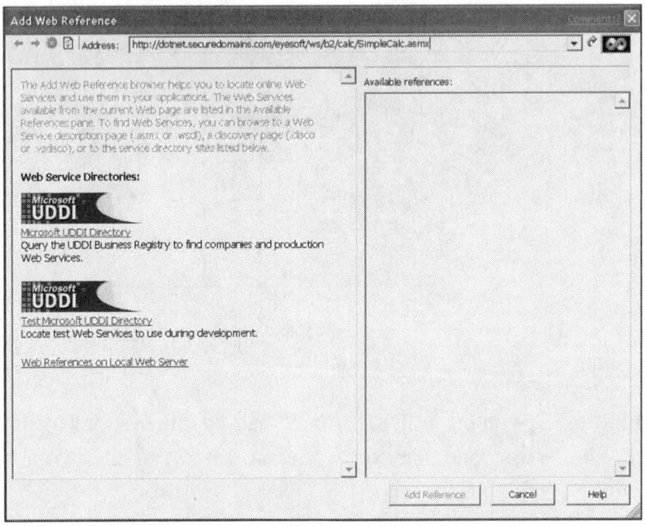

FIGURE 7.3
Visual Studio .NET's Add Web Reference dialog box.

This dialog box enables you to create proxies from one of three sources:

- From the local server
- From the Microsoft UDDI repository
- From a URL that you provide

The local server option causes Visual Studio .NET to search for all Web Services on your computer. After it finds the list of available Web Services, it enables you to select the Web Service of interest. If you want to hunt for the Web Service, you can use the Microsoft UDDI repository to see what's available there. You saw this in Chapter 5. Finally, if you already know the URL of the Web Service, or, more correctly the Web Service's WSDL, you can type that URL into the address control and press the Enter key. This causes the dialog box to access the Web Service's WSDL, decipher the contents, and create the proxy source code, which, if successful, will be created and placed in the Web References subdirectory under your project's directory.

Synchronous Web Services

Probably the next thing you'll want to do is to bring the proxy source code into the editor so that you can see what you can do with the Web Service. We did just this using the URL you see in Figure 7.3, which returned the WSDL examined in Listing 7.1. The resulting proxy, edited for brevity, is shown in Listing 7.2.

LISTING 7.2   SimpleCalc's Proxy Source Code

```
//----------------------------------------------------------------
// <autogenerated>
//     This code was generated by a tool.
//     Runtime Version: 1.0.2914.16
//
//     Changes to this file may cause incorrect behavior and will be
//     lost if the code is regenerated.
// </autogenerated>
//----------------------------------------------------------------

namespace Calculator.com.securedomains.dotnet {
    using System.Diagnostics;
    using System.Xml.Serialization;
    using System;
    using System.Web.Services.Protocols;
    using System.Web.Services;


    [System.Web.Services.WebServiceBindingAttribute(
        ➡Name="SimpleCalcSoap",Namespace="http://tempuri.org/")]
    public class SimpleCalc :
            ➡System.Web.Services.Protocols.SoapHttpClientProtocol {

        [System.Diagnostics.DebuggerStepThroughAttribute()]
        public SimpleCalc() {
            this.Url = "http://dotnet.securedomains.com/eyesoft/ws/
                                    ➡b2/calc/SimpleCalc.asmx";
        }

        [System.Diagnostics.DebuggerStepThroughAttribute()]
        [System.Web.Services.Protocols.SoapDocumentMethodAttribute
          ➡("http://tempuri.org/Add",
          ➡Use=System.Web.Services.Description.SoapBindingUse.Literal,
          ➡ParameterStyle=System.Web.Services.Protocols.
            ➡SoapParameterStyle.Wrapped)]
        public long Add(long a, long b) {
            object[] results = this.Invoke("Add", new object[] {
```

LISTING 7.2   Continued

```
                         a,
                         b});
            return ((long)(results[0]));
        }

        [System.Diagnostics.DebuggerStepThroughAttribute()]
        public System.IAsyncResult BeginAdd(long a, long b,
              ↪System.AsyncCallback callback, object asyncState) {
            return this.BeginInvoke("Add", new object[] {
                         a,
                         b}, callback, asyncState);
        }

        [System.Diagnostics.DebuggerStepThroughAttribute()]
        public long EndAdd(System.IAsyncResult asyncResult) {
            object[] results = this.EndInvoke(asyncResult);
            return ((long)(results[0]));
        }

     ...


    }
}
```

You can see a couple of interesting things here. First, because the calculator application is written in C#, the proxy code was generated using C#. Had we used Visual Basic .NET, the proxy would have been generated in that language. Second, note that the proxy has a namespace, so, to make your code a bit easier to read, you'll probably want to add the namespace to your application. In this case, you would add the namespace like so:

```
using Calculator.com.securedomains.dotnet;
```

or

```
Imports Calculator.com.securedomains.dotnet
```

This enables you to create an instance of the proxy in this manner:

```
SimpleCalc pxyCalc = new SimpleCalc();
```

or

```
Dim pxyCalc As SimpleCalc = new SimpleCalc()
```

You're still free to use the fully qualified name (`Calculator.com.securedomains.dotnet.SimpleCalc`), but by declaring the namespace you can save yourself some typing. Returning to the proxy source code, you also can see the methods that the Web Service exposes. The `Add()` method, for example, uses this code:

```
[{attributes}]
public long Add(long a, long b) {
   object[] results = this.Invoke("Add", new object[] {
            a,
            b});
   return ((long)(results[0]));
}
```

The attributes associated with the `Add()` method are `System.Diagnostics.DebuggerStep ThroughAttribute` and `System.Web.Services.Protocols.SoapDocumentMethodAttribute`. `DebuggerStepThroughAttribute` enables you to single-step through the Web Service, assuming that the Web Service's security permissions allow you to do so (you can't step through the SimpleCalc Web Service using F11 [single-step remote debugging]—we checked!).

`SoapDocumentMethodAttribute` enables you to tailor the SOAP packets returned to the server through WSDL. Remember that, using WSDL, you can send information over the wire using either RPC or document encoding styles. If you're using the document encoding style, which from the WSDL you see in Listing 7.1 includes SimpleCalc, you'll need to respond to the Web Service using the template provided in the WSDL.

```
<binding name="SimpleCalcSoap" type="s0:SimpleCalcSoap">
  <soap:binding transport="http://schemas.xmlsoap.org/soap/http"
    style="document" />
   ...
</binding>
```

For example, you'll use the datatypes defined in the `<types/>` element, which are used in messages defined in the `<message/>` element, and so on. In this case, you're reapplying the request's target URI, reaffirming the WSDL SOAP binding style (from Listing 7.2, `Use=System.Web.Services.Description.SoapBindingUse.Literal`), and specifying how the parameters are to be placed within the SOAP Body (`ParameterStyle=System.Web.Services.Protocols.SoapParameterStyle.Wrapped`). Because these attributes reflect the WSDL provided by the Web Service, *it's best not to change their values* in the proxy. If you need to do that, you should modify the Web Service itself. If you can't, you should honor the settings that the Web Service requires.

However, for completeness, Tables 7.1 and 7.2 provide you with the values that the bindings and parameter styles may accept. This should help you better understand the proxy source code.

7

CONSUMING .NET
WEB SERVICES

TABLE 7.1 .NET SoapBindingUse Enumeration Values

Value	Meaning
Default	Uses the default encoding (if document, use Literal; if RPC, use Encoded)
Encoded	Produces WSDL that uses the RPC style encoding
Literal	Produces WSDL that uses the document style encoding

TABLE 7.2 .NET SoapParameterStyle Enumeration Values

Value	Meaning
Bare	Specifies that the parameters are to be encoded as independent elements within the SOAP Body
Default	Uses the default encoding style for the Web Service, which would be Section 5 encoding for RPC methods and Wrapped for document methods
Wrapped	Specifies that the parameters are to be encoded as embedded elements within the method element inside the SOAP Body

The Web Service itself is synchronously invoked using `SoapHttpClientProtocol::Invoke` (from Listing 7.2):

```
object[] results = this.Invoke("Add", new object[] {
            a,
            b});
return ((long)(results[0]));
```

`Invoke()` is meant to be a general-purpose method; as such, it accepts two parameters. The first is a string that contains the name of the remote method to execute. The second is an array of input parameters, both `[in]` and `[in, out]`. For `Add()`, this equates to the two long `[in]` values a and b.

Hidden beneath `Invoke()` is the magic that makes Web Services work within .NET on the client. You don't have to worry about the messy details. .NET takes care of them for you, and `Invoke()` is your portal into .NET's Web Service communication infrastructure.

Assuming that there is no problem, `Invoke()`returns to you an array of objects that represent the output parameters, including the return value (array element 0), `[out]` values, and `[in, out]` values. The order of the array elements is as specified by the order of parameters of the method itself, reading from left to right.

If the Web Service returns to you a SOAP fault packet, `Invoke()` will throw a `SoapException`. Because `Add()` doesn't handle the exception for you, you'll need to do one of two things if you want to handle the exception yourself. Nothing says that you can't modify the proxy source code, so you might put an exception handler directly into the proxy if you want. It is true that, if you regenerate the proxy, you will lose your changes, but it isn't often that you need to regenerate proxies. If that happens, make a copy of the original proxy source file and merge the proxy files after you've created the new proxy. Of course, the second alternative is to provide exception-handling support in your application's source file.

Turning to the application source file, you create an instance of the Web Service proxy using the operator new. For the Calculator application, lazy allocation is used here:

```
// Check for proxy creation if necessary
if ( !m_bLocal )
{
   // Check to see if proxy exists,
   // and if not, create one.
   if ( m_pxyCalc == null )
   {
      // Create one
      m_pxyCalc = new SimpleCalc();
   } // if
} // if
```

Lazy in this case refers to the tests that wrap the creation of the proxy. We'll create the proxy only if we're going to actually invoke the Web Service because we have the option of making the calculations locally. Here we also check to see if the proxy has already been created—no sense creating a new one if the one we have will do. Proxy creation is expensive in terms of time, especially if you have the System.Diagnostics.DebuggerStepThroughAttribute() set in the proxy. .NET will issue an HTTP POST packet to the Web Service when the proxy is created that establishes debugger causality (establishes deadlock prevention), so you'll sustain at least that round trip when you execute the new. Without the debugging attribute present, you'll still issue and receive a possible Domain Name Server packet, as well as a couple of packets to establish a connection (the standard TCP three-way handshake connection-establishment protocol). All in all, you'll see up to four round trips to the remote server even before you invoke the remote method. If the remote server is truly over the Internet, you can see that unwarranted creation and tear-down of proxies is not recommended.

To show this in action, Figure 7.4 shows the Network Monitor dump for the setup of the SimpleCalc Web Service. The HTTP packet that made the SOAP request is highlighted; in this case, the packet multiplied 9 by 6.

The system is indicated by the MAC (Media Access) address XEROX 000000, while the computer hosting the SimpleCalc Web Service has a MAC address of 6C0720000200. The data from the Netmon dump has been arranged in a sequence diagram, which you see in Figure 7.5.

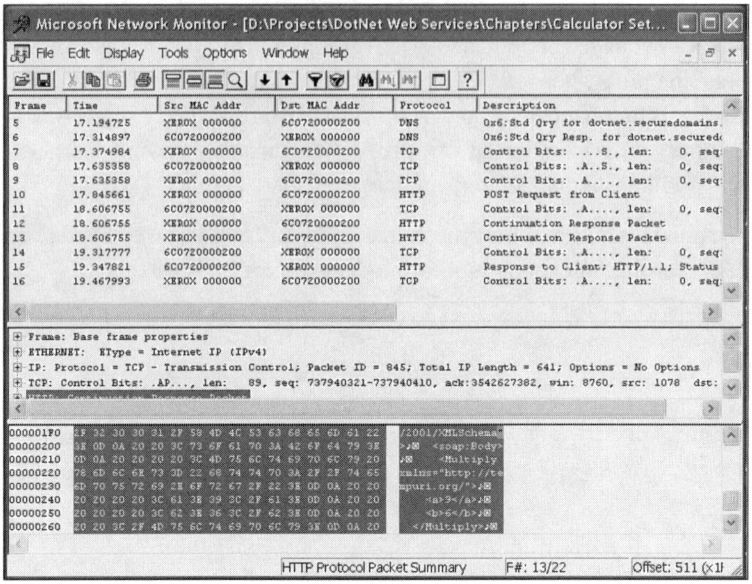

FIGURE 7.4

Netmon output indicating setup of SimpleCalc Web Service.

From Figure 7.5, you see that it took essentially 1.4 seconds to initialize the dialogue between the client and the Web Service. Granted, we're running this over a 64KBps ISDN line instead of a 100MBps local network, but even with the higher bandwidth, it will still take time to establish the connection with the Web Service and begin operations. On my system, which is a 1.7GHz Pentium IV Dell Dimension, you can bet the local calculation took a handful of nanoseconds, so the Web Service is several orders of magnitude more costly in terms of time. Don't reestablish connections if you have no good reason for doing so.

As you've seen, synchronous communications take time. You wait for one call to complete before you turn to another. Application developers often create the illusion that something is happening when the system is actually locked up while waiting for something else to complete. Let's look at one way to better manage time and user perception with Web Services.

Asynchronous Web Services

Being a savvy designer, you probably wouldn't choose a Web Service over a local capability without a good reason for doing so. You most likely already know what Figure 7.5 is telling you—network calls take time. They don't just take a little more time; they take a *lot* more time. But perhaps the cost-to-benefit ratio that the Web Service offers is worth the network hit, so you insert the Web Service into your design.

7

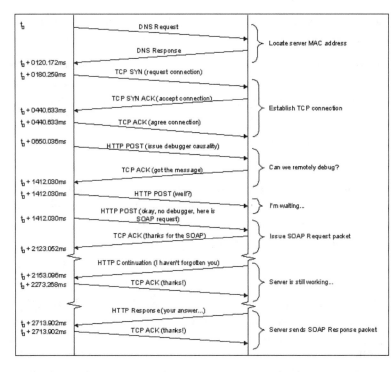

FIGURE 7.5

Netmon output as a sequence diagram.

This evaluation process is a good one to practice. You did your homework, and if Web Services offer something you can't create using local resources, then, by all means, use Web Services. But, depending upon your application, you might have to play tricks to boost performance—or *perceived* performance. And remember, by "application," we don't just mean end-user apps. Web Services and server components could just as easily consume other Web Services, and the time penalty is additive for each network hop.

One good trick that you can use is to make your Web Service call *asynchronous*. With synchronous communications, such as you saw with the Calculator application, you invoke the remote method and stop processing until the Web Service returns an answer. My application stopped working for 1.4 seconds while the Web Service multiplied 9 by 6. You can't do anything about the setup time; it will take some amount of time to establish communications with the Web Service, and that is not negotiable. That's part of the cost of doing business with the Web Service, given the bandwidth of the connection.

However, in some cases you might not need to stop processing and wait for an answer. For example, imagine that your application invoked Web Services exposed by the very bogus car rental agencies Hurtz, Aviz, and Aloha, with the goal being to request pricing for a midsize sedan for several days. (Forget the compacts—you've earned a midsize by now.)

So, your initial implementation used synchronous Web Service invocations in which you first asked Hurtz, then Aviz, and finally Aloha for pricing. If the timelines for each are nominally 1.4 seconds to create the proxy and invoke the Web Service (which is optimistic because the Web Service will almost certainly need to access a database), the total time will be as follows:

```
3 * 1.4 seconds = 4.2 seconds
```

Your user will wait about 4 seconds for an answer.

However, if you invoke the Web Services asynchronously, you again begin by firing off the request to Hurtz, but the Web Service returns control immediately instead of *blocking* (stopping to wait for the Web Service to continue). This means that you can execute each Web Service concurrently, so the total time to get all three responses will be (nominally) 1.4 seconds. This reduces the user's wait time by 66%, which is well worth the effort to make the asynchronous calls.

Asynchronous communication involves callback functions. Within .NET, callback functions often take the form of a *delegate*, which is actually a type-safe generic function pointer. When you initiate the communications, you also register a delegate that the operating system will use to notify you of the results of the communication. In the Web Service case, the delegate takes the form of a method that implements the .NET IAsyncResult interface. Methods that initiate asynchronous communications return objects that implement IAsyncResult. In this case, delegates accept IAsynchResult and act upon the values returned therein. If you refer back to Listing 7.2, you'll find a couple methods defined that fit this description:

```
[System.Diagnostics.DebuggerStepThroughAttribute()]
public System.IAsyncResult BeginAdd(long a, long b,
        ➥System.AsyncCallback callback, object asyncState) {
   return this.BeginInvoke("Add", new object[] {
                a,
                b}, callback, asyncState);
}

[System.Diagnostics.DebuggerStepThroughAttribute()]
public long EndAdd(System.IAsyncResult asyncResult) {
    object[] results = this.EndInvoke(asyncResult);
    return ((long)(results[0]));
}
```

With asynchronous Web Service communication, you no longer have a single method. You have two. The first initiates the communication, and the second retrieves the results of the Web method call. To actually retrieve the results, you'll need to identify the delegate that .NET will use to notify you when the Web Service has concluded its tasks.

Let's demonstrate this and then discuss the results. First, you need a Web Service. Because Hurtz, Aviz, and Aloha are fictitious, we instead created the overly simplistic "Hello World" Web Service on our local machine. To follow along with this example, create a new Web Service project using your favorite language, uncomment the lines that expose "Hello World," and compile. You should now have an identical Web Service that you can use to test— remember that the asynchronous behavior is client-based, not server-based. What the server does is immaterial for this discussion.

With the Web Service in place, create a console-based application, again using your favorite language. We'll create one using C# and Visual Basic .NET, to demonstrate both. Add the Web Reference to the Web Service that you just created as well as the reference to the namespace (which should be *{project name}.localhost*). At this point, you're ready to add the asynchronous call.

> **NOTE**
>
> You can work asynchronously with the Web Service in at least two other ways, but we find that they're not as useful, so they're not presented as alternatives here. Both involve blocking the main client application thread or using polling techniques, which are inefficient for this purpose. They're more parlor tricks than anything else. The technique that you see here is by far the most valid.

> **NOTE**
>
> Of course, as soon as we wrote the previous note, we realized that it isn't precisely true. We're actually going to create *three* client applications to demonstrate asynchronous Web Service communication. This is because, with the second beta of .NET, a bug within Visual Basic .NET prevents what would normally be correct operation from completing correctly. So we'll also provide you the workaround solution, in case you're using .NET Beta 2. This situation also uses the polling method that I mentioned. The true asynchronous behavior should be fixed when the released version of .NET arrives.

The client application for both C# and Visual Basic .NET will be a simple console application that initiates the Web Service asynchronously and then continues processing within the main application thread. Actually, we wait for you to press the Enter key, but the point is that you could continue processing through the main application thread if you needed to do so.

Listing 7.3 provides the C# code for this application.

LISTING 7.3 C# Asynchronous Web Service Client

```csharp
using System;
using CSAsyncClient.localhost;

namespace CSAsyncClient
{
   /// <summary>
   /// Summary description for Class1.
   /// </summary>
   class Class1
   {
      static void Main(string[] args)
      {
         // Beginning test
         Console.WriteLine("(main) Beginning asynchronous communications
                         ➥test...");

         // Create instance of proxy
         Service1 objHelloSvc = new Service1();

         // Make asynchronous call
         objHelloSvc.BeginHelloWorld(new AsyncCallback(Handler),
                                 objHelloSvc);

         // Simulate work...we'll wait for the user
         // to press the <enter> key
         Console.ReadLine();

         // Provide a response
         Console.WriteLine("(main) The main subroutine is now
                         ➥terminating...");
      }

      static void Handler(IAsyncResult iar)
      {
         // Retrieve the returned string
         string str = ((Service1)iar.AsyncState).EndHelloWorld(iar);

         // Notify user
         Console.WriteLine("(web service) Web Service returned '{0}'",str);
      }
   }
}
```

The application begins by printing a note to the screen. The next thing it does is create an instance of the proxy, as you've seen with synchronous applications:

```
// Create instance of proxy
Service1 objHelloSvc = new Service1();
```

Then it makes the asynchronous call:

```
// Make asynchronous call
objHelloSvc.BeginHelloWorld(new AsyncCallback(MyCallback),
                            ➥objHelloSvc);
```

At this point, .NET initiates the Web Service activity. But instead of waiting for the Web Service to complete, .NET returns control to you. Therefore, the next line of code runs nearly immediately:

```
// Simulate work...we'll wait for the user
// to press the <enter> key
Console.ReadLine();
```

We could have done nearly anything, but we elected to wait for the Enter key because this would delay the main thread from terminating before the Web Service could complete. This was for demonstration purposes; we wanted the results of the Web Service displayed before printing the application termination message. Unless you're really quick with the Enter key, you should see the output shown in Figure 7.6.

FIGURE 7.6

Asynchronous Web Service client screen output.

Of course, the call to `Console.ReadLine()` would be replaced with truly useful client code.

It turns out that the Visual Basic .NET code that you would write to perform this same action is very similar to the C# code that you saw in Listing 7.3. This is the code that you'll find in Listing 7.4.

LISTING 7.4   Initial Visual Basic .NET Asynchronous Web Service Client

```
Imports System
Imports VBAsyncClient.localhost

Public Class VBAsyncClient

    Public Shared Sub Main()
        ' Beginning test
        Console.WriteLine("Beginning asynchronous communications test...")

        ' Create instance of proxy
        Dim objHelloSvc As Service1 = New Service1()

        ' Make asynchronous call
        Dim acb As AsyncCallback = New AsyncCallback(AddressOf
                                        ➡VBAsyncClient.Handler)
        objHelloSvc.BeginHelloWorld(acb, objHelloSvc)

        ' Simulate work...we'll wait for the user
        ' to press the <enter> key
        Console.ReadLine()

        ' Provide a response
        Console.WriteLine("The main subroutine is now terminating...")
    End Sub

    Public Shared Sub Handler(ByVal iar As IAsyncResult)
        ' Retrieve the result string
        Dim objHelloSvc As Service1 = iar.AsyncState

        Dim strResult As String = objHelloSvc.EndHelloWorld(iar)
        Console.WriteLine("The Web Service returned {0}", strResult)
    End Sub
End Class
```

The comparison between the Visual Basic .NET code and the C# code is striking, but perhaps less so when you consider the influence of the .NET Web Service support classes. One additional step is required with the Visual Basic .NET version: You must explicitly create a reference to the `AsynchCallback` object that represents the delegate:

```
' Make asynchronous call
Dim acb As AsyncCallback = New AsyncCallback(AddressOf
                                    ➥VBAsyncClient.Handler)
objHelloSvc.BeginHelloWorld(acb, objHelloSvc)
```

The problem with the code shown in Listing 7.4 is the bug mentioned. When created, the delegate is not apprised of the address of the callback function, which, in this case, is `Handler()`. The reference remains null, so the call to the Web Service terminates with a `NullReferenceException` immediately after you press Enter. The solution to this is to poll the asynchronous invocation object and, if it has completed, retrieve the results of the Web Service call. Listing 7.5 gives an example of this.

LISTING 7.5 Beta 2 Visual Basic .NET Asynchronous Web Service Client Workaround

```
Imports System
Imports B2VBAsyncClient.localhost

Public Class B2VBAsyncClient

   Public Shared Sub Main()
      ' Beginning test
      Console.WriteLine("Beginning asynchronous communications test...")

      ' Create instance of proxy
      Dim objHelloSvc As Service1 = New Service1()

      ' Make asynchronous call
      Dim iar As IAsyncResult
      iar = objHelloSvc.BeginHelloWorld(New AsyncCallback(AddressOf
                                 ➥B2VBAsyncClient.Handler), objHelloSvc)

      ' Simulate work...we'll wait for the Web Service to return
      While (False = iar.IsCompleted)
         ' Print something to show we're working...
         Console.WriteLine("Still sleeping..." & DateTime.Now)

         ' Update iar...
         Console.WriteLine(objHelloSvc.EndHelloWorld(iar))
      End While

      ' Provide a response
      Console.WriteLine("The main subroutine is now terminating...")
   End Sub
```

LISTING 7.5   Continued

```
Public Shared Sub Handler(ByVal iar As IAsyncResult)
End Sub

End Class
```

As mentioned, to avoid the true asynchronous bug with the second beta of .NET, you can resort to polling the `IAsyncResult` object returned from `BeginHelloWorld()` to see if its `IsCompleted` property is set:

```
' Simulate work...we'll wait for the Web Service to return
While (False = iar.IsCompleted)
    ' Print something to show we're working...
    Console.WriteLine("Still sleeping..." & DateTime.Now)

    ' Update iar...
    Console.WriteLine(objHelloSvc.EndHelloWorld(iar))
End While
```

The `While` loop does the polling, with the internal call to `EndHelloWorld()` updating the `IAsyncResult` object for each iteration of the loop. We'll let you judge the efficacy of this workaround, but we'd use the C# version if we truly required asynchronous behavior.

So far, then, you've seen a couple of ways to consume Web Services. But if you look at the proxy's code, you'll find something interesting—the URL is hard-coded! So what happens to your proxy (and application) if the URL for the Web Service changes?

Web Service Configuration Files

Let's open the proxy file and take a look at something that can be worrisome. Here is some code from the "Hello World" proxy created for the Visual Basic .NET asynchronous test:

```
Public Class Service1
    Inherits System.Web.Services.Protocols.SoapHttpClientProtocol

    <System.Diagnostics.DebuggerStepThroughAttribute()>  _
    Public Sub New()
        MyBase.New
        Me.Url = "http://localhost/HelloWorld/Service1.asmx"
    End Sub
    ...
End Class
```

Here is the corresponding line for the C# proxy:

0

```
public class Service1 :
  System.Web.Services.Protocols.SoapHttpClientProtocol {

  [System.Diagnostics.DebuggerStepThroughAttribute()]
  public Service1() {
     this.Url = "http://localhost/HelloWorld/Service1.asmx";
  }
  ...
}
```

Clearly, when the proxy was generated, the URL for the Web Service was hard-coded into the source code. This is fine if the Web Service will always be available, but companies and Web sites come and go, enterprise servers change names, and Web Service code migrates from URL to URL.

Because of this, both WSDL.exe and Visual Studio .NET have mechanisms built in that enable you to shift the location of the URL from the proxy source code itself to the Web Service configuration file.

> **NOTE**
>
> .NET considers the Registry obsolete, or at least bad form to use for configuration information. Within .NET, configuration information is typically stored within configuration files, which are XML-based files that are accessible and that are used by the .NET Framework. However, nothing prevents you from storing configuration information in a database or within Active Directory.

When using WSDL.exe, you change the URL storage mechanism using the command-line option /urlkey:key:

```
wsdl /l:cs /o:Proxy.cs /urlkey:MyURL
     ➥http://localhost/HelloWorld/Service1.asmx?wsdl
```

Visual Studio .NET provides you the option of using a *static* or *dynamic* URL in the property settings for the Web reference. Static URL use refers to the hard-coded URL within the proxy source, and dynamic use indicates that the URL should be found in the application's configuration file. Figure 7.7 shows the URL Behavior property.

The advantage of using WSDL.exe is that you can select the key for the URL when you create the proxy. With Visual Studio .NET, the key defaults to `urlsetting`. However, you are free to change this by hand, if you want (don't forget to change the configuration file as well). The big advantage that Visual Studio .NET has over WSDL.exe is that it also creates for you the application configuration file. With WSDL.exe, you'll need to create this yourself.

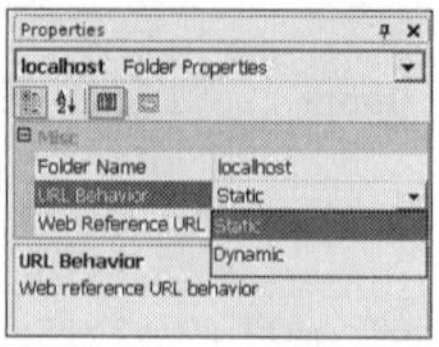

FIGURE 7.7

Visual Studio .NET Web reference URL Behavior property.

After you create the proxy using WSDL.exe and the /urlkey:key command-line option, or after you change the proxy to use a dynamic URL using Visual Studio .NET, the Visual Basic .NET code will look like this:

```
Dim urlSetting As String =
    System.Configuration.ConfigurationSettings.AppSettings
      ➥("VBAsyncClient.localhost.Service1")
If (Not (urlSetting) Is Nothing) Then
   Me.Url = String.Concat(urlSetting, "")
Else
   Me.Url = "{Default URL here...}"
End If
```

The C# code changes to this:

```
string urlSetting = System.Configuration.ConfigurationSettings.AppSettings
                    ➥["CSAsyncClient.localhost.Service1"];
if ((urlSetting != null)) {
   this.Url = string.Concat(urlSetting, "");
}
else {
   this.Url = "{Default URL here...}";
}
```

The resulting configuration file then looks like this (for the C# case):

```
<configuration>
   <appSettings>
      <add key="CSAsyncClient.localhost.Service1"
        value="http://localhost/HelloWorld/Service1.asmx"/>
   </appSettings>
</configuration>
```

One thing to note is that the URL is a public property of the proxy class, so if you'd rather maintain the URL outside the proxy, you can easily do so. The proxy's Url property is as easily changed as any other public class property. This means that you can decide whether you want the proxy to be self-contained or whether you want an external URL manager of some type to maintain the URLs for your proxies, thus enabling you to set the specific URL at runtime.

Now that you've seen how proxies are created and how Web Services are consumed by client applications, it's time to return to Web Service operations. As you might recall, you can establish a SOAP Header using .NET's SOAP classes when you create the Web Service itself. How are they managed on the client?

SOAP Headers

As you might recall from Chapter 6, your Web Service might require the client to process SOAP Headers. Perhaps the client needs to create the Header and provide your Web Service with the appropriate information. Just as likely, your Web Service will be sending the client information in addition to the result of the remote method invocation.

Listing 7.6 consumes the Visual Basic .NET Web Service from the previous chapter, which required the client to complete a Header. The value placed in the Header itself would be returned as a string to prove that the Web Service actually did read and understand the Header. Listing 7.7 shows you the equivalent C# code.

LISTING 7.6   Visual Basic .NET Client SOAP Header Processing

```
Imports System
Imports Ch7VBEx3.localhost

Module Module1

    Sub Main()
        ' Create the Web Service
        Dim objHdrSvc As Service1 = New Service1()

        ' Create the Header itself. This Header will go to the
        ' Web Service for processing
        objHdrSvc.Header1Value = New Header1()
        objHdrSvc.Header1Value.Header = "This is a test!"

        ' Call the Web Service
        Dim strResult As String = objHdrSvc.Foo()

        ' Display the string
        Console.WriteLine("The Web Service returned '{0}'", strResult)
    End Sub

End Module
```

LISTING 7.7 C# Client SOAP Header Processing

```csharp
using System;
using Ch7CSEx3.localhost;

namespace Ch7CSEx3
{
   /// <summary>
   /// Summary description for Class1.
   /// </summary>
   class Class1
   {
      static void Main(string[] args)
      {
         // Create the Web Service
         Service1 objHdrSvc = new Service1();

         // Create the Header itself. This Header will go to the
         // Web Service for processing
         objHdrSvc.Header1Value = new Header1();
         objHdrSvc.Header1Value.Header = "This is a test!";

         // Call the Web Service
         string strResult = objHdrSvc.Bar();

         // Display the string
         Console.WriteLine("The Web Service returned '{0}'", strResult);
      }
   }
}
```

To begin, you will do as you always do—create an instance of the proxy (of course, this is after you've added the Web reference or used WSDL.exe to create the proxy):

```
' Create the Web Service
Dim objHdrSvc As Service1 = New Service1()
```

Unlike the previous clients you've seen, in this case, you'll need to assign a new value to the associated SOAP Header, which is referenced as a public property of the Web Service's proxy class:

```
' Create the Header itself. This Header will go to the
' Web Service for processing
objHdrSvc.Header1Value = New Header1()
objHdrSvc.Header1Value.Header = "This is a test!"
```

The proxy class Service1 contains this code:

```
Public Class Service1
    Inherits System.Web.Services.Protocols.SoapHttpClientProtocol

    Public Header1Value As Header1
    ...
    End Class

<System.Xml.Serialization.XmlRootAttribute([Namespace]:="http://tempuri.org/",
➡IsNullable:=false)>  _
Public Class Header1
    Inherits SoapHeader

    Public Header As String
End Class
```

The Header information contained within the proxy code is italicized. Hopefully this makes it a bit easier to see the correlation between the code that you write to create the Header and the proxy code that supports the Header.

From there, both Listing 7.6 and Listing 7.7 simply invoke the Web Service, which reads the Header and returns the value that it finds there as the return string. There is nothing unusual about this code.

There is another facet to the examples from Chapter 6 to cover before leaving this chapter. In each of the SOAP Header server examples used here, you probably noted the server code also implemented a SoapExtension to dump the contents of the SOAP packets to a log file. Can you do something similar on the client?

Intercepting and Modifying SOAP Packets

As it happens, you can. The proxy source code that WSDL.exe or Visual Studio .NET provides is nothing more than that—source code. As with any source code that you write, you are free to make modifications.

> **NOTE**
>
> That doesn't mean that the modifications you make are safe from automated revision. Because a tool created the proxy source code, the same tool can overwrite any by-hand changes that you make if you regenerate the proxy source file for some reason. Be sure to save a copy of the edited/modified file if you need to re-create the proxy source code. You'll certainly lose your edits if you don't. But, as mentioned, do you change proxy source code that often?

Listing 7.8 shows you the C# source code created to execute a Web Service that implements a SOAP Extension, shown in Listing 7.9, to decrypt a method parameter and send it back as a clear-text string. For the Web Service to decrypt the parameter, the client must encrypt the parameter. This encryption/decryption is all done by SOAP Extensions—.NET default Web Service processing is not involved. The test application itself is very simple: It sends a string to the Web Service and displays the resulting string returned from the Web Service.

LISTING 7.8 Client-Side SOAP Extension Test Application

```
using System;
using Ch7CSEx4Cli.localhost;

namespace Ch7CSEx4Cli
{
    /// <summary>
    /// Summary description for Class1.
    /// </summary>
    class Class1
    {
        static void Main(string[] args)
        {
            // Create an instance of the Web Service
            // and execute...
            Service1 ws = new Service1();
            string strResult = ws.EchoTest("This is a test!");
            Console.WriteLine("Returned string was '{0}'", strResult);
            Console.Write("(Press <enter> key to quit...)");
            Console.ReadLine();
        }
    }
}
```

LISTING 7.9 Client-Side Web Service Proxy with SOAP Extension

```
//------------------------------------------------------------
// <autogenerated>
//     This code was generated by a tool.
//     Runtime Version: 1.0.2914.16
//
//     Changes to this file may cause incorrect behavior and will be lost if
//     the code is regenerated.
// </autogenerated>
//------------------------------------------------------------
```

LISTING 7.9 Continued

```csharp
namespace Ch7CSEx4Cli.localhost {
   using System;
   using System.Diagnostics;
   using System.Xml.Serialization;
   using System.Xml;
   using System.Xml.XPath;
   using System.IO;
   using System.Web;
   using System.Web.Services;
   using System.Web.Services.Protocols;
   using System.Security;
   using System.Security.Cryptography;
   using System.Text;

   [AttributeUsage(AttributeTargets.Method)]
   public class SoapEncrypterAttribute : SoapExtensionAttribute
   {
      private string m_strFilename = "C:\\EncryptLog.txt";
      private int m_iPriority;

      public override Type ExtensionType
      {
         get
         {
            return typeof(SoapEncrypter);
         }
      }

      public override int Priority
      {
         get
         {
            return m_iPriority;
         }
         set
         {
            m_iPriority = value;
         }
      }

      public string LogFile
      {
         get
         {
            return m_strFilename;
         }
```

LISTING 7.9   Continued

```
        set
        {
           m_strFilename = value;
        }
     }
  }

  public class SoapEncrypter : SoapExtension
  {
     private Stream m_stmOld;
     private Stream m_stmNew;
     private string m_strLogFile;
     private byte[] m_key;
     private byte[] m_iv;

     public SoapEncrypter()
     {
        // Create the DES key...note this and the initialization
        // vector must be the same as that used by the server
        // or the value cannot be decrypted...
        m_key = new byte[8];
        m_key[0] = 104; // random data, but same as server
        m_key[1] = 91;
        m_key[2] = 2;
        m_key[3] = 56;
        m_key[4] = 226;
        m_key[5] = 77;
        m_key[6] = 165;
        m_key[7] = 194;

        // Create the DES initialization vector
        m_iv = new byte[8];
        m_iv[0] = 69;
        m_iv[1] = 148;
        m_iv[2] = 67;
        m_iv[3] = 76;
        m_iv[4] = 139;
        m_iv[5] = 21;
        m_iv[6] = 89;
        m_iv[7] = 247;
     }

     public override object GetInitializer(Type serviceType)
     {
        return GetType();
     }
```

LISTING 7.9 Continued

```
public override object GetInitializer(LogicalMethodInfo methodInfo,
                                      SoapExtensionAttribute attribute)
{
   return ((SoapEncrypterAttribute)attribute).LogFile;
}

public override void Initialize(object initializer)
{
   m_strLogFile = (string) initializer;
}

public override void ProcessMessage(SoapMessage message)
{
   switch (message.Stage)
   {
      case SoapMessageStage.BeforeSerialize:
         break;

      case SoapMessageStage.AfterSerialize:
         EncryptInput(message);
         break;

      case SoapMessageStage.BeforeDeserialize:
         LogOutput(message);
         break;

      case SoapMessageStage.AfterDeserialize:
         break;

      default:
         throw new Exception("invalid stage");
   }
}

public override Stream ChainStream( Stream stream )
{
   m_stmOld = stream;
   m_stmNew = new MemoryStream();
   return m_stmNew;
}

public void EncryptInput( SoapMessage message )
{
   // Reset the SOAP stream to load into XPath processor
   m_stmNew.Position = 0;
```

LISTING 7.9   Continued

```
try
{
  // Load it and create a navigator
  XmlDocument xdc = new XmlDocument();
  xdc.Load(m_stmNew);

  // Query for the parameter.
  XmlNamespaceManager mgr = new XmlNamespaceManager(xdc.NameTable);
  mgr.AddNamespace("soap",
                    "http://schemas.xmlsoap.org/soap/envelope/");
  XmlNode nodeBody = xdc.SelectSingleNode("/soap:Envelope/soap:Body",
                                            mgr);
  XmlNode nodeParm = ((XmlNode)nodeBody.FirstChild).FirstChild;

  // Pull element's value as a string
  string strDecrypted = nodeParm.InnerText;

  // Convert the string to a byte array
  UTF8Encoding enc = new UTF8Encoding();
  byte[] bytClear = enc.GetBytes(strDecrypted);

  // Create a stream for encryption
  byte[] bytOut = new byte[4096];
  MemoryStream stmOut = new MemoryStream(bytOut);

  // Create the service provider
  DES des = new DESCryptoServiceProvider();

  // Create the crypto stream and buffer
  CryptoStream stmEncrypt = new CryptoStream(stmOut,
                              des.CreateEncryptor(m_key,m_iv),
                              CryptoStreamMode.Write);

  // Encrypt to memory stream
  stmEncrypt.Write(bytClear,0,bytClear.Length);
  stmEncrypt.FlushFinalBlock();

  // Write XML
  nodeParm.InnerText = Convert.ToBase64String(bytOut,
                                                0,
                                                (int)stmOut.Position);

  // Write encrypted output to stream.
  m_stmNew.SetLength(0);
```

LISTING 7.9   Continued

```
        XmlTextWriter xtw = new XmlTextWriter(m_stmNew,new UTF8Encoding());
        xdc.WriteContentTo(xtw);
        xtw.Flush();
    } // try
    catch (Exception)
    {
        // Do nothing, just pass decrypted value through...
    }

    // Create a file to contain the logged output
    FileStream fstmLog = new FileStream(m_strLogFile,
                                        FileMode.Append,
                                        FileAccess.Write);
    StreamWriter stmLog = new StreamWriter(fstmLog);
    stmLog.WriteLine("---------------------------------" +
            ➥ " (Encrypted) SOAP Response at " + DateTime.Now);
    stmLog.Flush();

    // Write the encrypted output
    m_stmNew.Position = 0;
    Copy(m_stmNew,fstmLog);
    fstmLog.Close();
    m_stmNew.Position = 0;
    Copy(m_stmNew,m_stmOld);
}

public void LogOutput( SoapMessage message )
{
    // Output logging is the same as for previous
    // SoapExtension (as seen in Chapter 6)
    Copy(m_stmOld,m_stmNew);
    FileStream fstmLog = new FileStream(m_strLogFile,
                                        FileMode.Append,
                                        FileAccess.Write);
    StreamWriter stmLog = new StreamWriter(fstmLog);
    stmLog.WriteLine("===================================" +
            ➥ " SOAP Request at " + DateTime.Now);
    stmLog.Flush();
    m_stmNew.Position = 0;
    Copy(m_stmNew,fstmLog);
    fstmLog.Close();
    m_stmNew.Position = 0;
}
```

7

**CONSUMING .NET
WEB SERVICES**

LISTING 7.9 Continued

```
    void Copy(Stream stmFrom, Stream stmTo)
    {
        TextReader trFrom = new StreamReader(stmFrom);
        TextWriter twTo = new StreamWriter(stmTo);
        twTo.WriteLine(trFrom.ReadToEnd());
        twTo.Flush();
    }
}

[System.Web.Services.WebServiceBindingAttribute(
  ➥Name="Service1Soap", Namespace="http://tempuri.org/")]
public class Service1 :
 ➥ System.Web.Services.Protocols.SoapHttpClientProtocol {

    [System.Diagnostics.DebuggerStepThroughAttribute()]
    public Service1() {
        this.Url = "http://localhost/Ch7CSEx4/Service1.asmx";
    }

    [System.Diagnostics.DebuggerStepThroughAttribute()]
    [System.Web.Services.Protocols.SoapDocumentMethodAttribute(
      ➥"http://tempuri.org/EchoTest",
      Use=System.Web.Services.Description.SoapBindingUse.Literal,
      ParameterStyle=System.Web.Services.Protocols.SoapParameterStyle.
      ➥Wrapped)]
    [SoapEncrypter()]
    public string EchoTest(string strEchoMe) {
        object[] results = this.Invoke("EchoTest", new object[] {
                    strEchoMe});
        return ((string)(results[0]));
    }

    [System.Diagnostics.DebuggerStepThroughAttribute()]
    [SoapEncrypter()]
    public System.IAsyncResult BeginEchoTest(string strEchoMe,
                    ➥ System.AsyncCallback callback, object asyncState)
    {
        return this.BeginInvoke("EchoTest", new object[] {
                    strEchoMe}, callback, asyncState);
    }

    [System.Diagnostics.DebuggerStepThroughAttribute()]
    [SoapEncrypter()]
    public string EndEchoTest(System.IAsyncResult asyncResult)
```

LISTING 7.9 Continued

```
    {
        object[] results = this.EndInvoke(asyncResult);
        return ((string)(results[0]));
    }
  }
}
```

Much of what you see in Listing 7.9 is similar to the `SoapExtension` work in Chapter 6. For example, you still declare a `SoapEncrypterAttribute` that references the `SoapEncrypter` SOAP Extension. This enables you to mark each pertinent Web method with the `SoapEncrypter` attribute that activates the SOAP extension when the method is executed. Note that the `SoapEncrypter` attribute was placed on the `EchoTest()` method (synchronous and asynchronous versions).

As before, `ProcessMessage()` routes the SOAP packet to the handlers, both before and after serialization. This is where you activate the code that will encrypt the single method parameter.

At the time the SOAP packet has been created ("after serialized") but not sent to the Web Service, you'll want to change the contents of the SOAP packet. To do that, we created the `EncryptInput()` method.

`EncryptInput()` begins by locating the specific method parameter, as represented by an XML node:

```
// Load it and create a navigator
XmlDocument xdc = new XmlDocument();
xdc.Load(m_stmNew);

// Query for the parameter.
XmlNamespaceManager mgr = new XmlNamespaceManager(xdc.NameTable);
mgr.AddNamespace("soap", "http://schemas.xmlsoap.org/soap/envelope/");
XmlNode nodeBody = xdc.SelectSingleNode("/soap:Envelope/soap:Body", mgr);
XmlNode nodeParm = ((XmlNode)nodeBody.FirstChild).FirstChild;

// Pull element's value as a string
string strDecrypted = nodeParm.InnerText;
```

When you've found the node, you read its text value and place that into a string that you'll later encrypt. Before you can encrypt the string, you need to convert it to a byte array:

```
// Convert the string to a byte array
UTF8Encoding enc = new UTF8Encoding();byte[] bytClear =
➥enc.GetBytes(strDecrypted);
```

7

We did this because the encryption classes expect a byte array rather than a string. With the input to the encryption process in place, you then can turn to creating an instance of the encryption class `DESCryptoServiceProvider`. This is but one encryption class we could have selected, and we had no special reason for selecting this class over any other, except for this caveat: We chose a symmetric algorithm over an asymmetric one.

> **NOTE**
>
> We selected a symmetric algorithm because we didn't want to generate the digital signatures and public/private keys that would be required by the asymmetric case. The difference between the symmetric and asymmetric encryption algorithms is essentially related to the key material. Symmetric algorithms use the same keys on both ends, while the asymmetric ones use public key/private key means (and are much more complex). It was simply a bit easier to show encryption in action if we simply created the keys by hand. We then code the key material into the Web Service, so both client and server have access to the same keys, and the encryption/decryption process works.

In any case, we needed to create a new stream to contain the encrypted information, a cryptographical service provider, and an instance of `CryptoStream` to actually perform the encryption activities:

```
// Create a stream for encryption
byte[] bytOut = new byte[4096];
MemoryStream stmOut = new MemoryStream(bytOut);

// Create the service provider
DES des = new DESCryptoServiceProvider();

// Create the crypto stream and buffer
CryptoStream stmEncrypt = new CryptoStream(stmOut,
                            des.CreateEncryptor(m_key,m_iv),
                            CryptoStreamMode.Write);
```

The tools needed to encrypt the string are now created and ready to perform their tasks, so you can perform the encryption:

```
// Encrypt to memory stream
stmEncrypt.Write(bytClear,0,bytClear.Length);
stmEncrypt.FlushFinalBlock();
```

You now have the encrypted method parameter in the temporary stream that you created, so you can extract the encrypted string data and place it back into the XML stream. Note that we convert the bytes to Base64 for safe transmission:

```
// Write XML
nodeParm.InnerText = Convert.ToBase64String(bytOut, 0, (int)stmOut.Position);
```

So far, you've encrypted the XML value associated with the method parameter, but you haven't actually written the stream with the revised XML information back so that you can send the SOAP packet to the Web Service. For that, you create an instance of XmlTextWriter and save the XML information to the stream that you'll eventually hand back to .NET:

```
// Write encrypted output to stream.
m_stmNew.SetLength(0);
XmlTextWriter xtw = new XmlTextWriter(m_stmNew,new UTF8Encoding());
xdc.WriteContentTo(xtw);
xtw.Flush();
```

The Web Service invokes a similar SOAP extension to pull the encrypted method from the XML stream, decrypt it, and provide it to the deserializer for processing in a normal manner. The actual Web method, EchoTest(), did not "know" that the string parameter was encrypted. This detail was handled behind the scenes.

Hopefully you'll find this technique interesting and useful. However, keep in mind that the point of this example was to show that you can modify the proxy source code to provide the functionality that you require to communicate with the remote Web Service. We simply tried to select a more compelling example.

More Deployment and Debugging

Finally, as in the previous chapter, we'll close with a few words regarding deployment and debugging. As with the Web Service itself, you are free to create a deployment project for your client application using Visual Studio .NET. The process that supports this is the same as the one that you previously saw in the last chapter. In many cases, however, you might be able to simply copy the executable from one system to another.

Debugging the Web Service is fascinating: .NET and Visual Studio .NET allow you to "step into" the remote Web Service. If you create a debug-enabled Web Service that is invoked using a debug-enabled client, you can step into the remote method just as if the code were resident on your local system (some people call this F5 debugging). This is a very handy technique for debugging your Web Services, so definitely take advantage of the capability.

Summary

This chapter was devoted to consumers of Web Services. Although it concentrated on executable applications as consumers, there is no reason that you can't have another Web Service as a client.

Visual Studio .NET was created with Web Services in mind. Because of this, it is easy not only to create Web Services but also to create clients for those Web Services. However, you are not required to use Visual Studio .NET. For example, WSDL.exe will create for you the proxy that you require to access the remote method. Both tools enable you to shift the storage of the Web Service URL from a hard-coded value to a value stored in the application's configuration file.

The chapter then looked at using the Web Service from both a synchronous and asynchronous perspective. For synchronous use, you simply call the method. For asynchronous use, you call the "begin" version of the method and provide it a delegate that .NET will use to call you back when the Web Service finishes its work and sends a response. After the callback is executed, you can decipher the results of the Web Service using the "end" method. All three methods are declared within the proxy.

Because Web Services might require SOAP Headers, you saw how the client would create the SOAP Header, which was wrapped in a class that the Web Service defined for this purpose, and assign it a value. From there, .NET takes over and created the necessary SOAP for you. If you needed to, you could manipulate the SOAP XML stream yourself using a client-side SOAP extension, which is programmed in the same manner as a SOAP extension within the Web Service. In the client's case, the SOAP extension is coded into the proxy, however.

Finally, we mentioned that you can deploy Web Service clients in the same way that you deploy the Web Services themselves; you'll find the techniques for that in the previous chapter. We also mentioned that you can relatively easily debug the Web Service using a client application. Visual Studio .NET provides you with some powerful debugging tools, the most important of which is one that enables you to step into the remote method from the client machine.

The next chapter, ".NET Remoting," deals with .NET's answer to Distributed COM. You'll see remoting in action, as well as learn more about the differences between .NET Web Services and .NET remoting.

More Advanced Web Services

PART

III

.NET Remoting

IN THIS CHAPTER

If you refer back to Table 6.1 in Chapter 6, "Web Services in ASP.NET," you'll see that we compared .NET remoting to .NET Web Services. This book is devoted to .NET Web Services, but we believe it's a good idea to mention .NET remoting and what it entails so that you are familiar with remoting and can make better design decisions when creating .NET systems.

.NET Web Services are the popular technological buzz today, and there is good reason for this. They're flexible, they're compelling, and they offer tremendous advantage over other forms of remote communication (scalability, coupling, and so on). But .NET is also performance-minded. Remember that even though today .NET is a Windows bolt-on technology, by tomorrow .NET will *be* Windows, and possibly even will be implemented natively on other systems as well. So, .NET was created with performance in mind, and it will continue to improve in performance as newer versions are released.

How do Web Services, remoting, .NET, and performance all tie together? Well, to achieve the scalability and loose coupling that Web Services offer, you trade some performance. Accessing Web Services, .NET-based or otherwise, requires additional processing that would otherwise not be required if you were to use a more tightly coupled communications system. This is the ultimate goal of .NET remoting—to bring many of the benefits of .NET Web Services into a slightly more tightly coupled communications architecture to boost .NET object to remote object communication performance.

.NET Remoting Architecture

The basic remoting architecture is as you see in Figure 8.1. The client creates a proxy that represents the remote object. When the client makes a remote method call, the proxy creates a message. The message is routed through message sinks, which process the message in some way, and the message is sent to a channel.

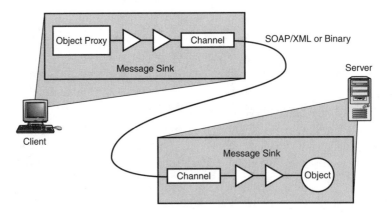

FIGURE 8.1

Basic .NET remoting architecture.

The channel is responsible for transmitting the message to the server, where additional message sinks process the message until the actual object is finally activated and invoked. Let's look at this process in a bit more detail.

Remoting Boundaries

.NET remoting provides you with differing functionality depending upon whether you cross a *boundary*. There are essentially four major types of boundaries:

- Context
- Process
- Application
- Machine

Context bounds are dictated within a given application so that all objects sharing the same runtime constraints also share a context. Objects that do not share similar constraints are placed in separate contexts. For example, security concerns often force particular objects into a context separate from other objects. Thread affinity and synchronization issues also force objects into particular contexts.

Process bounds are defined by the Windows process. That is, one executable application runs within one Windows process. Another Windows executable application runs in another process. Each process is assigned its own virtual address space and protection mechanisms so that if another process suffers a catastrophic error, other processes (ideally) should not be affected. But because each process has its own virtual address space, data (and objects) must be *marshaled* (converted) to values that can safely be sent to another virtual address space. For example, a reference to an object in one address space is meaningless in another address space because the addresses assigned to the object are invalid outside its originating process. Objects that are destined to be accessed by reference must then be converted to references in other address spaces to be valid.

Application bounds, which denote application domains, are specific to .NET and the managed environment. They are essentially logical processes that run within a single physical Windows process and are used to create more scalable systems. They do this because the cost to access data in another address space is relatively high. If you create logical processes within a single Windows process, you achieve the isolation between applications that Windows processes offer, yet you can share information using the same address space. Interprocess marshaling is not required, and your applications together run more quickly.

Machine bounds are probably the easiest to visualize. Objects on one machine that access objects on another machine cross machine bounds to do so (typically using a network connection). Just remember that process and context bounds are just as firm and require some of the same plumbing to operate correctly.

The reason boundaries are so critical is that if, when using remoting, no boundary is crossed, .NET wires the calling object and the called object together for the highest possible efficiency. Depending upon the boundary that is crossed, .NET brings increasingly complex systems into play to manage the communication required to link the two (caller and callee). Knowing this enables you to optimize the placement and runtime environments for your application objects.

Remoting Object Model

You can remote essentially four types of "objects" using .NET:

- Interfaces
- Context-bound classes
- Agile classes
- Value types

Interface remoting refers to exposing an object that you create by interface so that other objects access your object through the interface that you provide. In reality, you're accessing an object, but it is through a standard set of methods exposed by the particular interface.

Context-bound classes are classes that must be accessed via proxy outside their context. This guarantees that the code supporting the object will execute within the specific context—say, with some security constraint or thread affinity issue. The caller obtains the proxy and makes object method calls only through the proxy, unless the two objects happen to reside within the same context (no boundary is then crossed). This is very much like the traditional Web Service model that you've seen thus far—the Web Service runs on its server, and you access it through a proxy.

Agile classes come in two forms: those that are bound to an application domain and those that are completely unbound. Application-bound classes are remotable outside their application domain, but, as with context-bound classes, by proxy only. Within their application domain, no proxy is required. Unbound classes have no limitations with respect to context or application domain, and they can be shared and executed within the context and application domain of the caller.

Value types are simply .NET datatypes, such as integers, structs, and strings, that exist in memory on the method's call stack (versus out in general "heap" memory). These can also be remoted and could be considered unbound because no proxy is required to access their value.

The basis for the object model is twofold. First, you get a sense of the cost to access the remote object based upon its location in the remoting object model. For example, bound classes will require a proxy outside their binding locality. Whenever you use a proxy, performance is degraded to some degree (how much depends upon the objects in question and the locality of the caller). But if in your design you manage to stay within the bounding scope of the "remote" object, if this is possible, you garner increased performance. Second, you'll know precisely where the computations will take place—which specific context, which application domain and process, or even which machine. You can better plan workload optimization, network utilization, and so forth.

While we're talking about a remote communications process, there must be some way for data to traverse the distance between objects. With .NET remoting, this communication takes place over a channel.

Remoting Channels

Channels are themselves objects, and their sole purpose is to transfer messages from object to object. Their communications can be established to provide them with unidirectional or bidirectional capabilities, making it easy to plug different channels into your remoting system. For example, perhaps you send data to a remote object using TCP, but you prefer the response to the data transfer to come back to your local system using HTTP.

The basic interfaces for channels are `IChannel`, `IChannelReceiver`, and `IChannelSender`. Channel objects derive from `IChannel` and implement one or both of the communications interfaces.

Channels are shared resources. That is, when you initiate remoting, you register the channels that you require:

```
Dim channel As New TcpChannel(8080)
ChannelServices.RegisterChannel(channel)
```

In this case, we're registering with the TCP channel and using port 8080 (a port often available through firewalls, although this is not universally true). Other objects that register the same channels also share those channels with you. They might not receive the same messages that you do, though, because they and you are located at different endpoints. But they share the channel nonetheless; you can imagine the channel objects as implementing a form of resource sharing.

Channels are also one point within the communications path where you have the option of extending the communications framework. You can do so by providing a *sink*, which is an object that implements `IMessageSink`. Sink objects accept messages, which themselves implement `IMessage` and perform specific actions upon the message. Sinks are chained, so one or several sink objects might deal with a given message as it passes through the system.

Assuming that objects have access to channels of communication, what makes an object remotable? Let's explore that issue in the next section.

Remotable Objects

Not all objects that you create will be remotable. In fact, odds are good that most of the objects you create will not be remotable because there are some specific constraints placed upon them to allow the remoting system to transmit them from place to place. Specifically, remotable objects must either implement ISerializable (or use SerializableAttribute) or derive from System.MarshalByRefObject. Objects that do neither are not remotable outside their context.

Serializable Objects

Objects that implement the ISerializable interface (or, again, that use SerializableAttribute) are considered to be *serializable*—that is, they are remoted *by value*. When an object is remoted, the entire object—or, at least, its state information (internal values and such)—is copied from one domain to another, and an exact replica of the original object is created at the remote end. The extent of the communications process ends there because changes to the original object's state do not affect the copied object's state. To do that, you would instantiate another copy.

These types of objects are often referred to as *marshal-by-value* objects, and you'll see this term used often in remoting literature (we'll examine the corollary, *marshal-by-reference* objects, in the next section). You provide methods that the remoting system will execute that roll your object into a formatted form that is suitable for transmission.

The key there is *formatted*. The values that your object encapsulates must be formatted for transmission, and several built-in formatters are available:

- XML/SOAP (System.Runtime.Serialization.Formatters.Soap.SoapFormatter)
- Binary (System.Runtime.Serialization.Formatters.Binary.BinaryFormatter)

Which you select depends on the needs of your application. Binary is most efficient with respect to parsing and transmission. The SOAP formatter, however, offers the advantages of the SOAP protocol (XML, nonproprietary, and so on). An obvious use for each is to develop your objects using the SoapFormatter, to enable you to debug the network packets with relative ease, but switch to the BinaryFormatter when you're ready to ease your object into a production environment. Of course, this assumes .NET to .NET communication. If you happen to be remoting to an external system (non–.NET), you'll most likely maintain the SOAP message format.

NOTE

There is a 1:1 mapping between the formatter that you select and the channel that you use. That is, the binary formatter is associated with the TCP channel, while the SOAP formatter is associated with the HTTP channel.

You select the formatter that you want when you serialize your object's state. For example, in Visual Basic .NET, you might use code such as this:

```
Dim objFormatter As IFormatter = new BinaryFormatter()
```

In C#, you'd use this:

```
IFormatter objFormatter = new SoapFormatter();
```

You'll most likely, then, use the IFormatter's `Serialize()` or `Deserialize()` methods to actually read and write the formatted data.

Passing objects by value is fine in many cases, but sometimes you'll want to access the original object, not just a deep copy. For this, you'll need to access the object by reference.

Marshaling Objects by Reference

For an object to be remoted by reference, it must extend `MarshalByRefObject`. That is, the object must derive from this class:

```
public class MyRemotableClass : MarshalByRefObject
{
    ...
}
```

`MarshalByRefObject` is intelligent. If the object requires a proxy, such as when the caller and callee are on different machines, for example, the remoting system creates a proxy and makes all the calls to the remote object through the proxy. Method parameters and properties are serialized and transmitted, and the object is then invoked with the deserialized values. However, if no proxy is required, such as when the caller and callee coexist within the same context or application domain (depending upon the objects), the remoting system makes direct calls to the object because they share the same memory. There is no need to remote the object.

The essential design principle for using marshal-by-reference objects is that you'll need to use them when the state information contained within the object is meaningful only within the originating address space. Window handles, for example, have no meaning between remote machines, so an object that deals directly with a window handle would be remoted by reference. This enables the remote client to change facets of the window through the window handle, even though the remote client never actually sees or uses the window handle. Something to consider, however, is that the communications between the client object and the server object (caller and callee) may at times require significant time to complete if the objects are connected using reduced-bandwidth communications media.

So you've seen how objects are serialized, but what about activation and lifetime issues? How is a remote object activated, and how long will it exist before the operating system decides to collect it? That's the topic of the next section.

8

.NET REMOTING

Object Lifetimes

With respect to remoting, objects have a lifetime that begins when they're *activated*. If they're activated from a client, their usefulness continues through their *lifetime lease period*. Activation depends upon your point of view, client or server, and leasing is configurable but controlled by the client (server defaults can be established by the server, however).

> **NOTE**
>
> Activation and leasing are concepts that are related to marshal-by-reference objects only. Marshal-by-value objects have no need of activation and leasing because they are transmitted as a complete bundle of data and will exist for as long as the client wants them to remain uncollected.

Client-Side Remote Object Activation

The client creates an instance of the remote object when it executes `new` or `System.Activator.CreateInstance()` against the remote object's proxy (or the object itself, if remoting determines that this is possible). The client establishes the lifetime lease period, which will be a default value if none is provided. `new` is the easiest and most obvious way to create the remote object, but the `Activator` class allows for much greater control over the activation process. For example, with the `Activator` class, you can specify the *binding flags*, which, among other things, enable you to specify operation types and access settings with respect to the remote object. The `Activator` class is simply a .NET class designed to create remote objects on your behalf.

Server-Side Remote Object Activation

The server object is not actually created until it receives its first client method call. That is, even though a client executes `new` and creates an instance of the remote object's proxy, the remote object itself won't be created on the remote system until the client executes a method call against the remote object.

Server objects come in one of two varieties:

- SingleCall
- Singleton

SingleCall objects are activated so that they accept only a single method invocation before they are collected. After this one-time activation, they're destroyed and another instance of the object must be created if the server makes another call. You might use this type of activation if the object consumes a nontrivial resource yet is called infrequently.

The Singleton object may be used to serve multiple method calls, except that, instead of serving a single client, the singleton object serves *all* clients. That is, no matter how many different clients create proxies to this remote object, only a single object is ever created. This type of object has many uses, but it is most often used to maintain state across many clients (such as a counter) or when very expensive resources are involved (such as when controlling a machine).

In the case of client activation, we mentioned that the object exists on the remote server for the duration of the lifetime lease period. What's a lifetime lease period?

Object Leasing

A lifetime lease period is essentially a fancy name for a timeout. The object exists for a specific length of time, after which it is deleted and collected to be reclaimed by the system. Each application domain has a lease manager that is responsible for implementing the lease behavior, which has an interesting twist.

If a lifetime lease period is about to expire, the system's lease manager invokes a method on the client proxy that requests a continuance. That is, the remote system will first ask you, the *sponsor*, if you would like to extend the life of this particular object; if you want to do so, its lifetime lease is extended. If you do not respond, the object is destroyed if all other clients also deny the object additional time.

Lifetime leases are managed through the ILease interface, which enables you to access a collection of lease properties, or through simple object invocation. Each time you invoke the object, it receives a new lifetime lease period.

The actual lifetime of the object is the sum of the specified lifetime lease period and the *renew-on-call* time. The renew-on-call time is the time it would take to request a new lease on life from the sponsor. This prevents the object from being destroyed before you have an input. When the lifetime lease period expires, the remote object (through its lease manager) requests additional time from the sponsor. If the sponsor is unavailable, the object exists for the duration of the SponsorshipTimeout. All these values can be established through the application's configuration file or through code. For example, in code, you would adjust the lease settings through the InitializeLifetimeService() method, which comes from MarshalByRefObject:

```
public class MyRemoteObject: MarshalByRefObject {
    ...
    public override Object InitializeLifetimeService()
    {
        ILease lease = (ILease)base.InitializeLifetimeService();
        if (lease.CurrentState == LeaseState.Initial)  {
            lease.InitialLeaseTime = TimeSpan.FromMinutes(2);
            lease.SponsorshipTimeout = TimeSpan.FromMinutes(5);
            lease.RenewOnCallTime = TimeSpan.FromSeconds(5);
        }
```

8

.NET REMOTING

```
    return lease;
  }
  ...
}
```

If you override `InitializeLifetimeService()`, you have your *one shot* at setting the lease values. You won't get a second request for lease information with this object. You'll have to wait to create another remote object to establish its lease settings.

Configuring .NET Remoting

Many systems probably rely upon configuration files to establish remote object endpoints and lease values, although, as you've just seen (leasing), you can configure things programmatically. Configuration files, though, enable you to be flexible when you deploy your objects. Changing remoting values is as easy as changing XML information, which is quite easy to do.

You'll want to include four pieces of information in your configuration file:

- The channel registration information
- Any metadata associated with your remote invocation
- The type of activation that you require or desire (client versus server)
- The endpoint URL for the object

Although you might not have metadata to declare, you'll certainly need to provide information for the remaining three items in your configuration file. This is probably easier to show by example, so let's look at the client configuration file HelloNew.exe.config that you'll find tucked away in your .NET Framework directory (typically found in C:\Program Files\ Microsoft.NET\FrameworkSDK\Samples\technologies\remoting\basic\remotinghello\client\ consoleclient):

```
<configuration>
  <system.runtime.remoting>
    <application>

      <client url="http://localhost/RemotingHello">
        <wellknown type="Hello.HelloService, Hello"
          url="http://localhost/RemotingHello/HelloService.soap" />
      </client>

      <channels>
        <channel type="System.Runtime.Remoting.Channels.Http.HttpChannel,
                   ➥System.Runtime.Remoting" />
      </channels>
```

```
        </application>
    </system.runtime.remoting>
</configuration>
```

From this example file, you can see that the remote object is to be activated by the client because we see the `<client/>` element. You also can see that it will use the SOAP formatter because it is registering the HTTP channel and the well-known type uses the .soap-terminated URL. The type itself has this form:

```
type="assembly.class, assembly"
```

This provides the .NET Framework with the type information that it requires to create a proxy to the remote object without actually issuing a network call. To do that, you need the endpoint URL, which is given by the URL attribute to the `<client/>` element—in this case, that is `http://localhost/RemotingHello`.

.NET Remoting Example

In fact, an example now is actually in order. Several examples are available within the .NET Framework SDK, and some are more complex than others. For this example, you'll stick with something rather simple: You'll access a remote object that will give you the server's local time.

To begin, fire up Visual Studio .NET and create a new class library. We did this for Visual Basic .NET; we've shown the code that we inserted into the class library in Listing 8.1.

LISTING 8.1   The RemoteTimeServer Implementation

```
Imports System

Public Class RemoteTime
    Inherits MarshalByRefObject

    Public Function GetServerTime() As String
        ' Simply return the current time
        GetServerTime = DateTime.Now.ToString()
    End Function

End Class
```

Here you see a class, `RemoteTime`, that implements a method, `GetServerTime()`. The class will compile into an assembly also called `RemoteTime`. Because the class `RemoteTime` derives from `MarshalByRefObject`, you know that it's remotable by reference. The function `GetServerTime()` does very little—it returns the current time as a string, as you envisioned.

The client code is not much more difficult, and it's shown in Listing 8.2. For this, we created a Visual Basic .NET console application that you can use as an execution environment for the remote object.

LISTING 8.2 The RemoteTimeClient Implementation

```
Imports System.Runtime.Remoting
Imports System.Runtime.Remoting.Channels
Imports System.Runtime.Remoting.Channels.HTTP

Module RemoteTimeClient

    Sub Main()
        ' Inform the remoting infrastructure that all of the
        ' necessary information is contained within the
        ' application's configuration file...
        RemotingConfiguration.Configure("RemoteTimeClient.exe.config")

        ' Create an instance of the proxy
        Dim rt As RemoteTimeServer.RemoteTime = New RemoteTimeServer.RemoteTime()

        ' Invoke a remote method
        Console.WriteLine("Server's time was {0}", rt.GetServerTime())
    End Sub

End Module
```

Note that we created a configuration file named RemoteTimeClient.exe.config, the contents of which we've placed in Listing 8.3. After the main application configures the remoting infrastructure with the call to `RemotingConfiguration.Configure()`, it creates an instance of the remote object's proxy. If this is successful, you invoke the `GetServerTime()` method on the remote server object and display the results.

LISTING 8.3 The RemoteTimeClient Configuration File

```
<configuration>
  <system.runtime.remoting>
    <application name="RemoteTimeClient">

      <client url="HTTP://localhost/RemotingTimeServer">
        <activated type="RemoteTime.RemoteTime, RemoteTime" />
      </client>

      <channels>
```

LISTING 8.3 Continued

```
        <channel type="System.Runtime.Remoting.Channels.Http.HttpChannel,
                    ➥ System.Runtime.Remoting" />
    </channels>

    </application>
  </system.runtime.remoting>
</configuration>
```

To create the configuration file, we used the example in the previous section, "Configuring .NET Remoting," and made the appropriate changes (we've italicized these in Listing 8.3).

To run this, we inserted a reference to the class library DLL's project in the client application and ran the application.

Summary

This chapter outlined the .NET remoting technology and hopefully gave you an appreciation for how it differs from traditional Web Services, which you've studied throughout this book. For example, you learned about channels, formatters, and configuration files, among other things. Not once did we mention WSDL or UDDI, or the other .NET Framework Class Library attributes and objects that you've examined.

.NET remoting differs from .NET XML Web Services in that .NET remoting is .NET's answer to DCOM. Although for the near future we'll likely see .NET remoting used between .NET systems, the remoting architecture is extensible to other platforms. The goal of remoting is still to couple remote objects rather than publish consumable services.

The next chapter, "Extreme Web Services," returns you to the Web Service world and examines some advanced topics that you may find interesting, including transactional support, streaming, encryption, and more.

8

.NET REMOTING

Extreme Web Services

IN THIS CHAPTER

This chapter provides a blend of topics that are somewhat unrelated to one another but still necessary to the Web Service model. Here, we provide practical approaches to more complex problems, and we introduce some new technologies that might have significant impact on the way you build and expose your services.

We start by introducing several ways to carry XML payloads within a SOAP message. This is an important issue because a surprising number of systems already use XML, and you might encounter a situation in which you must wrap this XML within your own SOAP messages. This leads into the more general approach of handling payloads that consist of binary information.

The topic of how transactions might be handled in an unreliable Web world is also discussed. Two opposing viewpoints are provided so that you can formulate your own opinions and choose the approach that best fits your situation.

Some additional thoughts on debugging Web Services are discussed, with special emphasis on the client's capability to decipher the service's behavior.

Finally, we conclude the chapter by providing a framework that you might choose to follow when documenting your services.

Embedded XML

The growth of XML has been remarkable, and it has many developers just looking for a reason to use it. But because XML is being used so frequently, it brings up some important questions about how it should be used in combination with XML messaging. Let's first take a closer look at the issues, and then we'll introduce some ideas that you will want to consider.

Entity References

You already know that a SOAP message is nothing more than an XML document that applies some packaging and encoding rules to information. Listing 9.1 shows an example SOAP request message for a simple message logging operation. In this case, clients can log arbitrary messages with the logging service.

LISTING 9.1   SOAP LogMessage Operation

```
<SOAP-ENV:Envelope xmlns:SOAP-ENV="http://schemas.xmlsoap.org/soap/envelope/">
  <SOAP-ENV:Body>
    <LogMessage xmlns="http://www.mcp.com/Logger">
      <msg>This is a test.</msg>
    </LogMessage>
  </SOAP-ENV:Body>
</SOAP-ENV:Envelope>
```

However, what happens when a client decides to use XML within the message, such as `<This><is>a test.</is></This>`? Of course, .NET does the right thing by applying standard entity references to the string also known as *escaping*. Listing 9.2 shows the output that .NET produces. Notice the character replacements of less-than characters with < as well as other similar character substitutions.

LISTING 9.2   LogMessage with Entity References

```
<SOAP-ENV:Envelope xmlns:SOAP-ENV="http://schemas.xmlsoap.org/soap/envelope/">
  <SOAP-ENV:Body>
    <LogMessage xmlns="http://www.mcp.com/Logger">
      <msg>&lt;This&gt;&lt;is&gt;a test.&lt;/is&gt;&lt;/This&gt;</msg>
    </LogMessage>
  </SOAP-ENV:Body>
</SOAP-ENV:Envelope>
```

Manipulating the text in this way is necessary to avoid corrupting the XML structure of the SOAP message. However, the extra encoding in this example equates to an 83% increase in the size of the `<msg>` parameter. Because this example string is small, you'll see only a modest 24 extra bytes. For a large string (50K or more) with comparable tagging, this increase might start to have a noticeable effect on system performance. We also should mention that parsing this string and performing the reference substitution requires processor cycles that take away from system performance. Might there be a better way?

CDATA Sections

An alternative approach, although one that many consider a poor design choice, is to wrap CDATA sections around dangerous text. CDATA enables you to wrap *almost* any text in its original form without corrupting the tagging structure of the message, and you don't have to perform character substitutions. Listing 9.3 shows an example.

LISTING 9.3   LogMessage with CDATA

```
<SOAP-ENV:Envelope xmlns:SOAP-ENV="http://schemas.xmlsoap.org/soap/envelope/">
  <SOAP-ENV:Body>
    <LogMessage xmlns="http://www.mcp.com/Logger">
      <msg><![CDATA[<This><is>a test</is></This>]]></msg>
    </LogMessage>
  </SOAP-ENV:Body>
</SOAP-ENV:Envelope>
```

9

EXTREME WEB
SERVICES

This brute-force method resolves the message bloating that can occur with entity references, and it still solves the problem. But, wait—it, too, comes with some heavy baggage. CDATA sections do not enable you to nest other CDATA sections. In other words, you cannot do the following:

```
<msg><![CDATA[<This><is>a test of <![CDATA[some <tag> structure]]>
</is></This>]]></msg>
```

The semantics of CDATA sections are to continuously ignore characters until the parser sees an ending]]> character combination. So, to an XML parser, the previous example would look something like this:

```
<msg><![CDATA[{ignored text}]]> </is></This>]]></msg>
```

The inserted]]> characters cause the parser to prematurely stop processing the CDATA section. Of course, the superfluous tags cause the parser some grief. This example just emphasizes why CDATA sections are not a very elegant solution.

NOTE

In rare situations, when a parameter will contain a large quantity of XML and you know that the contents of a parameter will *never* contain CDATA sections (or extraneous]]> characters), you might consider wrapping that parameter with a CDATA section. But be aware that you will have to implement this functionality on your own because .NET automatically chooses to use entity references. Refer to the .NET documentation for information about the XmlTextWriter class and its WriteString method behavior.

Consider yet another approach, in which binary or text content is represented by a text-based encoding scheme called base64.

base64 Encoding

Although base64 encoding has been around for quite some time, very few people like to use it for XML messages. For one thing, base64 encoding hides information in an unreadable form. This is fine for binary data, but for text-based information, base64 encoding can lead to tunneled data that hides interface semantics.

Some developers believe that base64 encoding is a form of security because it's not immediately human-readable, but the reality is that anyone with base64 decoding software (such as anyone running .NET) can easily decode the information. Additionally, base64 bloats your data by an additional 33% (roughly). This is probably acceptable for small quantities of data, but large information blocks will have a noticeable impact on performance.

Listing 9.4 shows a simple Web Service that takes a fully qualified path and filename as input and returns a base64-encoded bitmap image from the specified location.

> **NOTE**
>
> This example illustrates just how dangerous a poorly designed Web Service can be. Because this service enables the client to specify any path and filename, it opens up a rather nasty security hole. You should view this example as a cute demonstration of base64 encoding, not as a realistic approach for a publicly exposed Web Service.

LISTING 9.4   base64 Encoding Server

```
[WebMethod]
public byte[] RetrieveBitmap(string fileName)
{
  if (fileName.Length > 0)
  {
    try
    {
      // Open the bitmap
      FileStream fstream = File.Open(fileName, FileMode.Open);

      // Read the bitmap
      byte[] buffer = new Byte[fstream.Length];
      fstream.Read(buffer, 0, (int)fstream.Length);
      fstream.Close();

      // Return the bitmap
      return (buffer);
    }
    catch(Exception){}
  }
  return (null);
}
```

The client application shown in Listing 9.5 requests a bitmap file from the service and displays the image on a form.

Let's take a closer look at the messages that are sent between the client and the service. Listings 9.6 and 9.7 show the request and response messages, respectively.

9

EXTREME WEB SERVICES

LISTING 9.5   base64 Decoding Client

```
private void button1_Click(object sender, System.EventArgs e)
{
  localhost.Service1 svc = new localhost.Service1();

  try
  {
    // Load the bitmap from the Web Service
    MemoryStream mystream = new MemoryStream(
                                svc.RetrieveBitmap(this.textBox1.Text));
    if (mystream.Length > 0)
    {
      // Display the bitmap
      Bitmap bmp = new Bitmap(mystream);
      this.pictureBox1.Image = bmp;
    }
  }
  catch (Exception)
  {
    // Clear the bitmap
    this.pictureBox1.Image = null;
  }
}
```

LISTING 9.6   base64 Request Message

```xml
<?xml version="1.0" encoding="utf-8"?>
<soap:Envelope xmlns:soap="http://schemas.xmlsoap.org/soap/envelope/"
               xmlns:xsi="http://www.w3.org/2001/XMLSchema-instance"
               xmlns:xsd="http://www.w3.org/2001/XMLSchema">
  <soap:Body>
    <RetrieveBitmap xmlns="http://tempuri.org/">
      <fileName>c:\triangles.bmp</fileName>
    </RetrieveBitmap>
  </soap:Body>
</soap:Envelope>
```

LISTING 9.7   base64 Response Message

```xml
<?xml version="1.0" encoding="utf-8"?>
<soap:Envelope xmlns:soap="http://schemas.xmlsoap.org/soap/envelope/"
               xmlns:xsi="http://www.w3.org/2001/XMLSchema-instance"
               xmlns:xsd="http://www.w3.org/2001/XMLSchema">
  <soap:Body>
```

LISTING 9.7   Continued

```
    <RetrieveBitmapResponse xmlns="http://tempuri.org/">
      <RetrieveBitmapResult>
Qk3GAAAAAAAAAEYAAAAoAAAAEAAAABAAAAABAAQAAAAAIAAAAATCwAAEwsAAAQAAAAEAAAAAAAAIA
AAAD/AAAA//8AACAQEBAQEBAQIgEBAQEBAQEiIBAQEBAQESIiAQEBAQERIiIgEBAQEREiIiIBAQERES
IiIiAQERERIiIiIgEREREiIiIiIRERESIiIiIyERERIiIiIyMhEREiIiIyMjIRESIiIyMjIyERIiIyM
JIyMhEiIyMjIyMjISIyMjIyMjIy
      </RetrieveBitmapResult>
    </RetrieveBitmapResponse>
  </soap:Body>
</soap:Envelope>
```

The TRIANGLES.BMP file is 198 bytes in its raw binary form, but, when encoded in base64, the image requires 267 bytes, making it roughly 35% larger. This is probably not a bad price to pay to be able to keep the image explicitly associated with the SOAP message.

Listing 9.8 shows a code fragment from the WSDL <types> section, where the base64 type information is shown in the interface schema.

LISTING 9.8   WSDL base64 Type

```
<types>
  <s:schema attributeFormDefault="qualified" elementFormDefault="qualified"
            targetNamespace="http://tempuri.org/">
    <s:element name="RetrieveBitmap">
      <s:complexType>
        <s:sequence>
          <s:element minOccurs="1" maxOccurs="1" name="fileName"
                     nillable="true" type="s:string" />
        </s:sequence>
      </s:complexType>
    </s:element>
    <s:element name="RetrieveBitmapResponse">
      <s:complexType>
        <s:sequence>
          <s:element minOccurs="1" maxOccurs="1" name="RetrieveBitmapResult"
                     nillable="true" type="s:base64Binary" />
        </s:sequence>
      </s:complexType>
    </s:element>
    <s:element name="base64Binary" nillable="true" type="s:base64Binary" />
  </s:schema>
</types>
```

As you can see from the listing, .NET's byte array is serialized as the `base64Binary` type defined in the XML Schema specification.

From a practical standpoint, base64 encoding is better for passing binary data than text, and .NET's byte array type makes base64 encoding an extremely simple task. Alternative approaches to base64 encoding have been proposed—specifically, multipart/related MIME and a new protocol called DIME. We will present more detailed descriptions of these proposals later in this chapter.

You've seen how base64 encoding can be used for binary data, but what should you do about text information? The most obvious approach is to incorporate that information as a meaningful part of the message. The next section suggests reasons for why and when this is a good idea.

Rich XML Messaging

In reality, using entity references or base64 encoding does solve the problem of protecting messages from becoming corrupted by harmful parameters. But if the intent is to purposely transmit XML inside a string parameter, you should consider a potentially better approach.

You need to ask yourself why you're trying to *tunnel* XML inside a string parameter. Would it be better to incorporate this XML into the overall message schema? The reason that you're defining an interface is to provide a client with information about the syntax and semantics of your service. The following example helps to illustrate this point.

Given the previously described `LogMessage` service, assume that you want to create log entries using an XML format. This is a reasonable idea that enables you to apply style sheets to your log files for filtering and sorting purposes. Consider the following format for each log file entry:

```
<logEntry>
  <time>2001-07-14T16:35:27-05:00</time>
  <file>MyFile.cs</file>
  <line>38</line>
  <description>Entered constructor.</description>
</logEntry>
```

The temptation is to simply place this XML into a string and pass it to the `LogMessage` service. As you've seen, this works perfectly well—.NET properly serializes and deserializes the XML, and the service places the text into a log file.

However, one day you realize that your style sheet suddenly doesn't work because another developer decided to use a completely different format for his log entries. This type of problem is quite common when you haven't clearly defined the syntax of your service.

Additionally, by tunneling information, you're burying interface details that eventually have to come out. This requires you to document the underlying syntax somewhere other than in a service description document.

NOTE

Most complicated Web Services probably have accompanying documentation anyway, so providing some additional syntax rules really isn't a big issue. But the less ambiguous your interfaces and parameters are, the better chance your clients have of using them correctly.

Microsoft's Favorites Web Service is an example of a more complex service that also contains API documentation. Refer to Appendix D, ".NET Web Service Resources," for the associated MSDN links.

A much cleaner approach is to define a more specific `LogMessage` structure than just a single `msg` parameter, like this:

```
<SOAP-ENV:Envelope xmlns:SOAP-ENV="http://schemas.xmlsoap.org/soap/envelope/">
  <SOAP-ENV:Body>
    <LogMessage xmlns="http://www.mcp.com/Logger">
      <time>2001-07-14T16:35:27-05:00</time>
      <file>MyFile.cs</file>
      <line>38</line>
      <description>Entered constructor.</description>
    </LogMessage>
  </SOAP-ENV:Body>
</SOAP-ENV:Envelope>
```

Given the schema shown in Listing 9.9, there's no question which parameters need to be provided to your service. It's also much easier for your service to validate parameters that have a clear and distinct purpose.

LISTING 9.9   An Improved `LogMessage` Web Method

```
<s:schema xmlns:s="http://www.w3.org/2001/XMLSchema"
          attributeFormDefault="qualified"
          elementFormDefault="qualified"
          targetNamespace="http://www.mcp.com/Logger">
  <s:element name="LogMessage">
    <s:complexType>
      <s:sequence>
        <s:element minOccurs="1" maxOccurs="1" name="time"
                   type="s:dateTime" />
```

LISTING 9.9   Continued

```
        <s:element minOccurs="1" maxOccurs="1" name="file" nillable="true"
                type="s:string" />
        <s:element minOccurs="1" maxOccurs="1" name="line" type="s:int" />
        <s:element minOccurs="1" maxOccurs="1" name="description" nillable="true"
                type="s:string" />
      </s:sequence>
    </s:complexType>
  </s:element>
</s:schema>
```

Yet another solution to the problem of sending XML is to package information at the application protocol layer, such as in HTTP attachments.

SOAP Messages with Attachments

Although the rich messaging approach promotes cleaner syntax and semantics, there are pragmatic reasons why this doesn't always work well.

The first issue is, of course, performance. When working with large XML documents that contain lots of tags, parsers can take an extremely long time to interpret a message. The recipient might not be interested in the majority of the message, but he still will have to wait for the entire message to be parsed.

The second issue is that you might not always know the exact schema of the XML document you're transmitting. This is especially true if your application has to treat the XML as an opaque document, regardless of its content. This can also be true when a data source provides XML in a structure that is inconsistent with your service.

> **NOTE**
>
> You might argue that rather than transmitting an inconsistent XML document, the service should simply return a fault response message. In many cases, this might be true. But what if you are writing a client that is responsible for correcting erroneous XML documents and does so over a SOAP connection? Clearly, faulting these messages would prevent your client from performing its intended job.

Finally, in some situations you might want to apply special encryption or MD5 encoding to the document, without affecting the original message. This will enable you to ensure that nobody else sees or tampers with the document.

> **NOTE**
>
> Efforts are underway to define a specification to use digital signatures within XML documents. Refer to Appendix D.

All these reasons lead you down the path of packaging documents outside the SOAP message. The "SOAP Messages with Attachments" specification provides details about packaging one or more documents (XML, binary, or other format) into attachments that are referenced from within a SOAP message.

SOAP and Attachments

In July 2000, a specification for using MIME multipart/related attachments was introduced to the SOAP community. This approach enables a SOAP message and zero or more attachments to be transmitted as a single *SOAP message package*. By using *media types* and specific *URI schemes* in this protocol, you can relate different parts of a SOAP message to attachments in the package. Figure 9.1 shows how the SOAP message package is organized within HTTP.

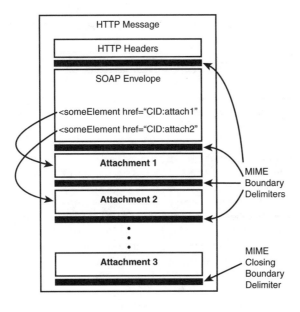

FIGURE 9.1

SOAP message package.

9

EXTREME WEB
SERVICES

As you can see from the figure, the HTTP message body contains an encoded data stream consisting of the primary SOAP message and its associated attachments. A boundary delimiter (as defined in the HTTP header) separates each part of the MIME message, and a closing boundary delimiter is used to denote the end of the MIME message.

Within each part of the MIME message, there exist the `Content-Type` and `Content-ID` fields. These fields are used to declare the type information of the part and its unique identifier within the message, respectively. In particular, the `Content-ID` value is used within the primary SOAP message to reference attachments as necessary. This is based on the `href` attribute usage, as defined in Section 5 of the SOAP specification.

> **NOTE**
>
> In February 2001, the ebXML organization announced that it no longer would be creating its own design for XML messaging and would be adopting SOAP.
>
> With this work now in place, the ebXML "Transport, Routing, and Packaging" specification uses "SOAP Messages with Attachments" to define how ebXML handles file attachments. Refer to Appendix D for more information.

Listing 9.10 demonstrates a sample RPC-based SOAP message that includes an attachment.

LISTING 9.10   Sample SOAP Message with Attachment

```
MIME-Version: 1.0
Content-Type: Multipart/Related; boundary=MIME_boundary; type=text/xml;
        start="<employee.xml@www.mcp.com>"


--MIME_boundary
Content-Type: text/xml; charset=UTF-8
Content-Transfer-Encoding: 8bit
Content-ID: <employee.xml@www.mcp.com>

<SOAP-ENV:Envelope xmlns:SOAP-ENV="http://schemas.xmlsoap.org/soap/envelope/">
  <SOAP-ENV:Body
      SOAP-ENV:encodingStyle="http://schemas.xmlsoap.org/soap/encoding/">
    <m:GetEmployeeInformation xmlns:m="http://www.mcp.com/Employee">
      <name>John Doe</name>
      <employeeId>003621</employeeId>
      <picture href="cid:employee.jpg@www.mcp.com"/>
    </m:GetEmployeeInformation>
  </SOAP-ENV:Body>
</SOAP-ENV:Envelope>
```

LISTING 9.10   Continued

```
--MIME_boundary
Content-Type: image/jpeg
Content-Transfer-Encoding: binary
Content-ID: <employee.jpg@www.mcp.com>

...JPEG image...
--MIME_boundary--
```

A few properties about this message should be pointed out. The very first `Content-type` dictates that the message is multipart/related MIME. It also includes a `boundary` definition that is used throughout the rest of the MIME message. In this case, we've chosen to use the text `MIME_boundary`, but you could use other names. Each boundary delimiter starts with the `--` character pair. The closing boundary delimiter starts with the same character pair but also ends in the character pair. Next, the `href` attribute on the `<picture>` element links to the attachment by using the `cid` identifier. The design for using attachments in SOAP is simple yet very effective because it uses SOAP's basic extensibility mechanisms.

Unfortunately, .NET Beta 2 does not natively support SOAP with attachments, although this will hopefully change by the final release of .NET.

Direct Internet Message Encapsulation (DIME)

One other specification that Microsoft has been developing is called *Direct Internet Message Encapsulation* (DIME). DIME has similar goals as MIME attachments, but it takes a slightly different approach in its design.

One of the performance-related problems with multipart/related MIME is that it uses boundary delimiters to separate attachments. Although this is a flexible approach, it requires that MIME messages be fully parsed to locate and process the entire attachment, resulting in extra buffering on both ends of the connection.

A DIME message provides a payload length and type, along with a unique identifier to solve the performance problems that were previously stated. More specifically, a DIME message consists of one or more DIME records, each having a type, size, and the capability to be chunked.

More information about DIME can be found in Appendix D.

Transactions

Over the last several years, transactional programming has regained momentum because developers have recognized its importance in Internet computing. You can see this re-emergence in the products that you use. Microsoft released MTS and eventually COM+, both providing a robust environment for transactional computing. Even Java2 Enterprise Edition (J2EE) supports transactions through mechanisms such as entity beans. Transactions simply make systems more dependable, and that's certainly a goal that we all try to achieve.

So how do transactions fit into the Web Service paradigm? This section takes a look at two opposing approaches to distributing transactions over the Web.

Transaction Authority Markup Language (XAML)

Traditional transactions use a Transaction Authority (TA) to coordinate the orchestration of *committing* data changes or *rolling back* data to its original state. This is a common design pattern that has existed for many years.

Extending this functionality to the Web Service model presents several challenges. The most significant challenges are these:

- A mixed-vendor environment
- Distribution across the Web
- Nonstandard, non–Web-based protocols

XAML intends to solve these problems by defining a transactional language, interface, and semantics using XML and other industry-accepted protocols such as SOAP.

At this time, the XAML specification is not currently available, but you can find a whitepaper on the topic at www.xaml.org.

The opposing methodology to XAML is based on data reconciliation using messages and validation, as presented in the next section.

Applying Transactions to Web Services

The idea is simple: Because developers currently use transactions to improve software dependability, it makes perfectly good sense that you would try to apply transactions in applications that are distributed across the Web, where potential for failure is extremely high.

Unfortunately, there is one difference—the issue of *trust*. Do you want your Web Service to be dependent upon some code that you know very little about?

Anyone who was fortunate enough to see the "Autonomous Computing" presentation by Pat Helland (an architect on the SQL Server team and transaction expert) at Microsoft TechEd 2001 is probably rethinking his stance on Web transactions.

The basic premise is: Independently controlled systems cannot and will not trust outside systems. Yet independent systems make up the fabric of the Internet. So how can you possibly manage transactions across Internet-distrusted systems? The proposal is that you can't!

Consider the case of a travel agency portal. The agency's system is designed to schedule airline and hotel reservations for a customer. The standard approach is to design the system so that an airline ticket and a hotel room are booked either successfully or not at all. One without the other is probably of little use to the customer. But to coordinate a transaction across the travel agency, airline, and hotel, they all need to trust one another.

Autonomous computing defines a design pattern that suggests that each independent entity in a computing relationship has private data that cannot be directly manipulated by other entities. Instead, outside entities must request that data be changed. Each request is authenticated, carefully validated, and either used or rejected. Remember that transactions increase the coupling between systems, and Web Services, by nature, should represent very loosely coupled systems.

Your service might choose to use standard transactions internally, but these transactions should never leave the walls of your system. When your service wants to share information to an outside entity, a snapshot of your data can be timestamped and then shipped out. By timestamping, you have stabilized the data, thus guaranteeing the accuracy of the data at some particular instant in time. Realize, of course, that snapshots of data increase in their staleness as time goes on. In other words, it will be easier to process requests that are based on fresh snapshots rather than to process those requests that are based on old snapshots.

The final piece to the puzzle is that your service also must provide ways to undo any changes that were made in previous requests. In the travel agency portal case, the airline and hotel services might each provide a way for reservations to be canceled. So, if a hotel room cannot be found, the customer would have the choice of keeping the flight and finding alternate housing or simply canceling the airline reservations.

The moral of the story is this: If you are building a service that will be used only within a trusted environment, you might have good reason to extend transactions to clients of your service. But any service that will be used on the Web should avoid exposing transactions and follow the stated guidelines.

> **NOTE**
>
> Appendix D contains information for locating Pat Helland's presentation.

Debugging and Web Services

As the consumer of a Web Service, you have to develop your client in a somewhat *blind* fashion. Generally speaking, you don't have access to the service's log files or other debugging mechanisms. For complex systems, this is a difficult arrangement.

Because most services probably will not want to provide general access to log files for fear of exposing proprietary information, one approach is to separate logging that is intended for the client from system-level logging. Additionally, client log files must be maintained separately so that client A doesn't see client B's activity. This configuration is shown in Figure 9.2.

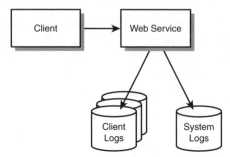

FIGURE 9.2
Web service logging.

Unfortunately, creating all these log files is far from scalable and simply won't work well for large numbers of clients. Rather than persisting debug information, it would be nice to provide transient logging information on a per request basis. One of the best ways to do this in SOAP is via the SOAP Headers.

To implement this in .NET, you add the tracing mechanism just like you would any other application-defined SOAP Header. First you must create a class that inherits from the SoapHeader class, as follows:

```
public class MyHeader : SoapHeader
{
  public string tracestr;
}
```

Next, you add an instantiation of this class:

```
public class Service1 : System.Web.Services.WebService
{
  public MyHeader trace;
  ...etc...
```

You then apply the SoapHeaderAttribute to the Web method to associate the trace variable in this example and to specify that the tracing header is optional and intended only for the client. This is shown in Listing 9.11. Notice that the name used in the SoapHeaderAttribute class must match the public instance of your Header class (trace).

LISTING 9.11 SOAP Header and Web Method

```
[WebMethod]
[SoapHeader("trace", Direction=SoapHeaderDirection.Out, Required=false)]
public int Add(int a, int b)
{
  MyHeader mh = new MyHeader();

  mh.tracestr = "Inspecting a:";
  // do something with a

  mh.tracestr += "Inspecting b:";
  // do something with b

  mh.tracestr += "Adding result:";
  trace = mh; // Assign the header
  return a+b;
}
```

Instantiating an instance of your `MyHeader` class within the Web method enables you to begin setting the Header value within your service. Once complete, you assign the Header value to the public `trace` variable of your service, which causes your tracings to be placed in the response message.

The client application code looks strikingly familiar to other client code that you've already seen. The one exception is that an additional property (`MyHeaderValue`) is available on the `localhost.Service1` class. The property enables the client to obtain the trace information, like this:

```
localhost.Service1 svc = new localhost.Service1();

int c = svc.Add(3, 4);

System.Windows.Forms.MessageBox.Show(c.ToString());
System.Windows.Forms.MessageBox.Show(svc.MyHeaderValue.tracestr);
```

Listing 9.12 shows the response message, including the trace information in the SOAP Header.

LISTING 9.12 SOAP Header and Web Method

```
<?xml version="1.0" encoding="utf-8"?>
<soap:Envelope xmlns:soap="http://schemas.xmlsoap.org/soap/envelope/"
               xmlns:xsi="http://www.w3.org/2001/XMLSchema-instance"
               xmlns:xsd="http://www.w3.org/2001/XMLSchema">
  <soap:Header>
    <MyHeader xmlns="http://tempuri.org/">
```

LISTING 9.12   Continued

```
    <tracestr>Inspecting a:Inspecting b:Adding result:</tracestr>
    </MyHeader>
  </soap:Header>
  <soap:Body>
    <AddResponse xmlns="http://tempuri.org/">
      <AddResult>7</AddResult>
    </AddResponse>
  </soap:Body>
</soap:Envelope>
```

> **NOTE**
>
> To keep the example simple, we've chosen to use colon-delimited strings to separate the trace messages. A more sophisticated approach is to use one of the collection classes in .NET that will serialize each trace message independently.
>
> You also will want to provide a mechanism for the client to enable or disable tracing. The proposed method is to use an input header field that the client can populate when tracing is desired.

Using the SOAP Header accomplishes two important goals, First, it enables the service to provide tracing information on a per-client basis without persisting the information. Second, it enables the service to isolate client-specific tracing from system-level tracing.

The final question that you need to answer is: What information should you be logging? The following list provides some suggestions that might be helpful to the client:

- Time of entry into the service
- Time of exit from the service
- Descriptions of the processes being executed
- Duration times of processes being executed
- User entitlement information

Of course, the particulars of your situation will dictate your logging requirements, but the listed items will be very helpful to your service's users.

Web Service Documentation

Most developers deplore the idea of writing system documentation. The reason is pretty clear—documenting systems usually involves tedious and uninteresting work. In the Web

Services paradigm, many developers think that a simple Web Service Description Language (WSDL) document and its associated XML schema are sufficient documentation for a service. Unfortunately, this just isn't the case.

So what do we mean when we say "documentation"? Generally, it's the information that describes a system's purpose, operation, structure, and data. More specifically, it's the definition of the syntax and semantics of a Web Service, including detailed descriptions of the public operations and their supporting parameters.

Rather than trying to recommend a particular format for your documentation, this section proposes several specific content items that you might want to include in your Web Service documentation. The names of these content items are not as important as what they represent. Ultimately, it's up to you to decide what information you want to present to your user and how you want to present that information.

> **NOTE**
>
> In the context of system documentation, we use the term *user* to mean the developer that is building application code to interact with your service.

Overview

To start, it's important for users to understand the essence of your Web Service, and this can be done with a simple introduction. The introduction should include general semantics, observations, and surrounding context for your service that will set the stage for the remainder of the document.

Design Approach

The design approach provides specific information about your service that transcends all your Web methods or operations. This includes information about the application protocols that you support, any special encoding that is used, security mechanisms, and so on. The following sections provide detailed questions that you should answer in your documentation.

Protocols

Because Web Services can be implemented with a variety of protocols, it's imperative that you explain how your service exploits these protocols.

In the case of SOAP, you need to be clear about how you're using SOAP. Some questions that you need to answer are listed here:

- Are you using SOAP as a document-based or RPC-based protocol?

- Are you using SOAP's encoding rules (see Section 5 of the SOAP specification)?
- Are you supporting HTTP, SMTP, or some other application protocol?
- Which versions of the protocols do you support?
- What language support do you provide?
- Are Header elements used by more than one operation?
- Are you using MIME attachments (MIME multipart/related)?

If your service uses HTTP, this section is also a good place to describe your service's uses of the SOAPAction HTTP field or other similar types of information.

Security

Users will want to see the types of security mechanisms that your service has in place. Because security involves a number of aspects, you need to tell the user how you have (or have not) addressed security concerns. Obviously, you don't want to provide any proprietary information that will tip off a hacker, but you do want to tell users what they might need in the way of security tools or libraries. Additionally, you will want to answer these questions:

- What guarantee can you make with regard to privacy?
- What authentication schemes do you use?
- Do you support SSL?
- Do you support digital certificates?
- How do you establish a trusted relationship with the client application?
- Do you require users to register their applications with your service?
- What are users entitled to do, and how do they obtain different entitlements?

Versioning

The topic of versioning is probably one of the stickiest areas of Web Services. Most users expect a Web Service to be around for an extended period of time. This means that you, the Web Service developer, simply cannot change an interface on a whim. This is true both syntactically and semantically. Instead you have to be willing to commit to that service and its interfaces for a fairly long period of time (several years or more). Ask yourself these questions:

- How long do you plan to support your service and its associated interfaces?
- In what way does your protocol support versioning of interfaces?
- How much notice will users be given before a change?
- How will you notify clients of such a change?
- What migration paths do you (or will you) provide for users of old versions?

> **NOTE**
>
> In reality, any guarantees or promises that you are making about your service should be included in a formal contract. In other words, this documentation is in no way intended to be a replacement for a legal and binding contract.

Remember that if you incorporate other services as functionality of your own service, you become responsible for ensuring that your users are not impacted by changes in those other systems.

Reliability, Availability, and Performance

Some attributes of a service are not necessarily obvious to the naked eye, but they're just as important as the interface. Reliability, availability, and performance are three such attributes that were discussed in Chapter 1, "Web Service Fundamentals."

A client cares whether your service is reliable. Will your service be capable of providing consistent results based on the client's request? Is your service impotent, meaning that the same request can be processed multiple times without adversely affecting the system?

A client cares whether your service is available. What level of redundancy does your system maintain? Are there any single-points of failure? Is your service dependent upon other systems in your organization that don't maintain a high level of availability?

A client cares whether your service performs well. Of course, good performance is defined by the context in which your service is being used. For instance, a stock quote service that is used to buy and sell stocks in a near–real-time manner requires completely different performance numbers than if the service were used to generate a business report on a company.

As users build systems on top of your service, they will want to know how your service can positively or negatively affect their application. This same principle should be something that you consider as you incorporate others' services.

Errors and Diagnostics

Whether you call them errors, faults, or exceptions, these are the anomalies that affect your service. Be sure to describe to users how your service will behave in these situations and how you expect the client application to behave. The specific errors will be covered in the API documentation (to follow), but your general approach to handling errors should be outlined in this section.

Something that tends to get ignored until problems arise is diagnostic information. This isn't necessarily a source-code trace of your Web Service. More likely, it is some other representation of how a request message flows through your system and the associated behavior that took

9

place. Diagnostic information can be system-level or application-level. In the first case, the developer consumes diagnostics to solve a technical problem such as locating a software bug. In the latter case, the developer still consumes the information but applies it to some end-user task, such as displaying a message to the end user.

> **NOTE**
>
> When using SOAP, it has been our experience that the SOAP Header is a great location to place system-level diagnostic information because it is out-of-band data that crosses operation boundaries. Alternately, application-level diagnostics usually tie into the semantics of your interface and should be placed in the SOAP Body (specifically in the body of your message) as an output parameter.

Questions that you should answer are listed here:

- What protocol error-reporting features are you using?
- Have you extended any of the protocol's error-reporting features?
- What type of diagnostic information are you exposing to users?

WSDL Documents

Finally, you will want to make a reference to your WSDL documents. Although there is redundant information shared between the WSDL document and your written documentation, clients will want to get a perspective on both sources of information.

API Summary

When providing a summary of the API, you should present the XML namespace URI(s) that your service exposes, as well as the Web methods that are scoped to each namespace URI. You also will want to include any helpful use cases, sequence diagrams, or other descriptions about how these operations relate to one another. This is especially true for Web Services that have complicated flows of information.

API Reference

The most tedious portion of your documentation is the detailed description of each Web method. This is where developers will spend most of their time learning how to use your service.

Table 9.1 provides a list of properties that you'll want to include with each Web method description.

TABLE 9.1 Web Service API Documentation Properties

Property	Description
Synopsis	This summarizes the purpose and behavior of the operation.
Precondition	Be sure to list any Web methods that need to be called, or any processing that needs to be completed before executing the specified operation. For example, to call the `GetStockQuote` operation, you are required to obtain an authentication token.
Post-condition	This describes the state of the system following the operation. For example, after successfully calling the `Authenticate` operation, you will have an authentication token good for one hour.
Logical Operation	It is helpful to provide a condensed representation of the messages by using one or more forms. When describing an RPC-based service, it is often helpful to use a standard API format such as `string MyMethod(MyStruct s, int a)`. The document-based service is best described using either an XML-like syntax or a table format with indentation representing the hierarchical XML structure.
Input Parameters	Be sure to list all the input parameters to the operation. You should include type information, size limits, ranges, optional or mandatory parameters, default values, any special syntax, and a description of the parameter.
Output Parameters	List here all the output parameters (and return values) for the operation. You should include type information, size limits, ranges, any special syntax, and a description of the parameter.
Errors	List here all the possible faults and their associated errors that can be generated by the operation. You should include a detailed description of each error and insight into how the service will behave when this error occurs.
Examples	Ultimately, example request and response messages will be the preferred reference documentation. Make sure that your examples are accurate and reflect a typical use of the service.

9

EXTREME WEB
SERVICES

Data Structures

Sometimes you will reuse data structures (for RPC-based messaging) or common message structures (for document-based messaging) across multiple Web methods. Rather than document the same structures in each operation's documentation, you might want to consider creating a separate section that contains these structure definitions.

A good example of this approach is the UDDI documentation, with the exception that the UDDI team decided to create a completely separate document for describing data structures.

Error Reference

By the time you finish documenting your API, it should be easy to aggregate all the errors into this reference section.

Arguably, you could have just created the error reference section and avoided the burdensome work of describing errors for each individual operation. However, it's much easier for a client application to know exactly which errors need to be handled rather than trying to handle all of the errors for each operation call.

This section should include client and server errors (grouped accordingly) that the client should expect to receive. You also might want to provide some suggestions or examples for how the client application might respond to the error.

Test Environment

If you happen to offer a test site where clients can play with your service without necessarily registering to use it, you will want to provide information about this environment. You should include references to the test site's WSDL document and describe any limitations that it imposes on the client.

It's also helpful to document which client implementations (such as Apache's SOAP implementation) might or might not work with your service. This includes the version information, any required workarounds, software patches, and related information that will make it easier for clients to build their applications.

Sample Document

So far, we've described a lot of documentation elements that you should provide to clients. The remainder of this section shows you sample document fragments that are used to describe an address book service. Although your document format might differ, the general idea and concepts should be the same.

Be aware that this example should not be used as a reference for legal doctrine. You should consult the appropriate legal counsel for proper wording and contractual processes.

Overview

The Address Book service enables users to store up to 200 entries in their personal address book. Each entry can contain the contact name, address, email address, phone numbers, and other related notes. Users can insert, change, view, and delete entries in the address book.

And so on... .

Design Approach

Address Book uses SOAP v1.1 in combination with document-based messaging to interact with clients. For more information about the message syntax, refer to the XML schemas as defined in the WSDL documents. All the XML messages use UTF-8 encoding.

Currently, only HTTP/1.1 and HTTPS are supported; a simple authentication approach that uses an `Authenticate` call as specified in the API reference, and a SOAP Header called `authToken` must be included on every subsequent request. Users are required to obtain a valid user ID/password by submitting a request to addressbook@mcp.com. This user ID/password combination must be provided in the `Authenticate` call over an SSL connection.

Based on the security scheme previously described, address book entries are protected by using SSL (HTTPS) connections. Address Book information that is associated with a particular user ID/password combination is accessible only to that specific user.

Client applications are not required to register with the Address Book service, but they are bound by the provisions stated in the attached legal agreements. By using this API, you are automatically bound to the terms and conditions of this agreement.

Address Book uses the URI to denote the version of the service and its interface. Future versions will be backward-compatible, unless otherwise posted on our Web site at www.mcp.com/ AddressBook. Clients will have 90 days from posting time to upgrade to compliant versions.

Because the Address Book service is free of charge, there is no guarantee of the reliability, availability, or performance of this service. However, clients should expect typical message processing to complete within 300ms of receiving the request (not including network transmission time).

Address Book uses standard SOAP fault messages, with the `<detail>` element containing a structure providing detailed error numbers. Error numbers are included in the API documentation for each operation.

And so on... .

API Summary

Address Book v1.0 uses a single interface, scoped to the http://www.mcp.com/ AddressBook_1_0.xsd URI, with the following operations:

- **Authenticate**—Authenticates the user ID/password and returns an authentication token to be used in subsequent calls

- **InsertContact**—Inserts a new contact into the address book (assuming that room is available)

- `DeleteContact`—Deletes the specified contact from the address book
- `RetrieveContact`—Returns information about the specified contact
- `GetContactList`—Returns a list of all accessible contact entries in the address book
- `ChangeContact`—Changes contact information in the address book for the specified contact

When inserting a contact, the client application may choose to persist the resulting contact identifier that is returned from the call. This identifier is used as a reference in subsequent API calls.

If the client application does not want to persist IDs, it can use the `GetContactList` call to retrieve a list of IDs for the accessible entries in the address book. These IDs can then be used in subsequent calls, such as changing or deleting an entry.

And so on... .

API Reference

InsertContact—Inserts a new contact into the address book (assuming that room is available).

Preconditions: The client must provide a valid `authToken` from the `Authenticate` call.

Post-conditions: The new contact has been added to the address book, and the resulting contact identifier is returned for future reference.

Logical Operation: contactId = InsertContact(contactInfo);

Input Parameters:

`contactInfo`—The contact information structure. This is a mandatory parameter with no default values. Refer to the "Data Structures" section for more information concerning this structure.

Output Parameters:

`contactId`—The unique identifier for the contact that has just been entered into the address book. This is an opaque string that is used to identify the contact.

Errors:

- `Err_InvalidContactInformation`—The contact information that you've provided is either incomplete or invalid.
- `Err_NotAuthenticated`—You are attempting to update the address book without providing proper authentication credentials.

Example Request:

```
<SOAP-ENV:Envelope xmlns:SOAP-ENV="http://schemas.xmlsoap.org/soap/envelope/">
  <SOAP-ENV:Body>
```

```
    <InsertContact xmlns="http://www.mcp.com/AddressBook_1_0.xsd">
      <contactEntry>
        <name>John Doe</name>
        <workPhone>(212) 555-1234</workPhone>
        <email>johndoe@mcp.com</email>
      </contactEntry>
    </InsertContact>
  </SOAP-ENV:Body>
</SOAP-ENV:Envelope>
```

Example Response:

```
<SOAP-ENV:Envelope xmlns:SOAP-ENV="http://schemas.xmlsoap.org/soap/envelope/">
  <SOAP-ENV:Body>
    <InsertContactResponse xmlns="http://www.mcp.com/AddressBook_1_0.xsd">
      <contactId>JD00001</contactId>
    </InsertContactResponse>
  </SOAP-ENV:Body>
</SOAP-ENV:Envelope>
```

And so on... .

Summary

This chapter introduced an assortment of topics that ranged from tracing to transactions to service documentation.

Embedding XML is a growing topic that isn't directly addressed by SOAP. You can embed XML in a number of ways, some better than others, but the best solution really depends on your particular situation.

XML and even binary data can be attached to a SOAP message by using multipart/related MIME encoding. This is the preferred method of the ebXML group and has been adopted by several non-Microsoft SOAP implementations.

Transactions are a hot topic in the Web Service arena, and they play an essential part in building dependable systems. This is clearly an area of Web Services that needs more thought.

Debugging client applications that use a service is a growing concern and requires forethought in Web Service designs. Use of the SOAP Header provides a reasonable and simple approach to providing out-of-band trace information to the client.

Client documentation is the single most important deliverable in publishing even a mildly complicated Web Service. By providing ample semantic descriptions, examples, and WSDL, clients will be capable of quickly constructing applications that can consume your service.

Chapter 10, ".NET and Web Service Security," is the final chapter in the story. Here, we describe aspects of authentication, authorization, and encryption as it applies to the .NET architecture and Web Service development.

.NET and Web Service Security

IN THIS CHAPTER

It would be great if you didn't have to worry about security and securing our Web Services, but the fact is, you probably will. Even the simple Web Services that you might provide as a public service will require some amount of security, if only to protect the server on which the Web Service is running. It seems that *some* people have extra time on their hands and take great pleasure in wrecking your servers.

But it's also true that security isn't just there to protect against malicious attacks. Sometimes you have important information that you simply want to keep private. Or, perhaps you have data that doesn't necessarily need to be encrypted, but you want to make absolutely sure none of the contents were modified (maliciously or otherwise) as the network packets travel the Internet. Of course, you also might be providing your service for a fee and want only registered (and paid) users to have access.

This chapter gives you an overview of the options that are available to you when securing your Web Services. In Chapter 7, "Consuming .NET Web Services," you saw how to encrypt a single method parameter. In this chapter, you'll look at other techniques and options that can be used to secure your Web Service.

Security Terms and Concepts

Before getting too deep into security, it's a good idea to make sure that we've defined the terms we'll be using throughout the chapter. It's easy to confuse authentication with authorization, for example. Table 10.1 lists some of the more important security terms you'll encounter when dealing with Web Services.

TABLE 10.1   Web Service Security Terminology

Term	Definition
Authentication	The act of verifying that a given user is capable of accessing the resource ("logging in")
Authorization	The act of verifying that an authenticated user is allowed to perform certain actions (delete privilege versus simply read privilege)
Data integrity	Mechanisms that provide assurance that the data transmitted from site to site has not been modified
Encryption	Mechanisms that render clear-text data unintelligible by outside agents that do not possess the cryptographical means to decipher the data
PK encryption	Encryption algorithm that employs a public key, which, when matched with a private key, allows decryption of the data

TABLE 10.1 Continued

Term	Definition
Denial of service	Malicious attack from an external agent designed to prevent valid users from accessing the Web Service or designed to break into the Web Service by repeatedly trying random user IDs and passwords

Authentication is used to make sure that a specific user passes the security checks to access the Web Service. Authorization specifies what that user can do with the Web Service. Some methods might be restricted for certain classes of users, for example.

Encryption and data integrity are somewhat related. Encryption transforms *clear text* into gibberish that is virtually unintelligible without the necessary keys to decrypt the information. Essentially two types of encryption algorithms are available—symmetric and asymmetric.

Symmetric algorithms employ identical keys on both sides of the encryption process. It would be like shipping a locked briefcase to your business partner in another city, and both she and you had identical briefcase keys.

Asymmetric algorithms, on the other hand, employ differing keys, called public and private keys. Someone encrypts the information using your public key, but only the (related) private key that you hold can decrypt the material. Data integrity is related to encryption because you can apply encryption technology to verify that no bits within the encrypted article have been modified or tampered with in any way. The decryption process will inform you if there have been attempts to modify the data.

Denial-of-service attacks are essentially network packet floods designed to hamper or disable your Web Service by sending more packets than you can handle at any given time. They also could be designed to discover by brute force a username/password combination. Your Web Service is so busy handling these invalid (and malicious) attacks that you have little or no resources left to handle legitimate user requests. One way to combat this is to employ authorization algorithms that very quickly ascertain whether a given entity represents a valid user and, if not, deny the request without accessing latent resources (such as a database lookup after a decryption process). If the password could not possibly be valid, you don't waste your time looking it up.

Many other terms and concepts are important to security—and Web Service security specifically—but these are the major concepts that you should be familiar with.

Application-Level Security Versus System-Level Security

Another security concept to be aware of is the difference between system-level security and application-level security. System-level security is implemented by the operating system or other systems that you require to expose the Web Service (the .NET runtime infrastructure and Internet Information Server, for example). If you can use system-level security, by all means take advantage of it. Generally, the system-level security software has been fairly well debugged and tested, and although at times security breaches happen, system-level practices largely keep the casual hacker out.

Application-level security practices are those that you implement yourself. Clearly, this type of code isn't something that you would assign to a junior technician. Rolling your own security system involves detailed knowledge of your system architecture, encryption techniques, authentication and authorization requirements, and so forth. However, often you simply must resort to bolting on your own security objects.

In this chapter, we'll examine both types of security, preferring the system-level implementations when available because they have been thoroughly tested and are ready to use with little or no additional development. I should note that some system-level methods will reduce interoperability, but for given situations, a slight loss in interoperability might be acceptable (such as intranet use where you control the network). Why are we dealing with security at all—or, at least, to the depth we will in this chapter? It's a good question, after all. Let's address that thought for a moment in the next section.

Web Services and Security

You might be wondering why security wasn't built into the SOAP protocol. After all, a chapter on Web Service security would be much smaller than this chapter if security had been addressed from the beginning.

The SOAP protocol avoided security for several reasons. For one thing, security is nontrivial to implement and maintain, which would invalidate the notion of SOAP being *simple*.

But there are a couple deeper reasons. Not everyone using SOAP would necessarily agree on security measures, practices, and protocols, making interoperable operations problematic. And security requires a much greater coding investment, as well as the associated testing and certification required to be absolutely sure that security is maintained under the conditions applied to the test (it's difficult to test for all conditions, for example).

Instead, the original concepts behind SOAP mandated that additional processing be layered atop the SOAP protocol, allowing system architects the freedom to use the systems and processes that make the most sense for their applications. It is because of this layering that we treat security *not* as an afterthought, but rather as a process that sits atop the network protocol itself.

As it happens, we apply security systems and techniques differently for differing situations. Security in an intranet sense can be managed differently than secure systems designed for Internet (general public) access. Let's take a look at how the differing breadth of the Web Service access changes the security horizon.

Breadth of Web Service Security

Web Services can be organized into two main categories—intranet and Internet. In the intranet case, you control the Web Service servers and the clients, and (in most cases) you have a limited network topology. You have a certain number of domains and users, for example. There may be a *great* many users, but the number is known and limited. *Internet*, of course, implies an infinite number of untrusted clients, and you must assume that those clients are or may become malicious until proven trustworthy—even then, they should be watched (with audit/use trails and so on).

Because the intranet case involves a limited set of users and servers, the security options available to you differ from those you'll consider when dealing with the masses. We'll first turn to the intranet case.

Intranet Web Service Security Alternatives

Intranet security measures differ from Internet measures primarily because of the number and type of potential Web Service clients and the knowledge of the network topography. It isn't difficult to target a specific IP address and allow a user from that address access to your Web Service. Applying the same concept to general Internet Web Service consumers is a lot less palatable because you probably want the general public to have access, even if that access is limited and monitored.

In this section you'll find the security options that make the most sense when you have control over the network topography and the user base.

IP Security (IPSec)

IPSec is a system-level security process that implements security measures at the network level. Because of this, you can secure your Web Service without changing a single line of code. IIS manages IPSec for you through administrative means.

Pure IPSec is defined through the Internet Engineering Task Force (IETF). In the IETF IPSec specification, you'll find an authentication header (AH) and an encapsulated security payload (ESP) header/trailer.

The AH provides assurance that your data integrity is maintained, and because the entire IP packet is signed (see Figure 10.1), you can also be sure that nobody is issuing this packet in a playback mode (trying to spoof you by throwing an otherwise valid packet your way).

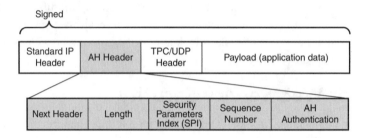

FIGURE 10.1

The IPSec authentication header.

The shaded areas of Figure 10.1 show the additional overhead required by the AH. Because the packet is signed but not encrypted, the data is transmitted in clear text and is therefore viewable over the Internet.

If encryption is important to you, you'll instead want to use the IPSec ESP header and trailer (see Figure 10.2). In a manner similar to that of the AH header, portions of the ESP packet are signed to be sure that the contents have not been molested. ESP takes the extra measure of encrypting several portions of the packet, as you see in Figure 10.2.

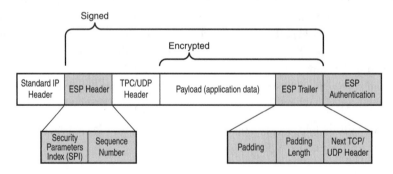

FIGURE 10.2

The IPSec encapsulated security payload Header/trailer.

Both packets export a Security Parameters Index (SPI) that indicates the security association (SA) and key with which this particular packet is associated. This allows a single computer to communicate with many other computers simultaneously without confusing the encryption keys.

Because IPSec deals with the network at the IP header level, which is a layer lower than HTTP, IPSec appears to simply happen for Web Services. However, IIS is responsible for implementing IPSec; IIS filters IP addresses and matches packets and IP addresses against security policies that you establish administratively. For more information regarding IPSec and how you might employ it within your intranet, see the MSDN article "IP Security for Microsoft Windows 2000 Server," at `http://msdn.microsoft.com`.

Firewalls

Nearly every Internet server probably employs a firewall to prevent outside agents from sending packets into the server using secured (locked) socket addresses. But you also can use firewalls to block access from groups of IP addresses; conversely, you can allow groups of IP addresses to send packets and have those packets pass through the firewall.

This is useful for allowing specific network domains to gain access to Web Services that reside behind a firewall designed to block packet access from systems that do not meet the firewall selection criteria.

An example is to establish a subnet for your Human Resources (HR) department and provide Web Services that the department can use to access sensitive personnel history information. Only computers on the HR subnet will be capable of accessing and using the Web Services because packets generated by computers belonging to the Accounting subnet will be denied access through the firewall.

Virtual Private Networks (VPNs)

Virtual private networks combine tunneling practices with PK encryption to form a private subnetwork using public network communications systems. You can see this from Figure 10.3. Physically, the client and server computers are using public network equipment (Internet or intranet), but because the packets are encrypted and tunneled, it appears to the client and the server that they are communicating using a private network.

Even though VPNs exist over the Internet, this technique is included in the intranet section because the VPN makes it appear to the network nodes participating in the VPN communications that the network is of intranet proportions. In other words, VPNs are most commonly used today to link remote members of the same department or department-level group.

The most common implementation of VPN technology is through the Point-to-Point Protocol (PPP). PPP is more often associated with dial-up connections, but this is by convention and is not a general rule. For more information regarding establishing a VPN, see the chapter entitled "Virtual Private Networks" in the "Internetworking Guide" section of the *Windows 2000 Server Resource Kit*.

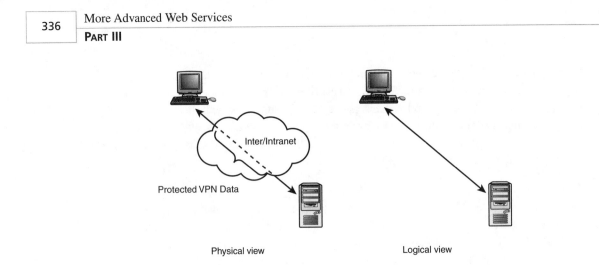

Physical view   Logical view

FIGURE 10.3

Virtual private networks.

HTTP Security

As IPSec encrypts and protects IP packets, HTTP also can help with security issues at the application (HTTP) layer through HTTP Security. IIS implements HTTP Security, which offers these authentication support levels:

- Basic
- Basic over SSL
- Digest
- Integrated Windows Authentication
- Client Certificates

Basic HTTP Security is essentially insecure because it transmits passwords over the network in clear text. But at least you must provide a password! *Basic over SSL* uses secure sockets to transmit the authentication information, which is to say that the packets in their entirety are encrypted (often referred to as *bulk encryption*). *Digest* authentication uses a cryptographical hash algorithm to hash the user ID and password, effectively encrypting only these two pieces of information rather than the entire packet, as with Basic over SSL authentication. *Integrated Windows Authentication* uses Windows security subsystems to request and verify user ID and password information. You might know of this option as NT Challenge/Response authentication. Finally, *Client Certificates* associate a digital certificate with a user so that the user must provide an individual digital certificate to the authentication server to gain access to the Web Service.

These HTTP-level authentication techniques use varying degrees of secure means to authenticate user access. At the low end, Basic authentication merely requests a password with no encryption. At the high end, client certificates request a user's representative digital signature as proof of that person's identity. HTTP Security is implemented through IIS, and you can establish the authentication that you want using the Internet Services Manager. If you select a virtual directory (for example, one that contains the Web Service assembly DLLs), you can right-click on the directory to bring up a context menu that has a Properties option.

After the Properties dialog box appears, you can select the Directory Security tab, which brings up the dialog box that you see in Figure 10.4.

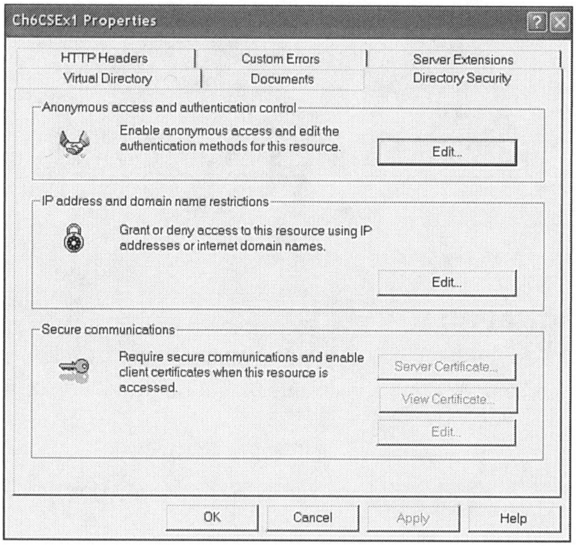

FIGURE 10.4
IIS virtual Directory security tab.

From there, you click the Edit button under Anonymous Access and Authentication Control to bring up the dialog box that you see in Figure 10.5.

By default, IIS allows anonymous access to the Web Service's virtual directory. However, if you uncheck anonymous access, the authenticated access defaults to Windows Integrated Access. This level of authentication works only with Windows systems (Unix systems typically won't participate, for example), but if the intranet is populated by computers running Windows, you'll get Windows authentication with little effort.

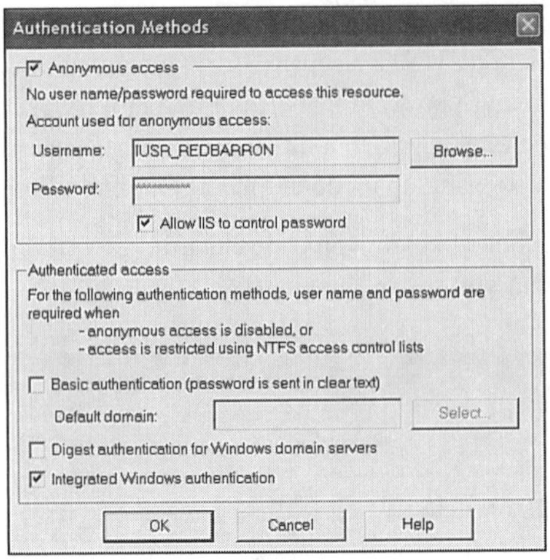

FIGURE 10.5
Authentication Methods dialog box.

ASP.NET Authentication

ASP.NET also provides for authentication, which you configure by editing the web.config file's `<authentication/>` element. ASP.NET uses authentication providers, of which there are three:

- Forms
- Windows
- Passport

You also have the option to select None, for no authentication.

Forms authentication enables you to specify a form that you've created to request a user's credentials for authentication. How you handle authentication is then up to you and the form that you use. *Windows* authentication is the same for ASP.NET as for HTTP in general, but each is applied separately (IIS first and then ASP.NET). ASP.NET Windows authentication will never dip below the level mandated by the IIS settings established for the Web Service, but you can more tightly constrain the Web Service at the ASP.NET level, if you want. Finally, *Passport* authentication uses the Microsoft Passport authentication service to authenticate user credentials. This also involves a user interface to authenticate—although this certainly will change for Web Services in the near future—and there are other requirements for using Passport as well. For example, you'll need to access `http://www.passport.com/business` to accept a license agreement, pay for the Passport SDK, and register your application with Passport. In other words, using Passport authentication isn't as easy as requesting it in the web.config file.

By default, the authentication setting is None, assuming that you used Visual Studio .NET to create the project (and the web.config file). This authentication element might contain more information, depending upon the setting:

<authentication mode="Windows" />

Forms authentication, as an example, will have child XML elements that specify the form to use.

More information is available regarding ASP.NET authentication in the MSDN *.NET Framework Developer's Guide* in the "ASP.NET Authentication" section.

Bulk Encryption Using Secure Sockets Layer (SSL)

Bulk encryption, or Secure Sockets Layer (SSL), is actually available to both intranet and Internet Web Services. Assuming that your Web Server has the proper certificate in place, Web Service clients can communicate with your Web Service using SSL through the use of the https protocol:

```
https://www.somehotservice.com/hotservice
```

Of course, you'd find this in the proxy source code or client configuration file. All the data transmitted between the Web Service and the client will be encrypted. SSL degrades performance a bit, but you can be sure that the information is protected. SSL is more commonly used to secure login and authentication than to encrypt mundane communications, but it could be used for this if the situation warrants the added overhead.

Internet Web Service Security Alternatives

The authentication systems that you've seen so far are really appropriate only when you're dealing with relatively small numbers of uses, such as a department-sized network or domain. When you scale to Internet proportions, the rules change. You still have secure sockets, but Windows authentication, for example, makes little sense. Likewise, Passport works well for authenticating users, but how do you authenticate a business communication under the guise of business-to-business Web Service use?

You turn to different alternatives when you're dealing with a wider scope. Two major alternatives are available to you: one for encryption (in addition to SSL) and one for authentication.

SOAP Digital Signatures

Not long after the SOAP 1.1 specification arrived, several engineers at Microsoft realized that it would be handy to encrypt a portion of the SOAP packet using PK encryption techniques. The public key could be transmitted in the SOAP Header, and the same XML Header element could indicate what portion of the SOAP packet was encrypted.

> **NOTE**
>
> You also have SOAP Digital Signatures as an option when dealing with intranet solutions. However, SOAP Digital Signatures involve quite a bit of processing overhead. Because other alternatives are available for intranet encryption (IPSec, for example), we didn't include SOAP Digital Signatures here.

SOAP Digital Signatures provide a standard SOAP Header entry that carries a signature compliant with the XML Signature specification, which you will find at http://www.w3.org. XML Signature relates a key to referenced octet data known as the *data object*. The data object is transformed (encrypted) using the key, and the transformation is included with the signature.

In the case of SOAP Digital Signatures, the data object is usually the SOAP Body, but any SOAP element could be used. Individual method parameters could be encrypted, for example. The identification mechanism is XLink, just as with Section 5 encoded multireference accessors:

```xml
<?xml version="1.0"?>
<Soap:Envelope
  (Other SOAP namespace identifiers)
  xmlns:SoapDS="http://schemas.xmlsoap.org/soap/security/2000-12">
    <Soap:Header>
      <SoapDS:Signature Soap:mustUnderstand="true">
        <SoapDS:SignedInfo>
          (Other signed info information)
          <SoapDS:Reference URI="#Body">
            (Transform/digest information)
          </SoapDS:Reference>
        </SoapDS:SignedInfo>
        (Other signature information)
      </SoapDS:Signature>
    </Soap:Header>
    <Soap:Body SoapDS:id="Body">
      (Encrypted Body information…)
    </Soap:Body>
</Soap:Envelope>
```

Processing SOAP Digital Signatures within an ASP.NET Web Service would require the use of the .NET SoapExtension because .NET does not support SOAP Digital Signatures as of Beta 2 of the .NET Framework. You would need to encrypt the payload before issuing it to the Web Service (SoapMessageStage.AfterSerialize) and then decrypt the payload before .NET Web Service processing (SoapMessageStage.BeforeDeserialize). However, it isn't hard to imagine that .NET will support SOAP Digital Signatures at some time in the future.

Application-Specific Authentication

Sometimes you simply have to take matters into your own hands and write the support code that you require. For authenticating users, custom authentication processes are sometimes required because the systems offered by the local operating system either won't scale or aren't meant for interoperable use.

How you implement your custom authentication is up to you and depends entirely upon your application's requirements. However, typically custom authentication architectures take this form:

Your Web Service requires the use of a separate login Web Service that returns a *session token* or *authentication token*. The session token is passed into secured Web Services, most likely in the SOAP Header, but it could also be passed into the Web Service as a method parameter. After you issue a session token, the session token is aged. When it expires, the user is forced to log into the system again to receive an updated session token. For efficiency, the session token can be quickly checked when used to prevent denial-of-service attacks. If the session token could not possibly be valid, you return a SOAP fault without taking the time to request authentication information from the database.

To demonstrate, we created a secured Web Service that requires a session token. To obtain the token, you must first be a valid user, which means that your name and password are stored in an authentication database. Assuming that you are a valid user, you must call an initial "login" Web Service and provide your username and password, which the login Web Service checks. If you are truly a valid user, the login Web Service then creates the session key and returns it to you. Note that the code we've written for the login Web Service sends the username and password in an unencrypted form, so you'd actually use SSL to transmit the SOAP packets.

Our session token consists of two GUIDs, or globally unique identifiers. Windows COM programmers will be familiar with them, but just in case you have not seen the details, a GUID is a 128-bit unique number. It is unique in time and space so that you can never create a random GUID like any other, for at least any practical time period. The algorithm for creating these values comes from DCE-RPC and isn't really important for your purposes other than to acknowledge that the GUID is unique.

Therefore, you have a "secret" GUID that only your application retains and a "public" GUID that you give to the authenticated user. You convert the GUIDs from their numerical values into string representations, concatenate them, and then encrypt them. Once encrypted, you can convert the resulting string to base64 to be returned to the client. Listing 10.1 shows how you can do this.

LISTING 10.1   The Login Web Service

```csharp
using System;
using System.Collections;
using System.ComponentModel;
using System.Data;
using System.Diagnostics;
using System.Web;
using System.Web.Services;
using System.Data.OleDb;
using System.Web.Services.Protocols;
using System.Xml;
using System.Security;
using System.Security.Cryptography;
using System.Text;
using System.IO;

namespace LoginServer
{
    /// <summary>
    /// Summary description for Service1.
    /// </summary>
    public class Service1 : System.Web.Services.WebService
    {
        protected string m_strWellKnownGuid;
        private byte[] m_key;
        private byte[] m_iv;

    public Service1()
    {
        //CODEGEN: This call is required by the ASP.NET Web Services Designer
        InitializeComponent();

        // Initialize the well-known guid
        m_strWellKnownGuid = "{33EEA85E-D343-4a6f-A8DC-293A3EBB4C31}";

        // Create the DES key...note this and the initialization
        // vector must be the same as that used by the server
        // or the value cannot be decrypted...
        m_key = new byte[8];
        m_key[0] = 254;
        m_key[1] = 56;
        m_key[2] = 72;
        m_key[3] = 244;
        m_key[4] = 30;
        m_key[5] = 144;
```

LISTING 10.1 Continued

```
    m_key[6] = 180;
    m_key[7] = 97;

    // Create the DES initialization vector
    m_iv = new byte[8];
    m_iv[0] = 103;
    m_iv[1] = 179;
    m_iv[2] = 216;
    m_iv[3] = 199;
    m_iv[4] = 37;
    m_iv[5] = 53;
    m_iv[6] = 122;
    m_iv[7] = 145;
}

(Code removed for brevity)

protected string GetNewSessionToken()
{
    // Simply create a new GUID
    Guid guid = Guid.NewGuid();
    return "{" + guid.ToString() + "}";
}

protected string EncryptToken(string strGuid)
{
    // Concatenate our "secret" GUID with the
    // public session GUID we just created.
    string strSessionString = m_strWellKnownGuid + strGuid;

    // Convert the string to a byte array
    UTF8Encoding enc = new UTF8Encoding();
    byte[] bytIn = new byte[4096];
    ((System.Array)enc.GetBytes(strSessionString)).CopyTo(bytIn,0);

    // Create stream for decryption
    byte[] bytOut = new byte[4096];
    MemoryStream stmOut = new MemoryStream(bytOut);

    // Create the service provider
    DES des = new DESCryptoServiceProvider();

    // Create the crypto stream and buffer
    CryptoStream stmEncrypt = new CryptoStream(stmOut,
                                des.CreateEncryptor(m_key,m_iv),
                                CryptoStreamMode.Write);
```

LISTING 10.1   Continued

```
        // Encrypt to memory stream
        stmEncrypt.Write(bytIn,0,strSessionString.Length);
        stmEncrypt.FlushFinalBlock();

        // Return base64 version of this encrypted value
        return Convert.ToBase64String(bytOut,0,(int)stmOut.Position);
    }

    [WebMethod]
    public string Login(string strUsername, string strPassword)
    {
        // Check input strings
        if ( strUsername.Length == 0 )
            throw new SoapException("Invalid username provided",
                new XmlQualifiedName("Client.InvalidParameter.EmptyUsername"));
        if ( strPassword.Length == 0 )
            throw new SoapException("Invalid password provided",
                new XmlQualifiedName("Client.InvalidParameter.EmptyPassword"));

        // Create a new (empty) dataset
        DataSet ds = new DataSet();

        // Pull the connection string
        string strConn = System.Configuration.ConfigurationSettings.
                        ➥AppSettings["ConnectionString"];

        // Create the search string
        string strSQL = string.Format("SELECT * FROM UserInfo WHERE username
                    ➥ = '{0}' AND password = '{1}'",strUsername,strPassword);

        // Create the connection, command,
        // and adapter objects
        OleDbConnection objConn = new OleDbConnection(strConn);
        OleDbCommand objCmd = new OleDbCommand(strSQL,objConn);
        OleDbDataAdapter objAdapter = new OleDbDataAdapter(objCmd);

        // Connect to the database and execute SQL query
        objConn.Open();

        // Fill DataSet with the results, if any
        objAdapter.Fill(ds,"UserInfo");

        // Check for data...we'll look at the id column...
```

LISTING 10.1 Continued

```
        if ( ds.Tables[0].Rows[0][0].ToString() == String.Empty )
            throw new SoapException("Invalid user, login denied"
                    new XmlQualifiedName("Client.InvalidUser.UserUnknown"));

        // If we got this far, we have a valid user, so we'll
        // create a session token, which is an encrypted
        // GUID.
        string strToken = GetNewSessionToken();
        ds.Tables[0].Rows[0][3] = strToken; // stored clear text

        // Now encrypt the token for transmission back to the user
        string strEncryptedToken = EncryptToken(strToken);

        // Get current date/time, add 5 minutes, and
        // write that to the database
        DateTime dtNow = DateTime.Now;
        dtNow.Add(new TimeSpan(0,0,5,0,0));
        ds.Tables[0].Rows[0][4] = ((Int64)dtNow.Ticks).ToString();

        // Update the database
        OleDbCommandBuilder objCmdBlder = new OleDbCommandBuilder(objAdapter);
        objAdapter.Update(ds,"UserInfo");

        // Close the connection
        objConn.Close();

        // Return the encrypted token...
        return strEncryptedToken;
    }
  }
}
```

The Login() method begins with a quick test of the username and password string parameters. If there is no data in either, you throw an exception to exit the method. If there is data, you open the database and look for the specified user:

```
// Create a new (empty) dataset
DataSet ds = new DataSet();

// Pull the connection string
string strConn = System.Configuration.ConfigurationSettings.
                ➥AppSettings["ConnectionString"];

// Create the search string
```

```
string strSQL = string.Format("SELECT * FROM UserInfo WHERE username
        ➥ = '{0}' AND password = '{1}'",strUsername,strPassword);

// Create the connection, command,
// and adapter objects
OleDbConnection objConn = new OleDbConnection(strConn);
OleDbCommand objCmd = new OleDbCommand(strSQL,objConn);
OleDbDataAdapter objAdapter = new OleDbDataAdapter(objCmd);

// Connect to the database and execute SQL query
objConn.Open();

// Fill DataSet with the results, if any
objAdapter.Fill(ds,"UserInfo");

// Check for data...we'll look at the id column...
if ( ds.Tables[0].Rows[0][0].ToString() == String.Empty )
   throw new SoapException("Invalid user, login denied"
            new XmlQualifiedName("Client.InvalidUser.UserUnknown"));
```

If the record has an empty id column, you know that the SQL query didn't return valid user information, and this user is rejected. However, if the user passes the test, you need to create a new GUID that represents this session:

```
// If we got this far, we have a valid user, so we'll
// create an authentication token, which is an encrypted
// GUID.
string strToken = GetNewAuthToken();
```

The GetNewAuthToken() method creates a new GUID and wraps it in braces, ({ and }). The braces are merely there to make it easier to visually inspect the GUID values, if necessary.

```
protected string GetNewAuthToken()
{
   // Simply create a new GUID
   Guid guid = Guid.NewGuid();
   return "{" + guid.ToString() + "}";
}
```

Because later you'll need to check for this GUID, you store it in the database so that it is associated with this user:

```
ds.Tables[0].Rows[0][3] = strToken; // stored clear text
```

You then pass it to the encryption method:

```
// Now encrypt the token for transmission back to the user
string strEncryptedToken = EncryptToken(strToken);
```

`EncryptToken()` concatenates the "secret" GUID with the "public" GUID that you just created. Then it encrypts the result:

```
protected string EncryptToken(string strGuid)
{
    // Concatenate our "secret" GUID with the
    // public authentication GUID we just
    // created.
    string strAuthString = m_strWellKnownGuid + strGuid;

    // Convert the string to a byte array
    UTF8Encoding enc = new UTF8Encoding();
    byte[] bytIn = new byte[4096];
    ((System.Array)enc.GetBytes(strAuthString)).CopyTo(bytIn,0);

    // Create stream for decryption
    byte[] bytOut = new byte[4096];
    MemoryStream stmOut = new MemoryStream(bytOut);

    // Create the service provider
    DES des = new DESCryptoServiceProvider();

    // Create the crypto stream and buffer
    CryptoStream stmEncrypt = new CryptoStream(stmOut,
                                des.CreateEncryptor(m_key,m_iv),
                                CryptoStreamMode.Write);

    // Encrypt to memory stream
    stmEncrypt.Write(bytIn,0,strAuthString.Length);
    stmEncrypt.FlushFinalBlock();

    // Return base64 version of this encrypted value
    return Convert.ToBase64String(bytOut,0,(int)stmOut.Position);
}
```

Because you're using a symmetric encryption algorithm, you need to specify your encryption key and initialization vector. Any Web Service you create that consumes the session token encrypted with these values will need the same key and initialization vector data. Although we selected different key values for this application, the technique is identical to the method parameter encryption application that you saw in Chapter 7. And because you're returning a byte array here that could contain bytes that match XML special characters, you convert the byte array into a base64 string.

At this point, you have an encrypted session token, but you need to record the expiration time that you'll associate with this token. If the user continues to use the Web Service, you'll allow the key to continue to be used. However, after the last use, the user has a brief time period in which to again access the Web Service. If the time limit expires, you force the user to reauthenticate. This code determines the current time, adds five minutes, and stores the value into the DataSet to be written to the database:

```
// Get current date/time, add 5 minutes, and
// write that to the database
DateTime dtNow = DateTime.Now;
dtNow.Add(new TimeSpan(0,0,5,0,0));
ds.Tables[0].Rows[0][4] = ((Int64)dtNow.Ticks).ToString();
```

Finally, you can update the database to record the new "public" GUID and expiration time, close the database connection, and return the encrypted session token:

```
// Update the database
OleDbCommandBuilder objCmdBlder = new OleDbCommandBuilder(objAdapter);
objAdapter.Update(ds,"UserInfo");

// Close the connection
objConn.Close();

// Return the encrypted token...
return strEncryptedToken;
```

The user then passes the session token to a secured Web Service, where you can reverse the process just described and check to see whether the user is allowed access to this Web Service. For this example, we created a Web Service that returns a string representing the current time on the server. Although this functionality isn't terribly compelling, the code to check the session token is.

LISTING 10.2 The Secured Web Service

```
using System;
using System.Collections;
using System.ComponentModel;
using System.Data;
using System.Diagnostics;
using System.Web;
using System.Web.Services;
using System.Data.OleDb;
using System.Web.Services.Protocols;
using System.Xml;
using System.Security;
using System.Security.Cryptography;
using System.Text;
using System.IO;
```

LISTING 10.2 Continued

```
namespace SecuredService
{
   /// <summary>
   /// Summary description for Service1.
   /// </summary>
   public class Service1 : System.Web.Services.WebService
   {
      protected string m_strWellKnownGuid;
      private byte[] m_key;
      private byte[] m_iv;

      public Service1()
      {
         //CODEGEN: This call is required by the ASP.NET Web Services Designer
         InitializeComponent();

         // Initialize the well-known guid
         m_strWellKnownGuid = "{33EEA85E-D343-4a6f-A8DC-293A3EBB4C31}";

         // Create the DES key...note this and the initialization
         // vector must be the same as that used by the server
         // or the value cannot be decrypted...
         m_key = new byte[8];
         m_key[0] = 254;
         m_key[1] = 56;
         m_key[2] = 72;
         m_key[3] = 244;
         m_key[4] = 30;
         m_key[5] = 144;
         m_key[6] = 180;
         m_key[7] = 97;

         // Create the DES initialization vector
         m_iv = new byte[8];
         m_iv[0] = 103;
         m_iv[1] = 179;
         m_iv[2] = 216;
         m_iv[3] = 199;
         m_iv[4] = 37;
         m_iv[5] = 53;
         m_iv[6] = 122;
         m_iv[7] = 145;
      }

      (Code removed for brevity...)
```

LISTING 10.2   Continued

```
protected bool CheckSessionToken(string strSessionToken)
{
    // We have two encrypted GUIDs smashed together, and the
    // one we want is the first. So we pull that out
    // after decrypting and check it against our "secret"
    // GUID...
    //
    // Convert the string to a byte array
    byte[] bytIn = new byte[4096];
    byte[] bytEnc = Convert.FromBase64String(strSessionToken);
    bytEnc.CopyTo(bytIn,0);

    // Create streams for decryption
    byte[] bytOut = new byte[4096];
    MemoryStream stmOut = new MemoryStream(bytOut);

    // Create the service provider
    DES des = new DESCryptoServiceProvider();

    // Create the crypto stream and buffer
    CryptoStream stmDecrypt = new CryptoStream(stmOut,
                          des.CreateDecryptor(m_key,m_iv),
                          CryptoStreamMode.Write);

    // Encrypt to memory stream
    stmDecrypt.Write(bytIn,0,bytEnc.Length);
    stmDecrypt.FlushFinalBlock();

    // Extract our secret GUID
    UTF8Encoding enc = new UTF8Encoding();
    string strSecretGuid = enc.GetString(bytOut,
                                         0,
                                         ((int)stmOut.Position/2));
    string strPublicGuid = enc.GetString(bytOut,
                            ((int)stmOut.Position/2),
                            ((int)stmOut.Position/2));

    bool bIsValid = false;
    if ( strSecretGuid == m_strWellKnownGuid )
    {
        // Session GUID is decrypted, so now we test the secret
        // session GUID we gave them previously
        //
        // Create a new (empty) dataset
        DataSet ds = new DataSet();
```

LISTING 10.2   Continued

```
// Pull the connection string
string strConn = System.Configuration.ConfigurationSettings.
                    ➡AppSettings["ConnectionString"];

// Create the search string
string strSQL = string.Format("SELECT * FROM UserInfo WHERE token =
                ➡ '{0}'",strPublicGuid);

// Create the connection, command,
// and adapter objects
OleDbConnection objConn = new OleDbConnection(strConn);
OleDbCommand objCmd = new OleDbCommand(strSQL,objConn);
OleDbDataAdapter objAdapter = new OleDbDataAdapter(objCmd);

// Connect to the database and execute SQL query
objConn.Open();

// Fill DataSet with the results, if any
objAdapter.Fill(ds,"UserInfo");

// Check for data...we'll look at the id column...
if ( ds.Tables[0].Rows[0][0].ToString() == String.Empty )
   throw new SoapException("Invalid user, login denied",
   new XmlQualifiedName("Client.AuthenticationError.UserUnknown"));

// If we got this far, they're valid, but are they over
// the time limit?
DateTime dtThen =
 new DateTime(Convert.ToInt64(ds.Tables[0].Rows[0][4].ToString()));
DateTime dtNow = DateTime.Now;
if ( dtThen.CompareTo(dtNow) <= 0 )
{
   // We haven't expired, so mark it as valid
   bIsValid = true;

   // Give them another time interval
   dtNow.Add(new TimeSpan(0,0,5,0,0));
   ds.Tables[0].Rows[0][4] = ((Int64)dtNow.Ticks).ToString();

   // Update the database
   OleDbCommandBuilder objCmdBlder =
                          new OleDbCommandBuilder(objAdapter);
   objAdapter.Update(ds,"UserInfo");
```

LISTING 10.2   Continued

```
                // Close the connection
                objConn.Close();
            }
            else
            {
                throw new SoapException("Login timed out, please log in again",
                        new XmlQualifiedName("Client.AuthenticationError.
                        ➥LoginTimeout"));
            }
        }
        else
        {
            throw new SoapException("Invalid user, login denied",
                    new XmlQualifiedName("Client.AuthenticationError.
                    ➥InvalidLoginToken"));
        }

        return bIsValid;
    }

    [WebMethod]
    public string GetServerTime(string strSessionToken)
    {
        // Check the session token
        if ( !CheckSessionToken(strSessionToken) )
            throw new SoapException("You are not authorized to use this
                        ➥ Web Service...",new XmlQualifiedName("Client.
                        ➥AuthenticationError.UnauthorizedUser"));

        // If we got this far, return the current time...
        return DateTime.Now.ToString();
    }
  }
}
```

The user will invoke the secured Web Service, which is GetServerTime(), in this case, at which time the Web Service will check the session token:

```
[WebMethod]
public string GetServerTime(string strSessionToken)
{
        if ( !CheckSessionToken(strSessionToken) )
            throw new SoapException("You are not authorized to use this
                        ➥ Web Service...",new XmlQualifiedName("Client.
                        ➥AuthenticationError.UnauthorizedUser"));
```

```
   // If we got this far, return the current time...
   return DateTime.Now.ToString();
}
```

`CheckSessionToken()` will remove the encrypted value from the base64 string, decrypt it, and check both GUIDs against values that you expect.

To help prevent excessive resource consumption when processing a denial-of-service attack, first check the "secret" GUID, which is *not* stored in the database. If that test fails, there isn't any chance that this session token is valid, so you can reject the user immediately. However, if the "secret" GUID is valid, you need to read the database to pull this GUID value and then retrieve the session timeout limit. The time is then checked, and the appropriate action is taken—you execute the Web Service or return an exception.

A client application might contain code that looks a lot like what you see in Listing 10.3.

LISTING 10.3   Client Application

```
// Create the proxy
localhost.Service1 wsLogin = new localhost.Service1();

// Retrieve the session token
string strSessionToken = wsLogin.Login("kenn","kenn");

// (Debugging note to the screen...)
Console.WriteLine("The session token was {0}",strSessionToken);

// Call the *real* Web Service with the
// session token we just retrieved...
localhost1.Service1 wsSecured = new localhost1.Service1();
string strServerTime = wsSecured.GetServerTime(strSessionToken);
Console.WriteLine("The server time was {0}",strServerTime);
```

A decision that you make as the secured Web Service designer is whether to force the session token to be passed to the server in a SOAP Header or as a parameter of the method. In this case, we chose the simpler option and passed the session token into the Web Service as the first method parameter.

Returning now to general Web Service security topics, the techniques you've seen here have been primarily implemented outside of .NET. As it happens, .NET also can help with security.

.NET Security

From the beginning, .NET was designed and implemented with security in mind. .NET enables you to specify security permissions and policies that, when associated with an assembly, authorize or prevent users and other code from accessing your secured component. .NET combines this with COM+ security as well, so you actually have two layers of code-based security available to you.

At the same time, ASP.NET allows for *impersonation*. Users logging into your Web Service may impersonate a local system account. That account will be administratively granted certain levels of secure access. So, if a user attempts to access code for which he is not authorized, .NET will throw an access or permission exception and the user will receive a SOAP fault packet for his efforts. Let's look first at .NET code access security and then move to COM+ security services.

.NET Evidence-Based Security

.NET bases code access on evidence, which is a combination of three components: permissions, policies, and evidence. *Permissions* are objects that represent authorization for secured resource access, such as to the file system or the Registry. When a user accesses a .NET assembly, the user rights granted them as a *principle* (a user) are carried with them in the form of these objects.

Policies are also administratively established by *role*. That is, groups of users are assigned to roles such as "administrator" or "power user," or even roles that you create. Policies carry with them the permissions assigned to the specific role associated with the principle. So, using administrative tools, you can lock down specific assemblies by allowing access to certain principles in roles with specific permissions. The .NET runtime environment then enforces the security settings you've established.

Evidence has a particular meaning to .NET. It represents information specific to the assembly that is known to the runtime environment. For example, the .NET runtime environment knows where in the file system the assembly is stored. You also may digitally sign an assembly, and this digital signature represents evidence that the runtime may use to determine access to the code. Through metadata, you also may add custom evidence and examine it when the assembly is called into play.

.NET combines these three aspects of code access security and makes a determination at runtime on whether the given user is authorized to use the particular assembly. .NET also is aware that secured assemblies may lie deep within the call stack. That is, you may invoke a Web Service that calls one assembly, which calls another assembly, which calls another, and so on. No matter how deep you go or how many assemblies you access, .NET walks the call stack and performs a security check for each assembly. If any assembly in the call stack fails the security check, the entire operation fails and the user is denied access to the code.

.NET Access Demands

This call-stack checking is called a stack walk. One way to force a stack walk is to apply a demand to secured resources. For example, instead of simply opening a file, you provide a permissions demand that forces a security check. If the demand fails, the user is denied access to the resource.

Demands come in two forms: imperative and declarative. *Imperative* demands use code to force a security check:

```
[WebMethod]
public string GetFileContents(string strFilename)
{
    . . .
    String fullPath = Directory.GetFullPathInternal(fileName);
    new FileIOPermission(FileIOPermissionAccess.Read, fullPath).Demand();
    // Read file contents into "strContents"
    return strContents;
}
```

Declarative demands are attribute-based, which means that they become part of the metadata associated with the assembly. And because they are metadata, they also become evidence:

```
[WebMethod]
[FileIOPermission(SecurityAction.Demand, Read = "c:\\temp\\myfile.dat")]
public string GetFileContents()
{
    ...
    // Read myfile.dat contents into "strContents"
    // (or change attribute filename...)
    return strContents;
}
```

.NET Strong Names

A *strong name* is really a digital signature that you apply to an assembly. Its purpose is to limit access to the assembly to specific users or businesses that are specifically authorized to access this particular shared component:

```
[StrongNameIdentityPermissionAttribute
    (SecurityAction.LinkDemand,
    PublicKey="00240000048000009400000006020000...",
    Name="MyWebMethod", Version="1.0.0.0")]
// Only MyWebMethod can use this class, and it is restricted
// (perhaps) by role...
public class MyCoolClass
{
    . . .
}
```

Strong names are applied to assemblies that are considered shared. Private assemblies are assemblies that the application loads into its own /bin subdirectory. Because the assemblies are not made known to the system as a whole, they remain private to the application. However, some assemblies are meant to be shared; at that time, they must be registered with the assembly cache (GAC). Doing so creates a strong name for the assembly, and it is against this strong name that you can enforce access (this is not required, but it is possible).

Today and for the near future, .NET bolts onto the Windows operating system. Therefore, COM+ also plays a role in security. Let's briefly see what COM+ offers.

COM+ Security

The COM+ runtime also provides security measures that you can employ to limit access to specific files, directories, and other resources. For example, you can denote a specific Web Service assembly as being accessible only by principles in the administrator role.

A nice feature that COM+ exhibits is that it is administratively based. That is, you may write code to force COM+ to enforce security, but you also may use administrator applications and, from a user interface, set permissions and role access. This reduces the security code that you need to write and generally makes securing resources easier to do.

Summary

This whirlwind tour of Web Service security options was meant to introduce you to concepts and options that you have available, to provide some measure of security for your Web Services. At this time, .NET–specific security information is available online at `http://msdn.microsoft.com`, but you'll probably find entire books devoted to security—as well as some written about .NET security specifically.

Here, we mentioned that you have differing options depending on the breadth of your Web Service audience. If the Web Service is exported to systems on an intranet, where the users and computer identities are known, you can use security techniques designed for peer-to-peer communications, such as IPSec or HTTP Security.

Wider-scale Web Services can't always take advantage of security techniques that smaller-scale Web Services can simply because you want the public to access your Web Service but you don't know the identity of every machine that might access your Web Service. Therefore, you'll turn to bulk encryption, SOAP Digital Signatures or other Body-encryption techniques, and application-specific authentication techniques to lock down your Web Service.

Appendixes

PART

IV

Example .NET Web Service

IN THIS APPENDIX

When you sit down to write a book, you have many decisions to make. Certainly one of those decisions is how you intend to handle examples throughout the book. Some books present complex examples that tend to mask the basic concepts that they present, while others present examples that target the basic concept but provide relatively useless test applications in the process. We've tried to strike a balance in this book, but, admittedly, the examples have been very simplistic.

With this appendix, we hope to correct that a bit. Given time, you would have seen a full-blown distributed application, with a rich ASP.NET front end, a SQL Server 2000 back end with cool stored procedures, and Web Services forming much of the business layer. There would be authentication services, data services, other business services, and so forth. But the reality of the situation is that this type of application can take months just to produce the code for, and that's not realistic for a book. Frankly, you probably don't want to wade through a couple of thousand lines of code to see how we implemented a certain feature.

Therefore, we decided to create two sample Web Services that are not terribly complex yet that could demonstrate a bit more than simple Web Service behavior. The first Web Service is written in Visual Basic .NET and serves as a "Tip of the Day" repository. The tips themselves are stored in an XML file, the location of which you specify in the Web Service's web.config file. You ask for a tip, and the Web Service opens the file and returns a random tip string. But you also can add new tips. This Web Service shows how to work with XML and the .NET Framework Class Library's XML support, to some degree.

The second Web Service is written in C# and shows ADO.NET and the DataSet in action. The intention was to simulate the old Unix finger command, where you provide finger with a name and it returns information about that user. finger was a little more intelligent, in that it would query a file that the user provided (and so it was distributed). In this case, we wanted to show database access, so the user information is centrally located. Nonetheless, if you provide the first and last names to the Web Service, it will return to you a DataSet with the user's job title, location, and phone number. A more interesting example would be to simulate HailStorm and have each user expose a set of Web Services that we can use to query for information—again, though, that would have taken quite a bit of time to develop and possibly would have smear code everywhere, obfuscating the details that you'll want to see.

So, let's take a look at these examples. With luck, you'll find the code here to be useful and interesting. We'll try to explain our thinking in some detail as we go through the code.

Tip of the Day Web Service in Visual Basic .NET

When we created this Web Service, we had a single goal in mind: to do something with XML using the .NET XML classes. We wanted to load a file, read it, change it, and write it back out.

Because we covered XPath in fair detail in Chapter 3, "Web Services and XML," we wanted to use another data access technique, through the XmlDocument object.

We've placed the XML document that we used for this Web Service in Listing A.1. The `<Tips/>` element acts as a container for the individual `<Tip/>` elements, each of which contains a string representing the tip itself.

LISTING A.1   Tip of the Day Tip Database File (XML)

```
<?xml version="1.0"?>
<Tips>
   <Tip>Do not run with scissors</Tip>
   <Tip>Learn everything you can about XML</Tip>
   <Tip>Beer is more than the sum of its parts</Tip>
   <Tip>It is not how much code you write...it is how well you write
      ➥ that code</Tip>
   <Tip>Free articles and code at http://www.endurasoft.com/educenter.htm</Tip>
   <Tip>No application is done being coded until at least three cases of
      ➥ Diet Mountain Dew have been consumed</Tip>
   <Tip>When in doubt, power it down</Tip>
   <Tip>They make fiberglass handles for golf umbrellas for a reason</Tip>
   <Tip>DOS 4 is out!...oh, wait, wrong Tip file...</Tip>
   <Tip>When you need code in a hurry, just any code will not do</Tip>
   <Tip>It is hard to soar with eagles when you work with turkeys</Tip>
   <Tip>The rats are winning...go home</Tip>
</Tips>
```

The Tip Web Service itself provides you with two remote methods:

- GetTip(), to retrieve a random tip
- AddTip(), to insert a new tip

GetTip() will read the XML file and extract a node list containing all the `<Tip/>` elements. Because it's possible to access an individual element in a node list as an array element, you can request a random number; from there you can dive into the node list and pull out a random tip string.

AddTip() accepts a string representing the tip and inserts it as the last `<Tip/>` element in the document. AddTip() does some basic data checking, but it doesn't check to see if the tip already exists. You can see both methods shown in Listing A.2.

LISTING A.2   Visual Basic .NET Tip Web Service Processing

```
<WebMethod()> Public Function GetTip() As String
    Try
        ' Find the path to the tip file
        Dim strTipPath As String = System.Configuration.ConfigurationSettings.
                             ➥AppSettings()("TipFilePath")

        ' Open the tip file for reading
        Dim objXmlDoc As XmlDocument = New XmlDocument()
        objXmlDoc.Load(strTipPath)

        ' Pull the root node...
        Dim objRoot As XmlNode = objXmlDoc.DocumentElement

        ' Pull all of its children
        Dim objTipsList As XmlNodeList = objRoot.ChildNodes

        ' Select a random number
        Dim objRand As Random = New Random(CInt(DateTime.Now.Millisecond))

        ' Return a tip
        GetTip = objTipsList.Item(objRand.Next(objTipsList.Count)).InnerText
    Catch ex As Exception
        GetTip = "Error retrieving the tip, " & ex.Message
    End Try
End Function

<WebMethod()> Public Function AddTip(ByVal strTip As String) As Boolean
    Try
        ' Find the path to the tip file
        Dim strTipPath As String  System.Configuration.ConfigurationSettings.
                             ➥AppSettings()("TipFilePath")

        ' Open the tip file for reading
        Dim objXmlDoc As XmlDocument = New XmlDocument()
        objXmlDoc.Load(strTipPath)

        ' Pull the root node...
        Dim objRoot As XmlNode = objXmlDoc.DocumentElement

        ' Add the new tip as the last child
        Dim objNewNode As XmlNode = objXmlDoc.CreateNode(XmlNodeType.Element,
                                                    "Tip", "")
        objNewNode.InnerText = strTip
        objRoot.AppendChild(objNewNode)
```

LISTING A.2 Continued

```
    ' Write the XML stream back out
    Dim objXmlWriter As XmlTextWriter = New XmlTextWriter(strTipPath,
                                                          Nothing)

    objXmlDoc.WriteContentTo(objXmlWriter)
    objXmlWriter.Close()

    ' Return
    AddTip = True
  Catch ex As Exception
    AddTip = False
  End Try
End Function
```

The first thing both methods do is search for the XML file's location web.config, where we added the italicized lines:

```
<?xml version="1.0" encoding="utf-8" ?>
<configuration>
  <appSettings>
    <add key="TipFilePath" value="c:\TipFile.xml" />
  </appSettings>
  <system.web>
    ...
  </system.web>
</configuration>
```

Each method then uses identical code to access web.config:

```
' Find the path to the tip file
Dim strTipPath As String = System.Configuration.ConfigurationSettings.
                    ➥AppSettings()("TipFilePath")
```

NOTE

You might need to edit the file permissions associated with the tip XML file to allow outside users to add tips. This will be especially true if the Web Service users are using the general Internet Information Server account.

After you have the XML file's path, you can open the file for reading:

```
' Open the tip file for reading
Dim objXmlDoc As XmlDocument = New XmlDocument()
objXmlDoc.Load(strTipPath)
```

The goal is to create a node list of all `<Tip/>` elements, but, to do that, you require their parent, `<Tips/>`, which also happens to be the document element:

```
' Pull the root node...
Dim objRoot As XmlNode = objXmlDoc.DocumentElement
```

With the parent element in hand, you can request the node list containing all its children:

```
' Pull all of its children
Dim objTipsList As XmlNodeList = objRoot.ChildNodes
```

After creating an instance of the random number generator, you can pick a random tip from the list of tips:

```
' Return a tip
GetTip = objTipsList.Item(objRand.Next(objTipsList.Count)).InnerText
```

Adding a new tip is also relatively easy. After retrieving the XML file's path, opening it, and retrieving the document element, you can create a new instance of `XmlNode`:

```
' Add the new tip as the last child
Dim objNewNode As XmlNode = objXmlDoc.CreateNode(XmlNodeType.Element,
                                                 "Tip", "")
```

You then can change the `InnerText` associated with this node to be the tip string provided as a method argument:

```
objNewNode.InnerText = strTip
```

But you have not yet inserted this new node into the XML document, so you should append it to the end of the children of the document element:

```
objRoot.AppendChild(objNewNode)
```

Finally, you need to save the modified XML information back into the XML file, which you can do using `XmlTextWriter`:

```
' Write the XML stream back out
Dim objXmlWriter As XmlTextWriter = New XmlTextWriter(strTipPath,
                                                      Nothing)
objXmlDoc.WriteContentTo(objXmlWriter)
objXmlWriter.Close()
```

We created a client for this Web Service then; you'll see the user interface in Figure A.1.

The user interface is little more than an edit control and a couple of buttons. If you retrieve a tip, the tip's text is recorded in the edit control. If you want to add a tip, the text in the edit control is written to the tip file. The code to do each of these is shown in Listing A.3.

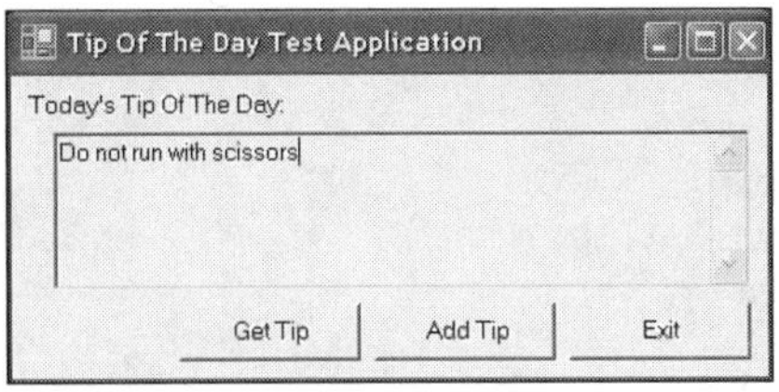

FIGURE A.1

Tip of the Day client application user interface.

LISTING A.3 Visual Basic .NET Tip Client-Side Processing

```
Private Sub cmdGet_Click(ByVal sender As System.Object,
            ➡ ByVal e As System.EventArgs) Handles cmdGet.Click
   ' Retrieve an existing tip
   txtTip.Text = m_pxyTipSvc.GetTip()
   txtTip.Modified = False
End Sub

Private Sub cmdAdd_Click(ByVal sender As System.Object,
            ➡ ByVal e As System.EventArgs) Handles cmdAdd.Click
   ' Quick check to see if there is really
   ' any tip text to add...
   If txtTip.Text = "" Then
      ' Nothing to add
      Exit Sub
   End If

   ' Quick check to see if any text was typed
   ' into the edit control
   If txtTip.Modified = False Then
      ' They didn't change anything...
      Exit Sub
   End If

   ' Add a new tip
   If m_pxyTipSvc.AddTip(txtTip.Text) = False Then
      MsgBox("Could not add new tip to tip database!",
            MsgBoxStyle.Exclamation, "Tip Of The Day Error")
   Else
      txtTip.Modified = False
   End If
End Sub
```

When the application's form loads, or when you click the Get Tip button, you access the Web Service to retrieve a tip:

```
' Retrieve an existing tip
txtTip.Text = m_pxyTipSvc.GetTip()
txtTip.Modified = False
```

Note that the text box's Modified property has been set to False—you'll need to know this when you add a new tip to the tip repository.

Adding a tip is nearly as easy. Simply perform some quick data checks to make sure that you don't issue unnecessary network packets:

```
' Quick check to see if there is really
' any tip text to add...
If txtTip.Text = "" Then
   ' Nothing to add
   Exit Sub
End If


' Quick check to see if any text was typed
' into the edit control
If txtTip.Modified = False Then
   ' They didn't change anything...
   Exit Sub
End If
```

Here you can see why it was necessary to set the edit control's Modified property to False when you loaded it with new tip information. If the user doesn't type something into the edit control, you assume that the information didn't change, so there is no need to write it back into the XML file.

Finally, you add the tip:

```
' Add a new tip
If m_pxyTipSvc.AddTip(txtTip.Text) = False Then
   MsgBox("Could not add new tip to tip database!",
         MsgBoxStyle.Exclamation, "Tip Of The Day Error")
Else
   txtTip.Modified = False
End If
```

The client application was created in the same manner as the applications you've seen throughout the book. We created the project, added a Web reference, and wrote the supporting code. This aspect of the client application is rather unremarkable.

That completes the first example Web Service. Next, let's look at accessing a database using C# and ADO.NET.

finger Web Service in C#

As mentioned previously, the old Unix finger command reached into a user's account and retrieved a file that contained user information. This information then was returned to the caller—perhaps the caller needed to know a phone number or location where the user could generally be found. This example won't access individual Window user accounts, but it will show you how to access a database using ADO.NET and C#.

> **NOTE**
>
> If you've done any database programming at all, you know that it's far better to place your SQL queries in a stored procedure than inline in your business layer. Yet that's exactly what we've done for this example. The reason for this is simply that it's easier to distribute a self-contained Access database file than scripts and such for a SQL Server 2000 database. Unfortunately, Access doesn't support stored procedures. But this code should get you up and working with ADO.NET, and you can then easily modify this code to invoke a stored procedure. (ADO.NET isn't *that* different from ADO from an object model perspective.)

This Web Service exports a single method, Finger(), that accepts as input two strings: one with the user's first name and one with the user's last name. Because this is a demonstration application, we don't handle the case with multiple users with the same first and last names (you could select based upon a middle name, for example). The resulting DataSet contains all users that match this criteria; the client assumes that only the first row is valid, as you'll see.

> **NOTE**
>
> If you're unfamiliar with the ADO.NET DataSet but you are familiar with ADO's RecordSet object, we can describe the DataSet in this way: An ADO.NET DataSet is like an XML-based ADO RecordSet that can store more than a single database table (and the relationships between the multiple tables). The DataSet is simply a container for tables, rows, and columns of database information.

The database itself, Finger.mdb, contains a table called Residents with the following columns:

- id (primary key)
- first (first name)
- middle (middle name)

- last (last name}
- title (job title)
- location (user's office location)
- phone (phone number)
- extensions (phone extension, if any)

To pull the user information from the database, you can use this SQL query string:

```
SELECT * FROM Residents WHERE first = 'first name' AND last = 'last name'
```

> **NOTE**
>
> If this were a production-quality application, we realize that you would probably not use the column wildcard, but instead you would select the individual columns from the Residents table. You also might want to place the SQL query string into the web.config file. The idea with this example is merely to show database access.

To make things more flexible, we stored the database connection string in the web.config file, just as we did the XML file's location for the "Tip of the Day" Web Service. We added the following italicized lines to the web.config file:

```
<?xml version="1.0" encoding="utf-8" ?>
<configuration>
   <appSettings>
      <add key="ConnectionString" value="Provider= Microsoft.Jet.OLEDB.4.0;
                                   ➥Data Source=C:\Finger.mdb" />
   </appSettings>
   <system.web>
      ...
   </system.web>
</configuration>
```

This enables you to easily configure your system by changing the connection string in the XML file rather than by recompiling the Web Service. When you try this example, be sure to insert the correct location of the Finger.mdb file, or you'll fail to connect to the database.

The Web Service's Finger() method code is shown in Listing A.4.

LISTING A.4 C# Finger User Information Retrieval Web Service Processing

```
[WebMethod]
public DataSet Finger(string strFirst, string strLast)
{
   // Create a new (empty) dataset
```

LISTING A.4   Continued

```csharp
DataSet ds = new DataSet();

try
{
    // Check input strings
    if ( strFirst.Length == 0 || strLast.Length == 0 ) throw new Exception("Not
➥used");

    // Pull the connection string
    string strConn = System.Configuration.ConfigurationSettings.
                        ➥AppSettings["ConnectionString"];

    // Create the search string
    string strSQL = string.Format("SELECT * FROM Residents WHERE first = '{0}'
                            ➥ AND last = '{1}'",strFirst,strLast);

    // Create the connection, command,
    // and adapter objects
    OleDbConnection objConn = new OleDbConnection(strConn);
    OleDbCommand objCmd = new OleDbCommand(strSQL,objConn);
    OleDbDataAdapter objAdapter = new OleDbDataAdapter(objCmd);

    // Connect to the database and execute SQL query
    objConn.Open();

    // Fill DataSet with the results, if any
    objAdapter.Fill(ds,"Residents");
} // try
catch(Exception)
{
    // Just return an empty DataSet...
} // catch

return ds;
}
```

The first thing you should do is to create a new, empty DataSet. If you sustain an exception, you'll simply return this empty DataSet. On the other hand, if you do run to completion, you'll fill this DataSet with the user data that you retrieved from the database. Here is how you create a new DataSet:

```csharp
// Create a new (empty) dataset
DataSet ds = new DataSet();
```

After a quick check to be sure that the user provided valid name strings, you can extract the connection string from the web.config file:

```
// Pull the connection string
string strConn = System.Configuration.ConfigurationSettings.
                    ➥AppSettings["ConnectionString"];
```

Next, create the SQL query string using the input method parameters for the first and last names:

```
// Create the search string
string strSQL = string.Format("SELECT * FROM Residents WHERE first = '{0}'
                    ➥ AND last = '{1}'",strFirst,strLast);
```

With the connection and SQL strings in hand, you can then create the ADO.NET objects that you'll need to access the data:

```
// Create the connection, command,
// and adapter objects
OleDbConnection objConn = new OleDbConnection(strConn);
OleDbCommand objCmd = new OleDbCommand(strSQL,objConn);
OleDbDataAdapter objAdapter = new OleDbDataAdapter(objCmd);
```

The `OleDbConnection` object maintains the connection, the `OleDbCommand` object encapsulates the SQL query and ties it to the database through the connection object, and the `OleDbDataAdapter` will be used to actually fill the `DataSet`.

Assuming that all goes well to this point, you can open the connection and execute the SQL query:

```
// Connect to the database and execute SQL query
objConn.Open();
```

If things work as hoped, you then fill the `DataSet` with the results of the SQL query:

```
// Fill DataSet with the results, if any
objAdapter.Fill(ds,"Residents");
```

The dataset is then returned to the client for processing.

To demonstrate this Web Service in action, we created the application that you see in Figure A.2. Essentially, you provide a first and last name in the edit controls and click the Finger button; the remaining information will be completed from the result `DataSet`.

The code behind this is shown in Listing A.5, where you see the handler for the Finger button's `click` event.

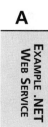

FIGURE A.2

Finger Client Application user interface.

LISTING A.5   C# Finger Client-Side Processing

```csharp
private void cmdFinger_Click(object sender, System.EventArgs e)
{
    // Retrieve the data from the FingerService
    try
    {
        // Create the proxy
        Service1 ws = new Service1();

        // Call the Web Service
        DataSet ds = ws.Finger(txtFirst.Text,txtLast.Text);

        // Extract the data from the DataSet
        lblTitle.Text = ds.Tables[0].Rows[0][4].ToString();
        lblLocation.Text = ds.Tables[0].Rows[0][5].ToString();
        string strPhone = ds.Tables[0].Rows[0][6].ToString();
        string strExtension = ds.Tables[0].Rows[0][7].ToString();
        if ( strExtension.Length > 0 )
        {
            // Add the extension here...
            strPhone += ", x";
            strPhone += strExtension;
        } // if
        lblPhone.Text = strPhone;
    } // try
    catch(IndexOutOfRangeException)
    {
        // No data is available for the parameters
        // given...
        MessageBox.Show("No Finger client available with that name...",
                    "FingerClient Error",
```

LISTING A.5 Continued

```
                        MessageBoxButtons.OK,
                        MessageBoxIcon.Error);
    lblTitle.Text = "*****";
    lblLocation.Text = "*****";
    lblPhone.Text = "*****";
} // catch
catch(Exception ex)
{
    // Check the error...
    string strMsg = "Error retrieving data from the Finger Web Service:\n'";
    strMsg += ex.Message;
    strMsg += "'";
    MessageBox.Show(strMsg,
                    "FingerClient Error",
                    MessageBoxButtons.OK,
                    MessageBoxIcon.Error);
    lblTitle.Text = "*****";
    lblLocation.Text = "*****";
    lblPhone.Text = "*****";
} // catch
}
```

To use ADO.NET on the client, you'll need to add the reference to `System.Data` (this is done for you when you create Web Service projects, but not for standard Windows applications). With this reference inserted, the client first creates an instance of the Web Service's proxy:

```
// Create the proxy
Service1 ws = new Service1();
```

With the proxy created and ready to go, you call the Web Service and accept the resulting DataSet:

```
// Call the Web Service
DataSet ds = ws.Finger(txtFirst.Text,txtLast.Text);
```

After the Web Service returns a `DataSet`, extract the data. Now, if there is data, these lines will pull the data from the `DataSet` and insert them into the label controls shown in Figure A.2:

```
// Extract the data from the DataSet
lblTitle.Text = ds.Tables[0].Rows[0][4].ToString();
lblLocation.Text = ds.Tables[0].Rows[0][5].ToString();
string strPhone = ds.Tables[0].Rows[0][6].ToString();
string strExtension = ds.Tables[0].Rows[0][7].ToString();
if ( strExtension.Length > 0 )
{
```

```
    // Add the extension here...
    strPhone += ", x";
    strPhone += strExtension;
} // if
lblPhone.Text = strPhone;
```

You know that there will be only a single table in this `DataSet`—hence, the `Tables[0]`. Also, you'll only ever access the first row (because the first user meets the search criteria), so the array index on the `Rows` property is hard-coded to be 0: `Rows[0]`. The second array index constraining the row is actually the column, and these are defined by the database schema. For example, you know that column 4 of the Residents table is the job title field, `Rows[0][4]`. Simply step through the remainder of the `DataSet` in this manner.

The code surrounding the phone number is there simply to produce a string in one of these two forms:

`123-4567`

or

`123,4567, x89`

If there is no extension, you display none; if there is, you concatenate it to the phone number itself for display purposes.

Notice that we wrapped the Web Service access in a `try/catch` block and that we're specifically interested in the `IndexOutOfRangeException`. This is because the user sometimes will request information for someone who is not included in the database; this is the exception that is thrown when you try to access an empty `DataSet`. So, this exception is handled a bit differently than some other generic exceptions.

Using ATL Server to Create Web Services

IN THIS APPENDIX

We've concentrated on the .NET Framework throughout this book. You've seen how Web Services are created and consumed using managed code, using both C# and Visual Basic .NET. But Visual Studio .NET also ships with a fascinating technology known as ATL Server. What is ATL Server, and why should you be interested in this technology?

ATL Server is to Web Services as ATL is to Component Object Model (COM) programming. If you're familiar with COM and ATL, you know that you can create extremely high-powered COM objects relatively quickly. The same is true for ATL Server.

ATL Server is really targeted more toward ASP.NET. That is, using ATL Server, you can create Web pages and back those Web pages with high performance C++ code (managed or unmanaged). For the purposes of this book, we're not going to discuss the Web site aspects of ATL Server. Instead, we'll concentrate on the Web Services end of the technology. We'll still start with an overview of ATL Server's architecture, however.

ATL Server Architecture

The main premise behind ATL Server is identical to that behind ATL itself—ATL Server is "lean and mean," and "you pay for only what you use." This provides you with some very performance-minded Web Services. It also serves as a bridge technology that lets you work with C++ as you have, yet still create Web Services in much the same way as .NET does.

Part of ATL Server's performance secret is that ATL Server uses Internet Services Application Programming Interface (ISAPI) directly. ISAPI is the Internet Information Server (IIS) portal to executable code, much like the Common Gateway Interface (CGI) is to traditional Web applications.

The design decision to separate Web presentation from page logic is a good one, and, like ASP.NET, ATL Server separates the basic HTML markup from the code that backs the content. ATL Server places the HTML presentation in *stencils*, which are stored in Server Response Files (SRF). The SRF files have markup within them much like you find with traditional ASP pages, where the markup is replaced at runtime by HTML-based results from some executable code you've provided. I mention these files not because they're used by ATL Server–based Web Services, but rather because they show up in the overall ATL Server architectural drawing that you see in Figure B.1. We don't use the SRF files when working with Web Services any more than we write user interfaces using ASP.NET when we create Web Services using .NET. The SRF files are shown in Figure B.1 for completeness.

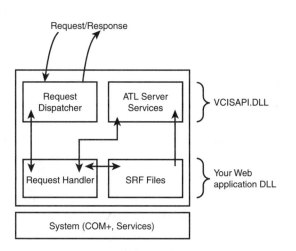

Request/Response

| Request Dispatcher | ATL Server Services | } VCISAPI.DLL |

| Request Handler | SRF Files | } Your Web application DLL |

System (COM+, Services)

FIGURE B.1
Overall ATL Server architecture.

Web Service requests and responses are handled through the *request dispatcher*, the functionality for which is provided by Visual Studio .NET. The dispatcher examines the incoming messages and routes them, as appropriate, to your own ISAPI extension DLL, where your *request handler* processes the request and formulates the response. Of course, you will need support from COM+ and the Windows operating system, as well as from ATL Server itself. Let's see how ATL Server works its magic.

Attributed C++

One of the things I noticed immediately when I created my first ATL Server Web Service was that the C++ language had changed! Microsoft extended the language to allow for attribute-based programming, much like the other .NET CLR-based languages could use attributes to control the execution of methods, classes, and so on. I saw many attributes that made sense from a COM programming perspective, and I saw attributes that were clearly designed to give the application its Web Service behavior. Microsoft also added a new extension C++ keyword, __interface, that provides the strong definition for interfaces in the COM sense. Let's look at some of the attributes first.

COM-Based Attributes

ATL Server Web Services are not COM objects—at least, not as they're created by Visual Studio .NET. Instead, they're simple ISAPI DLLs. Nonetheless, it was apparent that the attributes were meant to replace the traditional Interface Definition Language (IDL) file that described the COM interfaces that the object was to support. In fact, this is the case—the IDL file is no longer required, and all the information formerly contained within the IDL file may now be specified directly in the C++ code stream.

The reason for this was primarily to support COM directly in C++ rather than resort to a second language (IDL) with a separate compilation step (the Microsoft IDL compiler, or MIDL). If you were writing Windows applications in 1997, you probably noted Mary Kirtland's articles in the November and December issues of "Microsoft Programmer's Journal (MSJ)" that described COM+ as attribute-based additions to the C++ language. Of course, COM+ became something very different, but we now see Mary's predictions coming true (life must be wonderful when you have such inside information!).

The set of COM-based attributes are collectively known as Inline IDL, and I've shown you some of the more commonly used attributes in Table B.1.

TABLE B.1   Commonly Used Inline IDL Attributes

IDL Attribute	Purpose
coclass	Adds COM support to the class and to the underlying IDL file, if generated
dual	Creates the traditional dual interface (custom/IDispatch)
id	Specifies the DISPID for methods in interfaces that support IDispatch
in/out	Indicates the direction of the parameter in a method
progid/vi_progid	Specifies the ProgID for the component (versioned or version independent)
retval	Uses the parameter as the return value from a method
threading	Specifies the threading model for the component
uuid	Specifies a GUID for a class, type library, or interface

You'll see some of these attributes in action when you create an example ATL Server Web Service in the section "Example ATL Server Web Service."

Web Service-Based Attributes

As with the COM-based Inline IDL attributes, ATL Server adds a few attributes to directly support Web applications and Web Services in particular. I've included these in Table B.2.

TABLE B.2 ATL Server Web Application/Web Service Attributes

Attribute	Purpose
request_handler	Identifies a C++ class as capable of handling HTTP requests
soap_handler	Identifies a C++ class as supporting Web Services
soap_header	Identifies class members that will implement a request SOAP Header
soap_method	Designates methods within the class that are exposed to the Web using SOAP

You will definitely see these attributes in action in the example ATL Server Web Service. The first two, request_handler and soap_handler, are related. If the soap_handler is specified, only then does the request_handler become meaningful.

The C++ code that you write to support COM and Web Services must be compilable. Therefore, the compiler must support attributes. In fact, it does, and it uses the architecture that you see in Figure B.2.

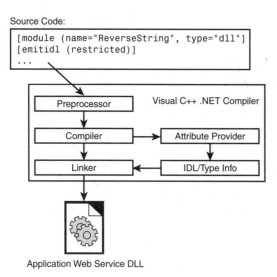

FIGURE B.2

Compiler attribute support.

B

USING ATL
SERVER TO CREATE
WEB SERVICES

Of course, all of these attributes (especially the Inline IDL attributes) are designed to work with an interface. Let's now look briefly at the new `__interface` keyword.

The C++ `__interface` Keyword

As you may know, COM interfaces are supported in binary form using a C++ virtual function table, or vtable. And if you've read this much of the appendix, it's probably safe for me to assume you're at least somewhat familiar with the C++ language. With that being the case, I won't provide the details surrounding vtables or tell why the COM architects elected to base COM on the vtable itself.

But if Microsoft changes the way you create C++ COM objects and provides all of these attributes for you to use, there had to be some way to lay out the COM vtable outside of using MIDL. Thus, the `__interface` keyword was created. Instead of creating classes with pure virtual functions, you can simply use `__interface`:

```
__interface IFoo
{
    HRESULT Bar([out, retval] BSTR* pbstrResult);
}
```

So far, you know that ATL Server supports high-performance Web Services because it deals directly with ISAPI, and you configure your code to run Web Services using C++ attributes and interfaces. When do you use ATL Server over ASP.NET?

When to Select ATL Server

If you're uncomfortable with C++, and ATL in general, then ATL Server probably isn't for you. ASP.NET-based Web Services are more appropriate, as you've seen in this book. However, if you are comfortable with C++ and ATL, Table B.3 provides some of the design trade-off decisions you'll need to make when selecting one technology over the other.

TABLE B.3   ATL Server Versus ASP.NET Web Services

ATL Server	ASP.NET
Enhanced control	Ease of development
Ultimate speed	Solid performance
C++ language	Any CLR-compliant language

Table B.3 tells you that if you like working in C++ but want to create Web Services, or if you want the tightest control over the execution of the Web Service with the greatest possible performance, then ATL Server is an optimum choice. On the other hand, if you need a Web Service up and operational very quickly, if you aren't terribly adept with C++, or if you are otherwise happy with the great performance that ASP.NET Web Services offer, then, by all means, continue to use ASP.NET-based Web Services.

Example ATL Server Web Service

To keep the code that you write as simple as possible, allowing you to concentrate on the code that Visual Studio .NET provides for you, I'll create a sample ATL Server Web Service that accepts a string and reverses the characters to be returned as an output string. I created the solution by using Visual Studio .NET's New, Project menu option and selecting ATL Server Web Service. I then selected a target directory for the solution files and named the solution ReverseString. I dismissed the resulting options dialog by clicking the Finish button, and I did this because everything that you require to create the Web Service project has been established by Visual Studio .NET.

After Visual Studio .NET finished creating the solution, I found two projects created for me. The first, ReverseString, implements the Web Service logic itself. The second, ReverseStringIsapi, implements the ISAPI extension logic that will intercept the Web requests and issue the responses.

To add the code to reverse the incoming string and implement the Web Service logic, I opened the file ReverseString.h from the ReverseString project. The resulting code is shown in Listing B.1.

LISTING B.1 ReverseString.h Source Code

```
// ReverseString.h : Defines the ATL Server request handler class
//
#pragma once

namespace ReverseStringService
{
// all struct, enum, and typedefs for your webservice should go inside the
➡namespace

// IReverseStringService - web service interface declaration
//
[
    uuid("8B57749E-80D9-4A18-96E4-F39E0DBEE610"),
    object
]
__interface IReverseStringService
{
    [id(1)] HRESULT ReverseString([in] BSTR bstrInput, [out, retval] BSTR
➡*bstrOutput);
};
```

LISTING B.1   Continued

```
// ReverseStringService - web service implementation
//
[
    request_handler(name="Default", sdl="GenReverseStringWSDL"),
    soap_handler(
        name="ReverseStringService",
        namespace="urn:ReverseStringService",
        protocol="soap"
    )
]
class CReverseStringService :
    public IReverseStringService
{
public:
    // This is a sample Web Service method that shows how to use the
    // soap_method attribute to expose a method as a Web method
    [ soap_method ]
    HRESULT ReverseString(/*[in]*/ BSTR bstrInput, /*[out, retval]*/ BSTR
➥*bstrOutput)
    {
        // Check the outgoing pointer...
        if ( bstrOutput == NULL ) return E_POINTER;

        // Reverse the characters
        *bstrOutput = _wcsrev(bstrInput);

        return S_OK;
    }
    // TODO: Add additional Web Service methods here
}; // class CReverseStringService

} // namespace ReverseStringService
```

I've italicized the changes I made to the file. Essentially, I removed the HelloWorld() method and replaced it with a method that I called ReverseString(). Therefore, I had to change the interface definition:

```
[
    uuid("8B57749E-80D9-4A18-96E4-F39E0DBEE610"),
    object
]
__interface IReverseStringService
{
    [id(1)] HRESULT ReverseString([in] BSTR bstrInput, [out, retval] BSTR
➥*bstrOutput);
};
```

I also had to add the implementation:

```
[ soap_method ]
HRESULT ReverseString(/*[in]*/ BSTR bstrInput, /*[out, retval]*/ BSTR
➥*bstrOutput)
{
    // Check the outgoing pointer...
    if ( bstrOutput == NULL ) return E_POINTER;

    // Reverse the characters
    *bstrOutput = _SysAllocString(wcsrev(bstrInput));

    return S_OK;
}
```

To keep things up-to-date, I edited the project's ReverseString.htm file to remove the reference to HelloWorld, but that isn't critical to the operation of the Web Service.

Turning first to the interface definition, you can see the __interface keyword in action:

```
__interface IReverseStringService
```

With it, I used several Inline IDL attributes: uuid, object, id, in, out, and retval.

> **NOTE**
>
> You might believe that this code will create a COM object that supports this Web Service. As I mentioned previously, this isn't so. The resulting DLL will be simply an ISAPI DLL with no COM plumbing. This is because _ATL_NO_COM_SUPPORT is defined in the ReverseString's stdafx.h file, which excludes ATL COM registration and support. You can modify this code and make the Web Service application DLL a COM server, but this technique is beyond the scope of this appendix.

I need the request_handler and soap_handler attributes applied to the C++ class to denote this class as a Web Service:

```
[
    request_handler(name="Default", sdl="GenReverseStringWSDL"),
    soap_handler(
        name="ReverseStringService",
        namespace="urn:ReverseStringService",
        protocol="soap"
    )
]
```

```
class CReverseStringService :
   public IReverseStringService
{
   ...
};
```

Note that the C++ class derived from the interface defined previously in the file. The handler is named GenReverseStringWSDL, so, to see the WSDL that this Web Service would generate, you can access the Web Service using the URL `http://localhost/ReverseString/ReverseString.dll?Handler=GenReverseStringServiceWSDL`. Of course, you would use the correct server URL had this Web Service been deployed on a different machine.

The final Web Service addition that ATL Server made is to define the `ReverseString()` method as a Web method through the `soap_method` attribute:

```
[ soap_method ]
HRESULT ReverseString(/*[in]*/ BSTR bstrInput, /*[out, retval]*/ BSTR
➥*bstrOutput)
{
   ...
}
```

If you make the changes italicized in Listing B.1 and compile the resulting file, Visual Studio .NET will create for you two DLLs, `ReverseString.dll` and `ReverseStringIsapi.dll`, and will copy them into a new virtual directory that it created to allow for Internet access. Not surprisingly, the virtual directory is named ReverseString.

To test this, I created a new C# console application and added the Web reference to the ATL Server DLLs just created. I then created the Web Service proxy and called the `ReverseString()` method so that I could print the results to the screen. You can see this code in Listing B.2. Because it's very similar to code you've seen throughout this book, I won't cover the code in detail.

LISTING B.2   ReverseStringClient Source Code

```
using System;
using ReverseStringClient.localhost;

namespace ReverseStringClient
{
   /// <summary>
   /// Summary description for Class1.
   /// </summary>
   class Class1
   {
      static void Main(string[] args)
```

LISTING B.2   Continued

```
    {
        // Create an instance of the ATL Server's
        // Web Service proxy
        ReverseStringService ws = new ReverseStringService();
        string strResult = ws.ReverseString("This is a test!");
        Console.WriteLine("The resulting string was '{0}'",strResult);
    }
  }
}
```

However, there is a bug in the second beta of Visual Studio .NET that might affect you when you try to add the Web reference to your client application. When Visual Studio .NET creates an ATL Server Web Service project, it creates an HTML file that, when rendered, looks very much like the Web page that ASP.NET would create when you view the .asmx file in the Web browser (you're performing an HTTP GET, which ASP.NET interprets and returns the HTML instead of the Web Service behavior). The link to the "service contract" is incorrectly generated by the AppWizard.

At the same time, Visual Studio .NET doesn't create for the ATL Server Web Service project a .vsdisco file—it creates instead the older .disco file. And here is where you'll get in trouble if you're not aware of the bug in the HTML file.

When you attempt to add a Web reference to your client that references the ATL Server Web Service, you'll find that Visual Studio .NET won't list the ATL Server Web Service among the locally available Web Services. Why? There is no .vsdisco file, so Visual Studio .NET doesn't "find" the ATL Server Web Service. Therefore, it isn't listed among the available services.

No problem—just find the URL that will produce the WSDL and type that into the edit control located at the top of the Web Reference dialog box. Go for the WSDL directly instead of relying upon DISCO. But if you use the URL contained within the HTML file, that URL is incorrect! The logic here is valid, but use the URL contained within the .disco file instead. This URL is the correct URL for locating the WSDL. While you're there, be sure to update the HTML file to use the correct URL as well.

This bug should be corrected in the released version of Visual Studio .NET, but, if not, at least the solution to the problem is a simple one.

XML Protocol and SOAP

IN THIS APPENDIX

This appendix gives an overview of the relationship between XML protocol and SOAP, beginning with a bit of history. XML protocol represents an acknowledgment from the W3C that an XML-based protocol is required by the industry. SOAP plays a big role in this effort by establishing itself as the dominant XML protocol currently being used in real-life applications.

The Birth of XML Protocol

In April 2000, the SOAP v1.1 specification was released to the public as a collaborative effort from Microsoft, IBM, DevelopMentor, Lotus Development Corp., and UserLand Software, Inc.

After releasing the specification, SOAP was submitted as a Note to the World Wide Web Consortium (W3C) for consideration. In May 2000, the W3C acknowledged the submission, following several months of soliciting feedback and evaluating the industry need for an XML-based messaging protocol.

It wasn't difficult to find evidence that such a protocol was needed and wanted. The W3C decided to take action by starting the XML Protocol Activity and creating the XML Protocol Working Group in September 2000. This working group consisted of W3C members, chaired by David Fallside of IBM, with the purpose of creating a simple foundation to support the needs of communicating applications.

As its first major deliverable, the working group developed a set of requirements for XMLP and released a working draft in March 2001. This set the stage for what an XMLP specification should and should not address.

Because the working group already had the SOAP v1.1 Note as a starting point, the members regularly compared it against their newly found requirements. Not only did this provide a sanity check, but it also helped them maintain an *issues list* for SOAP.

All of this has resulted in working drafts of an abstract model for XMLP and the SOAP v1.2 specification, both released in July 2001.

The XMLP Abstract Model

The development of protocols is difficult. This is partly because they are, by nature, abstract representations of protocols that must exist in the real world. The problem lies in the fact that humans typically gravitate toward describing abstract ideas using existing physical concepts. But for XMLP to be void of any particular implementation, an abstract model was created to define fundamental concepts that could be used in the XMLP specification.

Definitions

The XML protocol defines a set of terms that are consistently used throughout the working group's deliverables. Table C.1 summarizes the most commonly referenced terms.

TABLE C.1 XMLP Definitions

Term	*Definition*
XMLP application	An application that employs the services provided by the XML protocol layer. XMLP applications include consumers, producers, and intermediaries.
XMLP binding	The rules and semantics for transmitting an XMLP message on top of another protocol.
XMLP block	A logical set of data that can be interpreted as a single computational unit. This set of data is syntactically grouped together.
XMLP Body	The syntactical structure used to encapsulate zero or more XMLP blocks that are intended for the ultimate receiver in the XMLP message path.
XMLP Envelope	The syntactical structure used to encapsulate all other parts of the XMLP message.
XMLP fault	An XMLP block that contains fault semantics as defined by the XML protocol. An XML processor that determines that an XMLP message has not followed the XML protocol's syntax or semantics will generate a fault.
XMLP handler	Uses rules defined in the XMLP module to process XMLP blocks.
XMLP Header	The syntactical structure used to encapsulate zero or more XMLP blocks, intended for use by any receiver in a message path.
XMLP intermediary	An XMLP application that acts as both a sender and a receiver, which forwards XMLP blocks along a message path.
XMLP layer	An abstraction that provides XML protocol operations, which transfer XML protocol blocks between one or more peer XMLP applications.
XMLP message path	The XMLP sender, ultimate receiver, and zero or more intermediaries that an XMLP message passes through.
XMLP message	The basic unit of communication in XMLP.
XMLP module	The combination of an XMLP block and its associated handler that defines messaging-related or application-related services.
XMLP operation	A primitive service used to interact with the XML protocol layer.
XMLP processor	Uses the XML protocol rules and semantics to process XMLP messages.
XMLP receiver	An XMLP node that can consume an XMLP message that was received via an XMLP binding. The ultimate XMLP receiver is the final destination of the XMLP message.
XMLP sender	An XMLP application that can generate an XMLP message and transmit the message via an XMLP binding. The initial XMLP sender is the originator of an XMLP message in a message path.

C

XML PROTOCOL
AND SOAP

Let's take a closer at how these concepts are applied in the abstract model.

An XMLP Walkthrough

First and foremost, XMLP uses a layered architecture to separate XMLP from applications and bindings. Figure C.1 shows where XMLP fits into the overall picture.

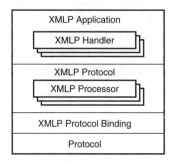

FIGURE C.1

XML Protocol layered architecture.

This extensible architecture allows XMLP to support multiple applications, bindings, and protocols. Before we can describe how XMLP messages fit into this architecture, you must understand the basic XMLP message structure. The structure shown in Figure C.2 depicts the relationship between the XMLP Envelope, Header, Body, and blocks.

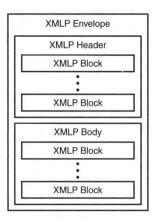

FIGURE C.2

XML Protocol message structure.

The Envelope's purpose is simply to wrap the remaining contents of the message. The Header and Body have similar syntactical representations but are designed for two semantically different purposes. The Header is responsible for carrying zero or more information blocks, with each block intended for one of the many XMLP receivers in the message path. In contrast, the body is strictly intended for the ultimate receiver.

To better understand how XMLP messages are transferred along a message path, Figure C.3 shows how the initial sender creates a message destined for the ultimate receiver. Notice that zero or more intermediaries can participate in transferring the message along the message path.

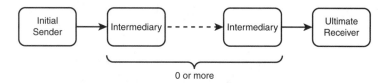

FIGURE C.3
XML Protocol message path.

Figure C.4 shows a more detailed diagram of this interaction. In this case, the initial sender application uses handlers A and B to create block 1 in the Header and block 2 in the Body, respectively. The entire XMLP message is eventually transmitted via the underlying protocol stack. Note that each layer in the protocol stack may route the message through protocol-specific paths that are orthogonal to the actual XMLP message path. For example, when using HTTP, proxies and firewalls may participate in the transfer of the message, without being part of the XMLP layer.

Each step along the way, intermediaries (not shown in the figure) may invoke handlers that consume XMLP blocks or possibly create new XMLP blocks destined for other receivers down the message path.

After the XMLP message has arrived at the ultimate receiver, handlers C and D are used to interpret the XMLP blocks, with block 2 being solely intended for this receiver because it is located in the message Body.

Although this description is not overly complex, the XMLP model can support rich orchestration of messaging yet remain a very simple protocol.

XMLP_UnitData

We've talked some about how messages are sent and received, at least from an abstract standpoint. XMLP defines a single operation called XMLP_UnitData, which uses four primitives or events as an interface between the XMLP application and the XMLP processor. Table C.2 describes the four events.

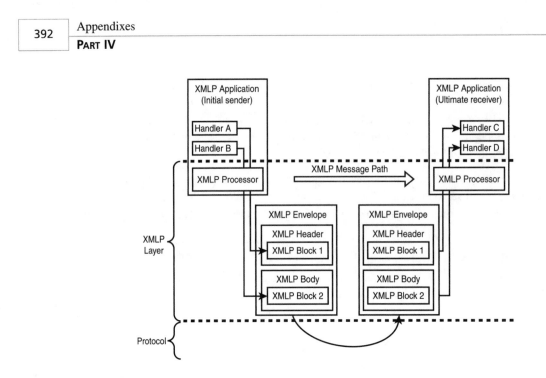

FIGURE C.4

XML Protocol model.

TABLE C.2 XMLP_UnitData Events

Event	Definition
send	Invoked by the sending XMLP application to the XMLP processor to initiate the transfer of an XMLP message.
receive	Invoked by the receiving XMLP application to the XMLP processor to receive an incoming XMLP message.
status	Reports the status of message delivery (success or failure) to the sending XMLP application.
forward	Invoked by an intermediary XMLP application to the XMLP processor to transfer an XMLP message to the next step in the message path.

Each event contains a unique set of parameters that are necessary for properly executing the event. Table C.3 provides a breakdown of these parameters.

TABLE C.3 XMLP_UNITDATA Event Parameters

Parameter	Definition
To	Denotes the initiating sender's intended final destination for the message.
From	Denotes the initiating sender.
ImmediateDestination	Denotes the very next intermediary in the message path.
Message	Is the actual XMLP message. An XMLP message contains three subparts, Message.Faults, Message.Blocks, and Message.Attachments.
Correlation	Denotes the relationship between XMLP messages. This allows for more complex message exchange patterns such as request/response. The Correlation.MessageRef subfield references a related message that was previously processed.
BindingContext	References information that is specific to the XMLP binding being used.
Status	Denotes whether a message has been *sent*, *delivered*, or *failed*, or possibly that the message is in some *unknown* state.

The following shows the abstract organization of the parameters from Table C.3 in their respective XMLP_UnitData events (optional parameters shown in square brackets):

```
XMLP_UNITDATA.send( To, [ImmediateDestination], Message, [Correlation],
                    [BindingContext])

XMLP_UNITDATA.receive( [To], [From], Message, [Correlation], [BindingContext])

XMLP_UNITDATA.status( [From], Status, [BindingContext])

XMLP_UNITDATA.forward( [ImmediateDestination], Message, [BindingContext])
```

XMLP defines additional primitives for exchanging messages, correlating messages, and handling errors. Using these primitives in conjunction with different protocol bindings results in a wide variety of XMLP messaging patterns.

Now that you've had a taste for the XMLP abstract model, let's take a closer look at a more concrete implementation, the SOAP v1.2 working draft.

SOAP v1.2

Aside from the simple fixes of typos and some minor clarification, SOAP v1.2 isn't all that different from v1.1. The following list summarizes the actual changes that have taken place:

- SOAP no longer stands for Simple Object Access Protocol.
- Bindings are now considered a component of SOAP.
- Namespace URIs and associated prefixes have changed.
- Version transition is provided from SOAP v1.1 to v1.2.
- Changes and fixes to examples have been made.
- SOAP schemas are compliant with the XML Schema recommendation.
- Changes to SOAP schemas have been made in both syntax and semantics.
- A defined mechanism has been added for communicating faults in regard to header elements containing the `mustUnderstand` attribute.
- A glossary of terms has been added.

Although the best reference for the changes to SOAP v1.2 is the specification, the following sections provide some detail of these changes.

No More Simple Object Access Protocol

From the beginning, SOAP was targeted to become an RPC mechanism that could eventually replace object protocols such as DCOM for Internet-scale applications—hence the word *Object* in its name.

With the growing interest in message-based applications, SOAP takes on a much greater meaning. Therefore, you will notice that the SOAP v1.2 specification does not continue the use of *SOAP* as an acronym, but it retains the name that is now so familiar to users.

Bindings

SOAP v1.1 defined three parts—the Envelope, encoding rules, and an RPC representation—as orthogonal elements of SOAP. It then outlined just two (of many) protocol bindings that the specification addressed.

SOAP v1.2 simply raised the importance of the protocol binding concept and added it as a fourth component to SOAP.

Namespace URIs

SOAP v1.1 used the following attributes for defining SOAP namespace prefixes:

```
xmlns:SOAP-ENV="http://schemas.xmlsoap.org/soap/envelope/"
xmlns:SOAP-ENC="http://schemas.xmlsoap.org/soap/encoding/"
```

Version 1.2 has adopted the W3C's URL in the URI syntax, and has removed the trailing slash (/):

```
xmlns:env="http://www.w3.org/2001/06/soap-envelope"
xmlns:enc="http://www.w3.org/2001/06/soap-encoding"
xmlns:f="http://www.w3.org/2001/06/soap-faults"
xmlns:V="http://www.w3.org/2001/06/soap-upgrade"
```

Appendix C of the SOAP v1.2 working draft outlines a scheme to transition from v1.1 to v1.2. Future work will eventually provide a generalized approach to versioning that will apply to all versions of SOAP.

encodingStyle

Although the SOAP encodingStyle attribute can be applied to any element in a SOAP message, SOAP v1.1 generally used the <Envelope> element to assign this attribute.

However, the more generally adopted form is to use the encodingStyle attribute on blocks within the header or body because there likely will be a need to have different encoding forms used for different portions of the same message. The examples in SOAP v1.2 accurately reflect this notion. Listing C.1 provides a simple example of this syntax.

LISTING C.1 encodingStyle Example

```
<env:Envelope xmlns:env="http://www.w3.org/2001/06/soap-envelope" >
  <env:Body>
    <m:GetTemperature
        env:encodingStyle="http://www.w3.org/2001/06/soap-encoding"
        xmlns:m="http://www.mcp.com/Temperature">
      <zipCode>12345</zipCode>
    </m:GetTemperature>
  </env:Body>
</env:Envelope>
```

mustUnderstand Faults

SOAP v1.1 did not provide an adequate method for communicating that specific header elements failed the mustUnderstand semantics somewhere along a message path. To correct this, v1.2 extends the use of the header by allowing you to denote the elements that failed this test.

Listing C.2 shows an example fault message.

C

LISTING C.2   mustUnderstand Fault

```
<env:Envelope xmlns:env="http://www.w3.org/2001/06/soap-envelope"
              xmlns:flt="http://www.w3.org/2001/06/soap-faults" >
  <env:Header>
    <flt:Misunderstood qname='ext:MyExtension'
                       xmlns:def="http://www.mcp.com/MyExtension" />
  </env:Header>
  <env:Body>
    <env:Fault>
      <faultcode>MustUnderstand</faultcode>
      <faultstring>One or more mandatory headers not understood</faultstring>
    </env:Fault>
  </env:Body>
</env:Envelope>
```

Here, a receiving party did not understand the MyExtension header entry, so a fault was generated stating this fact. Upon receiving such a fault, the sender can interrogate the specific header faults when applicable.

XMLP, SOAP, and the Future

Although the XMLP Working Group is still working toward developing a proper W3C recommendation for XML-based messaging, its work is already having a significant impact on SOAP development.

First and foremost, there's huge participation by a wide variety of industry experts. This has resulted in many excellent discussions about the issues surrounding XML-based protocols.

Secondly, the working group has reinforced the fact that SOAP is a very stable and robust protocol, even with a few minor blemishes. SOAP as it exists today should serve the industry well until the W3C delivers a final recommendation with the appropriate migration paths defined. So far, the changes that have been proposed in SOAP v1.2 do not present any serious conflicts with the current SOAP v1.1 specification.

.NET Web Service Resources

IN THIS APPENDIX

For more background or additional detail on topics in this book, the following Web sites, news-groups, articles, and books are excellent resources.

XML General

W3 and XML: `http://www.w3.org/xml`

XML Schema: `http://www.w3.org/xml/schema`

Microsoft: `http://msdn.microsoft.com/xml/default.asp`

XML in Action, William J. Pardi, Microsoft Press, 1999 (ISBN 0735605629)

XML Bible, Elliot Rusty Harold, Hungry Minds, Inc., 1999 (ISBN 0764532367)

XML Unleashed, Michael Morrison, Sams, 1999 (ISBN 0672315149)

Professional ASP XML, Mark Baartse et al., Wrox Press, 2000 (ISBN 1861004028)

Essential XML: Beyond Markup, Don Box, et. al., Addison-Wesley, 2000 (ISBN 0201709147)

General .NET Information

Microsoft: `http://msdn.microsoft.com/net`

Got Dot Net: `http://www.gotdotnet.com`

Discussion list: `http://discuss.develop.com/dotnet.html`

"ATL Server and Visual Studio.NET: Developing High-Performance Web Applications Gets Easier," Shaun McAravey and Ben Hickman, *MSDN Magazine*, April 2001: `http://msdn.microsoft.com/library/en-us/dnmag00/html/atlserv.asp`

"C++ Attributes: Make COM Programming a Breeze with New Feature in Visual Studio.NET," Richard Grimes, *MSDN Magazine*, April 2001: `http://msdn.microsoft.com/library/en-us/dnmag01/html/attributes.asp`

You will also want to subscribe to one or more of the newsgroups located at `nntp://msnews.microsoft.com`. The following list is just a subset of the available groups:

- `microsoft.public.dotnet.general`
- `microsoft.public.dotnet.faqs`
- `microsoft.public.dotnet.framework`
- `microsoft.public.dotnet.aspnet.webservices`
- `microsoft.public.webservice`
- `microsoft.public.xml.soap`

General Web Service Information

Microsoft: `http://msdn.microsoft.com/webservices`

IBM: `http://www-106.ibm.com/developerworks/webservices/`

Web Services Resource Center: `http://soap-wrc.com`

Web Service position papers: `http://www.w3.org/2001/03/WSWS-popa/`

Webservices.org: `http://www.webservices.org/`

Xmethods Web Service listing: `http://www.xmethods.org/`

Salcentral Web Services Brokerage: `http://www.salcentral.com`

SOAP/XML Protocol

Understanding SOAP, Kenn Scribner and Mark Stiver, Sam's, 2000 (ISBN 0672319225)

SOAP: Cross Platform Web Service Development Using XML, Scott Seely, Prentice Hall, 2001 (ISBN 0130907634)

SOAP Specification: `http://www.w3.org/TR/SOAP/`

Microsoft: `http://msdn.microsoft.com/soap`

XML Protocol: `http://www.w3.org/2000/xp/`

List of implementations and resources: `http://www.soapware.org/`

SOAP Messages with Attachments: `http://www.w3.org/TR/SOAP-attachments`

"SOAP in the Microsoft .NET Framework and Visual Studio.NET," Keith Ballinger, Jonathan Hawkins, and Pranish Kumar, November 2000: `http://msdn.microsoft.com/library/en-us/dndotnet/html/hawksoap.asp`

"Fun with SOAP Extensions," Keith Ballinger, March 2001: `http://msdn.microsoft.com/library/en-us/dnaspnet/html/asp03222001.asp`

SOAP discussion group: `http://discuss.develop.com`

SOAP builders list: `http://groups.yahoo.com/group/soapbuilders`

Remoting

"Microsoft .NET Remoting: A Technical Overview," Piet Obermeyer and Jonathan Hawkins, July 2001: `http://msdn.microsoft.com/library/en-us/dndotnet/html/hawkremoting.asp`

"An Introduction to Microsoft .NET Remoting Framework," Paddy Srinivasan, July 2001: `http://msdn.microsoft.com/library/en-us/dndotnet/html/remoting.asp`

UDDI

UDDI.org: `http://www.uddi.org` (version 1.0 and 2.0)

Microsoft: `http://uddi.microsoft.com/` (includes MS UDDI SDK)

WSDL

Microsoft: `http://msdn.microsoft.com/xml/general/wsdl.asp`

W3: `http://www.w3.org/TR/wsdl`

WSDL list: `http://groups.yahoo.com/group/wsdl`

Transactions

"Autonomous Computing" (DAT489), Pat Helland, Microsoft TechEd 2001 (presentation)

Xaml.org: `http://www.xaml.org`

Principles of Transaction Processing, Philip A. Bernstein and Eric Newcomer, Morgan Kaufmann Publishers, 1997 (ISBN 1558604154)

Tools

TcpTrace: `http://www.pocketsoap.com/tcpTrace`

Security

XML Digital Signatures: `http://www.w3.org/TR/SOAP-dsig/`

Applied Cryptography, Bruce Schneier, John Wiley and Sons, 1995 (ISBN 0471117099)

Programming Windows Security, Keith Brown, Addison Wesley Longman, 2000 (ISBN 0201604426)

Internet Protocol Security: `http://www.microsoft.com/windows2000/techinfo/planning/security/ipsecsteps.asp`

Web Service Security: `http://msdn.microsoft.com/vstudio/nextgen/technology/security.asp`

The OASIS organization is working on a standard authentication and authorization specification called Security Assertion Markup Language or SAML. More information can be found at `http://www.oasis-open.org/committees/security/`.

ebXML

General: `http://www.ebxml.org`

Specifications: `http://www.ebxml.org/specs/index.htm`

Sample Web Service

The sample Favorites Web Service and associated documentation can be found at the following locations:

`http://msdn.microsoft.com/library/default.asp?URL=/library/techart/ssf1over.htm`

`http://msdn.microsoft.com/library/?url=/library/en-us/dncold/html/ssfapiref.asp?frame=true`

INDEX

A

selecting ATL Servers, 380
semantics, Web Services,
    13-14
serialization, 128
    Body object, 134-136
        array, 148-153
        compound data types, 145
        remote method, 137-140
        simple datatypes, 140-145
        structs, 145-147
    embedded data, 147
    formats, 205-209, 211-222
    independent data, 147
    objects, 292-293
Server Response Files (SRF),
    376
server-side remote object
    activation, 294
servers
    ATL Servers
        architecture, 376-377
        attributed C++, 377-380
        code, 381-385
        selecting, 380
    base64 encoding, 305
    MTS, 51
services
    logging, 302-303
    providers, 14
    registry, 14
    requester, 14
    Web. *See* Web Services
    WSDL, 178
Session
    feature, 31
    object, 233
session-state management,
    203-205
shaping, data shaping, 209,
    211-222
signatures, digital, 339-340
Simple API for XML (SAX), 79
simple datatype serialization,
    Body object, 140-145
Simple Mail Transfer Protocol
    (SMTP), 17-19
simple type definitions, 89
simple-dimension arrays, 149

SimpleCalc, 255-259
simplicity of Web Services,
    26
sinks, 291
SMTP (Simple Mail Transfer
    Protocol), 17-19
SOAP
    defining need, 124-126
    digital signatures, 339-340
    future of, 396
    Headers, 225, 271-273
    message attachments, 310-313
    packets
        intercepting, 273-283
        modifying, 273-283
    v1.2, 394
        bindings, 394
        encodingStyle attribute,
            395
        mustUnderstand faults,
            395-396
        namespace URIs, 394
    Web sites, 399
SoapBindingUse, 258
SoapDumper, 231
SoapException, 232
SoapExtension class, 225-231
SoapFormatter class, 155-159
SoapMethodAttribute,
    206-209
SoapParameterStyle, 258
SoapRpcMethodAttribute,
    237
solicit/response operation,
    173
Solution Explorer window,
    38, 199-203
source code
    SimpleCalc, 255-257
    viewing, 199-203
sparse arrays, 150
specifying
    Headers, 224
    WSDL, 164-165
sponsor, 295
SQL (Structured Query
    Language), 79

SRF (Server Response Files),
    376
SSL (Secure Socket Layer), 26,
    339
standards
    Internet, 16
    OASIS, 22
start tags (XML), 81
states, Web Service manage-
    ment, 232-236
stencils, 376
strong names (.NET), 355-356
structs, Body object, 145-147
Structured Query Language
    (SQL), 79
structures
    bindingDetail, 188
    XML messages, 390
styles, encoding, 42
summaries (API), 322, 325
support, Visual Studio .NET,
    246-248
synchronous Web Services,
    255-260
syntax, Web Services, 13-14
System namespace (.NET
    Framework), 68-73
system-level security, 332
System.Net namespace, 72
System.Object methods, 66
System.Runtime.Remoting,
    73
systems, integrating, 23

T

TA (Transaction Authority),
    314
tags
    empty-element (XML), 81
    end (XML), 81
    start (XML), 81
target namespaces (XML), 89
TCP/IP (Transmission Control
    Protocol/Internet Protocol),
    16